I CAN'T WAIT 'TIL SPRING!

A Lifetime with Flowers

Keith Paul Nichols

ISBN: 978-1-78955-547-9

Published by New Generation Publishing
www.newgeneration-publishing.com

 New Generation Publishing

Typesetting by Linda Harris
Ryn Manuscript Services
Pillaton, Cornwall

Scanning of all photos and cover design by Dale Nichols
All images in this book are provided by the author,
unless stated otherwise.

Cover picture is from an old postcard,
painted by Ellen Warrington in the early 1900s.

Dedications

To my dearest wife, Debbie, who I married in 1972
at St. John's church, Walthamstow, East 17, on the 20th of May.

AND NOW TO OUR CHILDREN:

HEATHER born in 1976, husband Stuart,
children Tyler, Honey, Rose and Summer-Ray.

ADRIAN born in 1979 and wife Kaye

ROWAN born in 1982 and wife Jessica,
children Arthur and 'Teddy' Edward.

DALE born in 1991.

And all the Nichols, Ridley, Axford families and (appropriate for a
gardening book) Jessica's family name of FLOWERDEW.

Further dedications to Linda and Andrew Harris (Cornwall).

All at New Generation Publishing

Also to my wrestler pals Les Prest (and wife Carol)
and to Richard (Dicky) Swales who wrestled under the memorable
name of DIRTY DICK SWALES
and my friend Dennis 'Drop kick' Lord, and JULIA.

Also my dearest Romany Traveller friends, Joan and John West,
and Andy and Candy Sheridan.

Other books by the author:

They Seek Him Here... They Seek Him There... (True Tales of a travelling showman)
ISBN: 0 9526567 0 1

I've Got a Lovely Bunch of COCONUTS!" (Or is it the way I walk?!)
ISBN13: 978-1906710-46-0

Prices and details, plus copies of the above books,
direct from the author:

Keith Nichols
'Coniston Lodge'
20 Rider Haggard Lane
Kessingland
Suffolk
NR33 7PD

Foreword

(by John Jackson)

Keith Nichols is a man of many parts. He has been involved in various activities, all of them with the utmost vigour. I have known him for many years and our mutual interest has been horticultural. We talk plants like most men talk football. New plant introductions or discoveries are discussed and weighed in our opinions.

Most of all, Keith is a practical and hands-on person. If a job is to be done, then it will be done correctly and with enthusiasm.

I have followed all of his articles in the Kessingland Times and they are invariable informative and practical, often with a touch of humour.

It is a compliment to be asked to offer a foreword to his book, and I wish it every success.

John Jackson

Let John Jackson tell you a little about himself – and Joyce of course! So over to you John…

Keith Nichols

My life has revolved around two subjects – Music and Horticulture. I have been fortunate in both.

It was at the age of about ten, after seeing a performance of *Faust*, that I decided I wanted to be an Opera Singer. I was already a choirboy and loved singing, but it had not occurred to me that when my voice broke, singing might not be an option.

I was lucky and appeared in many operas over a period of about thirty years, most of them at the Royal Opera, Covent Garden…

My love of gardening never diminished, and my quite large garden received constant attention. My green house has been occupied with various plants until I finally became hooked on Cacti and Succulents, with which it is now completely crowded. Also being secretary of the Waltham Forest Branch of the BCSS [British Cacti and Succulent Society] I am very involved with them.

After I retired from singing, I was asked by the local Council to take over a class, teaching gardening etc. This went on for some years and I still get calls from former pupils (now friends) asking for advice and help.

Both occupations have been good to me and I consider myself very lucky to have been blessed with them.

My wife Joyce also assists and is membership secretary of the Haworthia Society – a fascinating group of Succulents – with members all over the world. If you are interested, view our website www.haworthia.org and you will learn much about them.

Finally, I know that Keith will join with me in saying that Horticulture and growing things is one of the most satisfying pleasures in life.

John Jackson

Let the author tell you about…

JOHN JACKSON

What can I say about my good friend John Jackson! John, now in his eighties, was genuinely shocked, yet so delighted to write the Foreword for this book, and he still can't believe why I chose him!

Me and my wife, Debbie, first met John when he opened his sign shop on the corner of Chingford Road and Kenilworth Avenue E.17. Chingford Road too was mine and Debbie's first house that we bought, in other words a mortgage! And a two minute walk to John's lovely shop. John was an excellent sign-writer, and did all my fairground signs for me, I being in that line of work for the greater part of my life. Other lovely signs that he did for me were of course for my Landscape Gardening business.

As we got more pally, John invited me to meet his wife Molly, a lovely lady who on first meeting her gave me a cheery wave whilst washing up at the sink. John showed me round his most delightful garden and greenhouse, which I hasten to add was full of cacti and Succulents. Our friendship now made, we spoke often about plants. Sadly, Molly died, and John was devastated, but a good few years down the line John met and married lovely Joyce. On the phone I have a brief chat with Joyce followed by a 'fifteen hour' chat with John! Well, it seems that long, for we both talk so enthusiastically about plants flower shows etc. and we never keep track of time.

John has a fine operatic voice, and has sung with the best of them – Pavarotti, Placido Domingo, to name but two. It's the Cacti and Succulents that are John's passion, and Joyce's too!

I think it's wonderful how we all get special people that enter our lives, and keep that very special friendship for years.

It is most certainly the plant world that got us together, so what a wonderful way to start nearly a lifetime of friendships, just simply marvellous!

Keith Nichols

Spring is here and the countryside rejoices,
Flowers abound, so many choices,
Young leaves and buds show through
Casting out winter for me and you.
The morning dew lies all afresh now
Whilst a dusting of frost lays on each bough.
Flowers banish those darkened days,
We welcome back those golden rays.

Keith Nichols
27th August 2010

Introducing you to my Book of Flowers

Well, gardening friends, I hope you like the title that I have chosen for this book, for I'm very certain that it's a phrase we all use especially around December, January and February in the depths of winter!

It's that anticipation of spring, for those first hints of green buds, usually the hawthorn being among the first to show, and very late winter for the 'Yellow Aconite' and 'Snowdrops' which also have that other very delightful common name of 'Fair maids of February' and they truly are.

I love everything about springtime, the newness, the lovely greens of all sorts of leaves, and abundance of thousands of spring flowers.

This book I hope is a lot different to most garden books, for I knew what I would do for a living even as a small boy – so did Mum, Dad, our relatives and neighbours – so I can say that I was born to garden!

This book is not an A–Z of plants by any means, but I will tell you about the various jobs that I have had in gardening, plants that I love, plus tips that I can give you from working in the garden and the world of plants. I'll also tell you of people who have given me the most encouragement, sadly most have now passed on, but really deserve all the credit. I dearly hope that there is an afterlife and that they are all sitting in a beautiful garden somewhere, hopefully resembling the garden as seen on the front cover of this book. I have the greatest fondness from when I was a boy living at Harold Hill, Romford, Essex, of course being my first years of life, and seeing the wonders of nature.

I was born in Thorpe Coombe Hospital, Walthamstow, London E.17 on the 4th November 1948. Mum's youngest sister, now 73 (2008) is my Auntie Rita, she tells me that I spent the first three years of my life sleeping in a drawer – a cot was something I don't think I ever had!

We moved from Walthamstow to Harold Hill when Mum and Dad had obviously heard of new council houses being built, so assume we moved to No. 8 Chippenham Walk around 1951.

In this book I will also tell you about the nice clients that I had… and still have, and of course the not so nice and a few oddballs too!

I'll tell you of my own 'experiments' in the world of gardening, which includes why so-called modern ideas do not work, and how I feel sorry for the young up-and-coming gardeners, especially those that have to work with ME! For I fiercely argue against modern ideas. I will also tell you of my ideas to make certain jobs easier to seeing them adopted on TV gardening programmes, not that they learned them from me, but I found it highly amusing to see those ideas used as if it was the best idea since the invention of sliced bread, and used as an up-to-date modern method, yet I adopted these ideas way back in the late '60s and '70s using common sense.

Well, that's enough of my ramblings! Grab your favourite armchair, have a nice 'cuppa' and 'bickies', sit back and read about **FLOWERS!**

Cosy Cul-de-Sac!

Directly opposite our house in Chippenham Walk (Harold Hill, Essex) were two fairly wide strips of grass, graced with two or three very young ornamental trees within a protective wire 'cage'; hand, on heart, they certainly did not need protecting from us kids, for we loved those trees, and never an ounce of damage was ever done to those trees in all my childhood. Those same trees exist today, but whether those trees were vandalised in later years… gladly, I'll never know.

Let's now go back to those strips of grass, for my main memory is of me sitting on the strip directly opposite our front door (No. 8) and me making buttercup and daisy chains, always on a sunny day, and a Sunday too, and knowing that Mum and Dad were at home just a few feet away gave me the greatest comfort, and knew Mum was preparing our roast dinner.

Chippenham Walk is a cul-de-sac, and my childhood world was within 'the Walk' and our front and back gardens, and never wanted those lovely days to end. They did of course, quite abruptly, when Mum's Multiple Sclerosis worsened, and Mum wanted to be near her family, hence moved to Chingford Hatch E.4 and not too far from family in nearby Walthamstow. My life changed dramatically at this point, and have covered this in other books, hence will stick to talking about my life with plants etc. which hopefully will make more pleasant reading! But I will cover the actual gardens where we have lived, both as a child and adult, right up to my garden right here in my present home in Kessingland, Suffolk.

Gentler Times No More

I have made my mind up here to cover as much as I can remember about my boyhood years at Harold Hill, Romford, Essex, then lead you on all through the years after leaving Harold Hill, albeit the name Harold Hill will crop up from time to time as certain memories come to the surface. For these were my favourite years, although I have always been saddened on leaving Harold Hill, I'm glad in a way that I never saw 'thuggish' 'yobbish' times there, nor witnessed vandalism, nor had any fear of being there alone in the streets at night, nor not the slightest temptation to ever bolt a door or back gate – no, these were post-war genteel times, and my boyhood.

On odd occasions reading the *Romford Recorder* local newspaper as an adult, it shocks and saddens me that I have to read of the most

3

terrible things, so in a way, I'm glad that we moved away on the 7th March 1960 and that my Harold Hill memories were not tarnished in any way. This proved beyond doubt, that since those times we have extremely weak governments, for health and safety executives can make rules and enforce them right down to the most idiotic rules, yet our so powerful governments cannot bring stiff punishments, like 'life' meaning 'life' etc. instead very lenient sentences for stabbings and violent crimes. To think that 99¾ of all crimes would be stopped if sentencing was harsher, we might then all get back to those lovely feelings we all felt pre-war or indeed post-war like myself.

I've rambled on, let's get back to the flowers shall we!

The Shed

The local council came round to Chippenham Walk and built cement bases for the forthcoming sheds that they were to put up. I loved it in there, and I would often go in there on colder or rainy days to believe it or not… write! As a seven or eight year old, I suddenly had this yearning to write and found it fascinating that I could do so, no matter how poor or amateurish it looked, and then liked making up stories.

The first, and only story that I remember writing was 'The Ducks that turned into Water Bottles' for Mum and Dad had bought my sister Sandra and I a pink… and one blue 1ft 6ins high approx. rubber water bottles (which were duck characters) in with other Christmas presents, hence made up the story, which sadly I have long forgotten. This was my first effort, my latter school years I always seemed to do okay in composition; I must at this point tell you the reader that I much prefer non-fiction.

The front of the shed where the windows were, I planted 'Sweet Williams'; this was also the run-off point for the rain, but washed away the soil slightly and leaving droplet 'holes' and exposing smallish stones.

One of my present day clients has a similar shed with the run-off point in exactly the same place and after rain, leaves those very same markings, and with the little stones showing minus of course any sign of 'Sweet Williams'. It was an odd feeling, for on looking down at this sight, I was that little boy again and expected any moment for Mum to call me in for my tea; in a flash, back to reality, I was no longer a little boy, and Mum died many years ago (1978) and it's true, that memories are more precious than gold.

On the left-hand side of the shed (window side) was our compost heap, which in latter years rose up a little higher above the now slanting chestnut fencing and far easier to climb over onto the very narrow

4

cinder path to see Mr & Mrs Brooks and Mrs Thornton whom you'll read about later.

At the back of the shed was a single climbing rose, probably more of a 'pillar' rose really, for it did never climb, this lovely rose was growing between the Jackson's house (No. 9) and our shed, but <u>every</u> year I'd squeeze through just a little to smell the flowers, although several weeks prior to this I always just loved to see the buds emerge, and the first signs of red breaking out of the bud.

Like most of the plants from my childhood, I make sure I grown them all today, all a very sweet reminder of childhood and people I knew, the lovely red rose at the back of our shed was 'Paul's Scarlet'.

The Jackson Four!

I just mentioned the Jacksons at No. 9 – Paul was my friend, and had a sister Glynis. Their mum and dad were Rose and Tom, and never really spoke to us kids, nor Mum and Dad, but every year 'Uncle' Tom would call me and Sandra and of course Paul and Glynis into the garden albeit stayed in our garden, he'd say "Watch this!". He'd then shake this enormous 'Butterfly Bush' and literally hundreds of butterflies in all species would cascade into the sky, what a sight that used to be. We had to wait a whole year before Tom would call us again, and a whole year for Tom to actually speak to us too! Even if it was only "Watch this!"

Rose, their mum, was the same, she always seemed serious, and never acknowledged me in the back or front gardens if I was playing out. Chestnut pales of fencing divided all the council gardens; Rose and Tom had built a one to two foot high long mound of soil all down our two adjoining gardens and planted the beautiful perennial 'Golden Rod' the length of it, so that grew to four to five feet or so in summer, it made a perfect screen!

Each year Paul and I would play 'Jungles' amongst the tall stems of the 'Golden Rod' usually with our toy tanks, tin soldiers or Cowboys and Indians, he in his garden, I in mine, but Rose always came out and stopped us playing, yet we did no harm.

Before the Jacksons moved in, the previous people made a long rockery in front of their kitchen window, and during its construction they made a home somehow for their tortoise, thus making a proper entrance for it to come out of, or go into hibernation each year, so when the rockery was built the tortoise's home was deeper under the ground. That tortoise had survived until they moved away, so I think they took the tortoise with them.

Our Lawn

Dad was certainly no gardener, and took no interest in it at all. I would say that I was about eight or nine years old when, out of the blue, I decided to dig up the whole back garden! I think Dad then levelled it over and put down grass seed, then he threaded milk bottle tops through lots of cotton, where Dad would put in pegs which the cotton was tied to. The glistening bottle tops (not metal ones) scared the birds away.

You do not see foil bottle tops nowadays, and folk use shiny CD disks instead. When these eventually go out of use I wonder what gardeners will use then, it might then be the case of simply doubling or trebling up the cotton!

Dad also made a concrete path right in the centre of the garden, with a sudden right turn that now led to the new shed. I watched Dad put in the 4" high or so shuttering, and went with Dad just down the road to what was the new Bosworth Junior School that was nearing completion. Dad borrowed a barrow from someone, and I helped him load the barrow with rubble for the path, so my dad was the first 'burglar' at Bosworth!(?).

Back in our garden I watched Dad doing the to-ing and fro-ing with a levelling board to get a good level. We never ever had a mower of any kind to my knowledge, the grass only being kept down by me and Sandra through our constant playing on it. There was certainly no mower in the shed. I remember that the front garden was cut by 'Uncle' Arthur next door at No. 7, for he kept his lawns immaculate.

Sandra and I loved our lawn in the spring and summer months. Mum would let us have our tea in the garden and we'd have mostly strawberry jam sandwiches and still love all jam sandwiches today! Sandra and I would long to 'trap' a stray cat or kitten that came into our garden, and make a cosy den for it, we'd both kiss and cuddle it until Mum insisted we let it go, which only happened once or twice to my recollection. I remember it well as it was a pleasant surprise for us to see a cat in the garden.

One day Mum and dad must have had an item delivered that came in a large cardboard box, and once again a new novelty in the garden and something different to play with. I did something very unique – I punctured holes on one side of the box and poked in all the different colour cellophane sweet wrappers. I'd lay on the grass with my head and upper body inside the box then look up to the now drooping wrappers that I poked through. It was sunny outside but darkish inside the box and the sight was marvellous! Probably reminding me of those oh so special nights at Southend-on-Sea's illuminations that drew crowds in their thousands in the 1950s.

Mum's favourite flowers were Gladioli – red ones! I don't remember ever having any in our limited garden borders, but Mum always bought bunches of them for our front room. Dad loved Fuchsias, although we didn't have any of those either! Just the once Dad took me to a Fuchsia show, I had no idea what a Fuchsia looked like! The show was in a building adjacent to… and probably part of St. George's Church. This Church wasn't far down the road as we turned right outside Chippenham Walk. Being small, I loved looking up into those lovely blooms, for I had a worm's eye view!

Our Front Garden

I mentioned earlier that Dad took no real interest in the garden, but did he on occasions? For I recall the whole of the front garden being planted up with mostly I think, Darwin Tulips and was a beautiful sight. I recall this once only for I cannot now remember any other flowers in that spot prior to this, so whether it had just remained bare earth or weedy I don't know, but soon after this flare of tulips, Dad must have seeded the area, and that winter built my first ever snowman right in the centre of the lawn, plus saw my first robin, who looked so lovely against the white snow.

Directly under the windowsill in the front garden was a small border of possibly 2ft wide and began at our doorstep (that Mum always kept bright red with Cardinal polish) and ended at the border of the alleyway that divided us from next door at No.7. Mum or Dad had planted the so superb 'Parrot Tulips' which grew to just above the windowsill and had much thicker stouter stems than the Darwins. Again I only witnessed this spectacle once in this border. The only other plants I remember on that spot were "Canterbury Bells" Campanula 'medium'. Also in the front garden was a long wire and short posts divided us from Rose and Tom Jackson's next door at No.9 and Mum always sowed this thin strip (between the wire and the concrete front path) with Candytuft. It always looked so nice, along with 'Virginia Stock', Nemesia, pansies, Viscaria and Linum, the red variety and resembled the lovely Viscaria. Mum always picked the pansies and put them in a dullish, yellowish bowl that had a thick 'blob' of removable glass in the middle which had holes in it to put the plants' stems. Today people use any sort of bowl with a strange 'material' called oasis.

Mum's best pal in 'the walk', or so it appeared to me as a child, was Vi Smith No.13. I mention Vi for each year I'd watch her plant rows of pansies at the side of her front path, and she would chat away very happily, unlike the Jacksons and other neighbours who were happy not to talk to us kids.

Most council properties which ours was, had Privet Hedges; ours was a mix of Privet and Hawthorn. Only one neighbour removed their hedge and planted Euonymus which made a fine evergreen hedge. I do remember this hedge well, not only because it was so different to Privet and Hawthorn, for one day I had a big shock, for on the leaves was a monstrous thick green caterpillar with odd markings on it! Many years later I realise now that it was either the 'Privet Hawk Moth', 'Elephant Hawk Moth' or 'Death's Head Hawk Moth'.

Of course, when I was very small my knowledge of plant names was almost nil, so you can imagine how excited I was when one day a 'curious' little flower came up under our hedge adjacent to the front gate. Sadly it never grew again. I remember this so well, for although my keenness to have more flowers in our garden, it never ever came about, I yearned to have more flowers, but at that age I never had the ways or means to buy any!

An Infant's Memory

The infant of course being ME! Apart from all those mentioned so far, I'd like to tell you about all the plants that were in our back garden, although some were annuals that were planted at various times over the years.

Let's start with the rockery and the rockery area that contained my own little plot. The rockery only had four really good spreaders on it, 'Snow-in-Summer', Aubrietia, 'Creeping Jenny' and Sedum 'Acre'. The only other plant that was different and that was what I assumed was the latest craze in the plant world and that was miniature roses; Mum bought a lovely red one called 'Tom Thumb' and she was so pleased with it, so was I, well I was pleased for Mum for I had no idea that this was a new type of plant, for as I said before I didn't know many plants back then, but I went along with all the excitement anyway!

If you, the reader, want deeper details of my time at Harold Hill, you'll have to purchase a copy of my childhood memories at Harold Hill, Romford, School Years, seasonal happenings etc. – see contact details in this book.

I can't tell you how much I loved my own little plot, this faced the other 'alley' that led to the kitchen door, therefore this little plot faced me each day as I went out into the garden. I suppose the tallest and most spectacular of my plot was the lovely rose 'Dorothy Perkins', yes and with the yearly mildew too! This rambled all over the fence, I have often wondered if our shed, Dad's path and screen, along with the rockery, Dad's crazy paving, 'Paul's Scarlet' and 'Dorothy Perkins' are STILL THERE! (?)

On the very edge of my plot was what everybody told me was the 'ice-plant', hence it took a good few years to eradicate this from my brain when learning that the correct name was Sempervivum or 'House Leek'. I waited several years for it to flower, it certainly grew in size with plenty of plantlets growing from it. Everyone back then used to say "they only flower every seven years", quite untrue of course, but hearing this I thought I'd never see it flower. They do in fact bloom every year, although mine didn't for some reason.

One day though, I noticed a subtle difference to my plant, when the centre started rising. A flower at last, I thought, and would have been, for horror of horrors, Sandra came running towards the alley to get to the kitchen when c-c-crunch! She stood on my prize plant! I remember being in such a rage, all the dreams of seeing a flower at last… gone! Mum or Dad told her off for being so careless (a word that was used on both of us at times!), but I just cried and cried, in fact it was the only time I ever cried without getting a smack for something or other from Mum and Dad! That sempervivum never did bloom, albeit the now squashed plant did actually slowly recover, but never flowered!

A few years down the line, and like siblings, do like to torment each other, as mentioned earlier, I dug over the *whole* of the back garden, Sandra then came back I think from playing in the street, and I said to her, "now don't walk on this will you, I've just dug the lot over," then Sandra put her foot out and squashed one of my proudly dug-over clods. I saw red and, sadly for her, I still had the garden fork in my hand and stabbed her in the foot with it; in fact it went right through the side of her heel! Boy, did I get told off for this! Thankfully, they were the only two incidents with Sandra, I think we both learnt lessons here, don't you!

Someone gave us two Chrysanthemum plants and I now suspect that it could have been my Uncle George Mansfield, the husband to my Auntie Iris, who was the next eldest to Mum. Uncle George was a keen Chrysanth grower, and did see them in all their glory when they lived at 169, Leucha Road, E.17, and also remember him mostly for growing the most beautiful Phlox 'paniculata'.

The Chrysanths in our garden were the large bronze type and large white, they were truly amazing, for this reason I expect after seeing the same flowers in bloom all year, to suddenly at the latter part of the year to see something burst open in bloom and flowers so very different to what was in the garden at that time.

Another 'curious' flower arrived in the garden and certain that it came from the Jackson's garden (No.9) for I sort of recall seeing it in their garden at some point, and as the plant seeds and germinates very well, it must have blown with the wind? The plant was "Rose of Heaven" Lychnis 'coronaria', although my plant died out and left no seedlings which is quite strange, for they often grown like weeds!

Next to it at some point, Mum or Dad bought a "Christmas Rose" Helleborus 'niger' the niger referring to its black roots. This was quite an unusual plant to buy in the 1950s, and have no Idea where Mum and Dad bought it from. Garden centres then were virtually non-existent at that time too, and I know I certainly never saw one until the sixties. All I knew was Woolworths where they sold seeds in very colourful packets.

On the subject of Woolworth's, sadly now just closed down (2008–2009), my Nan, Mum's mum, was the manageress at Woolworth's in Walthamstow E.17 when the original shop/store stood at the bottom of Walthamstow's famous market in the High Street. It stood on the corner of Blackhorse Rd and St. James' St. Almost 'facing' Coppermill Lane. My Granddad used to play the piano in the store to the great delight of all the customers. Imagine doing that today!

Woolworth's back then, like The British Home Stores and Marks & Spencer, all had the most wonderful wooden floorboards, this alone making these stores quaintly old-fashioned and most welcoming, each having long sectional counters with perhaps three or more staff per 'section', one of these being an area set for plants, seeds and garden sundries.

Dad planted two areas up with Hollyhocks, one batch against his 'screen' that I'll tell you about in a minute, the other batch at the back of the garden that backed onto Mr and Mrs Brook's garden, albeit divided us by a narrow cinder path. The Hollyhock was a fascinating plant to a small lad like myself, for they were very unlike any other plant that I had in the garden, they grew so tall.

Something I do remember doing, and that is getting up very early on summer mornings, getting on a kitchen stool, unbolting the back door of the kitchen that led to the alley then garden, I would make for the Hollyhocks and slightly prise open a bud on each plant to see what colour they were going to be in just a few days! I must confess I always longed to see the 'black' colour. It must be quite outstanding even nowadays, for seed firms have singled this one out and sell it as Althaea 'niger' (the botanists now changing the botanical name to Alcea for some strange reason).

The only other buds I remember peeking at were Paul's Scarlet (rose) which you remember from earlier, the other was a carnation, *red* of course, for no doubt that was Mum's choice!

Mum also bought Antirrhinums 'Bunny Rabbits' no doubt to amuse Sandra and me, and pansies of course with their little 'faces'. I wonder if my dad was the first hippy! for Dad used to tell me that during the war tobacco was hard to get hold of, and that he smoked three different types of leaves during the war years, he smoked the dried leaves of Lettuce, and Hollyhocks! and of course the leaves of the actual tobacco plant that grew in most gardens, possibly Nicotiana 'affinis'. Dad grew the common various coloured Nicotiana and it was these that he referred to for smoking, although it's possible that dad was mistaking this plant for 'affinis'.

The second from last plant that I remember in our garden was in fact the first successful cutting that I did. (The first one at school was a disaster!) Looking toward our house, at the end of our 'cul-de-sac' and my back to Chippenham Road, looking left was a group of shrubs, mainly Ribes 'sanguineum', "Flowering Currants", the very ones that had the insects – 'blood-suckers' – all over them, and we were told that they would indeed suck your blood! (but of course they don't). These shrubs cornered both sides of Chippenham Walk, and each had a sloping piece of grass on them on which we played, backing the shrubs were of course 'old people's bungalows' as we were taught to say!

The side I was now standing was the bungalow of Mrs Reid (I'm not certain which of the several versions of Reid is the right spelling, i.e. Read, Rede, etc.), the other bungalow belonged to a Mrs House, to describe her hairstyle nowadays would be an early 'Beatles haircut' albeit the Beatles were not then known, it was after all still the late 1950s.

Anyhow, I'm on the path with the left-hand shrub border, when I looked down and saw a semi-crushed stem that had been walked on. I do remember feeling so sorry for it. I took it home straight away, to plant it, and I planted it right next to 'Uncle' Arthur's fence, i.e. where the rockery of ours ended and the chestnut fencing began.

To my surprise the cutting started to pick up and sprout leaves, although over the years long grass used to cover it quite a bit, as I said earlier… Dad was no gardener, and me being so young obviously a lot of time was spent at school, and when we weren't I was out playing or indoors with my toys etc. That cutting grew no more than 1 ft high, but when we moved to Chingford Hatch E.4 and took my plant with me, and it grew enormous, sadly when the house was pulled down, that shrub went with it.

My last plant that I remember at our Harold Hill garden, was when I dug a 10ft square patch at the bottom left of our garden, hence I made it a sort of extension of Uncle Arthur's similar sized border next door, and dearly wanted to copy Arthur's patch if I could. Uncle Arthur had that area crammed with Dahlias of every description, and enhanced the colours even more by adding the clump forming varieties of Michaelmas daisies, and a pound to a penny one variety I'm certain was "Winston Churchill" the other plants were the yellows and bronzes of Heleniums.

Just one variety of Dahlia in my child's eye stood out from all the others and that was a very distinctive mauve and white variety which Uncle Arthur must have told me was called "Prince Albert". Some of you may know that there are various types of Dahlia, i.e. Pom-Pom, Cactus, Decorative etc. "Prince Albert" was the latter.

We used to have a Provident man call, and Dad was quite pally with him. Dad knew that I liked that variety of Dahlia and the Provident man it seems was an ardent Dahlia grower, so Dad told him about "Prince Albert" and the next week he brought a plant round for me. I remember being so delighted, my very first Dahlia! Mind you, it did look lonely in that big square that I'd dug over, and only Hollyhocks backed it; the rest of that patch was never planted up but I do remember weeding it a lot in case someone bought me some plants… they never did!

About 2ft or so from this border, I dug out another smaller 4'x3' approx. and planted all sorts of seeds: "Love-in-a mist", "California Poppy" and Lupin, the leaves of these looked particularly nice after a rainfall or heavy summer dew. The "Love-in-a-Mist always scared me once it had gone to seed, for when trying to get the seeds out, lots of earwigs would scurry out and make you jump! I felt really proud having two small plots of my own, which included the one by the back door. My new third plot on the top left of the garden by my 'Dahlia bed' was always full of annuals, mostly from seed firms doing 'Children's Mixture'. I used to stay with my Nan and Grandad for one or two weeks in the summer, and they bought me a small 4" or so toy yellow tractor, and remember taking it straight over to that second plot to play with it amongst my annuals! A lovely sunny day long ago.

1950's Sundries

Don't get too excited, readers, for I only remember three! My most favourites were little half-inch round tablets called 'PLANTOIDS' brownish in colour, and all you had to do was push one of these tablets into the ground, but about 1"–2" away from the plants and making sure that they were near roots – boy! They made the smallest annual become quite bushy, the bigger the shrub, I'd perhaps put two or three tablets, for in my child's mind assumed that bigger plants needed that extra boost. Logical really, and I was probably correct in what I was doing?

The next chemical sadly I can't recall the name, but it was a powder that actually worked to kill slugs and snails. I use the word 'kill' very lightly, for I think it was to act as a deterrent, for you simply did a trail of this powder either on your path adjoining the border, or just in front of your plants on the actual soil, this barrier of powder would stop slugs and snails crossing over to your plants. I do not recall seeing dead slugs, I never saw one snail ever in the Chippenham Walk garden, nor the really big slugs that you see today. We had the small creamy white ones and the odd small black slug now and again.

The third chemical was a bucket? full of water and Dad would throw all his old cigarette butts in it to make a nicotine insect-killer! Both Mum and dad were quite heavy smokers, of course back then, and during the war years, being told that it was good for them. Our ashtrays indoors were scallop shells, Mum and Dad had them for our duration at Harold Hill.

Dad's Screen

Whether people liked it or loathed it, I can't say! Dad built what he called a screen, it certainly was very colourful, although as children, Sandra and I never knew what its purpose was, it was many years down the line that I gave it some thought, and of course it was to screen off the people over the back to us – no, I don't think from old Mr and Mrs Brooks, but probably from Mr and Mrs Popple who had their flat above the Brooks.

Mr Popple, like Mr Brooks, was in a wheelchair and Mrs Popple would wheel him out onto the balcony and they'd give us a cheery wave. I don't ever recall Mr Brooks outside at all. I will tell you of Mr and Mrs Brooks shortly.

I can only assume that because we were overlooked, and Mum often at the kitchen sink, perhaps proved embarrassing for both parties, hence Dad's screen?

Dad started cutting up 5"–6" wide timber into various lengths, the thickness no more than 2" thick I should think. He then primed and undercoated these before painting them a gloss white. He then built it to a sort of framework, leaving 4'x3' wide squares in strategic places the length of the screen, all carefully planned out, then about three large openings some 8ft high by 4ft wide, on these he screwed in eyelets and threaded a red ¼" thick wire in an up and down pattern like long elongated V-style.

The still empty 4'x3' areas, Dad cut out exterior ply panels and affixed them to these empty square, then each was painted in an array of pastel colours of blues, greens, yellows etc. These panels had been meticulously worked out to be in a position to block out each of the balconies mentioned earlier, hence Mum could not be seen when at the kitchen sink, even the entrance through the screen had been carefully positioned, then Dad made the path down the garden that I mentioned earlier.

Dad was way before his time looking back now. He was in fact an Architect, and built and designed what was once the biggest power station in the world at Ffestiniog, Wales. He also designed weird very long sloping roofs of 'modern day' churches and schools. He used to take me to see some of them, some I think in Harlow for the then new town, and worked with a great pal of his with the surname of Gifford. Dad was studying at Fitzwilliam College Cambridge, he became a lecturer at Walthamstow College and was studying for a Professorship, but a heart attack put paid to this.

Dad was also an accomplished painter in oils, his best work in my eyes was paint and pastels, he sold many of his paintings on The Green at North Chingford. My Auntie Rita, Mum's youngest sister, used to take him a flask of tea over for him, not used today, but I have that same flask, given to me by Auntie Rita. Dad, for many years, wrote for the Amateur Photographer magazine.

Plants in our House

Yes, I'm still talking about No.8 Chippenham Walk! Let's start with the kitchen, a lovely red Cyclamen stood on our sunny kitchen windowsill, with red gingham curtains each side of it, it had many flowers on it, and I remember being sad when it died back for its rest period, and delighted when the first leaves and buds reappeared later on. It had a very large corm on it, I'm pleased to say I never saw its demise, I love red cyclamen even today (Mum certainly liked RED!) (Dad, yellow).

When I was small Auntie Rita bought me a bowl of Narcissi, a variety called 'Pheasants Eye'. The bowl was made of papier maché, and had a crinkly patterned edge to it for decoration. The bulbs were in their dormant stage, and it was here that I learned the term 'forcing', for Rita said that I must put these in a dark cupboard, then check each week to see them grow. I can assure you, the reader, that on seeing the very first spurt of growth from those bulbs I took a peek almost daily, such was my interest and dare I say it… impatience!

I couldn't contain my excitement when the yellowy leaves grew to about 6" high and time now to come out of the cupboard and onto the kitchen windowsill alongside the cyclamen. When the buds first came through, again it seemed forever as a small child, for of course I had no idea what a Narcissus was, so explains my impatience and excitement to see what the flower would be like!

As I grew up, I have always assumed that I was told that my bulbs were 'Pheasant Eye' Narcissus, or as some gardening books call it 'Old Pheasants Eye' but it could have been another old variety called Narcissus 'Actaea', sadly… I'll never know.

Again, someone knew my love of plants, and can only assume that Mum and dad bought me three nicely rounded small pots of three separate varieties of bulbs, these I nurtured on my bedroom windowsill. I'll never forget them, they were Muscari "Heavenly Blue", Chionadoxa "Glory-of-the-snow" and Scilla 'Siberica' "Spanish Squill".

The only other plant I tried to grow on my windowsill was some peanuts or 'Ground Nut'. Mum had bought her weekly mags *Woman* and *Woman's Own* and one of them had a garden article about growing your own peanuts, and actually showed you its leaves and lovely small yellow flowers. Dad was a peanut nut! so he must have given some to Mum to give to me to plant.

I planted them up, but the whole lot turned into a soggy mess. I remember being so disappointed. I was often looking out of my bedroom window, for it looked down on ours and other gardens, and see them change over all the seasons, and to see all the spent fireworks and bonfire of just ashes the day after Guy Fawkes night will stay in my memory, always.

Thank you, Mrs Gwyther!

One of my most favourite teachers at Bosworth Infants (and Juniors) school at Harold Hill, Romford was Mrs Gwyther, she knew of my interest in flowers. Yes, I was still in the infant school in the wooden annexes, the Juniors was brick-built (where Dad 'borrowed' some rubble for our path!). I think I must have asked Mrs Gwyther if I could show the class how to do a cutting, and Mrs Gwyther gave me that chance. I don't remember, but Mrs Gwyther in fact may have asked me to demonstrate a cutting, and bring one in, it's such a long time ago now it's hard to remember.

I have a superb photo of my Nan and Grandad (Mum's parents) at a seaside somewhere, I always thought it was taken at Southend-on-Sea or Clacton-on-Sea, but my Auntie Rita tells me that it could have been Bexhill-on-Sea as apparently they were very fond of the place. Anyhow, in this photo they're both smiling away standing next to a large shrub of Senecio 'greyii' "New Zealand Daisy Bush" which has bright yellow daisy flowers and literally smothers its own leaves with flowers.

I recognised this shrub in the photo from the shrubs that cornered each side of Chippenham Walk (mentioned earlier) so I took a 3"–4" cutting from the shrub, took it along to my class, and Mrs Gwyther asked me to show all the class how to take a cutting. I must have asked Mrs Gwyther for a pot of sand, no doubt from the school sandpit, for in my child's mind I thought of Nan and Grandad (Rose Ridley née Axford and Harry Bishop Ridley) at the seaside, put two and two together – shrub, seaside, sand – it must grow in sand! Sadly my cutting died. I thought about my first demonstration many times over the years after this, and sort of ashamed of my failure, although I must say no one else gave it a second thought! I felt silly thinking that the cutting would grow in total sand, but I now realise that I hadn't been wrong after all, for indeed you can get cuttings, moreso hardwood or semi-hardwood to grow in sand, providing you keep the sand moist.

Looking back now, perhaps my cutting was never kept watered? for I never saw it again after it left Mrs Gwyther's desk. Also, I suspect it was the wrong time of the year for cuttings. Many hardwood cuttings can actually be buried in sand, and even after a few weeks will even root at the right end! Roses are particularly good in rooting this way, and also in a compost heap!

Mrs Gwyther one day brought in an earthworm on a sheet of paper, and asked us to be completely silent, and said "Did you know that worms make a noise?" We of course all gave a resounding "No!", so we all stood silently only to hear the minutest "tut"!

A Lovely Flower Story

Still at Bosworth school and in my earliest infant days, and my first teacher Miss Evans, we all had the usual Janet and John books but one story in a separate book of stories stood out to me above all other, but sadly do not remember the title of the main book, however the story that I loved is called – 'THE NASTURTIUMS THAT GREW TOO BIG FOR THEIR BOOTS' – and had the most delightful colourful photos to depict the story. The story goes like this…

An old man and lady lived in a thatched cottage just outside the main village. One day the old couple decided to plant up some Nasturtium seeds in the man's old work boots, and the Nasturtiums grew and grew, they came into bloom with reds, yellows etc., climbed up the walls right onto the roof. But from the village looking across the fields to the thatched cottage, the villagers thought that the cottage was on fire! So all the villagers grabbed buckets and bowls full of water to form a chain across the field to the old cottage, of course the old man and lady came out of their cottage to see what all the fuss was about, then they... and the villagers all fell about laughing when they realised that it wasn't flames after all, and only the vibrant reds and yellows of the lovely Nasturtiums!

As an afterthought, I expect I was the only one in the class perhaps who actually knew what Nasturtiums were!

'My' Two Oak Trees!

One Oak tree to me stands out above all others, and saw it in all its seasons every day of my life at Chippenham Walk, for this giant oak faced our house at the bottom of the walk. It was a huge tree then and must have been some age, I'm glad to say that it's still with us! The other oak stood to the edge of our playground, and in the property of one of the prefabs. I remember this tree well because sadly a hedgehog had got trapped and died between the chain-link fence and the trunk of the oak, the hedgehog smelt awful.

I'm told the prefabs and Bosworth school are both no longer there, but did someone have the good sense to keep that lovely old oak when they built the then new housing? Somehow I doubt it.

Bosworth School – Gardening Club

You can imagine my delight when a gardening club was started up, when the teachers thought of something that was to be called 'House Groups' and each house group had a name and a colour, all of which I remember today.

The House groups were all named after places in this country, although I don't think at our ages back then in the early Juniors any of us had heard of any of the places! The House groups were as follows... there was BLUE HOUSE (Cambridge), RED HOUSE (Maldon), YELLOW HOUSE (Thaxted), GREEN HOUSE (Greenstead). I really can't remember now what house I was in, but suspect the latter as it has references to greenery!

Not many children chose the Gardening Club when it came to choosing what subject you wanted, and sadly do not remember any of the children's names in that club. I do, however, remember our very nice teacher Mrs Galloway, like Mrs Gwyther whom I spoke of earlier, was a homely lady with a nice pleasant manner.

The club was very good, but sadly no gardening whatsoever, but we learnt about birds, badgers, dormice etc. I realise now why there was no gardening, and that it must have been winter, for the gardening club was held in the afternoon and the classroom lights were on.

One child brought in something curious, and it had come from their mum and dad's loft (attic) and was I think either a wasps' or bees' nest, and the wasps or bees were still stuck on the next where they had been sprayed to kill them off.

Little did I know that my happy childhood at Harold Hill, and my school was slowly coming to an end, when Mum and Dad decided that we were to move to Chingford Hatch. 7th March 1960 and now I'm at the age of just turned sixty, finally now know why! For not until now did I ever wonder why Mum and Dad had to move. It was because Mum was expecting a baby (my brother Barry, born on the 18th March 1960) for there simply was no room for another child at Harold Hill, for there were only two bedrooms – Mum and Dad in the front bedroom facing the street (cul-de-sac!) and me and Sandra in the room overlooking all the gardens as I mentioned earlier.

I was now twelve years old and Sandra eighteen months younger, therefore both were getting older to share a bedroom. Mum had been 'diagnosed' with M.S. (Multiple Sclerosis) albeit not really being diagnosed until several years later to what it was. Mum was just twenty-eight years old when the first signs of M.S. appeared. I witnessed that first fall just behind the chip shop as Mum, Dad, Sandra and me were making our way back home a short distance away.

Right… back to the gardening club! Mrs Galloway one day out of the blue then spoke of gardening at last, and told us all that she was going to show us our new gardening plots, each plot would be shared between two children. She told us that our caretaker (school gardener?), Mr Trapp, had dug these plots out over the winter months, ready for our use come springtime. So off we trotted to the far end of the school field, and saw Mr Trap's hard work for ourselves. They were all along the fence line adjacent to the steps and path leading to the Briar Road shops and of course the Prefab estate.

One of Mum's pals Marie… (pronounced 'Marry, as the old music hall star Marie Lloyd) …lived in one of these prefabs. I thought them to be lovely homes and gardens, and would solve housing problems today, 99% of people did not want to leave them, so that tells you something, but as usual falls on deaf ears.

I only ever saw my plot once when Mrs Galloway showed us, for as mentioned, we moved away and of course the start of the gardeners' calendar, for it was now March. So I never did do any gardening in the gardening club, but have often wondered what I would have learnt had we stayed put, what was Mrs Galloway's knowledge like in the actual flower world? Sadly, I'll never know.

The only thing that I was apprehensive about was who I had to share my plot with, I sort of recall that I didn't like the child's manner (too forward?) or that I didn't know that boy at all, would we have got on well together? I have often thought of those so far off days, and wondered how the children and gardening club fared after I left it all behind.

The Tower, Geraniums and Me!

Mr and Mrs Dobson, and daughter Janet, lived at No.12 Chippenham Walk. Janet was a very smiley girl, older than us, and possibly must have started work or at least more or less leaving school. Sadly, I never knew Mr and Mrs Dobson's Christian names, but Janet's dad built her the most beautiful Wendy house, this is probably why she never played out – who would with that in your garden?

When you're small, life is new, and you have lots of FIRSTS, by that I mean the first time you see things for the first time. The front garden of Mr and Mrs Dobson was the first time that I had ever seen standard roses, these were underplanted with Geraniums (Zonal Pelargonium) which Mr Dobson loved.

When I was in my thirties I went back to Chippenham Walk, and took a chance to knock on the door of No. 12, hoping that Mr and Mrs Dobson still lived there, or indeed if they were still alive. Thankfully they were both alive and well. It goes without saying, I left Harold Hill aged just twelve years old, so I certainly would have changed a great deal from boy to man. It was Mr Dobson who opened the door, and so not to alarm him as I was a total 'stranger', I just blurted out with a cheery smile "Hello Mr Dobson, do you remember me?" of course he said "No". I then said, "Do you remember little Keith Nichols at No.8? he then smiled and said, "Not little Keefy Nichols!" I then said, "Yes, now I'm BIG Keefy Nichols!"

He and I were both overjoyed, then he called out to Mrs Dobson, who in turn was so pleased to see me. Mr Dobson's face then saddened, "Ah, Keith, it's not the same here any more, not like when you was a boy, there's murders, muggings, rapes, vandalism, burglary, etc., no, not the same."

Needless to say, my genteel days of boyhood at Harold Hill were totally shattered on hearing what Mr Dobson had just said, and how sad that Mr and Mrs Dobson themselves had witnessed that change through staying in that same house for all those years. And who do we have to thank for this sad change? It is of course very week governments, lawmakers, judges and police?

Mrs Dobson then cheered up again, when I told him what I did as a living, I think he more or less guessed, for in his next breath he said, "Do you remember when I took you out for the day?" I gave a very surprised "No!" Mr Dobson said, "So you don't remember <u>exactly</u> where I took you?" once again I gave a very resounding "No, I don't!" I told him that I do remember being with him standing next to a flower bed full of red geraniums and that he told me the variety was 'Paul Crampel'!

Mr Dobson was so surprised that I'd remembered the variety! He then totally shocked me by saying that it was THE TOWER OF LONDON that he took me to! But I remember nothing of the day whatsoever. I don't remember Mr Dobson collecting me from home, waving Mum and Dad "goodbye", the journey there and back by train and bus etc. I only remember those geraniums, and Mr Dobson said how I kept talking about them. I did visit the Tower again the '1st' time when married, not realising that I had been with Mr Dobson years ago.

Golden Leaves at Number Ten

Ted and Kit Lane lived at No.10 with son Alan who had just started work. They had a lovely friendly dog called 'Rusty' who loved to come into the street to see us kids. I remember him with great fondness.

Ted had a pigeon loft in his back garden, but they weren't a nuisance, in fact you rarely saw them flying about. Kit was a nice lady, in fact a friendly family who did speak to us children.

From Ted and Kit's path in the front garden, was a 1ft wide border either side of it, and had the same plants in for all of the years at Chippenham Walk. I could see them so easily from our front garden, looking across the garden of our next door neighbours at No.9, as Ted and Kit's house was up in the corner (the houses were set in a square, i.e. our block was 6, 7, 8, and 9, Ted and Kit's 10, 11, 12, and 13 plus of course the opposite side.

The plants were such a bright gold and Kit said they were called Matricaria, the old name for the 'Golden Feverfew' Chrysanthemum 'parthenium aurea'. Ted and Kit would cut these back each year to keep bushy, and without a doubt lots of seedlings would appear to thicken the borders even more.

Rumours in much later years said that Ted and Kit bought (or managed) a pub in Stowmarket area. I would loved to have seen Ted, Kit and Alan again. Sadly 'Rusty' will be long gone now. I put several letters in various newspapers and magazines to try to locate the family, knowing how many people use pubs, for you only want one person to pick up a pen or phone to tell you all you want to know, but alas folk do this less and less nowadays.

Over the Moon!

Mr and Mrs Bowen lived at No. 11; again, sadly I did not know their Christian names. They had two little boys – one named Terry, the younger one my dad called 'Buster' who had a cute rounded little face.

Again, these were lovely people, and on odd occasions they would ask me in to watch ITV, though my mum and dad always said that WE were the first people to have a television in 'the Walk'. ITV of course had adverts which I truly loved to see, but my main reason for going over there to No. 11 was to see *Rin-Tin-Tin* and *Boots and Saddles* and *Twizzle*, *Torchy The Battery Boy* etc.

Sadly, the Bowens decided to move away, and their kindness continued. Just before they left, for they knew that I loved flowers, they gave me permission to go into their back garden after the removal men had gone, and dig up whatever plants I wanted. I couldn't contain my excitement, but grabbed Dad's garden fork at the ready!

At the time when I used to go in their house to watch ITV, one day they called out to me with great excitement, and asked if I would like to go over and see the new BLUE rose. I remember them being so excited with their new acquisition. I, of course, at the time had no idea that a blue rose was so unusual. The blue rose went under the name of 'Blue Moon' and has remained a popular rose ever since.

I was over in their back garden like a shot once the removal men went away. Sadly they'd taken 'Blue Moon' but I was compensated with the old variety of pinks called 'Mrs Sinkins'. Unfortunately I have no recollection of what other plants I dug up – if any!

Mrs Thornton Over The Back!

It annoys me greatly that I cannot recall the lovely face of old Mrs Thornton who had the lower flat that was just to the right as I walked to the bottom of our garden. Mr and Mrs Brooks' garden backed onto ours, hence Mrs Thornton was their next-door neighbour.

On one very hot summer's day, Mrs Thornton asked me if I wanted to earn some pocket money by digging up a border for her in her front garden (Dunstable Road). This was my very first paid job! I can't remember what Mrs Thornton paid me now, but when I'd finished, she asked me into her kitchen for a glass of orange juice for I was very hot and tired, and knew then that if I chose to do this as a job, I'd be in for a very hard working life, as indeed it has been.

Whilst enjoying my orange juice, Mrs Thornton chatted to me, and then I espied two plants on her window-sill, one pretty pink flower growing in a glass vase with lots of roots that of course you could easily see. I'd never seen this plant before, so asked Mrs Thornton what it was called, and she told me that it was called 'The Japanese Water Plant'. Many years later as this plant grew in popularity it soon adopted another name, that being 'Busy Lizzie'. I have never heard that plant being called 'The Japanese Water Plant' since Mrs Thornton spoke of it way back in the mid-1950s.

The second plant had the tiniest leaves that I'd ever seen, so once again I said, "What's the name of that plant, Mrs Thornton?" Mrs Thornton retorted "Mind your own business!" I was stunned, and went quiet and extremely embarrassed and wished that I hadn't asked a second question. I need not have worried, for Mrs Thornton obviously saw my now very sad face, and in a split second said, "It's alright, Keith, that's the name of the plant, it's called 'Mind-Your-Own-Business'!" Of course we both laughed, and no doubt she offered me another orange juice to make me feel better, and to prove that she hadn't turned into a nasty lady!

The plant's other common name is 'Baby's Tears', and although Mrs Thornton had the plant indoors she may have not known that it grows perfectly well outdoors too, even if a frost catches it badly, often little bits survive, and you only need a tiny bit of it to re-grow, and it does, very quickly. There are two tender versions of the plant – a golden one and also variegated.

I look back very fondly to my early years, and to think that Mrs Thornton was someone's mother, sister, grandmother etc. and of course there was a Mr Thornton at one time. There must be some photos of her somewhere…

…And Next Door

And next door to Mrs Thornton was a very dear old couple, Mr and Mrs Brooks. I never knew Mr Brooks' Christian name, but I'm sure Mrs Brooks' name was Rose. I never called her by her first name though.

Mrs Brooks' face, thankfully, I do vaguely remember, and she was a great mentor to me, and *every* time she was in the garden I made a point of saying "hello", and asking her questions and what she was doing. I must have been a bit of a pest, but she never did seem to mind; she answered all my questions and demonstrated to me how to plant seeds etc. I'm certain the first seeds I saw her grow were the 'Annual Chrysanth'. She made a square out of old house bricks, probably not more than 1ft 6" square, with a piece of glass on top, which she explained kept the seedlings warm.

I had no idea what annual chrysanths looked like until she showed me the seed packet. I could see why she liked them.

As the seedlings grew, she showed me how to transplant the new plantlets, and she put them in different parts of her garden. Other seed varieties she showed me how to plant in long rows, and the seedlings then stayed put and looked superb all bunched up! Mrs Brooks then showed me how to mark the newly planted seedlings by putting in a 'stick' to mark the end of the row, and a stick or small garden cane pierced through the seed packet to mark the other end, plus of course to show you the picture of the seeds of what you have just sown, plus other details.

I asked Mrs Brooks about all the flowers she planted for I spoke to Mrs Brooks almost daily. I do so clearly remember her planting a rosemary plant (sub-shrub); she did this from a cutting, and planted it under the window of t heir kitchen (?).

When I was in my twenties and passed my driving test, one of my first priorities was to visit 'old' neighbours. 'Auntie' Vi and 'Uncle' Tom at No. 13 were sadly not at home, but thankfully our next-door neighbours 'Uncle' Arthur and 'Auntie' Ena were at home and made me so very welcome. I simply had to ask them if they knew that Mr and Mrs Brooks were still living at 77 Dunstable Road. They both lowered their voices and told me that Mr Brooks died some years ago, and sadly I'd missed Mrs Brooks as she'd died just three weeks ago. I was saddened. If I'd gone to Harold Hill just 6–12 months earlier I would have at least seen Mrs Brooks for the last time.

I'd made up my mind that day to see Mr and Mrs Brooks and their garden, and perhaps take a peek at our own garden that I'd played in all through my boyhood. I then drove round to Dunstable Road, and knocked on the door, and it seemed so strange for me doing that, for the last time (and only time) I knocked on that door I was a little lad, and Mrs Brooks came to the door and Mr Brooks gave me a very cheery smile and hello. I'll tell you the reason I knocked at their door at that time way back in the '50s a little further on…

The elderly lady greeted me at the door, and I explained who I was, and straight away she said "Would you like to see the garden?" I must have given a hearty "YES!", in fact I know I did! I told the lady where the rosemary shrub used to be and how I remember Mrs Brooks taking that cutting. The lady gasped, "I only dug that out just two weeks ago!" She never realised how old that shrub was.

I must admit my heart sank on not seeing that rosemary growing in its rightful place under the kitchen window. I also mentioned to the lady that Mrs Brooks' first name was Rose (possibly Rosemary?), but her daughter *was* Rosemary; she too was a lovely friendly lady, and looked like a really young version of Mrs Brooks and no doubting about the family resemblance. Rosemary had a little daughter called Pamela, although they (we) always called her Pammy or little Pam Pam! She had lovely blonde hair. They would visit Mr and Mrs Brooks often in summer when we were playing in our garden, or eating jam sandwiches, or playing with a clay bubble pipe – after the original contents were used up Mum would make up some soap suds for us to we could carry on playing.

I also told the lady where Mr and Mrs Brooks had their huge border filled just with the tall old-fashioned Marguerite Daisies. The lady listened with great interest, and told her that from my back garden (which I tried desperately – to no avail – to look at whilst talking to the lady), and the border of daisies was on the right-hand side looking from our garden. Mrs Brooks, looking back now, must have had an enormous task cutting this lot down to ground level each year, but the job must have been worth it to her for that so marvellous display of Marguerites that I most certainly looked forward to seeing every year of my childhood.

During the latter nineties, I put a letter into the readers' letters page of the *Romford Recorder* newspaper to try and find Rosemary and now a grown-up 'Pammy'. The letter was printed but nothing came of it. I also tried to find the two sons of Mum's best pal in the 'walk' (Tom and Vi Smith); the two sons were Keith and Alan, but again to no avail.

Right! As promised, I said to you the reader that I knocked on the door of Mrs Brooks as a little boy, for one day in the garden she said could I ask Mummy if it was OK to go and see them, for Mr Brooks had something in the gardening line that he wanted me to see. My mum said it was perfectly OK to go over. I was so excited, I went to the bottom of our garden, climbed onto our compost heap and over the very slanted chestnut paled fencing and onto the narrow cinder path (and they *were* cinders too!).

Once on the path, I faced right, then turned a sharp left, then through their alley where both front doors faced each other of our lovely neighbours, i.e. Mr and Mrs Brooks, and Mrs Thornton.

As mentioned earlier, Mrs Brooks opened the door to me, Mr Brooks was in his wheelchair. "Come in, Keith, come in! I thought you might be interested in seeing this." Mr Brooks went on to say that this huge scrapbook contained each and every strip of the *Daily Mirror's* Mr

Digwell. Superb drawings of an elderly man with a flat cap, moustache, and pipe, mostly all done with 'speech balloons' and written as most people talk, and every gardening tip imaginable.

Mr Brooks said that these 'cartoon' type strips went right back to when the *Daily Mirror* first showed Mr Digwell, and he was still adding to them. I have often wondered if Rosemary ever kept that so precious scrapbook and if it still exists today somewhere?

I am though a proud owner of Mr Digwell's soft-back booklet that was priced at 3/- 6d – a much treasured item of mine.

The Annoying Little Boy... Me!

Questions, questions, questions – that was me, a little lad so keen to learn. Mrs Brooks, Arthur Cox, our immediate neighbour, had to put up with me as well!

Ena and Arthur Cox were such lovely neighbours. Thankfully Arthur is still alive (2011). Arthur was very well known in Brentwood, Essex, as he owned a working man's cafe there in the High St(?), and I *think* was called Arthur's cafe (?).

Arthur's now well into his eighties, but I still do remember him as a young dad, an image I'll never forget, and that memory of him watering all his flowers on the nearest side to us, when on a warm day he'd give me and Sandra the odd squirt with the hose, and make us all laugh, and he did that each summer. He found it hilarious, and so did we!

Ena and Arthur's garden was always kept really immaculate, a lovely manicured lawn, never a weed to be seen and put our garden to total shame, but totally out of my hands as a little 'un, yet I dearly wanted to mimic Arthur's garden. I was always looking through the chestnut palings to see what Uncle Arthur was doing, what was he planting *this* time!

Behind our rockery, which fronted a panel of closeboard fencing, was Uncle Arthur's rockery, and furthered my very limited knowledge on 'rockery' plants, but each year I asked Arthur over and over again as each of the plants bloomed, so eventually they registered and knew their names at a glance.

Nowadays I can't recall the plants that he had on his rockery, except two – they being 'Yellow Rock Alyssum' and 'Rock Candytuft', i.e. Alyssum 'Saxatile' and Iberis 'sempervirens', although I of course didn't know their botanical names as shown here.

Every year Uncle Arthur, in summer, planted a blue and white edging annual, namely the blue lobelia and white Alyssum or 'Sweet Alyssum' to give its common name. These were planted alternate, and looked superb against the nice lawn, and these plants were backed by red salvia. The two annuals that I distinctly remember him planting and still today are two of my top favourite plants, were Mimulus or 'Monkey Flower' or 'Flower of the Incas', a lovely range of colours, often a double colour and each colour covered in spots. Apparently the Mimulus or Musk, was at one time very highly scented, then suddenly the scent stopped and has never returned.

The second plant was the Calceolaria 'hybrida' and looked like inflated cushions, again in various colours and they too were covered in spots. You never see this variety of Calceolaria sold as a summer bedding plant now, and now is sadly resigned to being a greenhouse plant, or a plant for the windowsill. Back in the 1950s, this plant was sold as all other bedding plants back then, and that was in *wooden* seed trays. If you buy Calceolaria today, they're sold as a biggish pot plant and a biggish price too! Lots of nurseries and garden centres today single out certain plants that you could once buy in a box of 25 or even 50, although these plants thankfully can still be bought as seed, like for instance 'Love-Lies-Bleeding', sold now as a single plant or seed, but never as several nice plants in a lovely old wooden seed tray.

Wooden trays, in my opinion, were far better than plastic, for the wood stayed damp for long periods with often the roots sticking to the wood in an attempt to try and grow through the timber. It was always a lovely sight to see plants in wooden trays, and they lasted almost as long as plastic ones, and looked very natural when stacked and stored until their next use, along with all those lovely old clay pots that you used to see until plastic came along.

As Ena and Arthur came out of their 'alley' that led to their kitchen, on the left was the other close board section of fencing (facing the other by our rockery), and on each of these sections of fence was good timber. Arthur zig-zagged planting boxes and hung them on the fence, and affixed singular strips of wood to the front of the elongated boxes. Each of these strips had an 'arch' shape to them for effect, and each strip of wood he painted pale blue and white and looked lovely with all the trailing lobelia hanging over the edges of the 'window' boxes. Both the trailing lobelia and the window boxes were so fascinating to me as a young lad. Another novelty Arthur had on the rockery was a large pinkish conch shell.

Sometime after the year 2000, I had a lovely meet up with Ena and Arthur again at daughter Linda's house in Brentwood, Essex. It was so sad seeing them old, but they were alive and that was more than good enough for me… and them! Their lovely smiles and voices were of course the same, and it was like being transported back in time when they spoke to me as a boy, right up to the time we left Harold Hill when I was twelve. It grieves me that I had no chance to say any goodbyes to all the people I loved the most. Arthur was so surprised at my memory of childhood, and they were both thrilled that I was a gardener.

Sometime before we actually met, Ena and Arthur sent me a lovely photograph of themselves at one of their anniversary do's, and a delightful letter, and I choked back tears, for they had put 'with love from Auntie Ena and Uncle Arthur'. Here I was, a man in his fifties and far from the little boy that I once was at Harold Hill, and they still put Auntie and Uncle – how very sweet and touching that was.

Arthur used to take us out for the day. One fine autumn day he took me, Sandra and his two daughters Linda and Wendy to a forest or woods as we knew them. We spent the day kicking about in the fallen leaves in the country lanes, that I do remember well. The woods had overgrown trenches in them. Arthur said they were used by soldiers during the war (was it WW1 or two I wonder?). I do remember deep holes in the leafy banks and frightened ourselves believing wolves lived in the. Of course there were fox holes. Uncle Arthur I think was amused at me trying to re-create the woods in my own garden when I pulled out tall weeds 1'–2' high from the edge of the woods, brought them home, planted them to make my own little wood, but they all wilted straight away, but the thoughts of that happy day stayed with me.

My wife, Debbie, and I on visiting Ena and Arthur on that nostalgic visit, passed a wood on our way to Linda's house. On reaching our destination and me bringing up that memorable day to Arthur, he said "you passed that very wood as you came in!" and Arthur said, "it's called Warley Wood", and that name sort of came flooding back to me in my brain. I hope one day I'll re-visit that lovely wood of boyhood.

Let's go back to Arthur's dahlias. In autumn, he would cut them all down and leave 6" or so of the stems, and on these he would tie a piece of wool or twine on with a label naming the variety. He would make a makeshift-type cloche and tuck them all cosily away for winter. The cloche was directly under their kitchen windowsill which faced south, so kept reasonably protected even during the coldest days. Under our windowsill, as I said before, was either a pile of coal or coke, Dad's push-bike, or Puch or Vespa motor scooter! (Lambretta?).

I remember taking the odd glance towards Arthur's cloche, although I couldn't see in it, but remember so clearly him taking the tubers out of the cloche in late spring/early summer, and see those tubers with ample greenery on them, all ready for a new season.

Now, let's go back to that visit to Brentwood when I saw Ena and Arthur, and Ena goaded Arthur to tell me the story about how my Mum told Uncle Arthur off and how he made me say my very first swear word! It was yet another day when I was peering at Uncle Arthur through the chestnut paled fencing, and to see what he was up to that day.

It turned out that he'd ordered a load of well rotted horse manure and wanted to move it onto the Dahlia bed, and as rainfall was due at any time Arthur was in a hurry and no time to talk to little boys asking questions! But ask a question I did! "What's that Uncle Arthur?" and Arthur said that on that day he was flustered and very keen to get the manure moved so answered me by saying s**t! Mum must have asked me who'd told me that word, and as a small child I told her! So Arthur said, "your mum told me off for making you swear!" I just loved hearing of that little story, of which I have no recollection, but I really do remember the pile of s**t... er, sorry, manure!

Looking back now, what an immense wealth of knowledge I gained as a small lad, and from people who actually bothered about me and knew my keenness for gardening. It was at this time, however, that people kept saying "He's got green fingers!" I honestly thought back then that I had some awful disease, although I couldn't see it!

A Bluebell Wood

Perhaps I should say *woods*, for I'm sure that there was more than one. Dad didn't take us out much as kids, and I suppose looking back now, the war hadn't been over that many years, and Dad being a young man then probably had little money. He did take us out each year though to a Bluebell wood, and one that we definitely walked to from Chippenham Walk. We went in the direction of what was to become Central Park, and had to cross 'deep' ditches. I have had a lifelong phobia of heights, a real terror, not like these people on TV today who do weird challenges and tell you they have a fear of heights – to then see them 50–60 feet high and a lot more besides, where my phobia can start at a mere 8 foot! And has caused me many embarrassing moments over the years. I suffered horrendous earaches all through my childhood, so possibly that has caused some imbalance?

Anyhow, Sandra and I were petrified to jump across, so Dad carried us and jumped across and I still recall that even that was scary in itself. Would Dad make it to the other side? Would he slip and fall in the water? Would he come back for me once he'd got Sandra safely over? All rather silly really, but to me it was scary, even knowing that we had to make a return journey to do the procedure all over again. All this possibly explains where the second wood came in and we went by car, for I'm certain that when Dad asked Sandra and I in subsequent years, we must have let known that we wanted to go but didn't like those ditches!

Looking at a Harold Hill map today, I can see woods marked on them and very possibly the two we went to, especially the nearest one to us. I'd love to go back there again one day to find both, to see if it jogs any familiar surroundings. We used to pick a bunch of bluebells each year to take back to Mum, and I distinctly remember the new buds on the hawthorn – why I should remember that I can't say, it's obvious I suppose, the newness of spring, the lovely blue of the bluebells growing in great masses throughout the woods, the sun shining, and being with our Dad.

Sorry! Or not so sorry?

Life really is so precious, and as far as we know, we are all only here just this once and that's it(?). Hence why I have been as much as I can, a vegetarian, in fact did not eat fish until I was just in my fifties. For like us, every animal and insect is here just once too. I have always (now don't laugh!) felt guilty having to kill slugs, snails, flies etc. for they too have their little lives and deserve to be in this world as much as us.

Once again, I turn back to Harold Hill (Essex) as that small boy, never knowing about death or dying, and took on, for a short while, this obsession to kill flies, beetles etc. Flies in particular, they would land on Dad's screen that I spoke of earlier, and I'd swipe them with a long garden cane, then make a small area by the screen to make a mini-graveyard, and make little crosses for them. Alive one minute, dead, buried in an instant the next... Oh! the guilt. I took away their little lives all those years ago, and it was wrong.

Over the years I have tried to make myself feel better for doing this, and this is what I think, as daft as it may seem! I believe of all the billions and billions of people that have ever lived, there is not all that much room in the place we call Heaven, so I think that the nastiest people come back as horrible creepy crawlies for then themselves to be destroyed i.e. with sprays, chemicals... trodden on etc. as payback for the wrong doings and misery they caused to nice people in life. Every wasp, bluebottle etc. was once a Nazi, warmonger, thief, rapist, vandal, murderer, burglar, etc., etc. It's these thoughts that then make me feel better – if my thoughts are wrong, then I can only say a big sorry for taking those little lives so long ago... silly eh! (?)

A Fern and Two Primulas

I seem to have left out three more… and final plants that were bought for me, and put in my bedroom. Mum and Dad must have given them to me as a present – one was the lovely 'Maidenhair Fern', but it slowly but surely Died. Mine and Sandra's room faced south and was a very sunny bedroom, but of course there was no central heating in those days, therefore once you left the front room or kitchen, the house went really cold.

The next two plants were Primula 'obconica', a variety that can irritate your skin if touched, and was something I learnt many years later, but never affected me at the time, and I'm certain that there was no warning on the label in those days. The other plant was also a primula, namely Primula 'malacoides' which had an array of tiny pink flowers, and the common name of 'Fairy Primrose' suits it perfectly. These two varieties were indoor types, both no doubt died of the cold.

Who was it?

As a boy in the 1950s I used to receive several gardening catalogues, and all of them with my name on, but Mum and Dad always seemed baffled and convinced me that it wasn't them who had them sent, and couldn't think who did, although we had plenty of relatives and neighbours alive at that time who could easily have done this lovely gesture. I felt quite grown up, seeing my name on the envelope of a catalogue I can tell you! I never ever did find out, and as you the reader can see I certainly have not forgotten.

Very sadly, I can only remember two names of the companies that sent to me. One was Keith Luxford, and remembered that cos of the Keith of course! They were Chrysanthemum growers, and one of their Chrysanths was called 'Keith Luxford'.

I have never in all these years seen this name since childhood, but on 7th February 2009, we went to Norwich to my son Rowan's house, to celebrate my youngest son's birthday, his eighteenth, hence Dale was now a MAN! (other son is Adrian, and daughter Heather). Anyhow, Rowan showed me an old gardening book, and lo and behold, one of the contributors was Keith Luxford! There was no date of print in this book, so I said to Rowan that it could easily be 1950s for they were certainly trading at that time, but how long before or after this time I can't say.

I often wondered if it was my aunt and uncle (Mum's sister and husband) – Auntie Iris née Ridley and George Mansfield – who had this particular catalogue sent to me, for as mentioned further back in this book, Uncle George was a keen Chrysanth grower. Uncle George's dad had a fruit and veg stall outside Toynbees butcher's shop in Walthamstow's famous High Street market for many years (Jack Mansfield). Jack's brother worked in Toynbees.

The next catalogue had a picture on the front of one (three?) ponies with their heads poking through a giant horseshoe, and a chance to win a pony! The competition was to name a rose. I now suspect that I was around nine or ten years old, and thought I'd try my luck at my first competition, but after I'd done it and went to send it off, I saw the concern on Mum and Dad's faces, moreso when they said, "If you win, where will you keep it? We've only a small garden!" I remember being so very worried, then hoped I wouldn't win, in fact dreaded it!

Mum and Dad though gave me high praise for thinking of the name of a new rose for that competition. The name of the company was Anderson's and I think they were based in Scotland? On occasions through childhood, on bright summer evenings when you *still* had to go to bed early, not quite ever understanding why you had to go to bed with the sun still shining! Dad would sit on my bed, being near the window, and read stories by Grimm and Hans Christian Anderson, the latter of course bringing the bright idea to my head and call the rose 'Fairy Tale' – I actually called it 'Anderson's Fairytale'.

I often wonder even today who actually won this pony and did they ever sneakily ever use 'Fairy Tale' in their rose collections, not ever thinking that the name was thought up by a 9 or 10 year old boy.

Several catalogues came my way, as today, with a very mixed bunch of trees, shrubs, plants, bulbs, veg, etc., and one catalogue plugged the plant Canna or 'Indian Shot' to give it its common name, and exclaimed – NEW! Canna Crozy! – Look in any gardening book today and you will not see a variety called 'Crozy', so where this name came from I have no idea. I never have trusted catalogues and plant companies regarding fancy names like 'Sunburst' or 'Liquid Gold' etc. for I'm certain they change the names to suit certain plants as things go in and out of fashion, or to change the name of a plant to boost it up to be something quite different to enhance its sales once again.

Another name that fell out of favour, was one used for the Hosta, and that was Funkia, and possibly a name more suited to today with the word 'funky' used in everyday speech.

I always wished that I'd known who had those catalogues sent to me, for I longed to thank them. If there really is a heaven, maybe I'll still get the chance! (?)

It was through these catalogues that I was able to learn of new plant names and see them in glorious colour, like Ixias, Tigridias, and longed to have a 'Tiger Lily'!

Leaving Childhood Behind

On the 7th March 1960, we moved away from Harold Hill, to Chingford Hatch, London, E.4. Dad was on the verge of leaving us all for another lady, and my brother Barry being born soon after our arrival at 'the hatch' on the 18th March, and Mum's M.S. getting slowly worse. 1963 saw the bitter winter, snow, ice, burst pipes in the kitchen, stand-pipe in the street to get water, and Dad long gone for a new life elsewhere. A multitude of bullies in and out of school, and yearned to be back at Chippenham Walk. My heart ached for No. 8 Chippenham Walk. My life changed forever after this, even more so when we moved from 'the Hatch' to Walthamstow, when I was just eighteen, and was planted with drugs by the police in Edmonton. I was brought to 'justice'; all the so-called police got away with it, and who else suffered under their evil hands? I looked at my lovely youngest son Dale recently, just celebrating his 18th; he, like me, a non-drinker and non-smoker. I tried to picture him in my place at the daunting Quarter Sessions court, an innocent. Looking at him now 18, was like looking how young I then looked at 18, only really just out of latter childhood. If there is a hell, those police will most certainly go there.

Our garden at Chingford Hatch (37, Bernwell Road) was a really good size, but I still had no money to make the garden really nice. The plants I did have were begged or borrowed no doubt. We had only been at Bernwell Road for a few days when we had possibly the very last rag and bone man down our road, and something scared the horse and the cart hit Dad's car. The poor rag and bone man was visibly shaken up, so Mum and Dad took him indoors and gave him a 'cuppa', thankfully the horse remained calm outside.

Dad always said that when he was a little boy, he would follow all the horse and carts and collect the horse droppings in a bucket and take it home to his mum and dad's garden at 80, Kenilworth Road, E.17. It goes without saying, I wanted to copy Dad, so in the two remaining years or so that this rag and bone man came along Bernwell Road, I was there with a bucket and shovel. I can safely say that I was the last person to pick up horse manure in Bernwell Road, and certainly the last person to have chickens there.

The Chingford Hatch Garden

Dad hadn't walked out on us at this time, and our new home did feel... well... homely! The forest was less than five minutes from our front door, relatives still called, little brother christened at the local church adjacent to the level crossing, and the vicar christened him as Mary Glen Nichols instead of Barry!

There was a tall Pyracantha 'fire thorn' to the left of our front door, and blackbirds nested in it each year. We had 'two' front gardens – one in front of the front room window (the room where Barry was born), the other adjoined the big double gates where a long wide path led to allotments, which in turn backed onto our garden, and beyond. The section of front garden joining these gates had an unkempt centre flower-bed in the lawn, plus side border that was filled with a new plant to me called a 'Siberian Wallflower', a short tufty wallflower with bright yellow flowers. These seeded readily, so this border remained full of this flower for the whole duration of our stay at Bernwell.

All the houses (council) had a privet hedge, and once or twice a year council gardeners would cut all the hedges with hand shears. They worked in gangs, and they worked really hard too, so the hedges were owned by the council too. I befriended one of the gang, he sort of looked like fifties' singer Buddy Holly, he was a friendly chap. In later years, like all authorities, they started to cut back, and then only cut one side of the privet, facing the pavements, and the tops. Later on the council notified everyone to say that hedge-cutting would now be carried out by the tenants only. Many people, especially the elderly, found this a task, and even the fit ones now realised what hard work it was to cut a hedge with shears, so then gave thought to all that council gang who had no choice to do it all day long, each day, until the entire estate was cut, then they were put to other duties.

As a lad of twelve then, I started doing private work, and something I had not done since working for Mrs Thornton all those years ago at Harold Hill. I dug the whole garden over for a Mrs Mee further down Bernwell. I remember it being arduous, for the garden was a sticky clay. I did hedge-cutting for a time too, along with washing cars with my then new-found friend Tony Barnard (still great pals today!). We had the hard job of digging out a huge tree stump at a house in Loughton, Essex, boy that was some graft!

A certain Mr Brownlow had just moved out of our house at Bernwell, and no doubt bought his own property? I was told he was a brilliant gardener, and mainly grew Chrysanthemums, albeit must have took each and every one with him when he moved, for there wasn't a Chrysanth in the whole of the garden when we moved in! We never knew that dad was going to walk out on us all, not an inkling at first, for Dad bought a 'Panther' push mower as we had a big lawn now, and after Dad went I had the job of keeping the grass down. Of course I was still a schoolboy, and had no ideas that mowers needed to be sharpened and oiled, and of course covered up. We had no shed there, so it eventually ceased up! Therefore in the end, a 10ft wide by 30ft long strip of grass remained uncut; the larger area that I did manage to keep cut right to the end was done with hand shears and took me hours!

On our left border (that had a well-made close board fence running down the side of it, with the arris rails our side) was edged with 'Mrs Sinkins' pinks, and were possibly cuttings from one original plant that I brought with me from Harold Hill, that once belonged to the Bowen family at Harold Hill. I had a 6ft long plank by 1ft wide, I'd rest one end on the arris rail and the other end on the path, therefore I was slightly raised above the border, and not crush any flowers and could manoeuvre it between taller plants when I was either weeding or dead-heading.

The right-hand side of the garden I grew mainly annuals and had a first go at growing vegetables. I grew the lovely orange Calendula 'Camp Fire' or 'Pot Marigold', plus all my old favourites from boyhood, Malcomia or 'Virginia Stock', Iberis 'Candy Tuft', Mathiola 'bicornis' 'Night Scented Stock', Viscaria, Linum 'rubrum' etc. I also came across a plant that the elusive Mr Brownlow left behind (I always thought he'd knock to check on his garden) and that was 'lemon balm' Melissa 'officinalis', and I suppose really classed as a herb.

As mentioned, I tried my first attempts at veg growing and was very successful, and I had plenty of room to do it. I grew radishes, carrots, beetroot, Cos lettuce, along with Mum's favourite 'Webbs Wonder' often called 'Webbs Wonderful'. I grew the most beautiful spuds too, and all from Mum's potatoes that were sprouting unused in the veg rack, and someone told me to take off all the shoots, but leave two of the strongest shoots, preferably right near to one another, then plant. I was then told the method on how to 'earth up' the 'taters' to make mounds and furrows, and keep the spuds in the dark. I was also told never to eat potatoes with the slightest green on them as they were very poisonous.

I bought a packet of seeds called Salpiglossis 'Painted Tongue', the flowers on the pack looked marvellous, and came in all colours with loads of very thin lines on each petal. I made a small square with bricks and put a sheet of glass on top to protect the seed, plus keep them warm, and hopefully to germinate. They did grow, and when my Uncle George (Mansfield) saw them he gave me a huge compliment and said that most people found them difficult to grow, and it was a great achievement. Praise like this was so good to hear. I must admit, although I have bought potted plants of Salpiglossis since those times, I've never again tried seed, so whether they really are difficult to grow I can't say – or was dear Uncle George just giving me a boost to gain confidence as a young lad. Sadly I'll never know, but for old times' sake I may just try and get some seed going, for after all it's quite a flamboyant annual!

My Auntie Rita and Uncle Jack came to visit us at the Hatch one Easter, and said that she'd bought Sandra and I a present each. She gave Sandra a large Easter Egg which she was so pleased with, then she gave me mine, and it was a really tiny egg! She must have seen the great disappointment on my face, although I desperately tried not to show it, for I was 'grown up' now and 'far too old' for Easter Eggs! So I gave a cheery 'thank you very much' and accepted what I was given. Auntie Rita soon put me out of my misery, and gave me the most beautiful Delphinium plant, with an unusual mix of lavenders, blues and pinks. Auntie Rita today cannot recall that 'cruel trick', but she was highly amused when I told her!

Earlier on in this book I mentioned the very small black plus creamy white slugs at Harold Hill, well, at Chingford Hatch. I couldn't believe my eyes when I saw these large 4"x6" black fat slugs, plus deep orange-edged paler types in my new garden, I'd never known slugs this big before. Mum, as I said earlier, loved 'Webbs Wonder' lettuce and 'Cos' lettuce too, so when the first ones were ready I picked them for our tea, and Mum made salad sandwiches, no doubt made from my other crops too.

Mum was literally mere inches from biting into her sandwich when we all shouted "Stop Mum!". She withdrew in horror when she saw one of these huge fat orangey slugs urging its way out of the lettuce between the two slices of bread, with its eyes almost level with Mum's!

Today, I simply can't eat orange peaches, for they so remind me of biting into a soft juicy slug! And I ask my wife Debbie to check all lettuce, cabbages, etc. for any hidden wildlife that may have clung on during the veg being washed etc. I'd also never seen large flying ants before, and each year at 'The Hatch' they swarmed just about every year we were there, they were just about everywhere.

In the top left-hand part of the garden, I made my first compost heap, and so surprised how hot it became, especially grass clippings, you very soon took your hand out of it in a split second I can tell you! Just beside it was a pear tree of a good shape; now this pear tree is something that I associated with our house at 'The Hatch' and didn't mention it among all the plants etc. that I had in the garden at Chippenham Walk, for it's Harold Hill where this tree started life, and was actually given to me as a present from one of Mum's pals who lived near Central Park, probably still came under Chippenham ROAD. I remember Mum's pal Ivy Paxton, née Warren, and husband

(Curly?) asking us round to look at this pear tree. It seemed that they had several fruit trees as I remember, I think I helped Ivy's husband dig it up and I remember it being a happy day. For the life of me, I cannot recall where the pear tree was planted in our garden at No. 8 just prior to our move, but suspect and vaguely picture it in my 'Dahlia Bed'. Do you remember further back in this book when I spoke of 'Prince Albert' all alone on the big empty plot? Hence must have been planted on this spot. It annoys me when I can't think exactly where it was, yet should do, being the only tree that I'd ever had.

Sadly, this pear tree and my first successful cutting of Philadelphus, both went under the bulldozer when they pulled down 37, Bernwell Road to make a new road and housing estate where the allotments were. Our house plus double gates to the allotments was now called Farthing Close, and is still there today.

The pear tree did bloom every year, but sadly the pears were what they call a 'wood pear', they were rock hard and didn't soften much even when wrapped in newspaper and put in a drawer for a few weeks. I think really these were a cooking pear, and would have softened straight away when boiled.

By coincidence? Ivy Paxton and Curly moved to Chingford Hatch at Simmons Lane at the top of Friday Hill. Both of their children were also in my class (Alan and Rita), but never recall Ivy coming to see Mum. Mum of course couldn't get to her because of the M.S.

I have always been a hard worker even if I say so myself, but have been so very unlucky for the whole of my life in the monetary sense, and beggars belief when I look back on life and recall what I have done, and should by now be fairly comfortable money-wise. It's not worth dwelling on this, for I turned 60 years old on 4th November 2008, so little chance of taking on or earning money in the big bracket, so won't bore you readers with my moanings and regrets.

Once at Chingford Hatch, I worked, over lengths of time at three newsagents as a paper boy, both early morning rounds up at four o'clock to mark the papers and deliver them, go to school, come home, then do an evening round. When I wasn't doing a paper round I was up at four again to load milk crates onto the float (Station Road, Chingford North, E.4) only on weekends and school holidays, the latter of course I'd work all day helping Vic the milkman, hence I was doing seven days a week during school holidays.

During my school years pals of mine told me of this amazingly well-paid part-time work that they had and it was at a Carnation nursery. The owners were I think English, with the name of 'Danes Nursery' which was in Mott Street, just off the Sewardstone Road, between Chingford and Waltham Abbey.

The staff at the nursery were nearly all Italians and had apparently been prisoners of war, but decided that they liked the area so much… they stayed! Some of the work was gruelling, shifting soil about and bags of a special fertiliser that had an odd smell.

The greenhouses were of course extremely hot in the summer when the carnations were regularly watered with heavy thick hosepipes. The carnations grew to 6–8 ft tall, and lots of dead-heading was done, plus carting and boxing freshly cut flowers for the florist and market industries. We worked from early morning to about lunchtime, and as my pals said, the pay was good, so good in fact that staff was never a problem for the company and they took on people who wanted to work. The more workers, the quicker the plants were grown, maintained and boxed in huge abundance, clearly a company who knew exactly what they were doing, and no one had a reason to complain about wages, for their profit was good, so paid the workers well for helping them get that big profit. If only all firms thought like that!

In hindsight, on leaving school, I should have gone to see Mr Dane and ask for a full-time job instead of going to work for the L.C.C. (London County Council) at £4 five shillings and tuppence! At the carnation nursery, yes still at school, I was earning £20 plus a DAY where the £4 plus at the L.C.C. was my weekly wage for several years, but I wanted to learn about more than one 'plant' and not learn to specialise in just one variety.

Back in my garden at 'the Hatch' I used to pick blackcurrants and loganberries when the odd fruits used to grow through the fencing. The elderly thin man with the black beret, or cap, had a large allotment directly behind our garden, a hard worker he was always there, but only ever said "hello" once in all the time we were there, yet just as I did with Uncle Arthur at Harold Hill, tried to work near that fence hoping the man would talk to me on occasions, and then I could learn about veg growing. The man must have known that I was a keen gardener for I was always in the garden as much as I could.

Two very well made paths were either side of the garden, and an incompleted one, which I used to put my seed trays on and potted up some primula 'wanda' which I believe Ivy and Curly Paxton gave to me from Harold Hill… there! that's another plant I'd 'forgotten' about!

My favourite bit of the garden was no doubt what someone told me could be a kitchen garden, for indeed, as you came out of the back door was this largish square area, containing a small lawn.

There were some nice times at Chingford Hatch, both before and after dad walked out on us all, and even some nice occasions even at school, unusual for I always hated school, from day one to me it was like a prison, and never ever believed that I would ever be able to leave. I almost counted the days that would release me. The day did come, and I went with pals to 'play' in the park, Pimp Hall Park, at the top of Friday Hill (everyone called it Pimple Park!) and we all rejoiced in trying to realise that we never ever had to go to school again. I cherish that memory still today.

Memory is very strange, as you readers can see. I like to think I have a strong memory, but there are many gaps, and suppose it's impossible to recall every day of your life. At Chingford Hatch, I did expect to see more relatives visiting, for we were now living a lot closer to all of them. Mum's mum and dad, my Nanna and Grandad, I only recall one visit, and that was the day there was a huge row when they were trying to stop my dad leaving us. What with Mum's worsening M.S., a baby brother, Sandra and I being so young, and too tender an age for all the upset that comes with the break-up of a family.

Uncle Alf, Nan's brother, came once (?) with Auntie Flo, albeit Auntie Flo visited many times, and you'll read about this very lovely lady shortly. Her daughter, Phyllis, was a regular too. How funny life is, when Sandra and I were at 'the Hatch' we always called her Auntie Phyllis. It all fell into place when I was in my fifties when of course Phyllis said she is my second cousin!

When Dad left, Auntie Flo Axford née Latchford did all our painting and decorating for us, and she was a superb wall-paperer! She was always a hard worker, probably learning of graft from her own dad who was sadly killed, he was a railwayman and tragically killed on the railway – an accident.

One Memorable Day in June

We hadn't been living at Chingford Hatch very long, when one day Auntie Flo asked me if I'd like to go out for the day with her to KEW GARDENS! I didn't need asking twice! Thankfully, it was a warm summer's day, and I had my dear Auntie Flo all to myself for a whole day! It was Rhododendron and Azalea time, and recall all the lovely smells at Kew. I'd never seen Rhododendrons or Azaleas before, and to a young lad like me, it was truly overwhelming.

I particularly loved the 'bearded' Iris. I'd seen this very common mauve variety many times, but had no idea they came in so many colours, and even moreso today with all the hybridising. I had also never seen orchids before, cactus, and many other tropical plants, including the giant floating leaf of Victoria 'amazonica'. Auntie Flo asked me if I'd like to work here when I left school, and said that I'd have to go to college. (I'll tell you about that later.) Auntie Flo then spotted some of the gardeners and she told them that I was a very 'keen gardener', a term I'd got used to through all of my childhood. Auntie Flo asked them what I had to do to get a job at Kew, but I was at an age where I didn't understand a lot of the ins and outs of what they were saying, but I really thought I would work at Kew when I left school, but alas!

I'll never ever forget that special day, and it truly was a lovely day. I was devastated when Auntie Flo died, she always worked so hard, even at Christmas she did a hell of a lot of walking when the postal service took on extra workers to deliver all the mail.

As Auntie Flo became more immobile, and Uncle Alf had died, she enjoyed doing numerous puzzles. They lived at Barclay Road, E.17. Uncle Alf was a doorman at Walthamstow Town Hall. (Flo and Alf Axford) Alf was my nan's brother.

I'll Work for the Queen of England!

Well, this was an earlier dream of mine, long before dreaming of Kew! As mentioned earlier, Mum used to have three magazines each week, *Woman's Own*, *Woman*, and *Woman's Realm*. In one of these mags they showed lovely colour photos of the Queen walking around lovely herbaceous borders of Buckingham Palace, and Mum said, "You might work there one day."

I'm glad I didn't for many years down the line I learned that the wages were pretty poor, and in line with most gardening wages, in other words damned hard work for little money, and things are still about the same today in jobs of gardening employment.

Gardening is still sort of classed as 'underdog' work, yet nearly everyone likes to see a nice garden, but not all the hard graft that comes with it I'm afraid.

Thumbs up, Grandad!

My grandad (Harry Bishop Ridley) who always called himself "The Bishop of Walthamstow!" used to demonstrate to me how to measure the depth to plant seedlings either singularly or in rows, by using his thumb, therefore the depth to plant was to the first knuckle (child's hand).

A Big Thank You to Nan and Grandad

I'm sure that you, the reader, realise now that it pays to nurture a child if they show all the very early signs of really liking a certain subject, and as you've read, I've had superb mentors in my early life, and I suppose I have a wealth of plant knowledge today, but certainly do not know it all, for gardening is a never-ending subject.

My big regret from childhood was that I wasn't bought a lot more plants, and would have been a fast learner. I also never had the tools. I used to stay with my Nan and Grandad for a week or so each year, and again I have no recollection of the journey to or from Harold Hill to Walthamstow where they lived, and where I was born. (Thorpe Coombe Hospital E.17)

I have vivid memories of those lovely days. I don't really know the reason why I stayed with them, was it because Mum needed a break, for she had both Sandra and me to look after, and the M.S. to deal with, or was it because I was Nan and Grandad's first grandson, and Harold Hill not just being round the corner to just pop in and see me, and as we know, kids grow up fast.

My lovely Nan – Rose (Rosina Alice Ridley née Axford) – used to pile up my breakfast bowl with cornflakes each morning. Grandad would be sharpening his razor on a long leather strap that hung from the door or wall. When I'd finished it she'd ask if I'd like another lot! I couldn't believe it, this never happened at home, not that I starved, but gave a quizzical YES PLEASE! And even when I had finished that she asked me if I'd like ANOTHER bowl! I always said "yes", not really quite believing it.

It's no wonder that Nan always said, "You must have a stomach like a dustbin!" and much later, as my voice developed, she'd say, "You need rubber heels on your voice!"

Nan and Grandad lived at 176, Leucha Road, E.17 (then at 169 and 69). In the front garden Grandad each year grew potatoes, yes EACH year, for Grandad either didn't know about crop rotation, or didn't want to know, for he had nowhere else to grow them, for the small back garden was full of gladioli and numerous roses. It was in Nan and Grandad's garden that I learnt a good few rose varieties, and keep on continuously asking Grandad to repeat the names each year, until they well and truly sank in!

I must point out that it was Mrs Brooks at Harold Hill who first taught me the big difference between hybrid 'tea roses' although she never said the word hybrid it was always the tea rose or a floribunda, the latter having a multitude of small buds. Mrs Brooks didn't have climbers or rambler roses, so I must have learnt that from a book much later on.

My Grandad was born in Hackney, London, in 1899. He had been in two world wars, and no doubt some of the rose names had significance to both Nan and Grandad, like say the 'Peace' rose that was bred in 1945. This rose, however, should not be confused with 'Chicago Peace' which came out much later in 1962.

Just a few years ago I sent off for a catalogue (2004) selling old and new roses, and tears were brought to my eyes, for on seeing some of those names that had been long 'forgotten' in my brain, came flooding back to me, and could almost hear my dear Grandad saying those names to me again.

As you came out of their kitchen to the right near the kitchen window was what I thought Grandad called 'Madam Butterfly' (1918) and all of my life I thought that this vigorous climber/rambler was 'Madam Butterfly' with its millions of petals dropping everywhere, smothering the path and first part of the lawn and border.

It turned out to be my own confusion as a boy trying to learn all these names, for opening a page on this catalogue, a name came screaming out at me and that was 'Dr Van Fleet' (1910), hence 'Madam Butterfly' was a hybrid tea rose, and what I thought was Madam Butterfly was in fact 'Dr Van Fleet'. Grandad served on HMS *Blonde*, and I still cannot separate the two, for in my mind that vigorous rose will always be 'Madam Butterfly' even though I know it's totally wrong!

Grandad also had 'Sarah Van Fleet' (1926), 'The Doctor' (1936), 'Picture' (1932), 'Piccadilly' (1960) and was possibly one of the last modern roses that Nan and Grandad bought. And lastly 'Josephine Bruce' (1952). Nan and Grandad had other roses too, but sadly don't remember any others, saying that, one particular one stands out above all others, and was always in bloom during my summer stay, and that was growing on trellis work on the left of their garden and that was 'American Pillar' (1909). I grow this today, and on seeing those very first blooms come out, brings a smile to my face, as if looking through little boy's eyes back in Nan and Grandad's garden all those years ago in the 50s.

One of the first houses that Nan and Grandad lived in was No. 2, North Countess Road, E.17, and adjoined an old bakery, thus had the old baker's wall partly in their garden. I always thought it was 'American Pillar' on this wall, but Auntie Rita tells me that it was 'Dorothy Perkins' a rose we had at Harold Hill on my own little garden plot, perhaps Mum bought that re. the memories of her stay at North Countess Road as a girl.

41

Nan and Grandad took over the property at 169, Leucha Road, where their daughter, my aunt Iris, and Uncle George lived, as they were moving a long way away to Bracknell, Berkshire. I helped my grandad put up his garden shed, but have no idea if they took it with them when they moved to the top of the road to 69.

And yes, as always, that shed too was painted with green paint!

My grandad often took me out, and he always found a pub, and there was me waiting outside for my lemonade and crisps. He often took me to Lloyds Park, Forest Road, E.17, former home of William Morris. He would take me to see all the plants in the greenhouses that fronted the park, vandalism with umpteen panes of glass broken saw the demise of these lovely glass-houses. Once we got into the 1970s, vandals turned into monsters, for one night sick yobs smashed down all the aviaries, and slaughtered every bird and animal in their pens/aviaries etc. I often wonder if these 'men' look back with pride today remembering what they did, and tell their children, then grandchildren and so on. See my story – SORRY! or not so Sorry – further back in this book and see what category these yobs will one day be in, it sort of makes you feel better doesn't it! (The same sickening incident happened at Oulton Broad, children's zoo, Suffolk.)

The Main Sixties

The latter part of the sixties, early seventies, we lived at 87, Coppermill Lane, E.17. Our house to me was a so unhappy one, the garden only 8'x6', well, the growing 'patch' anyway. I planted a handful of shrubs, and let them get on with it. I went in that garden possibly three times, I hated it there, and have more bad memories than good, and a happy gardening book like this one is not the place to talk about bad times. I was however, a lot closer to Springfield Park, Clapton E.5 where from Coppermill Lane could take a long walk past the old copper mills, onto Walthamstow marshes, cross the bridge over the River Lea, and reach the bottom of Springfield Park, albeit a long weary trek up the steep hills to our bothy. When I think of the arduous journey taking three hours or more to get to work at Springfield from Chingford Hatch, either cycling, moped, or buses, trains and two long walks, all to be there for a seven o'clock start, thankfully back then I was young and fit, even youngsters today wouldn't do it. It used to break my heart when I did my usual times and cancellations occurred on buses or trains, or even full up and wouldn't let you on, to then be late for work and they'd stopped your money, and because they stopped your money, I had no choice but to work over-time and weekends and that was always until ten at night, then a long trek back to Chingford Hatch, a very long day, therefore Coppermill Lane was nearer.

Broom! Broom! Don't get me started!

I was glad to move out of Coppermill Lane and moved to a ground floor maisonette, 7, Hancocke House, The Drive, E.17. Debbie and I were courting then. We married on 20th May 1972 and Hancocke House then became our first home together before getting a mortgage and buy our own house.

The ground floor flat was a sunny place really, and I had the benefit of a front garden 30'x40' approx. and my first proper garden in adulthood, and the first time we encountered a nasty neighbour plus others whispering behind your back. Thankfully we have only encountered two in all the houses (6) where I have lived, and a good majority of the lovely neighbours are still on my Christmas card list today.

Our favourite neighbours at The Drive lived upstairs but one, Peter and Betty Harrison. They loved flowers, the outdoors, and deeply loved the Lake District. Peter was a groundsman on a sports ground owned by the Franch Banks, namely Credit Lyonnais, and stood (still stands?) at the bottom of the Manor Road cul-de-sac adjacent to the old now defunct Chingford Hatch level crossing. Peter grew flowers and shrubs on the ground and planted numerous varieties of trees around the whole of the perimeter of the ground, and I like to think that they are still there? He was a quietly spoken, smiley friendly man. Sadly Peter died quite suddenly a few years ago now, and I lost a good friend and close neighbour. I am thankful that I am still in contact with Betty, a lovely very sweet lady, losing Peter was a very bitter blow for her and their son Mark.

Years ago The Drive was full of large houses owned by the very wealthy, and was full of top doctors, solicitors etc. Our through lounge and kitchen had the lovely view of a few trees and a perfect view in the winter of Walthamstow Town Hall, Assembly Hall and College, the latter where my dad did lecturing on Architecture.

The Drive, when the big properties were all pulled down thankfully they had the good sense to retain the massive London Plane trees that still grace The Drive today.

Being a front garden, and a very low wall, all sorts of people would jump over as a short cut to the maisonette doors to deliver items etc. Ours was a block of six, but two sets of three a side. Quite a lot of my plants were broken, so somehow needed protection, I certainly didn't want anything thorny, for it would be me who had to work near to them.

I treated myself to a garden magazine and saw an unusual advert which read as follows – Multi Coloured Broom for sale, write to Dingley Dell, Dyke, Morayshire. I have long forgotten the lady's name and what I paid for them. They all arrived safely, around 50 I should think, and only about 6"–8" high, but I knew that Broom (Cytisus) was a fast grower, so providing I could given them some protection they'd come along very nicely.

I had the bright idea of setting in 1' 6" high chicken wire, just temporarily, and two foot from the low wall to make it fairly difficult for anyone wanting to make that short cut. It was about a day after when our first nasty neighbour reared her ugly head, and yelled from her window – (she was Italian, he was English, and had always been nice people) – she said "What do you think you are doing, it looks like a concentration camp!" I thought that she spoke cruelly, and very harsh words over something so trivial, like me protecting plants, and the chicken wire barely noticeable really, as most people said to me, you had to be looking for a row to even warrant picking on someone for that silly reason. I laughingly retorted back and said, "If it was a concentration camp, you could've just stepped over the chicken wire and escaped!" She then screamed back, "You Laugh, you laugh", I said "Yes, I do laugh, for you insult each and every person who was inside a concentration camp, you're disgusting!" With that, she slammed her window shut.

My multi-coloured broom grew and grew, and was such a spectacular sight, that nearly all the people I knew nearby wanted the address of where to buy it, and I readily gave it to them. I now had the perfect 6ft–8ft barrier, and I was then able to widen the borders to put in new plants. I was thrilled with my plot, and at this time took great enjoyment in sending away for plants and bulbs, some I knew, others I'd seen in books and magazines etc. and others I'd never heard of but wanted to give them a try. Peter (Harrison) whom I mentioned earlier, did the same, and chose unusual bulbs to try indoors on their very sunny windowsill and balcony.

I remember one bulb that Peter was overjoyed at seeing and he called me upstairs to show me his great achievement of growing, and getting to flower, the unusual plant of Moraea. I had always wanted a Rhus 'typhina' and the ferny variety 'laciniata' ("Stags Horn Sumach") and thought this would look fine in the centre of my lawn, so set about digging just a 1ft 6" square hole, and similar depth to plant it in, then all of a sudden the nasty neighbour once again threw open her window and screamed "What you do? What you do?" I retorted back, "I tell you what I do, I do build a pond, or swimming pool!" She ranted on and slammed the window once again. I thought, don't get me started, or I'll flare up! And I did! I raced up the stairs, banged on their door, they did answer, he stood at the background wearing a ladies' pinny! So I shouted at her hell for leather, asking what was wrong with her, why did she keep picking on me and my wife. All the other neighbours heard, and suspect that some were on my side, for Debbie and I didn't know if the neighbours had dealings with her in the past. I went on to say that she could clearly see that I was planting a large shrub.

There was an enclosed doorway to an undercover type hallway, all the women were tittle-tattling about us. We caught them mid-stream so asked 'all' of them what their problem was. "We all take turns to clean the steps and 'hall' way, you never help at all and take a turn", directing their eyes at Debbie. We were so angry and said that we didn't know what the routine was. We both worked, so had no idea what went on during the day, and that nobody told us that you had to take turns cleaning. Everything was resolved there and then, but we mistrusted these women thereafter.

After just a few weeks on, the Italian woman had yet another go at Deb and me. This time Deb was putting out the washing, when the woman screamed, "You can't use that line, it's Tessa's line!" We were dumbfounded, for Tessa was the lady who had had our flat and had been dead for three years! Once again I had a go back. "Right then, I'll remove the line, put it in the dustbin and put our own line up!" and that's exactly what I did!

On the left of our garden as you entered the door to the maisonette, was a small brick-built raised bed, and a favourite place for cats to do their 'business' in the part undercover dry bed. I soon planted this up and kept it moist from then on. The raised bed already had a bit of trellis work affixed to the wall, so sent away for a very expensive climber, namely Lapageria 'rosea' which grew well for it was well sheltered being in that bed, and facing south too really helped.

Around this time Deb and I took our first visit to the Spalding Flower Parade in Lincolnshire, the floats back then using some nine million tulip heads! (a lot less nowadays), and the subject then was 'Wildlife'. There were also hundreds of all sorts of plants for sale, and we bought a large clump of Zantedeshia 'aethiopica' the lovely white 'Arum Lily' at just one pound for the clump, and was really cheap even then for the early 1970s.

The arum took pride of place in that raised bed, but knowing that it was a moisture lover, had to keep an eye on it. I patiently waited for the first bud to appear, and didn't have to wait long before the first flower came into bloom. Deb and I were so elated, to us this exotic looking plant was one that only the rich could afford, hence my elation on seeing this large clump of arum for a mere pound.

Soon after the flower came into bloom, Deb and I had been out shopping or whatever, and on our return home we had a big shock, for someone had taken that lovely flower head off! It was nowhere to be seen, we'd never had trouble with yobs or vandals all the while we were in The Drive, so assumed it was a paper boy/girl or other tradesman calling to the area and taking the bloom.

About a fortnight later, our mad Italian lady had calmed down a little, and was now somewhat more friendly towards me and Deb and asked us if we would like to have a cup of tea with her and her husband, both perhaps now feeling very foolish, the lady moreso, and he for not correcting her or stopping her with her very adult-child behaviour. Deb and I went upstairs to their flat, and she gave us a warm welcome, asking us to come in and we were only just in the hallway when we glanced at a narrow ornamental table, on which was a small bowl type narrow vase with a figure of Jesus attached to it, and in that vase... wait for it!... was our Arum flower! We were both totally shocked, moreso when she actually made a point of asking us to "look at my little Jesus" and unbelievably saying "I picked a flower for my little Jesus."

I thought, yes, you've *stolen* a flower for your little Jesus, and gone into our garden to take it as well! Deb and I were dumbstruck on what we saw, how could she be so blatant? But she carried on talking, made our tea etc. as if she'd done nothing wrong. Thankfully, by the time we left The Drive, the plant was big and healthy and produced masses of blooms, and in flower when I had to dig it up to take it to our new house (a mortgage!).

Thinking back now, I'd bought a small conifer, about a foot high, and planted it in front of our bedroom window; this too was stolen during the night, or at least when becoming darker. It was only two weeks from Christmas, so was it taken for a present or as a small 'Christmas tree'? Was it a passing stranger who had taken it this time, or was the culprit living right under our noses? We couldn't prove anything, so if it was that lady again, she'd get away with it for a second time!

Reed All About It!

My son Rowan has his own business today, doing wetland management on the Norfolk and Suffolk Broads. (Reed and Sedge cutting etc.)

The Plant You Couldn't Smell!

Whilst at The Drive, I grew several plants from seeds. One very new to me was Eccremocarpus 'scaber' or 'Chilean Glory Vine' plus purchased Allium 'triquetrum'. I paid a fair bit of money for these, and all these years later know why! for they multiply readily and disperse seed everywhere, therefore once you've paid for them you never need buy them again, therefore the bulb firm know that you'd not need more! This is a very pretty bulb, around the same height as the common Bluebell, and in fact in some ways resembles a white BLUEbell if you know what I mean! Each petal has a green stripe on it, and seems to flower forever once established, it can bloom in September, October, November, December, January, February, March – the biggest showiest flash is April into May, then the lot die down to a soggy mess at first, then the leaves shrivel to a dry state during June and July. You can then pull them away, but by August they start to grow again and even expect the odd bloom. Heavy frosts knock them back quite a bit if in flower too early, but soon recover when temperatures rise again.

This next story I'm going to tell you about I have never lived down since the day it happened! I bought a plant for indoors at The Drive, although this plant is perfectly hardy outdoors too, and that plant is Tolmiea 'menziesii' or 'Pig-a-back plant' or 'Mother-of-Thousands', the latter name used on several plant species, hence confusion at times. This of course is why we have botanical names, for wherever you go in the world the botanical name is universal. Common names vary in different parts of the country. Tolmieas have an abundance of leaves (also variegated form) and carry 'young' on the leaf where the leaf joins the stalk. All you do to propagate is to take off one leaf, and where the 'baby' is just put on a stone to weigh it down at that point, and it will soon root away. The main leaves then die as the new baby plantlet grows to form a new plant.

The Tolmieas have thin wiry stems carrying dull brownish flowers, and when the flowers were fully out I wondered if they had any scent at all, for none could be smelt when standing near it, so thought I'd take a closer sniff, but then something odd happened – as I went to smell the flowers, the stem moved away from me! I made several attempts on other stems and from different angles and each time the stems drew away from me, the closer I got the stems bent back further!

At this point, I honestly and truly thought I'd found a novelty in the plant world that no botanist in the land had discovered! For the flowers are dull and uninteresting, like say trying to see if a stinging

47

nettle had scent, it just looks a boring flower and not even worthy of a scent! and indeed not worth trying to see if it had any.

I amused myself on the odd occasion trying to smell this un-smellable plant, and considered writing to Kew Garden first to see if they knew about this odd happening, for I'd checked each and every gardening book, but none spoke of this plant's curious habit.

I thought, I can't keep this to myself, so called my wife Debbie, and told her all that had gone on, and made my way over to the windowsill to show her a demonstration.

Deb cried out in hysterical laughter, "You silly fool, it's your beard pushing on the stems!" I felt so stupid, for then I did have a thick bushy beard, and of course the lower whiskers below the chin were pushing the stem below the flowers. I'm so very glad that I didn't send that letter to Kew!

Kicking up a Stink!

At The Drive I bought two more 'smellies', one was a succulent called Stapelia, the other was Arum 'Cornutum' or "Voodoo Lily". I think Mum or Dad had bought one of these for me as a boy at Harold Hill and was a 4"–5" roundish corm, and apparently eats itself away to make it flower! for it did not need soil or water, and you simply stood it on a windowsill and waited. Sadly, my corm at Harold Hill faded to nothing, not a shoot… nothing. So it wasn't until I got married that I, and Peter Harrison bought one each to try. Peter and Betty couldn't stand the smell and put it out on their balcony!

I knew when mine came into bloom, for when we let our first dog 'Bobo' into the front room, she made for the windowsill and barked furiously at it, and had to hold her back as she tried to jump up at it. This worried Deb and I, for we thought of the word 'Voodoo' and wondered then what triggered off Bobo's unusual behaviour – could she see something we couldn't?

The Arum 'cornutum' has the typical arum flower, but mottled with dull brownish spots and blotches, after the bloom fades, and by then the plant had fed on itself. You are supposed to plant it, and then it forms 'palmate' type leaves, I've never seen this by the way, but imagine it to look very similar to the foliage of another outdoor smaller Dracunculus 'Vulgaris' or "DRAGON ARUM" the name is spelt… or should say pronounced as Drar-Cun-Q-Luss. This corm was originally given to me by our next-door neighbour's (Mrs Clarke) brother, Bertie. He was a grand cheery elderly man, and used to sharpen all my shears, secateurs etc. Bert knew that I liked unusual plants, and all these years later I still have it. To think how long that is, for we'd then bought (buying!) 162 Chingford Road. E.17, the same year when the group 10CC had their song 'I'm not in Love' played constantly on the radio all that lovely sunny summer.

Mrs Clarke was a lovely neighbour, and a good plantswoman. She enjoyed her life in the garden and was always on a coach tour to somewhere or other. Mrs Clarke hated slugs (don't we all!) and each morning you'd see her relentlessly walking up and down the garden picking them off, putting them on the path, and with a sharp knife cut them in half!! aaaargh!! a grizzly sight I couldn't watch!

Sadly, most books on gardening hardly ever list Dracunculus, and when they do, they tell you very little about it, so I shall relate here on what to expect.

The plant likes a sunny spot, although mine is in light shade and grows and flowers very well. The sharp looking shoots appear in early spring, and look like mottled snakes rising from the earth. The Arum bloom is quite a large one, and is a 'sickly mauve', although does have a beauty of its own, for it's a deep mauve, so is the spathe – the rude bit often called the 'dog's dibble'! When the flower comes out the smell is putrid and smells of rotting meat, and attracts bluebottles and flies. Bert told me that they then get trapped down lower in the flower, but not killed, and after they have pollinated the plant they are set free. The smell stops usually after about three days, after this the plant then starts to die down, and like most arums, they leave a stout stem carrying the poisonous berries. After a short while you'll see nothing of the plant all summer, so you have to mark where it is for fear of digging it up in error. I usually just throw a few annual seeds down on this spot, the seeds root find their own way through or alongside the corms, and pull away easily by the end of summer, where you can mark the spot again with a label.

Our Garden at 162, Chingford Road, E.17

My wife Debbie worked at Gestetner in Tottenham as an offset duplicator, and earning more money than me, even though I was working for the Thames Water Authority, and paid very well considering it was for gardening, which was always lower paid, and even today folk think they can pay you a pound an hour!

Our combined wages was so good, we thought we'd apply for a mortgage, and got one! Little did I know I'd still be paying for it in 2009 and just turned sixty, and has been very, very hard to pay at times over the years.

As a warning, always refuse if someone wants you to view their house on a Sunday, for although we fell in love with it, and knew the area well, there wasn't any noticeable traffic, but boy when we moved in it was horrendous – lorries, buses, cars, main routes for fire engines, police and ambulances storming past at all hours and the grime on the windowsills was terrible, and inside the loft was covered in soot and worn-off rubber from tyres on the road, compared to our now seaside bungalow loft which is spotless!

We had been so enthralled in viewing our first house that we were oblivious to the main road. It was around 1975, and one year later our first baby was born and was the blazing heatwave of 1976, and Heather came into the world in the blazing August. On my first glance at the back garden, I was pleased to see a blank canvass, well… not that blank, for the grass was two foot high or more from end to end, and lovely old lilacs right at the bottom of the garden, and Mrs Clarke confirmed that they were at least seventy years old or more.

I got to work on the grass first, and got it very short, this of course yellowed, but at least because it was so dry I was able to cut out, then dig over new borders. The ground was a sticky soil, and clay less than 1ft down, so I decided to trench it. Each trench I poured in sharp sand, then the soil on top of that, covered then with Moss Peat, by the time we left there and during the time we were there, the soil became pliable and pleasant when trying to plant.

The garden was about seventy feet long by about twelve foot wide, and long before the term 'Garden Rooms' came about, divided the garden into three plots 'rooms'.

As you came out of the kitchen door to the left was a small 'shed', perfectly tiled, on which I knocked up a soggy, clayey, sticky lump, embedded some house-leeks into it, and set it on the tiles, and they grew fantastically, never having to water them, the plants only relying on rainfall. The old folklore was that if you had house-leeks (Sempervivums) on your roof, your house would never be struck by lightning. This little shed I kept my pots and seed trays in, and suspected it to once have been an outside loo. On the side wall I affixed a bookshelf to put potted plants on, and special ones at that. One I recall being the rarely seen Sternbergia 'Lutea', very much resembling a yellow crocus. This bookshelf was made by Dad's grandad or great-grandad, and was used by me for my books as a little boy when living at Harold Hill, and I'm glad I've still got it! The shelf has been in sheds of mine where we have lived, but hopefully now it will stay indoors, for I've known this all my life. I think the original colour was a greyey colour, but it's now pale blue. To the right of the kitchen door I planted Solanum 'Jasminoides' or "Potato Vine". This used to be a rare climber to see, and catalogues priced it at £5 upwards, today supermarkets sell it for just a pound! I paid £5 for mine, which was a lot of money back then.

The Solanum bloomed from May right up to the first frosts, and grew right up the drainpipes, my sole purpose of planting them there to hide those pipes. There was a drain cover in this first plot, set in with crazy paving that I laid, drain covers are eyesores, but of course a necessity, so bought my first low half-barrel and planted it with Hyacinths. The edges of the cover I cemented and stuck in fossils that we brought back from Lyme Regis – they looked really nice, and a good base effect to the barrel. Our other nice next-door neighbours, Peter and Maureen Noye, had a beautiful Laburnum tree that overhung this area, but like all blossom when it falls, a bit messy, and trod or blew into the kitchen, but was worth it for the lovely yellow blossom each year, plus they had a lovely looking rose that I identified for them called 'Kronenberg'.

My father-in-law, George Ward, bought himself a greenhouse. I helped him bring it home in my van, and I was shocked, for one week later he bought me one too! My very first one, and last to date! What a lovely man, a very kind thought. I affixed trellis work all round it so that Heather (later on Adrian and Rowan) didn't fall through the glass, plus I put in various climbers which gave very dappled shade in high summer and protected the seedlings within the greenhouse from being scorched.

I grew the weird and wonderful, but always grew Mimosa 'pudica' or "Sensitive plant", to amuse the children, for when the leaves or leaf stalk was touched, the leaves would fold up instantly. So, this was plot 'one', and divided it by putting in our first arch, and affixed a gate to it, either side of the arch I put in a low fence and planted taller shrubs to eventually take place of the fence once grown.

The second plot 'two' was to become the larger main area of the garden, surrounded by flowers, and a stone bird-bath in the middle of the lawn, the very same bird-bath graces our front garden today here in Kessingland, Suffolk. At the base of the bird-bath at Chingford Road I made a little square flower bed around it, and first planted it with black and white tulips – it looked really lovely. The first summer I planted Iceland poppies, that centre bed always looked superb. The borders were crammed with all sorts of perennials, climbers, shrubs, bulbs, etc.

Plot 'three' which merged with plot 'two' was a flat piece of border that led to the very shallow part of a concrete pond that I made. The flat bit I planted Gunnera 'manicata', the giant leaf from Brazil whose leaves can reach enormous proportions! The shallow part of my pond

51

had an overflow point, thus the soil that I dug out to make the pond formed the rockery. My van was parked in Farnan Avenue, a now blocked road, and it was from here that I carried large heavy rockery stone (Westmorland Stone to be exact); I liked this rock best because of all the cracks, strata lines, moss etc.

I found it quite funny that when completing the concrete pond, a frog stood staring at me from the middle of it, and must have guessed that it was going to be a pond! When making the pond, I bought lots of chicken wire for the bottom and sides of the pond for reinforcement, plus rolled-up chicken wire to use as a ridge round the pond… slap a load of concrete on it, so when it dried it would retain the soil and stop it sliding into the pond.

I always make a pond look natural, and that starts with the rocks, and always place them hanging at least half way over the pond edge, this then leaves lots of little hiding places for frogs, newts etc.

Plot 'four' was the area beyond the pond, which still had the other side of the rockery, but here stood those seventy-year-old lilacs that I spoke of earlier. It was here that I made a mini-woodland path to take you to the very back of the garden. This little mini path led from just at the side of the first shed that I ever bought, and *still* have it! Because this was a 'woodland walk', I planted up bulbs suiting this area.

The year 1976 was a real scorcher, and so very unbelievable to wake up to sunshine every day for weeks on end, but I made a real bloomer, for I'd sent off for a catalogue which was small and compact, and the prices were so unbelievably low that I bought one of every single plant in it! I received lots of varieties of primulas, but sadly because of the hose bans, lost the majority of most of them. When I did water you couldn't keep up because of the so intense heat. The other mistake was buying lots of unusual varieties of Meconopsis. One of the years at Chingford Road I bought lots of varieties of Lilies, plus a large box of the very highly scented Lilium 'Regale' "The Regal Lily". What with that and smothering the garden with Nicotianas "Tobacco plant" and mostly the white ones, the air of scent at night was exquisite. In London, the hot summer nights were unbearable, so Deb and I would still be out in the garden until two in the morning, but I have never forgotten the atmosphere out there on those so special nights, for tobacco plants mostly have their heads hung low during the day, and spring up at night; the white ones stood out with the whitest whites you'd ever seen!

On the arch I grew Clematis 'Vyvvan Pennell', a beautiful double clematis, looking more like a Paeony or old-fashioned rose; this variety was quite new at the time and I couldn't wait to show people. So, I knocked for old Dan, two doors down. Dan and Betty were both very elderly, and lovely people. Dan was the gardener for Walthamstow Town Hall (Daniel Doyle); he was responsible for the beautiful gardens there. Dan came to see me, he loved my garden and had also never seen a clematis like this before.

I Upset the Neighbours!

The age old Lilacs, Syringa 'Vulgaris', regardless of my great attempts to remove the suckers, were so tough that it was really a losing battle, for the prolific suckers strengthened each year piercing through every inch of soil and ruining all the planting. When I moved each rock, because of the shade and dampness under each one, the suckers had thick matted roots. Very, very reluctantly I decided to take the Lilacs out. This back bit of garden had a low four-foot high chain-link fence, so even with the tree-like lilacs the neighbours at the back were side onto us and we could both see each other very clearly even in summer when they – Mr and Mrs Bedding – were sitting in their deckchairs more or less facing us all the time. So as it was only the thick lilac trunks that did the 'shielding', I thought no more of it and dug them all out, and what a task that was I can tell you. They have tough old roots, which now at this point reminds me of the time I dug up my first Lilac when we moved to Chingford Hatch. Just a mile or so away was Highams Park Lake, and near there was an estate of now demolished prefabs, but all the gardens were as the owners had left them.

I had always wanted a Lilac, so took along the only gardening tool I had at that time, Dad's garden fork. I tried with all my might to dig it out, I did succeed, but bent the fork very badly through my hearty efforts! The Lilac did survive, and grew very well. I planted it next to the chicken-run that I made, rather crudely made I might add. I'll tell you about my chickens further on in this book. The lilac sadly went under the bulldozer.

As I was digging out the Lilacs, Mr and Mrs Bedding asked what I was doing, not that I had to explain for it was MY garden and could do what I like! They of course were very annoyed and upset. Not that I had to, but I did explain the problems with the Lilac suckers, and of my plans of what I was to do in that area. My plans were to plant several Buddleias, for they were fast growing and very colourful, and would make a nice backdrop to my garden, and very colourful for Mr and Mrs Bedding to see too.

I went ahead, planting the Buddleias, plus added two colourful trees for WINTER interest – they were Prunus 'subhirtella autumnalis' "winter flowering cherry", this had pink or white flowers, usually commencing to flower on leafless stems around November/December through to around April/May. I had the pink variety 'Rosea'.

The other tree did actually look like it had cherries growing on it, but they were in fact small red crab apples, and in the spring had the usual pinky-white blooms typical of the apple family. So it was a colourful tree. The apples stayed on all winter, and as the trees grew and merged together, it was a lovely sight to see on cold winter days. After I'd done all the planting, Mr and Mrs Bedding were still showing their disgust and one day when I went into the garden Mr B. was putting up an eight-foot high solid panel of fence! I approached him and said that surely he could wait for all the shrubs to grow and the short wait would be well worth it, but he didn't want to know and blocked us out. Deb and I didn't mind too much for we were no longer overlooked, for Mr and Mrs Bedding always sat dead in line with our garden, when they could have sat in other private areas of their garden.

A few years down the line, and still in Mr and Mrs Bedding's Road (Farnan Avenue) I was called in to remove… wait for it… a Lilac! So I started digging it out, and the next minute the lady over the back in the next garden came out ranting at me telling me not to take the 'tree' down as she liked it and it gave her a bit of privacy. I had no choice but to tell my customer, and the customer relayed what I was to say to her neighbour. So out of the house I went, back to the bottom of the garden where the woman was still fuming!

I told the lady that the customer said that "this was her lilac, her garden, and that if you want a lilac plant one *your* side of the fence, I don't want one!"

The woman stormed off, so I don't know what the outcome was after I left, but I did enjoy telling my customer all about the 'Bedding Saga' a couple of doors down! They say that lilacs are unlucky to have indoors; they're not too clever outside either as you've read!

A few doors down still, I was asked to do some turfing, a new company had started to advertise in our local paper, although they were cutting, and based in Kent. I asked for a sample turf, and it was the best quality that I'd seen in a long while, so gave him the order for this new job. The customer was delighted, it was January, and longed to see how this new turf looked in the proper growing season.

April soon came, and I had an unexpected call from the customer, who looked angry and just said, "Come and see my lawn!" I could tell by his fact and tone of voice that something was amiss, so went with him straight away to see what the problem was. When I did see, I couldn't believe my eyes – the lawn was covered in clover!

I was on the phone like a shot to the new turf supplier, and he casually said "sorry" and he would bring me another load. I said "and who is going to lift up all the others, pay for disposal and re-lay the second lot?" He didn't want to know. He did deliver a second lot, hence I did the whole job all over again. Had he given me compensation for all my work and played fair, he would have got work from me for many years after, hence he would then have pocketed many thousands of pounds. I then found a good firm in Cuffley Herts. who did 16 varieties of turf! Several people said that how come I never saw the clover when I was laying the turf – the answer was that it had all died back during that very cold winter, but the grass itself was a longish very lush top quality turf, so the clover was very low under the bases of the grasses and couldn't be seen.

A Garden Centre Genius!

Who am I talking about? Why me of course! I got a weekend job working at Northfields Garden Centre, Sewardstone Road, Chingford E.4 and I was taken on firstly to tidy the then quite untidy nursery, and soon I was there in an advisory capacity. I started weeding all the pots, and asked for an indelible pen; they asked why, I said that I knew my plants, and some of theirs were not marked and I could then write the botanical name one side of the label and the common name (if it had one) on the other. They all seemed impressed, but what they didn't know was that I had vast plant knowledge, and it soon came to light in the weeks ahead.

On one of these days I was clearing out a really overgrown bay of plants and noticed them actually coming into bloom, so I weeded them thoroughly, labelled them, cleared out the bay and the plants looked respectable again. The plants in fact were the bright yellow 'Rose-of-Sharon' or Hypericum 'calycinum'. Customers saw these bright blooms and they started selling like hot cakes! so much so that whoever was on the sales counter asked the owners where these flowers had suddenly appeared from, as just one day prior to me tidying them up, none came to the shop counter, but the next day they were turning up at the counter in their hundreds. One of the owners came over to see me to ask where these plants had come from, so of course I told him that they were over in the far corner of the nursery in a very neglected state, and that I'd cleaned them up etc. and went on to say that there were a lot more plants and shrubs that needed the same treatment.

The owners of course were overjoyed at this, so they left me to it. Visitors to the garden centre soon started asking me for advice, at first all innocently asking if 'we' sold such and such a shrub, or is this shrub okay for shade, or does this head need pruning etc. and quite thankfully I was able to answer most of their questions. Don't read me wrongly here, reader, for I'm not intending to sound big-headed, for I most certainly don't know it all, but was luckily enough to have questions thrown at me that I knew the answers to! (It's always easy when you know the answer!)

My weekend work was very poorly paid, and I was so shocked that when I decided to leave to take on a higher paid weekend job, that counter sales had risen quite a lot since I started working there. This information came my way from a friend who worked behind the sales counter (he was a Dahlia fanatic and avid exhibitor of this plant), for he knew first-hand that it had been me who boosted the plant sales as customers bringing the plants to the counter all said that "the chap outside told us all about these" or words to that effect, and they had been grateful to me for all the information that I was able to give them. Whilst I was there I was getting more and more into it, and enjoying talking to the public, and at peak busy times I didn't know who to speak to next, for I was trying to do people in turn for they all had a question for me or wanted advice. I had to talk for hours, and of course whilst talking to one lot of potential customers, other people stood very nearby ear-wigging all that I was saying, hence then making even more people wanting to talk to me!

As my presence in the garden centre was getting more well known, I asked the owners if I could have plant catalogues, garden books etc. They asked why, and I went on to tell them that lots of the shrubs and plants were not in flower, and if I was suggesting to a customer that a certain shrub would suit what they wanted, needed to show them a picture to hopefully encourage a sale, and boy it worked! For don't forget there were few coloured picture labels back then, hence unless you knew the plant, the others would just sit in the garden centre until the day it came into bloom, for more or less *anything* will sell if it has a flower on it.

My pal behind the sales desk was so taken aback when I left, even though he'd sung my praises to the owners, but they made no attempt to put my money up, and considering the revenue that I was bringing in, surely it was foolhardy to let me go? But it was gruelling for me to stand there all day talking, and making so much money for someone else.

Many years down the line in the mid-1990s in my present hometown (Kessingland, nr. Lowestoft, Suffolk) is a smallish nursery and farm shop about eight miles away at Wangford. The owners went to Lincolnshire a lot to do buying, as do most owners of garden centres and nurseries. They bought cheap and gave me a good trade price on everything I bought, therefore I could keep my prices low for my customers. On occasions, their customers often mistook me as one of the garden centre workers. They always said sorry, I said that that's okay but perhaps I can help you, and they then would reel off all sorts of questions.

One particular man came in one day, and again offered my help as I could clearly see that he had no clue on what to buy. At this point in time, one of the owners neared to us and heard some magic words come from the customer's mouth, "I'm so very pleased with this man's help (me!), for I intended to buy just two shrubs for my garden, but hadn't a clue which ones to buy, but now have happily spent over £300 and this chap... me again!) ...has given me lots of information which he's written down for me."

The owner then admitted to me that this had happened before when I'd come in and gave advice. He asked me if I'd like to work there weekends, but neither of us could come up with a suitable solution regarding pay, for I was honest with him and said that the choice of shrubs, trees and plants at the nursery was very limited. Had there been a far greater choice for me to use my knowledge and give them better advice I would not hesitate for a second to work for him.

Wouldn't you think lessons could be learnt from this? For today you have 'bits of kids' working on sales counters and outside in the nurseries and most seem to be totally clueless.

Acacia!... Bless You!

When I was a little boy, and when Mother's Day came around, Dad would nip out to a local florist at Harold Hill to buy Mum a bunch of the lovely yellow, fluffy flowered, highly scented Mimosa or 'Florists Mimosa' as it was more known as in the 1950s. Dad would make out that it was a present to Mum from Sandra and myself.

It always seemed sunny on Mother's day in those far-off days, and I suppose the very first time I was aware of what Mother's Day was, and Mum came in from our very sunny kitchen into the front room, and can still see the delight on Mum's face even now. Dad, I think, bought Mum chocolates etc.

When Mum died in 1978, aged just 54, through complications brought on by the M.S. I was so totally devastated, and like us all, you just don't believe loved ones would ever die. That year I bought a Mimosa shrub, Acacia 'dealbata' to give its correct name, a three-foot spindly-looking thing it was too! Anyhow, this was planted around the time Mum died (August 7th) and boy did it put on some growth for the remainder of the summer and growing months.

The 'shrub' grew to its tree-like proportions and reached a height of some 25 feet or more with a 12-foot spread! and hung over Maureen and Peter's garden next door, growing into their Laburnum!

It grew up to the bedroom window of our then little daughter Heather's room. I used to make her laugh and say "The Mimoza's getting Closza!" and indeed it was a lovely sight looking at it from window height.

Mimosa is grown more in warmer parts of our country, especially Cornwall, and I was told at the time that most of this country's Mimosa was imported from the south of France, where it is a prolific grower.

On hearing this I contacted our local newspaper *The Walthamstow Guardian* to ask if they'd like to see it. They got back to me straight away, and interviewed me, plus took a photo of me amongst all the greenery! I had a big shock, for they put me on the front page! with my own title of 'Touch of the Tropics'. Oddly, the Duke of Edinburgh had visited nearby Loughton and only had a very small write up and no photograph!

It was still only March, and Mimosa is an early flowerer, so I hoped it would flower, for the buds had formed in their millions by the end of that first summer, and if frosts didn't get to it, then I'd have a truly lovely display – and it was, I can tell you!

When my photograph appeared on the front pages I started to receive odd, but concerned phone calls, and each and every one asked why I was a victim of hate! I said I wasn't but each person said that it mentions that I was, for it's on the front page. I couldn't understand what they were on about, but soon realised their error, and was very comical. The wording 'Victim of Hate' was written in large print just above my head near the photograph, and was referring to the racial hatred that was going on at that time, but it did indeed look like it was referring to ME!

Everyone of course laughed when they realised their error, and I had to point out that the smallish article on me was *below* the photograph!

Several lots of people wanted to come and see my Mimosa and, as the article mentioned that I was a landscape gardener, it brought a little work in for me, and that was good for early in the year although my work always picked up come March when the better weather arrives and hopefully the worst of the winter is behind us.

Just a week or so after my picture 'hit the headlines', an elderly lady, whom I didn't know, appeared on the inner pages with the headline of

'The Grass is always Greener!' and indeed the editor of the *Walthamstow Guardian* newspaper must have got a map out, and the elderly lady did live near me in one of the roads… 'over the other side'! to complete the well known saying!

Sadly, all my glory came to an end, for the next winter we had sub-zero temperatures, and my lovely tree was no more, it virtually died overnight and all the bark broke open and peeled off.

It was many years later, not long after we moved here to Kessingland, that I bought another one, and knowing really that it was perhaps doomed for we are only a five minute walk to the beach and the open North Sea. Although the tree only grew to twelve or so feet and about half that in spread, bits died back each year, although new growths came each year, but the harder the frosts, the more severe was the die-back and I made all clean pruning cuts to try and save it. But alas, like in Walthamstow, one very severe frost put paid to it, sad really, for here (Kessingland) we only get about 3–4 frosts a year, and that's not counting the almost *daily* frosts we have had in the very cold winter of 2008 into 2009.

I've not read this in books anywhere, so like to think this is my own discovery! and that is if you have an eyesore to hide, or you are overlooked, plant the fast-growing Mimosa, and better still alternate with the fast-growing Eucalyptus, this evergreen will help to protect the Mimosa, which in itself can be evergreen in milder areas. I've found this combination far faster even that the now very common 'Leylandii' conifer, and far prettier to look at.

I have even added climbing and rambler roses to the bases of these trees to add colour for the summer months, the more vigorous the trees grow you can put in vigorous roses to match i.e. Rosa 'Paul's Himalayan Musk'.

When my glory days were over with that very first Mimosa, I truly believed that perhaps it was my dear Mum that was looking down on me, and gave me a big boost of happiness, after laying Mum to rest in Queens Road Cemetery E.17, for on seeing all those lovely small ball-type fluffy blooms on that tree, it very much reminded me of Mum's smiling face when receiving those bunches of Mimosa on Mother's Day in those far-off days of the 1950s.

On a very last note on the subject of Mimosa, Deb and I had a coach tour to Cornwall. We went to Bonython gardens, The Eden Project, and 'The Lost gardens of Heligan'. It's the Eden Project that I now refer to…

As we made our way down the winding slopes to reach the entrance, we saw a very unusual shrub right in the centre of the main outdoor borders. Lots of folk commented on it, for the colour of the leaves were truly unusual, being a misty greyey-bluey and deeper purple at the growing tips. Everyone who saw it said, 'Cor, I'd like one of those in my garden!" I could see that it most certainly had the Mimosa leaves and, never seeing this particular shrub before, just thought that perhaps it was an unusual shrub bought in by the Eden Project to match all the other weird and wonderful things that they grew.

The very next day we went to Bonythan gardens, down by The Lizard. This was a private garden and the owner showed us all around. We walked round the big lake, and on coming to the end of it, we turned the corner to literally see a grand specimen of this 'Mimosa'? again, twice in two days! This time we were all very close to it, and it was spectacular.

It took just a few seconds for one of our party to ask the lady owner what it was, at this point, and being close up, could see that it definitely was a Mimosa, and a variety that I certainly had not seen in all my life (September 2008). The lady swiftly replied "it's Acacia 'baileyana purpurea'… a Mimosa! and she went on to say how really spectacular it was in spring, for it still had those bright yellow, fluffy scented flowers to enhance the shrub even more.

On reaching home, this shrub was on my mind, I just had to have one! A friend of mine, Steve Malster, a true plantsman, who has his own fantastic nursery at Beccles, Suffolk – send for his catalogue, to Goose Green Nurseries –

Anyhow, Steve didn't sell these, but managed to get the very last two from another nursery, so I purchased the last two – one for me and one for a very dear client, Iris Jones, Darsham/Yoxford, Suffolk, who so sadly died in November 2008. Her birthday had been on August 18th, and I always bought her plants or shrubs etc. as a present, and this time she wanted something with berries, of which there is a huge choice, but I wanted something unusual, as I'd always done. I kept making all the excuses that I couldn't find anything at present with berries, but I had Callicarpa, or Gaultheria in mind, but I still wasn't happy.

Sadly, the two Mimosas came when Iris was on her last. It had been a long search for Steve Malster, and I least of all knew that time was running out for Iris. It's strange really, because on our arrival home from Cornwall, I told Iris all about our lovely break, and that I'd found her something very special (she already had new Mimosas in her garden at Darsham). I held back from telling her what it was, but then one week before she was due to go into hospital (thinking she would be out again shortly) I had this overwhelming feeling that I should tell Iris what it was. I had the feeling that she wouldn't ever see this plant. Yes, Iris had Cancer, and for a good while too, but I, and she, never thought it would come to an end at this particular time, for she was always bright and cheerful, a very kind lady.

In the end, I blurted out all that I knew of this plant, and she seemed very delighted on me giving her this description, and I so wished she could have seen it.

My own unusual Mimosa, I'll plant in my garden (Spring 2009) and further back in the garden for more protection I hope, at this point in time I have no idea how tall or how wide the 'tree' 'shrub' will grow to; the two that I saw in Cornwall stood about 8 foot high and similar spread, so I'll sit back and wait and see!

Senior School Surprises! ... and Sadness

Moving from Harold Hill, Romford, Essex, was a great wrench for me, and one of the horrors of this was having to go to a new school. Like most folk, we are not happy in the company of strangers although the old saying of 'strangers are only people or friends that you don't know yet' and that of course is very true, but none of us like that FIRST day at school, nor that first day at a work place.

Whitehall Junior and Infants School at Chingford was a series of wooden buildings, under the London County Council, and all the kids in our Juniors called it "The London County Cow-sheds" which it did actually resemble! It seemed to me to be a building from the past, for Bosworth Junior School at Harold Hill was brick built and modern, although the infants school there very much resembled Whitehall School in every way, but after spending longer periods at Bosworth, it did seem odd to me to go back to very basic buildings again.

My only teacher there was a very well spoken man by the name of Mr Jevoh (pronounced Jer Vo). He went on I think TV's *Panorama* programme once, and took us out on my one and only school day trip to Wivenhoe, West Mersea, and Colchester Castle, the latter I remember because of the very steep stairs and a Sycamore tree that grew out of the brickwork on top of the castle, and it's *still* there today!

A really lovely old lady by the name of Mrs McPherson took 'a shine' to me, perhaps because I reminded her of her son or grandson, she was always smiley, an elderly lady and I'm certain she was the head-cook – she always gave me extra food, and stuck up for me when a teacher on dinner duty used to walk round the tables observing each child to make sure that they ate *all* of the food whether we liked it or not!

I've had a lifelong hatred of meat – stringy, stretchy, tubes, bones…
aaaaargh! and refuse to eat it I did! Mrs Mac (as she was affectionately
known) told them to leave me alone, and that she would give me more
vegetables instead. She was a lovely lady, and I often wonder what
happened to her, although I never saw her again once I left Whitehall
to attend Heathcote Senior School that joined on next door.

Before I move on to tell you about Heathcote School, on my first
days at Whitehall School, all the kids said "You speak funny!" which
bothered me a lot for I didn't think they spoke any different to me. It
came to light later, that I and Sandra had adopted an Essex accent in a
'country-bumpkin' type style, rather than an East End of London
Essex style. For in later years I met new friends in remote Essex
villages, and noticed that they did have a country Essex dialect, for
where other folk would say "You daren't do it" my pal would say "You
doosen't do's it". Therefore I must have had twangs of very broad
Essex, and of course I would sound very different. Much the same now
if my own now grown-up children had gone back to London, for they
have adopted Suffolk amongst their cockney mum n' dad! … us!!

Heathcote School not only did it have the large modern area, but it
still had old annexes, so I only went into the modern bit for morning
assembly led by Mr Pollard the headmaster (Mr Gridley was our head
at Bosworth Junior School). One delight I had was when a workman
was affixing new guttering to the walkways through the annexes, and
it was my Uncle Sid! A lovely man who had served in the 8th Army
during World War II.

I was delighted at Heathcote because they did have a Gardening
Class. The girls did needlework, or needlecraft as it was also known.
Now I'm not sure on the spelling of the teacher's name, but the
pronunciation was Koons (Khunes?) and we all thought he was
German going by the way he pronounced things, like when showing
you the green house he'd say "Mind your fingass in zer door" (mind
your fingers in the door), or "Don't forget to put on your wellinks"
(don't forget your Wellingtons). It was a very small class of boys of
around ten pupils, most thought the class odd, and an unusual school
subject, and didn't really take it that seriously. I on the other hand
would have gratefully missed all the other lessons and garden all day.
On rainy days we'd spend our time in the classroom learning about
John Innes Composts, and different methods of digging, i.e. single
digging, double digging etc. and only two of us, out of the whole class
were asking questions and taking a real interest.

My pal's name was David Bolton, a very thin boy back then, with a
public school hairstyle, glasses, college scarf and a satchel. He was

bullied constantly when any chance could be taken by the many bullies who were rife in Chingford and Chingford Hatch at that time.

David came from what most folk would call a middle-class family, and had a biggish house as I remember. He really wanted to go into farming and I do clearly recall him and me having a debate on what he should do, for he said that farm pay was the next lowest to gardening. We were surprised to hear this, for even back then in the early sixties, you heard the familiar saying 'You never see a poor farmer' – maybe not, we thought, but there are poorly paid labourers!

David never did go into farming or gardening, which I thought was sad really, for such was his keenness back then. I met him one day by chance when making a visit to Chingford, sometime in 1988. He did remember me, and of course I asked him if he took up agriculture or horticulture; he told me that he was a security guard! This didn't really surprise me, for now he could perhaps be the 'bully', hide behind a uniform, he now had the authority to do 'payback time' to all those that he caught. He wasn't this skinny schoolboy anymore, but a bigger built man. I now could see what all the cowardly bullying had done to him all through his school years, and all that superb farming knowledge that he had was now totally wasted, for it was he now that had the 'power'.

Before I get back to the gardening, I'll tell you of another lad that I knew – he was plump, and had ginger hair, and once again a target for the bullies in his own year at school, a couple of years above me. I went to see 'The Beatles' at Granada Cinema, Hoe Street, E.17 – there were massive queues, right along Hoe St. through the then arcade, and right down Walthamstow High Street itself (Europe's longest market).

I then saw this lad, now left school, and was now a policeman, he acknowledged me with a smile as we did know each other, but he was brutish with the crowds who to everyone seemed to be in perfect order. He was pushing people violently, and really enticing trouble; here was yet another man masking his own bullied years behind a uniform, that power again. From that time I have often wondered what has gone on in the past when I see anyone who wants to wear a uniform – was it a broken home? awful parents? resentments, being put down in life? being bullied? I have certainly met several in all of the above in my life and it's very worrying.

I always loved the smell and atmosphere when going into Mr Khunes' lovely green house, the bottom half had separate doors and was *really* hot! Mr Khunes taught us how to do budding and grafting of fruit-trees and roses, which I found fascinating, and admit I've never done any since my school days. We grew an odd vegetable called Kohl

Rabi, and Mr Khunes let us take a couple home for our mums to cook, but none of us liked them. On the day I took mine home, Mum had an old school pal visit, and I remember Mum and her laughing at this weird looking vegetable!

Each half-term, or the break up for the school summer holidays, the school yobs smashed Mr Khunes' greenhouse to smithereens, which of course meant that all the plants were severely damaged too, especially the hot-house end, and I wonder even today how the urgent repairs were carried out. Mr Khunes must have been so broken-hearted, and wonder if those boys now men of my age (60 years old in 2009) feel any guilt of what they did all those years ago? None to my knowledge were ever caught because there were far too many of them, and all had to pass the greenhouse to reach the quick exit out of the school. Occasionally one or two teachers were put on guard, but this often meant nothing to those that were leaving school for good, they just took a chance.

Because David Bolton and I were the keenest of all the boys in the class, Mr Khunes each year took turns in putting either David or me at the top of the class for the set gardening exam, for we both couldn't be first... could we?

David and I didn't know it, but all the schools in the borough were each looking for the best two gardeners at each school, and David and me were chosen to represent Heathcote School for a tree planting ceremony that was to take place at Mansfield Park, along The Ridgeway at Chingford. David's mum decided to come along, and sat on the bonnet of the Mayor's car to put on her wellingtons!

Each child had one tree per two children (?) for the schools that were represented. I cannot remember if all the trees were of different varieties or not, but we had a flowering cherry. I did go back and look many, many years after leaving school, and saw a row of now mature trees, but had no idea which one was the one that David and I planted.

After all this we got ourselves into the local paper, and we were so pleased with that, and certainly a first for me in a newspaper! Soon after this, David and myself were chosen to load up lots of plants at the ancient Pimp Hall, where I think the local council had nurseries; all the loaded plants were taken back to our school as a display to the front of the stage for the forthcoming Prize presentation evening.

The day came for the prize giving, and as there was very little to do in Chingford Hatch in those days, me and a pal (Charlie Brennan or Tony Barnard) on the off-chance and out of the blue, decided to go along to this event. It was all rather boring really, and mainly fifth and sixth formers going up to the stage and being presented with silver cups, certificates etc. Then to my total shock, I heard the word gardening mentioned, and then *my* name being called! I was so totally surprised and still believing that there must be another Keith Nichols when my pal urged that indeed it was me! So off I went, a complete nervous wreck, and have had a lifelong hatred of being in the limelight and avoid it at all costs if I can.

I was, however, presented with a lovely gardening book called 1,000 PLANT PORTRAITS by A.G. HELLYER, and reads 'Intermediate Gardening Prize presented to Keith Nichols (1964)' and I am proud to say I still have it, and even spotted one photograph upside down!

Valentine Deliveries

When I was first able to drive, two friends of mine Peter and Betty Blackford, owned a florist's shop at the 'Bell corner' Forest Road, E.17. I often used to see them working until very late at night, preparing flower bouquets etc. for weddings, funerals etc. but their really busy times were on Mother's Day, and Valentines Day, the latter being even busier than the first! They asked me if I could do all of their deliveries for them, so I said yes straight away! and really enjoyed the shock – albeit very pleasant – on people's faces on receiving bunches of flowers and potted plants.

I did this lovely job until Peter and Betty sold their shop, aptly called 'Peter's Florist'. On one occasion they sold a very large bulb called 'Elephant flower' Crinum 'Powellii'. I wondered for years how the common name came about, but I suspect that the large bulb itself represents an elephant's head, and the long bended growing point the trunk!

Beatrix Potter

One year prior to Debbie and I getting married we visited the Lake District and simply had to visit the home of authoress and farmer, Beatrix Potter. Back in 1971 her house and garden was never really busy at all, unlike when we went there in the year 2000 and the queues to get in were enormous!

On that first visit, Deb and I were the only people being shown around, including our very first dog 'Bobo' (a breed of Manchester terrier) that I bought from the world famous Club Row animal market adjacent to Petticoat Lane, in London's East End.

Our dog 'Bobo' (pronounced 'Boe Boe') was only able to go into Beatrix Potter's house if she could be carried; luckily enough she was a small breed, so I carried her all round the house! She lay like a baby in my arms, tummy upwards, and looking all around as if taking it all in!

We were in the room where the scarf that was used in all the 'Peter Rabbit' pictures (and other items that were used in all the stories) in a glass cabinet. An elderly lady, and being one of the attendants, remarked "Oh what a lovely little dog. If Beatrix had been alive today she would love your little dog." We gathered by this assumption that the lady had possibly known Beatrix Potter personally, who later married William Heelis.

When we visited the second time in April 2000, the garden (and Mr McGregor's garden) all still seemed very atmospheric. we went the week before Easter, and I'd always wanted to see William Wordsworth's daffodils. I was not disappointed. When I think back now, I realise how far Deb and I walked to Beatrix Potter's home – we walked to and from Broughton-in-Furness… miles! (1971)

Always Double Check

I refer now to the very many errors made in gardening magazines, newspapers, radio and TV. At one time, as my wife Debbie will vouch for me, I would almost leap out of my chair when seeing a blatant error being made, by the very people who are supposed to be professionals, and paid very highly too, far more than I'll ever see in my gardening life. So it makes my blood boil – if you're going to learn about gardening and plants, then learn 100% first before going on TV or whatever, so as not to show the nation wrongful knowledge.

I don't bother to write in anymore, although most people, be it an editor, or owner of a garden, would write back to me with a sort of "sorry" and a kind of apology. Over the years I've mentioned these errors to owners of garden centres and nurseries (they too make many bloomers, as you'll read).

The trouble with all the complaining, the people to whom you write to or speak to direct, often think you're being very big-headed. I like to think that I was able to help *them*, yet at the same time able to test my own knowledge on what I'd learnt. I've always tried to be jovial and very light-hearted when telling folk that they're wrong, and not appear pompous as many will do to show their superiority.

I'm very sure that my very first letter went to… wait for it… Kew Gardens! The shrub should have been marked as Cornus 'Nuttalii' but was labelled as something completely different and a million miles from the Cornus family. Kew did write back and said the public often changed over plant labels – believe that if you will – but then nothing ever surprises me nowadays with the human race, many of course being 'adult children'.

A florist was put out when I went into his shop to say that there was a wrong label on one of his indoor plants; it was marked as Platycerium 'The Stag's Horn Fern' when in fact it was a Syngonium 'Goose Foot'. I never knew if he changed the plant's name to the correct one, but a year or so on I took on the 'gardens' at Walthamstow Building Society E.17, and up went my credibility in this man's eyes, when he saw what I was achieving, creating these new gardens. The chap became more friendly, perhaps now realising that I wasn't being 'clever' after all.

All this was around the time when I had planted *hardy* Freesias, a new introduction back then. I'd bought a huge box-load in about five or six colours and this chap on seeing them all in bloom couldn't believe that he was seeing… Freesias, outdoors, surely not! He asked me if I could get a box for him to sell in his florists shop in nearby Wood Street, a good buy indeed for him for he sold the lot and of course praised my display from that previous year of introduction, and thousands of people must have seen them on that very busy crossroad. So he was able to tell his customers that they were lovely and that there were thousands of them in the building society last year and asked if they'd seen them.

Many people find it hard to believe me when I tell them that there are hardy Gardenias. Many folk often want these, for people nowadays spend lots of holidays abroad, and Gardenias grow in abundance in exotic countries, and try to emulate that holiday by buying a Gardenia, without a doubt taking them back to their sunny holiday memories.

Another garden centre sprang up almost alongside the now defunct, but once very popular Larkswood Swimming Pool in Chingford, and I was of course very keen to see this new venture. I didn't take me very long for me to see that they'd made a very big error concerning a mass of hundreds of the same potted bulb, and each had a handwritten label simply saying 'CANDICANS'.

The nursery only had the bulb half right, so I thought I'd better mention their error before it rebounded on them. Again, in a jovial way, pointed out that they would never see a plant in any gardening book with the name CANDICANS. They argued to say that this was the right name "It's the 'Summer Hyacinth'" the nurseryman said. "Yes," I said, "I know that, but it is actually a Galtonia or to be more precise Galtonia 'candicans'!

How many people today still have those bought bulbs for their gardens and tell their friends and relatives that the lovely flowers are called candicans?

This is the reason that many garden centres get very annoyed when various TV garden shows get the name of a plant wrong, for the public jot down the name that comes up on the screen, then order that plant via a catalogue or garden centre, and when the flower blooms after they've bought the plant that they thought they saw on TV, to then be totally different, then the arguments ensue.

All this brings me on to errors made on *Gardeners' World* over the years. Now I truly love this programme, but on occasions in the past have had cause to get the ol' pen out and have a moan!

The now late gardener, Arthur Billet of Clacks Farm went to interview the Head Gardener of a grand house, and the plant that was being discussed was right close up to the screen, therefore there was no mistaking what the plant was. Arthur and the gardener stood directly behind the 5ft or so plant. Arthur said, "I've always loved Eryngiums … 'sea holly', I was almost inside my TV set! Eryngium I thought, that's not Eryngium, it's Echinops 'Globe Thistle'. I listened on for Arthur had clearly made a mistake, so perhaps the Head Gardener would correct him? I just could not believe my eyes, or should I say *ears*, for the Head Gardener then went on to say that he too loved Eryngiums and had grown these for many years!

I straight away wrote to the BBC *Gardeners' World* production team, to let them know of this major error, and again visualised folk looking at the Echinops, placing an order, and their plant grows to be Eryngium! I received a very basic "sorry" – 'Dear Mr Nichols, we did not realise that there was a mistake on *Gardeners' World*. We are sorry about this, you must be a very observant gardener.' Was I the only person in the whole country to spot this error?

I have seen several plays and TV programme dramas make mistakes on these next plants, which shows you that no proper research could have been carried out: the poisonous Aconitum "Monkshood" and Eranthis 'hyemalis' or "Winter Aconite". The TV programmes always say he or she, has been poisoned with Aconite, then they show you a bunch of Aconitums!

If my memory serves me well, such an error was made on the popular programme *Heartbeat* amongst others.

I went for a job years ago when Forest bark first came about. The head gardener was a cocky so-and-so and showed me round the gardens, and couldn't understand how he was getting severe losses of plants and shrubs. He was quite embarrassed when I said that you're only supposed to do minimal thickness of mulch to suppress weeds – he had planted everything in 2½ feet of just bark!

Yes, I have done mulches of mushroom compost as much as 3ft deep, but this was to starve light on a huge area of celandine – the garden contained no other plants, so this area was left to rot further down for almost two years. All the celandine was completely starved of light and it all died off. As I laid the mulch I trod it all solid, making any penetration of shoots impossible, especially for a tiny weed. I then had a blank canvass to work on, then plant up, and continue mulching for mainly effect with a graded bark or even leaf mould.

You may now be wondering how I go about sorting out the tougher deeper rooting weeds like dock, dandelion, Alkanet, Alexanders etc. I do exactly the same principle (this is assuming that the client hates using weed-killers), I put the heavy mulches directly on top of the weeds, you can just knock these over sideways first, but usually one good weighty barrow load will knock 'em over! I then continually tread, add mulch, tread again and so on, so assuming this is very early spring, the best time to do this particular job really, for during the year you can see which of those deeper rooting weeds make it with new growth to the surface again, and it's not many I assure you. As and when they start to appear, put one or more barrow loads of mulch on top of each one, this of course starves them of light, making their already weak growth even weaker; after growing through the first lot of mulch you can keep adding mulch to all those weeds that just refuse to give up. You should then get a firm grip on them and then by rights pull out with fair ease as if they were growing in a bag of sand.

Really troublesome weeds like Alexanders, or the awful Japanese Knotweed, I simply cut them down during the main growing season, and pour virtually any tough weed-killer neat down the now hollow stems, and to aid 'the kill' even further, run a steel rod, or long screwdriver, right down the hollow stem to penetrate the thick parsnip type roots, hence the week-killer reaches its target.

Life's a Beech!

I bet you every time you see a house or car etc. crushed after a severe gale or storm, the tree that has landed on it is a Beech tree. I always look at these drastic scenes and nine times out of ten it's a Beech.

Hogging all the Garden!

One of the most extraordinary scenes that I have ever witnessed in a garden was when a lady who lived on her own in a house, just off Lea Bridge Road, Leyton, E.10, called me on the phone one day and told me that she was literally trapped in her house by gigantic weeds! I was intrigued, so went along to see what the problem was. To be honest I was dumbstruck, for indeed the lady could not get out into her back garden whatsoever.

I looked out to the garden from her dining room, and all I could see was solid thick stalks, not unlike a very weird fantasy forest. I checked the back door in the kitchen, that strangely, if the stalks had not been there, opened OUTWARDS! If it had opened inwards, the normal way, I could at least start to cut down from the kitchen door, but alas. I did however manage to push open very gently one of the dining room windows, but fearing that it would either bend or break, I told the lady that at a push I could possibly somehow get out of the window to actually be able to commence working. The job would have been a real nightmare to do; I didn't get the job, my quote was turned down.

I expect you are now intrigued to know what this weed was! The weed was "The Giant Hogweed" or "Cartwheel Flower" Heracleum 'mantagazzianum'. A real brute reaching some 12 feet high or more, with giant white umbels of white flowers at the tops of the stems. Because this lady's plants were so dense, a lot of the ferny foliage had died off, therefore you had to look skywards to see any leaves, and of course the massive blooms.

I have, over the many years since the 1970s, wondered how the lady sorted this out, and who the brave gardener was!

Cheats!

I'm very certain that some editors of newspapers and magazines cheat when writing gardening columns or odd gardening features. I suspect cheating because there is no name at the end of the article, and my suspicions are that the editors or whoever, pick up random gardening books and simply copy other people's work, for there are lots of magazines and newspapers who do have the person's name mentioned, more so on features like – what to do in the garden this month. All the editor then has to do is to jumble the words about a bit, plus pick up numerous gardening books to then fill in to make an article, and when they've done this successfully, why indeed would they want to pay an expert to do their articles for them?

Cheating and Ignorance

Always each year TV stations all over the country will in January, February and March, show on screen how spring is getting far too early through global warming, and always show you close-ups of blossom on trees. To the layman it does indeed look like blossom time has come really early, but to us in the gardening world we easily see that all these blossom trees are meant to flower in the bleak months.

Prunus 'subhirtella autumnalis' is the one usually portrayed on TV as "being far too early and it's May when it should bloom". This particular variety can bloom some two weeks before Christmas, and occasionally October or November depending where you live; the name 'Autumnalis' alone tells you this. Excited reporters each year come out with their cameras and report to the public that global warming is playing havoc with nature!

Picture of Ignorance!

One major publication had a photograph of 'blossom' literally covered in frost, and wrote how wonderful this blossom was to stand up to such harsh treatment. I could clearly see that this wasn't blossom at all, but in fact was the bright seed capsules in red and orange of Euonymus 'Red Cascade'.

Just Plum Stupid

A chap I knew many years ago was bought a garden centre by his rich parents, and the area was noted for its very expensive properties, therefore he certainly knew how to charge. He eventually wrote a gardening column, and later had his own programme on a local radio station. It's an article that he wrote for his February column, and went on to tell readers of all the jobs to do for that month.

One part of this article astounded me and read – 'Now is the time to prune plum, damsons, peaches, etc' –

I couldn't believe what I'd just read, for the golden rule is that you never prune any 'stoned' fruit in winter for risk of silver leaf disease which can kill your trees. The correct time is between April and August. If you even have a branch snap in winter during high winds or heavy snow, these wounds must be treated right away.

I wrote to a couple of gardening magazines to check on what I was sure was a great error, imagining now all the general public killing off all their trees because an 'expert' told them that this was the right time.

The magazines both wrote back to say that I was indeed correct, and that the rules hadn't changed, and that no way should this work be carried out in the winter months; the rules are strict on this.

Eye Eye!

TV and radio presenters of gardening shows for certain have all been to college or training courses to learn their trade of horticulture, but there are occasions where I doubt it very much. Okay, so many of us have our own ways of pronouncing the complicated botanical names, but some of the easiest are pronounced incorrectly. One rather well spoken lady spoke of her Astilbe in bloom; she pronounced it 'Astul bee', instead of 'Ass still B', yet she must have heard others pronounce it the correct way many times.

TV gardeners seem to be the worst, for they are the presenters, top of their profession, the letters ii at the end of a plant or shrub's name is pronounced E I; for example Buddleia 'davidii' on telly becomes Buddleia 'davidi' (David Eye), but should be pronounced as' Da viddy I'.

Once again, I wrote to a couple of magazines to ask if there had been name changes for 'davidii' 'greyii', 'thompsonii', 'Darwinii' etc. for I told them how I was taught way back in the early 1960s. The magazines kindly wrote back to me and said that I once again was correct, and that it was just pure laziness on behalf of the presenters.

It's no wonder there is great confusion in the plant world, for is it Clermaytuss or Clemertiss for the popular clematis? I have old gardening books and they have a page of 'signs' on how a plant's name is given; it'll tell you a common daily word, so you get the gist of the pronunciation like an 'a' for example… Can't and Cat. Hence you then know the sound you should be making, say when talking about Carnations or Camellias.

One of my nicer customers when I worked in Hampstead, London, kept saying "I've grown a penis" or "I like the penis". I was in my early twenties then and used to blush up each time she said the word 'penis', for I knew what she meant to say, but hadn't the heart, more so the courage, to correct her! She was referring of course to the botanical name of the Pine tree i.e. 'Pinus' pronounced 'Pie-nuss'.

Assumption

Many years ago now when Deb and I first got married I kept seeing an advert for a rarely seen perennial for sale. I knew of the plant and had always wanted one; it was the tall Bupthalmum (pronounced 'Boo thall mum'), so I telephoned the man and said I'd be over. He had already told me it would be £2 for a large clump, so off I went. A poor looking unshaven ill-looking, but very pleasant man came to the door, he told me that I was the only person who had heard of the plant, and was so delighted when I told him of two other varieties of it!

He did at times seem a little sad; I assumed he lived alone, and assumed that he was ill. Moreso I assumed he was hard up, for he kept asking if I'd like the other clump too, but I hadn't come with any more money and he was almost willing me to buy it, for I think he knew he'd have no other buyers for this plant. I felt so guilty, and still do all these years on. I should have gone back!

Precious Gift

As a boy, then teenager, I was admired by a Mrs King (Chingford) for helping Mum through her M.S. Mrs King bought me a very expensive garden tool set; sadly I only have one piece of the set today. Mrs King had something to do with the M.S. Society.

Green by Name, Green by Nature

How folk say green is an unlucky colour makes the mind boggle, for surely it's the very best colour of all, for it is the colour of nature itself.

I'm now going to tell you about a very lovely lady by the name of Mrs Green. I don't think anyone ever knew her first name, nor that of Mr green. They were both near neighbours of Dad's mum and dad, who lived at 80, Kenilworth Avenue E.17. Dad's parents of course being one set of grandparents to me. I have no idea if Mr and Mrs Green were friendly with them, for I say *them* but I think my paternal grandfather had died by the time Mum was courting dad, for he had been in the Home guard in world War Two, along with his best pal Percy Clayson, and always said "Perc" (short for Percy, pronounced as 'Purse') "if anything happens to me, look after Rose for me (Rose Nichols née Coggin), and that's what he did do to the end of their days. You, the reader, will have to buy my book on my Earliest Memories at Harold Hill to fill you in with the story why my mum hated my nan; this being the reason, because of Nan's cruelty to Mum, and why possibly Mum became great friends with nearby Mr and Mrs Green.

Looking at an old photo recently, I assume that my great-grandmother (Minnie Nichols) knew Mrs Green, for the photo is signed – 'to Mrs Green from Mrs Nichols' – note the surname formality! I assume from this that my great-grandparents too lived very close by, hence there had been a very long association with the Greens and the Nichols.

Mr and Mrs Green never to my knowledge ever visited us at Harold Hill, Essex, but Mum always took Sandra and me to see them both, avoiding number 80 at all costs I should think!

Old Mr Green was a friendly soul, and rarely saw him standing up. He wore an embroidered rimless hat, that probably does have a proper name!

Ah!… Chocolate fingers! Every time, even now when I have these I think of Mr and Mrs Green, for this was I'm sure, the only time we ever had them! The same reason I think of my dear Nan, Rose Ridley née Axford, for as kids she always gave us those lovely 'iced gems'! Their home was quaintly old fashioned, and we always enjoyed our afternoon stay with Mr and Mrs Green. Mrs Green would take me on my own out in their garden, and left Mum, Sandra and Mr Green indoors, no doubt polishing off some more chocolate fingers! Mrs Green was the very first person to show me orange and lemon plants, all grown from pips; I asked to see these on every visit, and loved her garden.

When we moved to Chingford Hatch, we never saw Mr Green ever again, for he was by this time (1960) either infirm, or had perhaps passed away, but as soon as we moved to 'the Hatch' Mrs Green became a very much welcomed visitor, always happy and smiling, and even now I'm 60, I can still partly recall her voice (yet my mum's won't come to mind at all, possibly through shock of losing her?). Mrs Green never ever came empty-handed, we always had sweets, and she gave Mum bunches of flowers from her garden, magazines etc. even items of clothing that she either bought or found suitable for us all.

On occasions Mrs Green would perhaps bring a bunch of roses from her garden, and when they wilted I planted the 'twigs' just outside the kitchen door, right on the part of the garden where we shot the tea-leaves several times a day, therefore a very good spot for these numerous cuttings that actually did start to grow rapidly, no doubt because of the ever constant moisture around them.

On the 20th May 1972, Debbie and I were married at St John's Church, Chingford Road, E.17, and as we were going into the church a smiling face outside the fencing beckoned me and Deb over – it was lovely Mrs Green! She gave us a present of a crystal bowl, which so thankfully we still have. I was so longing to talk to her, but so many people were milling into the church, our "hello" and "goodbye" was too swift.

When we came back from our honeymoon (wait for it… in Kessingland!) I made a point of going to see Mrs Green. She opened her front door ever so slightly, although she smiled and knew who I was, there wasn't that beaming smile that she always had, and in some ways she looked so very sad. Was Mrs Green ill, was Mr Green perhaps still alive, and not dead as we thought when Mrs Green visited at

Chingford Hatch? All these thoughts went through my mind, for I was not asked in. What I would have given to go back into that lovely house and see that garden again, and talk to Mrs green as a proper adult, and yarn about flowers. Sadly, when that door shut, after I thanked her for that beautiful crystal bowl, I never saw Mrs Green ever again. Today I wonder where they both are buried, and would dearly love to pay my deepest respects to them both.

Chocolate fingers... Ah, those lovely chocolate fingers!

Three in a Row!

When I gave up my garden round at Hampstead etc. I carried on being self-employed, back in Walthamstow where unbeknown to me I got three jobs all in a row which proved very enjoyable – except for one inconsolable dear lady who had not long lost her husband. The lady was Mrs Penny, a very sweet elderly lady, who I don't think stopped crying for all the time I carried out her job of work.

I just did not know how to console her, it was so very sad, and as you can see, I've never forgotten that dear lady, and can only hope that there is an afterlife and Mr and Mrs Penny are reunited once more.

Mrs Penny gave me one of her husband's unusual gardening tools, and if she had been alive today, she would be so delighted that I still have it, albeit when I even see this tool, I think of Mrs Penny with tears streaming down her face.

The tool is on a long handle, and has a thin metal 'blade' which you could fit in the narrowest of gaps between plants when weeding; it's a fabulous gadget, and like Mrs King's precious gift that you read about just now, Mrs Penny's gift too is a very precious gift indeed.

Mrs Penny didn't have flower borders as I remember, if she did they were small, for the whole of this garden was crazy-paved. The paving looked dull, and a new type of garden paint was now on the market, with a rough sandy texture and came in several colours; she chose the green, for once down it resembled 'green grass' and it did look very cheerful too!

I think Mrs Penny told her next-door neighbours about me and how very happy she was with my work, the next-door neighbours, again, two elderly ladies one much older than the other. Back then, like now, I had my hair long, but I was greeted with a very cheery smile by these two ladies, one of them, Mrs Youlden, exclaimed "You look just like my nephew Vivien!" I, of course, happily replied "do I?" Mrs Youlden said, "Yes, he's in a famous pop-group," so now full of interest I said "What do they call themselves?" She replied, "The Bonzo Dog Doodah Band," then I thought, Ah, this all now makes sense. Vivien? Of course, her nephew was the lead singer Viv Stanshall. I said I knew a lot of their songs like 'I'm the Urban Spaceman' and of course their L.P. entitled 'The Doughnut in Granny's Greenhouse'.

The two ladies of course being Viv Stanshall's aunt and grandmother. Viv Stanshall I'm certain was living in Walthamstow (Grove Road) around that time.

I did an enormous amount of clearing and planting in this garden. I think the two ladies had only just moved in, for they had a skip outside which was full of old furniture, mirrors, pictures in beautiful wooden frames – all real good antique stuff. Boy, I wish I knew then what I know now, for that skip was full of wondrous items.

When I finished their job, I worked for Mrs Penny's other neighbour on the other side of her. It turned out that I knew the man who I knew simply as Ted, he had a stall for years down Walthamstow's famous market, and sold toiletries.

New houses had been built next to Mrs Penny, and of course Ted had the first one. This was a time when builders were now told to leave mature trees on plots of ground, and plan properties around them, so Ted had some good ornamental and fruit trees, and I laid turf end-to-end in this garden.

All in all, this was a good run of jobs, full of surprises and employed every bit of my time at each. I hope time was a healer for Mrs Penny.

Explosive Situation!

Another visitor who, once we moved from Harold Hill to Chingford Hatch, was Mum's school pal Betty Kebby née Moore. we got to call her Auntie Betty. Betty made sure that now she'd met up with Mum again, the friendship would stay, and Betty came to see Mum every Friday. Betty had lived the whole of her life at 32, Fleeming Rd., E.17, taking the house on when her parents died. Betty was also a brilliant artist, especially the drawing of all types of animals.

Betty asked me to 'landscape' her back garden, for there was only a small patch of lawn and no borders, and she wanted a proper garden.

I could see that my biggest task was to remove the monstrous growth of probably this country's fastest climber, that being the "Russian Vine" or its other name that suits it best "Mile-a-minute Vine", botanically named as Polygonum 'Bauldschaunican' and I'll tell you a little further on how I first came across this plant. Once established, this rapid climber is very capable of covering 50 sq. feet per season, and seems to grow almost in front of your eyes!

Auntie Betty said that it had been there for donkey's years, and only by looking either side at the bottom ends of her neighbours' gardens, could I tell how long her garden should be. All Betty's neighbours had all chopped away at it to keep it from encroaching onto their gardens, and the vine had taken over Betty's garden so much… hence the now very small patch of lawn adjacent to the house.

The job was a total nightmare, and the whole job was done by me, single-handedly. I had to cut, then dig out, cut and dig out, continuously, and at the same time making a huge stack of this climber. I burnt the lot on site, and took three long days, and it burnt away on its own throughout the nights too.

When the whole lot was burnt, Betty and I could now see the full proper size of her garden, something she had not seen for many years. My next task was to rotovate thoroughly the whole of the garden, getting rid of the last remnants of vine roots, etc. It was then a case of raking the area level, continuous rolling and treading, the latter where you keep your feet together and keep your weight to your heels, for then this will find all the weak spots, and make all size depressions in the soil. This method is called 'The Gardener's Shuffle'. After this you rake level again, then roll, tread, and so on until your heels make no more dents; you can then rake again to a fine tilth before you seed or lay turf.

If the preparation is not carried out correctly, just a mere few weeks down the line, your so-called 'levelled' soil starts to sink to find its final level. Of course by then your turf would be sinking too, resulting in what we call in the trade 'Rockery Turf' because that's exactly how they'll look. Yes, okay, laying the turf is the relatively 'easy' part, but the preparation is most essential.

I was now almost ready to do the 'pretty bits' i.e. the turfing and planting up, but still had just the very final levelling to do, and of course started at the back of the garden where the vine first started life! I was soon about ten foot down the line so to speak, when my rake hooked up a lump of stone or iron. It was a hot day, and the object dried very quickly, so I knocked it about with my rake to knock off the now dry and crusty soil. I then could see that it was 'iron' of some sort and had loads of squares on it. "No! Oh heavens, it was a hand grenade!" I made my exit a bit sharpish to tell Auntie Betty, she was dumfounded – how did it get there we both wondered? For Betty had lived here all through her life as did her mum and dad. But Betty said she thinks that during the war there was an ammunitions shed in one of the nearby houses over the back, but it still didn't explain this stray one.

I telephoned the Walthamstow Police Station in Green Leaf Road, E.17, and expected the bomb squad to turn up, but no, just one policeman arrived in his car! The officer came into the garden and confirmed that indeed it was a hand grenade, and confirmed too that the grenade was a live one, and worse still, the pin had worn away!

I relayed to the policeman all the work that I'd done – the bonfire on top of it for three days and nights, the rotovating, rolling, treading and levelling. He was so shocked for this could have gone off at any time! He then asked if Betty had a shoe box to put it in – I said is that to shoo (shoe) it away!? He laughed, but then was concerned that he had to pick it up and put it on the passenger seat. The windows were closed, so I tapped on the window to say that perhaps he should leave all the windows open in case the heat built up too much and set it off, for it was a scorcher of a day. I still wonder today why the policeman never called out the bomb squad, for I've had to since then when my sons and I found mortar bombs in a garden on the main road at Darsham, Suffolk. Both shells lay on the border of the lady's garden and the farmer's field. The bomb squad did come out this time!

Something in the Clay

Another weird find was when I was digging out an area for a pond. I had decent soil for the first twelve inches or so, then thick yellow sticky clay. I'd gone to a depth of 4 feet or so, and alive in the clay were black leeches!

The Great Plague and Me!

Whilst working for the Hackney Borough Council, at Springfield Park, Clapton, London, I was sent to do a pleasant job at a very small park adjacent to Hackney Police Station. My job was to scarify all the lawns with a petrol scarifying machine, to the layman a scarifyer (lawn rake) removes all the dead, dying and thatch from your lawn. The old method was to use a hand 'spring-bok' rake, and that plays havoc with the ol' stomach muscles!

I started up my machine, and commenced on the main lawns, but the ground that I was walking on felt hollow, and made a hollow sound. When it was time for me to go to the bothy for my tea-break, I told the main gardener of the strange feeling beneath my feet.

The man said "I don't want to shock you, but beneath this whole park are buried the victims of the plague of London!" He said, "Come outside a minute, I want to show you something of interest." Once outside he showed me one wall of the bothy building, and that one brick was missing and replaced with glass. This, he said, was to let them know of any subsidence – if the glass cracked then the building needed underpinning. The chap said that the lawns and paths often had to be re-levelled. I was never certain, but assumed the burials were of possibly so-called important or rich people underneath in private 'chambers', hence all the sounds of hollowness. I was to be even more shocked the following day, for on another part of the park, it sounded even hollower, so was scary to say the least. It was in this area where across the lawn was an old brick wall with various climbers over it; two of these I'd never seen before in 'real life' only in my gardening books and magazines, but recognised both straight away, those being the "Russian Vine" and "Dutchman's Pipe" Aristolchia 'sipho'.

The gardener said, "Go and dig a bit out of each, but leave the border tidy after!" I didn't need telling twice, off I went and commenced digging. I'd hardly dug a spade's depth when my leg fell through a deep hole and I banged my head and arms on the wall and was left with one leg up to my knee – the rest of my leg was with the plague victims! I was horrified, then thinking that the whole of this border would collapse!

Needless to say, both plants came out very easily. The "Dutchman's Pipe" I planted on the thick ½" x ½" trellis that stopped my children falling on the greenhouse and the "Russian Vine" went to near the shed at the bottom of our garden in the first house that we bought in Chingford Road. The trouble is, even now when the subject of these two plants comes up I think of those poor victims!

Crooked Eye!

One job that I had on my own went off without any problems, but two very skilled builder friends of mine had great problems with this same customer. He kept saying "my eye seems to be taking me to the left" (or right), referring to the levels that my pals were doing on fences, paths and walls. Their work was perfect, and under their breaths they kept saying "I'll poke his bloody eye out if he keeps on!"

Two Lots of Tears!

Another job that I did on my own was for a then, youngish couple, and like at my auntie Betty's had to put lots of newspaper, polythene and cardboard down all through the house from the front door to the back, for there was no back gate, so I had to carry all the rubbish in bags into a skip, and like at Betty's carry all the turf through the house!

This was a small garden, and because it was small, you could spend little money to fill it. I made a small pond and rockery, lovely borders etc., and it looked like a mini-Chelsea Show exhibit garden.

As I started getting the turf in, the man of the house was sitting on the bottom stairs right in front of me as I came through the front door, but his hands were over his face crying his eyes out! I felt really daft, moreso that any passers-by could see him too, and all I could do was shrug my shoulders as a gesture that I didn't know what was wrong. On reaching the kitchen and carrying several turfs, the woman was standing at the kitchen sink bawling her eyes out too! It was so embarrassing for me, for they both carried on crying, not making any attempt to go upstairs out of the way. As you can imagine, I had a good few turfs to carry through, and even took my time, to give them time to get upstairs, it was all rather odd, for there was certainly enough rooms for each of them to go in, it just didn't make any sense.

Much later in the day, when I had completed their work, they both came out into the garden together, both praising me highly, and paid me too. I was pleased about that, at least it wasn't anything that I'd done, but today I still think back to that day, it truly was a very weird experience, for surely there were rooms upstairs where they could have gone!

Cheats at Chelsea?

When living in London (E.17) I made a point of going to the Chelsea Flower Show every year. One lot of exhibits however baffled me each year, and I wondered how the exhibitors involved got away with it each time.

I refer to at least two exhibitors who just simply cut off a section of their shrubs each year, stuck it in a vase of water, and literally got 1st prize every single year!

Each pal whom I went with I'd say just round the corner here are cut-off branches of shrubs I bet you'll see a sprig of Enkianthus 'campanulatus' in one of those vases with 1st prize written on it, and it always was!

Ad-Libbing at Chelsea

One very nice pal of mine would come to the Chelsea Show some years, and was a proud holder of the R.H.S. Certificate (Royal Horticultural Society), but to me he often seemed clueless when it came to plant names and the totally wrong pronunciation of almost every plant that he spoke about! He'd say things like "Oh, I love that Wisteria" which in fact was Weigela or "I love the Nemesis" instead of Nemesia!

It was one year at Chelsea that I simply could not believe my ears, for we were both standing together, and he hadn't heard of this particular rose that I pointed out to him. At that point, two elderly ladies were standing next to me and overheard some of what I'd just said. I was in fact talking about Rosa 'Nazomi' and Rosa 'Snow Carpet', the so-called latest craze in ground-cover roses. I'd grown these before, just one year prior, so was able to tell the ladies what to expect.

As we all moved on, my pal and I got separated by two other people walking between me and my pal, as he was still admiring these roses. A lady spotted my pal, noting that he was showing some interest in the roses, and he said to the lady, "Do you know anything about these?" The reply was "No," my pal then reeled off all that I had said, which was fine – at least he'd taken it all in, but then he started to add other things that I never said! He told the lady that the plants were suitable indoors for a window sill, etc., etc., and he actually sounded very convincing!

R.H.S. NIL!

Another nice pal *told* me that he had the R.H.S. certificate. Yes, he liked plants, but one day he came to my garden in Chingford Road where I crammed in around 700 varieties of plants, and I'd say "you know this one don't you?" but on every plant he was totally baffled, yet somehow became a foreman at a park! He was there a very short time, and I believe he either left through some embarrassment or was asked to leave. Yes, he did have the certificate and no doubt showed it on his initial interview, but was not actually tested by anyone at that interview to see what his plant knowledge was like. He never ever worked in horticulture again. My theory on what actually happened is logical really, so read on…

Remember, Remember!

After the above 'happening', I was truly wondering if many R.H.S. holders should hold the title at all, and to me it seemed back then to be handed out as easy as ice-cream!

Now to my theory, like ANYONE who sits and studies for an exam, you go over and over and trying to learn all that you're likely to be tested on. Yes, the next day you may pass, but what of the days, weeks, months and years after – how much do you actually remember? It seems like my pals studied like mad, remembered it and an R.H.S. Certificate given to them.

Wanted – Two Holes to Swallow us up!

Carrying on further with my theory, and proving a valid point, I had a young chap come and work with me on a garden in Waltham Abbey, Essex. Again, a nice lad, and hard working. He was very excited, telling me that he couldn't help me on one of the days as he was sitting for the R.H.S. exam. I was pleased for him, and thought that if he passes he'd be a handy chap to stay on with me, and have a labourer who really liked the job, rather than someone coming out just to earn a day's pay.

So off he went to his exam, and I spent the day planting up on my own. The next morning I picked him up from home, and he proudly waved his 'PASS' certificate in front of me. He was totally over the moon with his achievement, and I was so happy for him. He talked excitedly about it all the way to Waltham Abbey. It came to roughly mid-morning I should think, and we'd done a lot more planting of trees, shrubs, plants and bulbs, and I suddenly rubbed my hands together and said, "Come on, mate, it's testing time again – let's see how much you know!" … this to my horror was the worst sentence that had ever come out of my mouth, as you'll now read!

I said "Right, I think we've planted around sixty-odd plants etc. I should think, so let's start here – what's this called?" "er… dunno" "What about this one?" "er, can't think for the minute" "Well, what about this one, mate, this is an easy one" "ooh! don't know that either!" (That shrub was the very common Forsythia!)

This was now getting extremely embarrassing for both of us; to put an end to this, the chap managed to identify just *one* plant (shrub) and that was Kerria 'Japonica'. He said, "I feel really silly now, Keith," and he went on to say "boy, haven't you got to know a lot?" I said that indeed you did have to know a lot, and I certainly, no way, knew it all, but I was totally honest with him and said that "if I had been an employer I'd use that certificate to light a fire with, so don't show it to too many people – go away and study a hell of a lot more, or you'll be caught out again during an interview." I never knew if he took my advice or not, whether he stayed in the business, I can't say.

This is why I warn all my clients, and say if you have a gardener in to estimate, do a simple test, by saying "This is a lovely shrub/plant, what's it called now, I can't think of its name?" and carry on like this in similar lines. Of course you may know all the names of your plants, but if the gardener can't tell you nine out of ten names, then you don't want them loose on your precious plants.

Right and Wrong

By this I refer to a tree surgeon that I knew many years ago now, and he was excellent at his job with the larger trees, i.e. Oak, Ash, Sycamore etc.

He knew that I did not do the big stuff and I only specialised in the restoration of fruit and ornamental trees. He saw that this always kept me busy, and he wanted to 'muscle' in on this too. Of course this never affected me, for London is a huge place. The chap had already told me that he'd never done fruit trees before, but it wasn't long before I saw his work on fruit trees first-hand.

The chap said, "I've just pruned two apple trees for two elderly ladies and they wanted a new lawn." I must admit I was quite shocked at what I saw. My pal certainly wasn't a con man, but he truly believed that he'd done a good job. The two ladies both said to me, "Your friend has done a lovely job, hasn't he?" I could only mutter a muffled "yes", and change the subject quickly, for I saw branches leaning on each other, dead-wood etc. and the centre quite congested. I couldn't understand it, and wondered why he hadn't done some of the principles used on the larger trees.

I tell customers that an apple tree should resemble an up-turned umbrella, with the air and light reaching the centre of the tree, and pears should be sort of goblet-shaped. I would dearly have loved for him to have done one of the trees, and me do the other, and see the contrast. The chap had seen my work many times, so I still find it strange how he thought his work resembled mine.

Well Stumped!

Around 1990 I was talking to a lady who said that her friend needed to see me urgently as she'd had the feeling that she'd been conned, and asked if I could go round and see, to put her mind at rest.

Conned was putting it mildly. The lady had a sixty-year-old Bramley apple tree, and each branch was now a three-foot stump! The lady said, "It doesn't look like it's been pruned properly, but he did take a hell of a lot of wood away." I asked the lady for the name of the people who did the job, and it all made good sense. I had to tell the lady that these chaps actually sold logs for a living. The poor lady was truly devastated.

I did try and console her by saying that I could get her tree back to good shape again, although it would be many years before it got to a reasonable size again. Strangely, the lady never asked me to put the tree right again, even after reeling off how I would tackle such a job. I also had to point out that quite possibly a tree of that age might even die of shock because of the so drastic 'pruning'. I even offered to take the lady over to another client's house to show her one of my successes in 'bringing back to life' an apple tree that another 'cowboy pruner' had hacked at so to speak, but still my estimate was not accepted, yet the cowboys had been paid in full!

A Rolling Stone

Two clients of mine, Hannah and Cyril Percival called me in one day as Cyril had cut out an 'island bed' in the middle of the lawn, and wanted me to plant it up. As quick as a flash I said to Cyril, "I know what will suit that bed!" Cyril could see that I was very excited about something, and I went on to tell him that a garden centre that I knew of had a lovely huge rock, the rock had all worn 'pockets' all over it, and visualised the likes of sedums, Jovibabas, and Sempervivum planted in them. Cyril and Hannah said that we should go for it even though they hadn't seen the rock. The rock arrived on the back of a tipper truck all 5 foot long, 4 feet thick, and we slowly lowered it onto two scaffold boards that lay across my very small trailer.

Cyril, me and my helper Bob Patnell, tried to not only push the two-wheeled trailer, but tried to balance it too! How this small trailer stood up to this weight heaven knows, the tyres too pushed almost flat!

All of a sudden, the rock slipped, fell against a fence and the trailer balancing on one wheel. We somehow got it back on the trailer and had to muster all our strength to do this, and it was nothing more than a miracle when it was safely balanced again. Once we got to the edge of the lawn, we put down scaffold boards, let the trailer tip up, and the rock fell onto the boards. We then put ropes round the rock and hauled the rock for all our might onto the centre of the flower bed, and as I thought, it looked so right to set this bed off.

I vowed never ever to come up with a bright idea like this again!

Lost the Plot... I Don't Think So!

Bill Day had a plot, a very large vegetable plot, and to date the very best kept plot that I've ever seen in my life; award winning doesn't come into it, not a single weed in sight, beautiful neat rows of veg, every garden cane placed so perfectly and a shed on a large scale that I'm certain you could live in! Although regretfully I never did see inside it.

I met Bill whilst working for Mary and Harry Lloyd, and restored their garden, albeit scaring them both half to death when seeing actual scarifying on their lawn and 'harsh' pruning of a very overgrown Forsythia, and to see their faces the following year with their 'new' garden and restoring their faith in me too!

Bill day's allotment backed onto the garden of Mary and Harry's and Bill could see that I was a true gardener by the way I restored everything instead of looking to dig things out because they are old.

When I took on the – at the time – so-called gardens at Walthamstow Building Society, Bill was so overjoyed when I gave him permission to take away barrow loads of bulbs, plants (late Spring, early Autumn) and couldn't believe his luck, I knew that everything would be looked after. As a sort of reward if you like, Bill gave me loads of nylon ropes for tying down rubbish on my trailer etc. but mainly for marking out where lawns and borders would be. Bill got these from his son who was a long-distance lorry driver, and I'm proud to say that I still use these very same ropes today.

Bill has been dead for many years now, and I'm proud to have known him. Being a young man back then, I was too busy with self-employment gardening, but so wished I'd made an effort to keep in contact with Bill. I'm certain I would have learnt so much from him about vegetables, he of course being of the old school with the old-fashioned – in my view – proper ways of growing vegetables.

Little Boys' Thoughts

I have tried twice, very unsuccessfully to get an allotment going, but hard arduous landscaping all day long leaves very little time and energy for that matter to keep up such a project, so never really ever got going! And of course I'd never be so lucky as to get a golden allotment from the likes of Bill day, so always had very neglected plots to sort out, and could see that it was partly a retired man's game, where you could spend all day every day on a plot working at your own pace.

Today, in Northampton, my brother Barry and wife Maura have an allotment. He's a top chef so loves the ol' veg and the total friendship of all on site, like one huge family!

When Bill Day passed away, I took on a very neglected plot on the same allotment site as Bill's, and by now had my second child and first son Adrian come with me over to the allotment and small old shed, whilst I was preparing this new plot and getting lots of spuds in to break up the soil for the first year, Adrian was playing with a very long piece of string amongst all the tall weeds.

I always took a flask with me plus sandwiches etc. for me and Adrian, he was around four or five years old I would think. One day, he sat on an old milk crate, and I could see he was in deep thought and thoroughly enjoying the surroundings of being on an allotment, when he out of the blue said, "Isn't it nice and peace and quiet, Daddy?" I thought, how cute, and agreed that "yes, it was nice and peace and quiet!" even my other little son Rowan had veg on his mind for he suddenly said, "Dad… Do pickles grow on a pickle tree?" I then had to explain!

Humane with Moles!

Some gardens and agricultural land are plagued with moles, and are often gassed or caught in traps by rodent officers. I couldn't do that sort of job, so I often look for humane ways of sorting out problems.

Many years ago whilst doing a garden for my aunt's pal, who had a nice house just a few hundred yards from Highwayman, Dick Turpin's cave at High Beech in the heart of Epping Forest, I came across the most curious plant, a biennial called 'The Mole Plant' or 'Caper Spurge' and a member of the Euphorbia family (Euphorbia 'Lathyrus').

Classed really as an old English weed, at this first sighting I knew nothing of the plant, except that it was supposed to keep moles out of the garden, and possibly push them into someone else's! One evening in the mid-1970s, I was waiting to watch 'Top of the Pops' and saw the tail end of 'Tomorrow's World' when suddenly they were all talking about this mole plant, so I was then all ears! The presenters were interviewing a grower, and on a huge scale grew polyanthus plants to supply to the trade, and the grower told how until fairly recently had been plagued by moles for many years that was until someone told him to plant 'Mole Plants' in his fields. He thought anything was worth a try, for it was getting time-consuming setting traps, and of course the rising costs of rodent inspectors.

I didn't catch where the grower got the seeds or plants from, but he said the plants most certainly did their job, and all the moles disappeared! It was said that the 'mole plants' didn't for some reason, work in all parts of the country, but he was so pleased that they worked in his part of the world.

'Tomorrow's World' also showed you the plant in a liquidiser, and demonstrated how the milky sap powered an engine, and said that one day all cars could run on this old English weed. I must admit that many years have passed since that programme was shown, and cars today still run on petrol, diesel and the fairly new bio-fuel.

I'll tell you now my dealings with 'mole plants' for over the years, virtually none of my own gardening books, be it on cultivated or wildflowers, tell you much about this plant. The seeds, which you can find you can literally throw anywhere and they seem to find a niche and grow away nicely, and at first sight resemble Chinese bamboo shoots, so are easily recognisable. They really are a true biennial and grow rapidly through the year, and even on maturity reach varied heights up to 3'–4' approx. The following year they flower, those being very tiny yellowy, greeny almost inconspicuous flowers, set in a sort of calyx. These flowers soon fade, to reveal the now forming seed pod or 'caper', the seed pod resembling a single garden green-pea vegetable, hence the botanical name of 'Lathyrus' which is the sweet-pea family, i.e. Lathyrus 'odoratus' etc.

Although none of my gardens where I lived in London ever had moles, I grew them anyway as they are always spotted as a curiosity when visitors come, when they all say – "What's that!"

The very first house we bought (Chingford Road, E.17), where you may remember when my father-in-law, George Ward, bought me my first greenhouse, was a house but one from a corner, and large advertising hoardings were a great favourite for kids and local yobs to throw stones and bottles at. Needless to say I was really worried about my new greenhouse. Nothing ever did land in our garden, or that of Mrs Clarke's directly next door to us, for she was even more vulnerable being the now corner house.

At times, until I found the 'culprit' I could hear my greenhouse and panel fencing being hit by small stones or grit, albeit still no sign of anything in the garden. This went on mainly around mid-summer, and it wasn't until one evening whilst sitting in the garden on a very calm night, then I noticed one or more of my mole plants moving, just as if something had given them a prod! Whilst this action was taking place, I could hear very clearly little shots of 'stones' being fired. It was of course the seeds bursting out from the mole plants at quite a force too! This too explained why when we thought kids were aiming stones at our greenhouse or windows and back door, and I'd rush out the front door, round to the hoardings and catch the kids, only to find not a single soul to be seen, hence had always remained a mystery about these 'shots'.

When we moved to Kessingland, Suffolk, two weeks before Easter 1987, after about three years, moles all of a sudden appeared in our garden, and then for the first time experienced what other folk had to put up with and it was truly heart-breaking to see all my precious plants and shrubs ruined overnight, and the lawn too!

One of my customers at that time offered me some mole plants; strangely they'd telephoned me to come in and identify these strange plants that just appeared in their garden one day, so I was delighted to be reunited with these plants once again. I kept in mind what the grower had said on 'Tomorrow's World' all those years ago, and that was that the mole plant didn't work in all parts of the country.

Anyhow, I planted up the small plantlets, and true to form they grew rapidly. At this point I must add the seriousness of the problem, and that our caravan was leaning badly due to the many mole runs. As the plants grew *all* and I mean *all* the moles went away! At the time of writing (2009), they have never ever come back. One lot of elderly weird neighbours that we had back then yelled "we've got all your moles in our garden!" Referring to when the moles suddenly arrived in my garden from literally nowhere. I shouted back "What do you mean MY moles! They're certainly not mine, perhaps they're yours!" They were most put out by my remark – isn't it funny how folk are quick to blame, and start a row?

The strange thing is that when 'my' moles went, so did theirs! I have given many mole plants away to people in the last twenty-three years, and all had an amazing result. The only thing that I cannot advise them on is how many plants are needed to do the job, for I haven't seen any advice in any gardening books.

I let my mole plants just seed as and where they grow, be it borders or crevices in a path, the more the merrier, so assume the bigger your garden, the more plants you need? Or do just a few radiate out whatever sends the moles on their way? There are still lots of questions concerning this plant – what part in the plant's growth gets the moles on the move? Is it when the roots bruise when penetrating the soil? Is it when the plant flowers? When the plant is dying? Or indeed when the actual seeds land on the soil – now there's a thought! (Moles do keep at least 60 feet from this Euphorbia.)

Beverley Nichols

Not a name possibly remembered today? But well-known in the 1960 TV ads for cat food, for Beverley Nichols loved his cats, and was known as 'the cat man. Many people, even back then, never knew that he was an amazing gardener and plantsman, and had books on the subject of gardening. My wife and I particularly like 'Merry Hall' all about a property that he'd bought, and how he created and restored the garden.

My dad, Walter Herbert Edwin Nichols, when a lad of ten, used to attend family parties and get-togethers at Beverley Nichols' house at Snaresbrook, Woodford, Essex. The house has long been pulled down, and now a shop or parade of shops I'm told takes its place. Sadly, my dad died many years ago now, but could have filled me in on a lot of the family history. Dad always told me that Beverley Nichols was a great uncle, that's all I know. When I was in my late teens, I wrote a letter to Beverley Nichols when he lived at Ham Cottage in Surrey, and his last home? I had very little to tell him, but asked if he knew of any family connection. His reply was short, to say the least, more or less saying "not that I know of."

I told him of my lifelong keenness for plants, and Dad and his grandfather strongly involved in building and architecture.

I do hope one day that I could afford to have Dad's family history followed up, for it looks a very interesting one.

Dad's grandad (my great-grandfather) designed and built the Kingfisher Swimming Pool in Woodford Green, and have a lovely photo of him on site there. Dad also used to take me to nearby Knighton Wood, and showed me an area where there were large rocks and old Rhododendrons etc. Again, I can't remember if this was one of my great grandad's projects, or the remains of a family home of one of the Victorian Nichols? for dad always said that one part of the family were indeed very wealthy people.

My Great Grandad (also called Walter Herbert) built and designed many houses in the Woodford area, including so Dad said, the very house that Dad lived in and where Dad died, at Monkhams Avenue. We also think that there is a Beverley Road or Close on the Monkhams Estate, hence still that very near family connection?

Dad's brother, Eric, also said that the Nichols family at one point, owned Woodford Green's large property called 'The White House', later owned by the Mallinson family, and where I later worked as their Head Groundsman at Wadham Lodge! The photo of my Great Grandfather at the Kingfisher Pool was taken on 12th June 1934.

The Kessingland and Broadland Times

We had only lived here in Kessingland for a year, when a local magazine was started up by authoress Maureen Long. Word soon got out that I was a landscape gardener and also a plantsman. Maureen asked if I'd like to do a gardening column for them, and I heartily agreed, and twenty-six years later I'm still doing articles for them, and more's the pity that all that lot can't go into a *really* big book, for I'm sure that in all those years I've not repeated myself once! The last couple of years, the magazine has become a bi-monthly, so unless you either collect the mags or have a good memory, it makes it difficult when doing an article that is long and needs to go in parts, and you have to keep referring back.

I only had one stipulation, and that is *all* that I write must be printed, and no editing whatsoever, for I'm not going to sit for ours writing, for half of it to be scrapped. I used to be a prolific writer on bygones etc. for magazines etc. to see it all heavily edited, to then see editors complaining that 'it's your magazine, it's thin this month, it's up to you to support us." Of course they had a mile of stuff on their desk, and other people's too, so we all gave up writing, for none of our stuff was hardly used. We found it an insult, especially as it was just the very few who actually bothered to pick up a pen.

The real beauty of writing your own column is that I tell it like it is, all my knowledge on plants, the odd happenings, tips, plus other gardeners and growers/garden centres, and places where I've visited in the horticultural world, all get a mention, and all helps to make my articles very different.

It's also brilliant when you get a bit of feed-back, when someone has tried out one or two of my tips, plus new things that I have experimented in, and actually work! My column is called '*Let Keith Lead You Down The Garden Path*'.

Flowering at the Wrong Time?

To a non-gardener, some of the things I do, baffles them, for soon after certain perennial plants have finished flowering, even in early summer, I cut them down to near ground level, give them a feed, and then sit back and watch them re-grow and flower again, after this last lot of bloom you can leave them to die back naturally, and cut back in late autumn or early winter, but don't forget to then apply a slow acting fertiliser like say bone-meal as you've now exhausted your plant twice, moreso if I've decided to let the first flowerings go to seed.

It's mostly the earlier flowering perennials that baffle people, for once cut down, they'll often be in bloom again around July, August and September, plants like Lupins, Delphiniums, Pyrethrum etc. It's not only my customers who are surprised, but also their friends and relatives.

You can expect remarks like "your Lupins are late." I always say, "no, they're not late, just too early for next year!" One of my other remarks is when someone says "what's the best time to prune roses?" I always say "ooh, around 4.30 a.m. I'd say," definitely not the answers they were expecting! Other plants to cut back are Papaver, echinops cranes bills, centranthus, etc. (try and experiment with many others).

The Dissolution of Clay Pots

Albert Danahar, one of the well known boxers of 'the fighting Danahar Brothers' from London's Bethnal Green, worked as a Park Keeper at Springfield Park, Clapton, London. As a mere teenager I worked alongside Albert many times. In the nursery section of the park, run by the austere Annie Hanks, Albert was asked to make a large storage shed. I helped Albert doing this task.

The very sad part of this job was that this was a time in the very early sixties, and the slow decline of the still much-loved clay pots. The nursery area had hundreds of them all lined up along a long wall, all in sizes from the really big ones to the minutest, and we had to smash every one of them up to use as rubble for the base of the forthcoming large shed.

I shudder to think what all these pots would be worth today, and often wonder if the big shed or at least the solid base is still there?

Making a Monster!

Being a landscape gardener, no matter how well you know your job, doesn't always mean you'll be busy all the time, and I've had some very lean times even in summer. One of these times I was browsing through our local paper and saw that the Walthamstow Building Society that stood on the crossroads of Forest Road, Fulbourne Road and Wood Street E.17 were advertising for a self-employed part-time gardener, so thought anything better than nothing, so made arrangements to be interviewed by the manager, and turned out to be the most lovely man by the name of Pat O'Brien. He explained that there were no gardens to speak of, only grassed areas that needed to be kept short, and at least half a day out of those three days were to be spent picking up litter, and included beer bottles and cans from local drunken yobs.

The meeting that day with Pat O'Brien was to lead to something quite wondrous, although he and I didn't know that then. I was left to my own devices, no one ever bothered me. As the weeks rolled on, my actual landscape work was non-existent, yes, even in a big place like London!

I gradually spent more and more time at the Society's ground, and at first only being paid my three days. I said to Pat, is it okay to create borders, flower beds, plant trees etc. and Pat was delighted, and thought it a good idea to brighten up the place. Pat said that he'd leave the lot to me, get whatever I want and he would give me the cheques for the materials. Luckily I was able to charge the building society retail prices, and get a trade discount that I could keep for myself, and help boost my money up quite a bit, for now I was on the loose with someone else's money!

My first task to get started was to plant lots of varieties of ornamental trees, the more unusual the better, like Davidia 'involucrata' "The Ghost Tree" or "Handkerchief Tree", Caragana 'arborescens' etc. then cut out a circular bed around each. It was late winter, so still had ample time to plant up bulbs and spring flowering bedding plants.

Gardening books still today tell you to plant up in September, yes a good time if you have space, but as climate changes have come about, summer flowers last for longer, and you certainly wouldn't think of taking them all up. (Hence today, plant bulbs in Jan and Feb!)

I created and planted up hundreds of bulbs and made up my own design patterns for continual spring colour i.e. for tulips, double early, double late, single early, single late, mid-spring season… and so on. I used plants like Polyanthus, Myosotis, Bellis, Viola, Primrose, Pansies, Wallflowers etc., etc. and was a magnificent show.

As a surprise Pat O'Brien (now of late) had a photographer come round and these photos were used on the front covers of the building society's customer newsletters, and a compliment along with that when Pat said that since the creation of the gardens, the counter sales had gone up, for people wanted to see the gardens. This was the very same compliment that I got when working weekends at Northfields Garden Centre (E.4) many years earlier, as you've already read.

The summer bedding schemes were equally as nice, for there was a much wider choice of plants to use, and I could create further beauty. Pat wasn't sure if it was worth planting up the raised beds alongside the building society's large windows, and they always seemed to be dry and dusty, and when it rained the 'mud' splashed up onto the windows. I soon put Pat's mind to rest, for I said I'll put in plants en-masse, and plants that needed little water, and to stop the water marks simply put in three inches of gravel around all the plants and covering the whole beds, this would stop the soil splashing on the windows until the plants grew to mask the raised beds.

I remember Pat thinking me so clever with such a simple idea, and indeed it did work fine. Lots of people spoke to me about plants whilst I worked there, and it was a very busy corner. Pat was thrilled with the gardens, and so were all the staff, and got to know lots of them.

One spring, loads of just one variety of tulips were stolen, they were 'Red Riding Hood, and stolen to order I should think for the approaching Mother's Day. Ironic when you think that when I bought all the boxes of bulbs, left them in my van, whilst I carried out a small job of work for a Judge! I'd known Alan for some years, and his wife Hilda was my daughter Heather's teacher. I'd worked for them many times creating their new garden on the Monkhams Estate, Woodford Green.

Let's backtrack a little, for as usual I've digressed!

Me and a pal, who was now assisting me at the building society and the now flourishing landscaping, drove past Woodford Green Police Station on my way to Alan and Hilda's prior to taking all the boxes of bulbs back to store at the building society. A police car was coming out of the driveway of the Police Station, and my pal said "That copper's really staring at you, Keith!" I said that I saw him do so, and I expected to be pulled over. He did actually follow me all the way to Judge

Hitching's (Allan) house! It was there that he got out of his car, and I just couldn't wait to tell him that he was outside a judge's house and that I should knock so he could confirm who I was! He then asked, "What's in the back of the van?" So I showed him all the boxes of bulbs (my van was fully sign-written) and told him where they were for, I also made the point of showing him a brand new sign that I'd had made by my friend John Jackson, a brilliant plantsman. The sign read – *These gardens are maintained by Keith Nichols, Landscape Gardener and Plantsman* – along with my telephone number. Pat said that I could keep the sign out on each day that I worked there, which did bring in a lot of work.

It was now my turn to ask the policeman some questions. I asked where was he when all the tulip plants were stolen the year before, how come he never saw the thieves or caught them, where was he when some of the trees that I planted were vandalised, where was he another time when other plants were stolen – all of these thieves and vandals all got away with it, yet it's me who gets pulled up and questioned just going about my daily work. I would have been a very soft target for him, and hasten to add have been many times before and since then.

I'll tell you now of a couple of incidents at the building society. It was early autumn and time to lift all the bedding plants and commence the spring display. Me and my pal started digging out all the summer plants at one end of the building, and soon time for a cuppa, so we sat on a low wall where we had been working. Our eyes were soon out on stalks! for a woman came over to the raised flower beds and frantically pulled out lots of plants and put them in a bag! She even turned round to see if anyone had seen her, and oblivious to us drinking our tea, we just could not believe it, she then calmly walked away, crossed the road and into a café that faced the gardens.

Had this woman waited, she could have had as many plants as she wanted, for we'd stack everything in one prominent place and tell the public to take what they liked, for they would only go into a huge bin. I said to my mate, that it did explain missing plants at times, but this was broad daylight, where again was that copper I wonder?

Another lady blatantly told me that "you know all those daffs that you have planted along the rose hedge, well, each year I come along and take the odd bunch" – once again, I thought, where was that copper?

On site there is a huge 'London Plane' tree, and Pat asked if we could turf under it to smarten it up. I ordered screened top soil to get a nice level, when all of a sudden a woman came up to me with her small Jack Russell dog, "Where's my dog going to do his 'jobs' now, I always bring him here!" I said that no wonder this area was a mess, and told her it was going to be turfed. She still acted defiantly, making out to haul this dog off our levelled soil, she was making out this was an effort to hold the dog back and acted as if it was an Alsatian!

It certainly goes to show that on many occasions, it may not be kids or yobs stealing or doing damage, when adults can do this and actually get away with it, *knowing* that kids will be blamed for everything.

The Haringey Council used to have numerous old-fashioned horse troughs scattered around the borough, the troughs all still in their original positions from the years of horse transport. We used to plant these up twice yearly with bedding plants etc. We were near Spouters Corner, Wood Green one year, and planted up lots of Muscari bulbs, and bedding plants, and went along the next day to carry on the watering to help them establish, but *all* the plants and bulbs had gone! Me and our 'gang' were going on about vandals etc. when a chap stood at his front gate (adjacent to the trough) and said "I took all the plants, for if I didn't take 'em the yobs will, and they'll just rip 'em up and throw them like they do each year."

Again, we were all totally dumfounded, and after what he'd said, we did actually wonder if he was actually doing the lesser of the two evils?

Human Waste and Council Waste

Many years ago whilst working for the Haringey Council, I had several projects under my belt, for the foreman, an ex-SAS man Ron Nunn, saw that I was keen and knew my trade, and picked the right chap for these projects. Just off White Hart Lane, the Tottenham end, was a brand new housing estate, and it was to be officially opened by the local mayor. It was my job to spruce the area up with bedding plants, these of course, making an instant splash of colour against the 'on-off' blooms of shrubs that seemed to be just greenery with the odd bouts of flowers on them. We planted up hundreds of geraniums (Zonal Pelargoniums), Standard Fuchsias, Standard Geraniums, Abutilons etc. these were there as 'dot' plants and underplanted with Ageratum, Salvia, Tagetes etc. Whilst these were maturing up we did a lot of tree planting, by now it was far too late for bare rooted stock, so we used mature large potted trees, and a bit of a job to prise from their pots!

After about a month, we noticed that the stakes that we were given to support the trees… started sprouting into leaf! and we were asked to leave them there because of the time factor for the grand opening. It looked so odd with ornamental trees of all sorts being tied to a growing stake! These were, if my memory serves me correctly,

Lombardy poplar, hence in time would tower above all the proper trees.

Just as all the bedding plants were coming along nicely in one part of the estate, some of the tenants beckoned us over as there was a vast weed problem in the beds that we first planted out, so we went along to see the problem for ourselves. We were totally shocked to see *thousands* of fifteen-inch high tomato plants! All the residents thought they looked like tomato plants but remained unconvinced as each tenant said that they hadn't planted any.

I soon found the problem, once we started pulling them out from the now almost covered bedding plants, it was a very blocked manhole which was full of raw sewage! Apparently tomato seeds do not digest in the human body, hence the seeds finding light and soil again, all germinated!

We were not asked to attend the opening of the new estate, and did not see it again until the end of the summer, when we were asked to clear all the beds for now the ceremony had been long over and the beds now in future to be filled up further with shrubs, the residents were very sad hearing this apparently, as all summer the estate had been a riot of colour.

We painstakingly lifted all the plants, discarded the actual annuals, but I put all the saveable plants in named groups, therefore keeping each group separate, and then take them back to the parks nurseries.

The head nurseryman, a nice chap, called George, was panic-stricken when I took all the plants back to him. "No, take them to the dump, Keith, for if you gave all these back to me, they wouldn't allocate me my full budget for nest year!" but he thanked me for my kind effort to mark up and separate the numerous varieties of geraniums fuchsias etc. including all the standards too, which also included Plumbago 'capensis', Lantanas etc.

I took the whole lot back to the estate, and not to the dump as George suggested. I picked a good area too pile the thousands of plants, my workmates said, "Why have we put them here, Keith?" I said that it's criminal to dump such beautiful plants, let's knock on each and every door on the estate and offer the plants to the residents. They thought this a brilliant idea, well at least all the plants had another chance of life. The residents took the lot!

A Laburnum Tree and Me

During my first stint at Springfield Park, Clapton, I was asked to dig out a Laburnum tree, a fairly mature one, that the birds had obviously dropped a seed of a few years prior. The reason I was asked to dig it out was that it was growing right in the centre of a large Rhododendron bed, this bed was enclosed by a thick well-made four foot high picket fence. The Laburnum did look out of place in such a bed, but that wasn't the problem; back in the sixties there was a national scare on around the country, because adults and children had eaten the poisonous seeds, and died so we were told, and Laburnums were felled in their thousands and being a park where children played, the only Laburnum at Springfield Park had to go too.

As long as I can remember, I've hated digging out to destroy perfectly good plants, trees, etc. and as a sixteen year old, point blank refused to dig that tree out. The foreman asked me why not, and I said that kids should not be playing in an enclosed rhododendron bed anyway, and that we'd never seen kids in that bed at any time, so made no sense to dig a perfectly good tree out.

Needless to say, I was sacked straight away. Sadly, I cannot now remember how the problem was resolved, for by the end of the week I was told I could stay! and strangely the tree stayed put too for several years, and for all I know may still be there!

My First Official Job

I say official, for it was my very first job on leaving school, on the cards so to speak, and paying tax and insurance. I also say official, for I'd always worked hard in my young life, and you'll have to read my first two books to see all that I have done.

The job was working as a trainee gardener at Springfield Park, Clapton, an area sandwiched between Stamford Hill and Hackney.

My story at Springfield really starts with my Grandad (Mum's dad), Harry Bishop Ridley, and his brother, my Uncle George Ridley. George was the Head Keeper at a place called Millfields, consisting of football pitches, tennis courts etc., and often went to see Uncle George there. He eventually moved on to a higher position, and became Head Keeper at the vast acreage of Hackney Marshes, and still boasts very many football pitches etc. George kept his position here until he retired.

Between my Grandad and Uncle George, an interview was arranged for me to see a Mr Gardner (or could it have been Gardener!). My Uncle George must have praised me up to Mr Gardner for me to get that interview at County Hall, London, and it was my Grandad who took me there. I was 15 and the year was 1964, so I was now to be in the world of the working man at last.

I passed the interview with flying colours, and I was to work at Springfield Park under three authorities; the first was the L.C.C. –

London County Council, the second was the G.L.C. – Greater London Council, and my last time I worked there was under the H.B.C. – or Hackney Borough Council.

Back then my hair was long, as indeed it still is aged 60 (at the time of writing), but back then a mere Beatles haircut! but very much frowned on, and even since those times have experienced many bad incidents through my hair being a few inches longer than most other people's, and got to know how the black and foreign people felt with such prejudice. I've been barred from cafes, trains, theatres, etc. people have got up and walked away from me if I sat next to them on a bus or in a café, in fact it even happens today on odd occasions. In the '50s you saw the colour bar with wordings like NO BLACKS, etc. The '60s had signs up NO LONG HAIR or even down to clothing – no jeans or leather jackets, etc. Even today you see such signs like 'ties must be worn' etc. To see these same so-called smart men pulverising someone outside a club or pub etc. where perhaps the black man, foreigner or the guys with the long hair would be totally non-violent?

Every job interview that I went for, I always put in writing at the end – 'I think it best to mention that I do have long hair, I do hope this is not a problem' – many a letter for an interview was not answered. Other employers wanted to take me on, but worried greatly what their clients would think. As an example, I must have applied to every removal company for a job. I was young, strong honest and reliable and a hard worker, and wanted to be a removal man, travelling the length and breadth of the country. I never got one single interview.

Today it amuses me seeing long hair on men of almost all job descriptions, vicars, archaeologists, scientists, doctors, and is a very huge list. I've stuck with my long hair through thick and thin, and that just about describes my hair too over the years!

When being interviewed by Mr Gardner, again asked if it is okay to have my hair long, he laughed and said "You can have your hair down to your arse for all I care, as long as you work hard we have no problem." Mr Gardner's words were to ring back a couple of years down the line, and will tell you about that later on.

Our foreman at Springfield Park was Mr Chris Galleyhawk, and a very knowledgeable plantsman, and lived above our bothy (tea room), and Ron Crabtree lived next door to him, his house was above the large tool shed (former stable?) and the main office, and Ron was based at another park. The under-foreman, and usually the one to come into the bothy and read out our daily tasks, his name was Ernie Howes, and at that time not long for retirement, and Bill Brotherton took over from him. Ernie Howes proved to be a hard task master, and like many of those in charge back then, as they say – from the old school. Although we all disliked a lot of the work back then, it has stood me in great stead ever since, you learnt the old ways, and still do much of it today, for to me it's the true and only way.

Ours was a 7a.m. start and I'd already been up at five, moreso when travelling from Chingford Hatch E.4, therefore from seven o'clock until tea-break at ten, we all had our allocated paths to sweep. We did this every day for several years, the paths all year were spotless. Many's the day too when if your paths were particularly messy through the fallen blossom, catkins or leaves and you hadn't finished your round, you had to complete it after tea-break and when done report back to the foreman for your new duties.

If someone was ill or away on holiday, you had to do their route too, and then it usually meant that you'd be sweeping nearly all day.

Parks in those days came in Classes; for instance, Victoria Park, Finsbury Park were 1st class parks, Clissold Park perhaps 2nd class, and Springfield was a 3rd class park. This was not for appearance sake, but for size. Springfield Park was a very picturesque park, very hilly to walk, and steep banks where an abundance of daffs grew each spring, other flatter areas and small grass areas were planted up with crocus, Dot King was a lady gardener, and did what I called proper gardening, and was meticulous when splitting up perennial plants, re-planting, staking etc. This border was adjacent to our Superintendent's house, a nice Scottish man, Mr Lindsay.

Dot worked mainly with Annie Hanks in the parks nursery. I had drugs planted on me as a mere eighteen year old, and Dot came to the rescue and loaned me the money for the fine, or it meant prison. The fine was £30, a hell of a lot of money back then. Detective Sergeant Gordon Ball and all his cronies all got away with what they did to me and two other pals. I'm sure they will pay for it, and assuming there is heaven and hell, the latter they will go for certain.

Dot always had aspirations to live in America, but I never saw Dot again after I left Springfield Park all those years ago. I've wanted to repay Dot so many times since that time, to also thank her for believing me, a hard thing to prove or disprove in the drug-crazed age of the '60s. I know I will swear my innocence to the day I die.

On the Lake in Winter (Springfield Park)

One job that was *always* allocated to me was the job of rowing a boat round and round the lake, all day long, and every day whilst the lake remained frozen. The idea was that by me keeping rowing, it stopped the lake freezing over and helped the fish to breathe. My upper body was always warm, but when the breaks came I literally had to be helped out of the boat, for I couldn't move my bottom half. This was the *only* time too when I was allowed an afternoon tea-break, in those days it was ten o'clock until twenty past, and it was *really* strict too, plus one house for dinner. On hot summer afternoons, the parks café would open, we'd look out for a foreman and dash in for an ice lolly and cold drink!

On the Lake in Summer (Springfield Park)

Me and my pals always thought that sweeping was a bit prissy, so I invented the word 'Grip Work', this meant we asked the foremen for men's work, something we could get our teeth into, and hopefully enjoy. I've never been a macho man, but in my younger years really did enjoy hard, heavy work, and at times when on a project that needed hard workers we sometimes got out of the sweeping.

There were many times that I dearly wished I'd kept quiet about wanting to do hard physical work when many were shying away from it, but often the work was interesting.

One day one of the foremen said, "Right, I've got a task for you, I want you and two others to dig up all of the very old shrubs around the lake, and a good few on the island." He then said that he'd allocate a full week. We literally so totally shocked him and ourselves when we did the lot in three days! They were massive shrubs, deep old roots that even a tractor had to pull to the edge for four of us to load onto the tractor trailer, driven then by Johnny Johnson.

The foreman couldn't believe his eyes, but then we worried, for we may have shot ourselves in the foot, and back on the ol' broom again! but no, we were set to the task of planting hundreds of new shrubs. If it had been nowadays, I would have insisted on those old shrubs being restored. I watched a gardening programme around 2006, and they said the shrubs were old and past it – in my opinion they should have shown viewers how to restore a very old neglected shrub bed and show the results one year on; they could still have planted a new shrub bed elsewhere if they wanted to. When you think what you'd have to pay for a large mature shrub, it makes you weep.

The TV show could also have shown off the skills of the gardener, this in turn would've made the public think twice before discarding something because it's too old.

Rock On! (Springfield Park)

"Grip, Grip, Grip"! Grip work it certainly was, getting to grips with a very heavy sledge hammer and crow bar to break up the very thick man-made pond that had probably been made in the year dot!

Me and pal Michael Neal were put on this enormous task, and possibly the only time in my life when the Health and Safety executives would have had a field day had they been around then. The American people had bought the old London Bridge as a tourist attraction in the USA, but not all of it went across the water, and I'll tell you about that in a minute. Mick and I alone, smashed up this easily two-foot thick concrete pond, from seven in the morning to almost six minutes to five in the evening, the sledges and crow bars were swung by us relentlessly. It wasn't long when huge blisters came, broke open, then wearing down further tender skin, we were given old rag to wrap round our hands, but the blood still started to show through, and at no point were we relieved of this duty.

I remember fellow workmates and all the park keepers being so disgusted with the foreman who set this arduous task for us, but it all fell on deaf ears, and we were kept on this project until the very end. As I said, we were truly under the old task masters.

If I remember correctly, the broken-up rubble was all left where it was, and several tons of soil was used to back-fill between the rubble, and eventually fill, or overfill the now broken-up pond. All this soil had to be well trodden in too.

The last remnants of the old London Bridge were kept at Victoria Park, huge rocks easily 4x4 or 5x5 in size, and we manually had to 'roll' them up scaffold boards onto the trailer, I think we only took two at a time. Once back at Springfield they were put just inside the entrance to our yard – we all thought this daft, for they could easily have been dropped onto the pond site, but instead we had to manually move them again, then once more to put them in position to now make a new rockery area which we planted up with all varieties and colours of Heathers or Ericas. We also planted Lings, Callunas, Daboecias, and also the very first time I saw 'Tree Heathers' which eventually grew to some eighteen feet or more. The majority of these of course are lime haters, so we put down bales and bales of peat to make the soil more acidy, albeit all the plants were planted in solely peat (peat being a dirty word now!).

On the subject of peat, peat was cheap and had they made alternatives as cheaply, many of the peat bogs would have remained untouched. Good graded bark is expensive, so is cocoa shells etc. and not nearly as much in a bag. Even today I look for the more bulkier or 'swollen' bags of peat or compost, for I assume the loading machine went wrong and jammed in a lot more!

All this hard graft with these huge boulders seemed to me to be a total waste of time in the end, for once in the yard, the foreman marked out a chalk line all around each rock, supposedly to show the best side, and also to show the depth that the rock was to be 'sunk' to. I found this odd, for now looking back, for where we all thought the foreman clever for knowing what was the best side, the rocks never actually moved from the positions once we unloaded it in the yard, so you couldn't see the other sides, for indeed they could have been the best sides?

We had a real hard job digging out the areas for the rocks once on site, for we kept hitting just some of our own large boulders that we'd broken up and buried, thankfully these were very few, for the depth of the soil covered all the others.

In my opinion, and I do it today when making a rockery, is to just lay the rock in position, for when making a new rockery with the best will in the world, as much as you think you've trod or rolled a site, it will sink further to find its own level, and so it had on my last time at Springfield. In fact because at the time we'd put in several tons of soil, a lot of it of course hadn't filtered through all the rubble even though we tried at the time and was an impossible task. Over the years of course, the soil and the rocks found their final level, and those huge boulders from London Bridge could hardly be seen, for they too with all that weight on freshly applied soil, sank to level.

I have often wondered if the rocks are still in existence, or if it was dug up at some point, what a shock for the person who had the task, seeing only two foot or so showing out of the soil, then lifting some five foot or so! The person, *if* the site has been cleared no doubt using a digger, not even knowing literally of blood, sweat and tears behind the original project. Perhaps I will go back one day to see what has changed.

Sickles, Scythes, Sweat and... Billhooks!
(Springfield Park)

All now easily done with modern-day strimmers, but back in the sixties, we were still using very old tools to cut the grass banks in the main park and further down the hill in the kids' area. We'd use scythes all day, and very often had hard graft doing all sorts when we volunteered to do overtime, and peak summer meant working until ten at night – we had to, the wages were so poor. If you worked a weekend, all

Saturday's money would go in tax, a few extra shillings could be earned if you were cleaning out drains etc. you'd then get 'dirty money'.

A lovely lady, named Lil, looked after the kids' area, and always made us teas when working there. I think she was always grateful when if a pervert was hanging about and the keepers not yet on duty, the call would come for us to race down the hill to sort out any problems. Perverts were rife at Springfield, and you always knew when something was amiss, for mostly the younger keepers would band together and would be seen hurrying along frantic.

I remember one particular incident when a grown man was making love to a girl in one of the park shelters, done *with* the girl's consent, they were caught – the girl was just ten years old! I remember one of the park keepers bringing the girl's white-tyred pump-up scooter back to the office. I still remember her unfortunate name!

The Park Keepers (Springfield Park)

We used to be quite envious of the park keepers, for they didn't start work until ten or eleven o'clock in the morning, but of course didn't end work until the same times at night, by the time they checked to see that no one was in the park before locking up the numerous gates. You don't see park keepers at all these days, and wonder how many are at Springfield today?

Back in the sixties there was a good few at Springfield, and in those days even took on men well past retiring age like Doug Duggan, and Taffy – we never knew his first name, he had a beautiful singing voice, and he told me how he fought at the battle of the Somme. Doug always looked regimental, immaculately turned out, he'd often leave Springfield, but liked the job a lot and come back; we were always pleased to see him, he was well into his seventies. I seem to now recall that Taffy's name was Tom, for although Tom was Welsh, we also had an Irishman called Tom, from the day he started he'd say, "Hello, my name's Tom, I'm the new boy!" and that's how he introduced himself to people… for years!

John Cumisky, another Irish chap, like Tom, was a real laugh, and a favourite with the ladies, some of his sayings are unprintable! Then there was Brian, alias 'The crow! –he took over from Johnny Johnson, on the tractor. (After Johnny retired, several people took on the job as tractor driver, Adam Sennok and Michael Neal, Mick took on the job solely.)

Albert Danahar was the one and only park keeper who was the most feared, although yobs didn't know that until they were confronted with Albert, for Albert was one of the famous Fighting

Danahar Brothers of Bethnal Green. (Read more of Albert in my first two books.)

Going back to 'The Crow', he got this name because he made crow noises whilst driving the tractor! He was a funny chap, we got on well. I met Brian many years later when I was working in Haringey, and have never seen such devastation on a man's face, when he told me of his sorry tale, and that was when he'd got very drunk one night and walked out into the road, got hit by a car, and lost a leg as the result.

Then there was Pete, a jovial chap; big Terry, who sold me a 'bubble car'! Ted Ellis who sold me a 1930's 'New Hudson' early motorbike-cum-moped, the accelerator was the same as that for a motor mower, and rode much better at night! and of course Ron Platt who took over the reins at Wadham Lodge Sports Ground, before I too took over as Head Groundsman there.

Park keepers were everywhere, and knew where to find each other if needed. Occasionally you'd see a group of them chatting away, then they'd disperse, each with a metal spike to pick up litter, and you'd hear the odd "Oi you, keep off the grass!" for grass areas still had these metal signs then.

The Dennis Drivers (Springfield Park)

A Dennis machine was a large motor mower, and had a coupling pin to put on a seat with added roller below you, so you felt all the bumps! The mower had a huge grass box, that alone was heavy to lift off, although there was a method where you could tip it and pile it on the path and the tractor driver would take it away. When I first started at the park, a lovely chap named Bert Dearing was the park's Dennis Driver – he was small in stature, well spoken, and a lovely man, and often ridiculed by some behind his back regarding his downfall from having his own orchestra to now driving a motor mower. How Bert ever got the machine going because of his stature, for the machine only started with a starting handle. There were two 'holes' and each had a separate pressure for starting, I suspect one was a cold start? Poor Bert one day lost control of the machine and it landed in the lake, when it came to my turn to take over a few years later, I dreaded having to go so close to the lake edge, especially late spring trying to dodge all the now faded bulbs. My mates often shouted "Don't do a Bert!"

Michael Neal took over from Bert until Mick took over as the main tractor Driver. Mick was able to show me all the do's and don'ts. One 'don't' was to keep your thumb well clear, for the handle under pressure could spring back and it was the thumb that could be so easily broken. Bert broke his arm with the kick-back of the handle. The

103

Dennis had its own little shed up in the far right-hand corner of the yard, so became my own little domain to clean the mower and check oil levels etc. at the end of each day.

Being a Dennis driver was hard graft, it was a heavy machine to manoeuvre, and not very often much chance to use the seat. My main job was to cut the grass at least six foot from the edges of all the paths, so that the tractor with its 'gang mowers' or 'triples' didn't run over the path's edges or hit bins etc. and gave the tractor driver a clear run. My other task was the park's theatre area, and the outfield of the cricket squares. I also did all the small areas that the tractor could not get to, like the seating area for the park's café.

One fairly big area that I did was the large putting green that faced the lake. I was lucky to be the Dennis driver twice at my times at Springfield, and the last time there were two workers who just wouldn't really speak to me – one, a chap called Alan, a fellow long-haired man, and his mate an older man aptly called Dennis! They just used to stop and stare at me working, and they'd do this for ages, and had no fear that the foreman would perhaps just walk round the corner. In my early days at the park we always talked and worked at the same time; the foremen back then weren't too keen on that – it was work, work, work!

The putting green had always been cut in straight lines, i.e. light and dark green stripes. I did exactly the same, but cut it *my* way and made a 'sunflower' effect, making sweeping arcs across the green. I remember the foreman coming over and he actually liked it. I said that was how I did it last time I was at Springfield, and they liked it then too! Yes, I still did it the old way so as to keep the grasses in different directions and so as the public could see the straight lines or the 'rainbow arcs' from whatever direction that they approached the green. wages were always bad, so although I loved it at Springfield, decided to leave and never go back, and I never did. One of the keepers, Ted (Ellis), told me about a job going at the Leyton Orient football ground, they wanted a Head Groundsman, this was around 1970/1971 I should think. I'll tell you about that later.

Feathers and No Birds! (Springfield Park)

We enjoyed most of the seasons at the park, and to quote an old saying, we were like one big family – all getting to know each other, and like with all people, some are much nicer than others. You didn't know with whom you'd work with each day, or what your duties would be.

It goes without saying the harder you worked, the more chance you got to work with the older chaps. This is why I liked being the Dennis driver, for I was my own man and knew what I had to do each day. I got to know the areas that had to have priority, before even thinking what area of grass to cut next.

Once the grass-cutting season had ended, I was back with the men again, and an array of different tasks to do. Our duties were not always in the park itself, but often had work outside the park too. As you come out of one of the gates on the top path, it led you to Clapton Common Pond (not to be confused with Clapton Pond which was the Lea-Bridge Road end, or Hackney end).

The large pond was always full of ducks, and had an outside café where all the bus drivers and conductors met to have eats and teas, and must have been their eating place for very many years, because a long shed still had the long poles with hooks on the end to disconnect the power from the trolley buses or possibly trams. This longish shed adjoined the keeper's hut, which in turn adjoined the café itself. The main keeper was Ron Platt, he had a really cushy number here, just picking up litter around the café and pond area. The café did a strange but beautifully tasting minced meat in a roll, a lovely taste, and certainly no one else for miles around did such a delight.

We were sent to the common to do a job called 'tree feathering' or remove 'feathers from the trees'. We were all intrigued to know what this job was all about. The 'feathers' in fact was the thick twiggy growths that come from the bases of mainly lime trees, and if left, all grow into thick branches themselves. Back then we were only armed with secateurs and a saw; it was an arduous, difficult, boring job which we worked hard at and soon cut enough 'feathers' to fill the tractor trailer.

I also did a lot of grass-cutting on the common itself, and even across the road facing the pond, we used Hayter machines which were good for rough cut. On the subject of mowers and the 'Flymo' came on the market, we were allocated one mower at Springfield, for the Superintendent Mr Bailey (Mr Lyndsay had retired) he said that this could be a chance for us never to use a sickle again, for the 'Flymo' could easily be used on the steep grass banks, or even possibly hauled in an up-and-down motion by the aid of ropes. The 'Flymo' turned out to be a duff one, for it started without any trouble, but sort of rumbled, and the only time it worked properly was when it was on its side, the position of course if you were changing or sharpening the blade! No one could believe it, for its only use would have been if someone had a lawn up the wall of their house!

Haul Away Boys! (Springfield Park)

I befriended a Jewish lad of my age at Springfield, his name was Paul Schaer, I'm not certain of the spelling of his surname, but it is pronounced as 'share' or as the pop singer 'Cher'. Paul had always wanted to see the singer Cat Stevens and asked me if I'd like to go to a theatre somewhere in London to see him too. The show was called 'FAME IN '67', the main act being Georgie Fame and the Blue Flames, so off we went. Georgie Fame, I remember, had to keep saying sorry, for he had a sore throat!

Poor Paul, he was accident prone, and to me was just a series of bad luck. We were allocated for a short while, a dumper truck, now if you've never handled one of these before, you too would be accident prone. I drove one at Springfield and Finsbury Park, and they have a mind of their own! To anyone who doesn't know, the power is in the back wheels. One day we were all sent to Clapton Common Pond, and the time had come to actually clear the pond of all the sludge which had built up over some years, and perhaps had started to smell a bit, and the odours drifting to the very nearby café that I spoke of earlier. Paul was to be the dumper truck man, we had already drained the pond of water using large hoses and power pumps. Paul drove to the centre of the pond and got firmly stuck! The poor chap was a laughing stock, and was annoyed with himself for driving to the centre instead of clearing the sludge from the outer edges first, then gradually work your way to the centre.

The public were gathering, and all the London Transport staff thought it hilarious seeing Paul on a dumper truck in the middle of Clapton Common Pond, and feeling so helpless.

One of us had to make our way back to Springfield to find one of the foremen, and to Paul the wait must have seemed like days! He must have felt really silly, just sitting there with now hundreds of people looking on. The foreman came to assess the situation, and decided for us all to go back with him to fetch extra scaffold boards, for although the dumper truck had been lowered into the pond on heavy boards, we needed to make it very strong to get a tractor down too.

Eventually, the tractor drove carefully into the pond without any mishaps, and ropes tided to the tractor and dumper truck and hauled away until Paul was at the pond's edge, to the delight of a very red-faced Paul and a cheering crowd!

This mucky job took us several weeks to do, again hard graft loading who knows what into the dumper.

After this project, Paul, Mick and myself were all given the job of using this dumper for various jobs of work around the park, even taking over boxes of bedding plants over to Dot or 'Little Dot' as she was so affectionately known! The Parks foreman made sure that the dumper was put to good use for the short time that it was on loan. Paul was to come unstuck again on the dumper, for he came sailing down the steep hill, lost control past the Superintendent's house and straight onto the Erica border, smashing into the ornamental low metal fence and twisting it all up, that fence had been there years too!

Here We Go Round The Mulberry Bush!
(Springfield Park)

I never knew much of the history on Springfield Park, but the huge white house was the home once of I think, silk weavers? All along the top path was (are?) old Mulberry trees Morus 'nigra', when the mulberries fell off, that path was a terrible mess, they also landed on the greenhouses the other side, and on the roof of the gents' loos (see-through plastic). The White House as it was known to us, housed a park keeper and his family; he worked at another park. The house also was the park's café which was extremely busy when it opened in the spring and summer. The basement too was huge, dark, dank and very cold, and on really snowy days and heavy rain each of us was allocated a room down there to chop wood all day long! I say wood, they were logs of all different shapes and sizes, they were already cut to what they call 'cheeses', for they did resemble a round slab of cheese. It was our job to cut these cheeses into logs and a suitable size for a fireplace, the logs of course were all free fuel for the already rent-free houses for the keepers, foreman and superintendent
.0. Wielding an axe all day was no fun!

Albert Danahar, who I spoke of earlier, apart from being a keeper, was the park's main handyman, along with Bill Brotherton. Albert's workshop was in that cellar, and had every tool imaginable, and quite rightly didn't like any of us in there for too long. Albert and I got on really well together, when Albert left for home of an evening, we'd walk, or bus, to Clapton Station which was on the Liverpool Street line. He'd get off at Highams Park Station with me; Albert lived at Highams Park, but I still had the long trek from there to my home at Chingford Hatch, where Mum always waited for me to do my tea. Often after a hard day's graft, the foreman would spring on us "Anyone want any overtime?" as wages were so meagre, so it was always a "Yes" from most of us. Albert wanted a labourer, so chose me, hoping now to be on lighter duties, but no, it was lifting and setting very thick paving slabs and did this until ten at night! There were times when just a broom in the hand was a welcome chore.

As you turned left outside the office door, Albert built a low wall for a flower bed – I often wonder if that's still there? I'm still in contact with the Danahar family today.

Dorothy King (left) affectionately called 'Little Dot', and Teresa Peck, planting up the newly-built small rockery at Springfield Park, Clapton, London E5 (1960s). The 'White House' which stands a few yards from the entrance, is the only remaining property in the park. (Dorothy lived in Walthamstow.)

Michael Neal driving the big 'Dennis' Mower, Derek Bobbin in the grass box! I took this photo one sunny day in the spring or summer in the 1960s. Derek later left Springfield Park to go to Kenwood, Hampstead, London NW3.

George Patterson, working on the top path outside the park's offices. Springfield Park, Clapton E5.

The park was a private estate until 1905 when at the time it opened to the public on the 5th of August.

My uncle George Ridley. Someone took this nice photo of him on his way to, or from work. Uncle George is wearing his Head Keeper's uniform. He was Head Keeper for Hackney Marsh. Uncle George is my Grandad's brother.

Note Lesneys' factory in the background, at Hackney Wick.

Photo by kind permission of my second cousin Ann and husband Michael Green. (Ann Green née Ridley.)

Uncle George Ridley and Auntie Flo, née Nichols. Photo taken at Windsor Castle, sometime between 1967–1969 (Ann's parents).

Photo: with kind permission of Michael and Ann Green née Ridley.

My first client on the industrial side of things was Charlie Boarder, who ran Kessingland Cottages (chalet site) just across from our bungalow.

My very first client on the private side back in 1987, was Peggy Cavill (not certain of the spelling of Cavill). Husband Peter, and Peggy's brother Frank.

Photo shows Peggy and son George at the front door of her home at Lloyds Avenue, Kessingland. Peggy was 91 in November 2014 – photo taken in 2011. (Photo by kind permission of Peggy Cavill.)

I managed to get all the chaps together, well, nearly all of them! For this nice shot. I took the photo just outside our bothy. Chris Galleyhawk's front door and large doors of the main tool shed (old stable block).

Left to right: Sid Butfoy, Tom 'Taffy' (who fought at the battle of the Somme), Terry Brown, Fred 'Johnny' Johnson, (tractor driver) , Chris Galleyhawk (foreman – he knew his plants too!), Paul Shaer, George Patterson, Michael Neal, Bill Brotherton (under-foremen).

The chaps kneeling: Derek Bobbin, Harry ____? Brian Jackson, John ___? (1960s)

A very sad photo for me, two of my chickens a day before slaughter, early 1960s in our back garden 37, Bernwell Rd, Chingford Hatch E4 (all now built on). The other side of the picket fence is the huge allotment site. Top far left of photo was my first compost heap, and chicken run. Behind the 'run' was the solid close-board fence which was the wide pathway leading to the big gates for the allotments. 16th May 1964.

Tom Tansley and Susan Mills, the ground behind them was where the Wallflowers were all grown for the park. The building in the back (top windows) was the home of Park Keeper Ron Crabtree and his family. The below window was the office for the superintendents. The window at the bottom of the photo is the 'girls bothy'; our bothy then was next door (not in view). Chris Gallyhawk lived upstairs to our bothy. Springfield Park, Clapton E5.

Two more of my pals who were Park Keepers, Left – Doug Duggan (73) Dougie and Ted Ellis, posing outside the Park's cafe. (1960s) Ted sold me an early motorbike '1955' called a New Hudson. Ted felt sorry for me having to catch trains, buses and lots of walking to get to the park by 7am from Chingford Hatch E4, on a very meagre wage of four pounds, five shillings and tuppence! (Ted lived in Walthamstow.)

The likely lads! Our tree pruners, who visited our park as and when needed.

Left – Colin, Jack, Les/Len? and Jim. Springfield Park (1960s).

Just behind Colin's head is the entrance to the park's greenhouses; our bothy is behind the second hedge. Chris Gallyhawk's front door and upstairs flat, also the double doors of the tool shed.

Me clearing out my transit van after another gruelling landscape project, outside our then house at 43 Guildford Rd, E17, (Upper Walthamstow) circa 1980.

Me aged 17 at Finsbury Park, London.

The GLC (Greater London Council) built a training centre, where I helped create the plots and make a *huge* loam heap! Also did plant I.D where our foreman at Springfield Park came along to test us, albeit we had to use a cabin to start with for classes until the centre was complete. The main gates of Finsbury Park were further along to the left of the photo. (Springtime, 1960s)

Me and my cousin Robin Nichols when I was Head Groundsman for the Wadham Lodge Sports Ground, Brookscroft Rd, E17. (Owned by Sir Terrance and Lady Mallinson.)

Sir Terrance (J.P.) always complimented me on my work. I was told that nobody in the history of the ground had ever cut the hockey pitches, running tracks etc., in the striped fashion (light-green dark-green) before.

I used a 'Dennis' mower. Sometimes I used the seat which had the roller underneath but mostly *I walked it*!

Queenie and Arthur Golding's house was right up in the far right-hand side corner as shown.

Alf Andrews, now late of Garner Rd E17, showing off his prize Chrysanths and cups. Alf had hundreds of varieties! Alf was the Secretary for either Leyton or Leytonstone FC.

Photo shows all the reinforced ironwork for the Kingfisher Swimming Pool, Woodford Green, Essex.

This photo belonged to my great-grandfather Walter Herbert Nichols, who married Minnie Robinson (both born 1876 and later married in 1899).

We were always led to believe that Walter that designed and built the pool.

119

Me and Vincent Crane of the Rock band 'Atomic Rooster' 1975. At his home in Wanstead. Vince co-wrote the 1968 No.1 'FIRE!' with Arthur Brown (The Crazy World Of Arthur Brown). When Vince split with Arthur, he formed Atomic Rooster with Carl Palmer (of Emerson, Lake and Palmer) and had a No.1 hit with 'Tomorrow Night' and 'Devils Answer' plus numerous albums.

(To find out more you can search said bands on Google/YouTube.)

Little ol' me, on the steps of the alley that led straight ahead to the coal cellar and turned right to the kitchen. I've got my dungarees on ready to work on my little plot! (Which was four feet or so in front of me.) Photo taken at Chippenham Walk, Harold Hill, Essex. (1950s)

My sister Sandra. There's 18 months' difference to us in age. Sandra's pram stands on the spot (next to the Jacksons) where my little plot was soon to be. Harold Hill, Romford, Essex (1950s)

This book is also dedicated to Sandra and late husband Ray, plus my nephews/ nieces.

Me in the garden at Harold Hill, and could be Linda Cox standing by the fence, and her younger sister Wendy in the pram at number 7 Chippenham Walk. Early 1950s.

This was our newly-built house, looks like my dad had already started to build the rockery, long before he made his privacy screen.

I was 18 months old !

Springfield Park – having our dinner hour in the sun 1960s... Harry _____.? eventually took over driving the tractor for a while. I used to pester poor Harry to let me have a go! Me seated in the front with fellow gardener Tom Tansley.

This was a pose, for I was still too young to drive a tractor! Note the big shed where I screened soil some days from seven in the morning until ten at night when the park closed, phew! The Dennis Mower was kept in a shed in the far corner just past the soil shed. Photo circa 1965/66

Springfield Park 1960s, outside the tool shed that still had the old cobblestones when it was a stable. Left to Right: – Michael Neal, Tom Tansley, Ken Crowther… Ken worked on the bowling green under the guidance of Charlie Swaby; John Growcott was another young chap under Charlie for a time. Lastly we come to Peter Reason who went on to be in charge? at Lloyd Park E17 (old home of William Morris).

Me posing (1965/66) with the Lilac that I dug out from a garden where prefabs had been pulled down. Note my Pear tree that I brought with me from Harold Hill to 37 Bernwell Road, E4. Note too the sapling of an Ash that grew in with my Salpiglossis seeds! The corner too where my compost heap was and eventual chicken run.

My dear dad, Walter Herbert Edwin Nichols, born October 5th 1922, died in 1987. Dad had many achievements in life, sadly some were when designing for other people, and they took all the credit. Photo taken when Dad moved to Monkhams Avenue, Woodford Green, Essex. (1971) Dad's third wife is Meg née Cordell.

Another nice shot that I took of my pals (1960s) at Springfield Park.
Left to right: Brian Jackson, Michael Neal (back), Paul Shaer, Harry (our nice
mild-mannered tractor driver), and Colin, one of the visiting tree gang
employed by the Parks Dept.

Three of our girl gardeners, having a break outside their bothy (tea room).
Left to right – Theresa Peck, and Sue Mills. Dorothy King 'Dot' is not in the
photo, she had her breaks with Annie Hanks in the park's nursery.
Sadly, I have no photos of Ann, or of Lily Nash. Lily's pal there was the very
nice Bert Dearing. Bert was the park's 'Dennis' driver, I took over this job
from Bert.

Me with my Beatles' hair cut! My pal David Bolton (left) ... and dignitaries. We were chosen to represent our school for a tree planting ceremony, at Mansfield Park E4. This was 1963 we were both apparently the best two gardeners at Heathcote School E4! Our job here was to stake and plant a Prunus species – wonder if it's still there?!

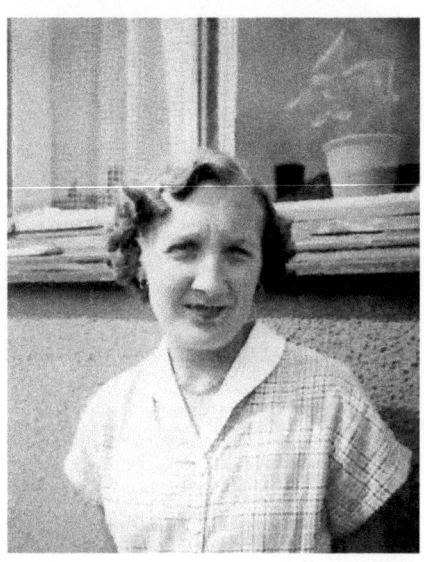

My dearest mum, Irene Eunice Nichols (née Ridley) known as Rene or Renie. Photo taken outside our kitchen window at 8, Chippenham Walk, Harold Hill, Essex (1950s)
Note Mum's gingham curtains, and the red Cyclamen that we kept alive for several years.
Mum (born 1923) married Dad 1947; she died in 1978 (complications with MS).

A lovely photo this, it's my great grandmother (my mum's nan) Rosina Alice Axford (née Jewel) 1872– 1961. The photo was taken at her friend's house either at or very near Southend-on-Sea, Essex. I have often wondered where this garden actually was?

My great gran made top headlines at the age of 87 when she saved many residents from a fire, I still have that Walthamstow news clip.

My great grandmother (left) and her pal Mrs Fricker – could this lady be the owner of the nice garden at Southend? (Photo late 1950s.)

My mum, Irene Nichols, with her best pal at Chippenham Walk, No. 13. Her friend's name was Vi Smith.

This was when we all had a nice day out at Southend during the school summer holidays, when the menfolk were at work.

Vi grew lovely pansies all along the left of her front path.

My mum loved Virginian Stock.

W. H. E. NICHOLS, A.N.INST.E.

BUILDING TECHNICIAN.

80 KENILWORTH AVENUE,
WALTHAMSTOW, E. 17

This is one of my grandad's early business cards, and is somewhat a mystery, for we have never found out what those initials stand for? And a further mystery that he was a building technician and a qualified plumber too , but was said to be mainly a very skilled electrician.

Joan and Johnny West, with grandson Jay

In their own words:

"… with our grandson Jay, he has been travelling with us since the age of three. We used to travel from North Yorkshire to Lincolnshire picking daffodils, lettuce and sorting onions etc. We also travelled through Norfolk and Suffolk working in the fields. It was in Suffolk at a Steam Rally where we first met Debbie and Keith, whom we have been friends with for many years. We also travelled to Kent where we picked hops, then travelled on to Worcestershire to pick apples, then made our way back north doing farm work, like cutting hedges / hedge laying and ditching with our horses 'Dolly' and 'Tommy' who both pulled the wagon. Even though we are old-age travellers now, we still enjoy travelling, and meeting with our old friends, and also pulling into our old stopping places."

(Photo by kind permission from Joan and John West.)

John and Joan at Bildeston (1997)

Me and my wife Debbie first met Joan and John at the Grand Henham Steam Rally, Suffolk way back in 1987 (September) and we meet at various events when they exhibit their beautiful wagon, and sell lovely wares, and we often are placed together alongside my old vintage juvenile equipment. Joan and John are true Romanies and the nicest folk you could ever wish to meet, both my wife and I are proud to call them friends.

(Photo by kind permission from Joan and John West.)

Upsetting the Applecart (Springfield Park)

Brian Jackson and I got on well with each other, and we often worked together on the 'Grip work'. Brian though was very quick tempered, and possibly not his fault, for he had a very serious accident falling from the back of a newspaper delivery van, in the days when the newspaper lads hung from the backs of vans and literally threw out the bundles of papers to the news-stands and newsagents. Brian longed for the day that he could receive his vast compensation, and couldn't get his hands on it until he was 21. Brian was around 17 or 18 then, and we were in the grip of the Mod and Rocker era. Brian called himself a 'moddy boy' and dressed like a mod when not in his working garb.

One year Brian was very keen to get a mate a job at Springfield. Brian said that his mate was a mod from Hackney, and liked lots of trouble. His pal did get the job, and we only knew him as Nobby Clark. He was a large(?) sort of chap, and was okay with me and seemed to get on with everyone. Brian though, had a slight dislike of Paul Schaer, and made a point of telling Nobby that. Nobby took the bait and punched Paul full on in the face. Nobby of course was sacked and Brian frowned upon for even thinking of bringing someone like this to our normally friendly 'family' group.

Keep the Workers Skint (Springfield Park)

As mentioned before, parks wages was very poor pay, but one day I found a good way of earning good money once our work was over for the day. There were two or three bays that adjoined the Dennis shed; these bays were for all the park's prunings, grass cuttings and other greenery. One day I noticed lots of trays of bedding plants just dumped, and all in perfect condition, so I said to Mick, we'll borrow a parks trolley, load it up and knock round the houses and split the profit.

Our venture and good fortune lasted just one evening! For someone, obviously jealous, reported us, and from then on Annie Hanks and Dorothy King 'Dot', were told to smash all the bedding plants face down, thus they were no good to anyone. A lot of the staff felt so sorry for us, and it seemed such a sad waste of perfectly good plants.

I Was Soiled! (Springfield Park)

One job that I really hated, and had to do it on my own, and that was sieving soil. No, this was a giant sieve some 8 feet high and 5–6 foot across, and had to be leant at an angle and propped up with a long piece of timber. The sieve was under cover, so that when the soil was sifted it remained in the dry, and I stood outside.

Several tons of soil would be dropped next to me, and the method of using this sieve seemed to suit the days of the Ark! For each full shovel load, you had to aim the soil as hard as you could against the sieve to filter the soil. Once again, I did this from seven in the morning until five, or if I wanted to carry on until ten at night, and I did too, all for just that little bit of money that mostly went to the taxman, but you had to do it if you wanted the extra cash.

Our working day ended at six minutes to five each day, the odd six minutes we were told made up the forty-hour week, and believe me, they would not let you go a minute earlier. We all gathered in the yard until a foreman or the Superintendent came out of the office and said "Goodnight everybody!"

As you can see with the whole of my working life, it doesn't always pay to be well-built and strong. I don't mind hard work, but some days I felt so very exhausted, for I did all the weekends and overtime offered, except when travelling the fairs.

Eyes Well Lit Up! (Springfield Park)

The above title was very appropriate at the time for there weren't any young lads in our group who didn't look keen – what am I on about? Well… girls of course! Not only did we have the park to look after, but also all the girls' (and mixed) schools' gardens. We all loved going to the girls' schools, nearly all the girls would wave or say hello, they'd all be looking out of the classroom windows etc. Our foreman used to get annoyed, we know that they were just jealous and wishing that they were young like us and getting all the attention! Even the teachers would get angry with the girls, for you'd think that they hadn't seen a male for years!

I spoke of Mulberry trees earlier; I noticed that a lot of the schools that we went to had at least one Mulberry tree in it which I found unusual, for it's not one of our most popular fruits.

Leaf It To Us! (Springfield Park)

I'm now on about the leaf compound that stood (still stands?) at the very bottom of the park next to a toilet block and facing the tennis courts. This blocked-in fenced area was totally packed with well-rotted leaf mould, and of course in another part of the enclosure all the latest leaf falls from not only our park, but also of the schools, Clapton Common Pond, etc., therefore tons and tons of leaves for future years' use later on when well-rotted down.

Leaf clearance was almost our sole job in winter, with everyone out with a broom or rake, plus two rough square pieces of wood to act as grabbers. Again, a long hard arduous job that seemed never ending. All the leaves would be put into huge piles all over the park, and when the tractor driver came round, we'd help him load the huge trailer which now had high-sided mesh grids added to hold even more leaves that in turn had to be well-trodden down. The leaf clearance used to get even harder, for once a year huge eight-wheeler lorries used to come, and every 'man Jack' among us had a dung fork in hand and load up these huge lorries. Well-rotted leaves were fairly weighty when on the end of a fork, to then hope you had the strength to get the clod of leaves over the high sides.

Still to this day, I never knew where all that lot went to, for I doubt if they went to any other parks, for each park had more than enough of its own. Therefore I was also very baffled when we'd go to Victoria Park and other places to pick up their leaf piles and bring them back to Springfield.

I've worked with all sorts of manures and fertilisers over the years – pig, chicken, hop as an example – but rotten leaves to me smelt the worst, and people were none too pleased to sit next to me on the bus or train I can tell you!

The Barnardo's 'Boy' and Me (Springfield Park)

I was fifteen and Mick nineteen, and we were pals straight away. Mick, for some reason, was not liked by some of the staff, well not at first anyway, and staff would say keep clear of him, but as young as I was then I wanted to make by own judgements on people for myself. Mick was living just down the road near Clapton station, and had a one-roomed flat. Mick used to come in very upset some mornings, for although he was a big strong chap, he was a gentle soul. He'd tell me know the other lodgers, navvies, got into his flat and take his sandwiches and other food, and even one day tried to push his mattress out of the window.

I told my mum what had happened, and she made Mick sandwiches for me to take to him. This act of kindness though seemed to annoy some of our workmates, and knew of my own sad circumstances at home – Mum with M.S. and Dad just walking out on us all. One or two of the chaps told Mick off for 'sponging' but he didn't, the other guys saw otherwise, many telling Mick that he was earning far more money than me, and to sort out his own lunches. I felt sorry for Mick, yes he was older than me then, but when I look back now, he was only really just out of boyhood himself.

Mick's mum had abandoned him, and he had been in Dr Barnardo's homes until he was able to start work, and that was with the Kent County Council, at Tonbridge Wells. I eventually got him lodgings at Chingford Hatch E.4 and have a room at my pal Tony Barnard's house, until Mick found his feet and moved in with Mr & Mrs Finesilver at Southend-on-Sea (Essex). It was there that we lost touch, when I last saw him he was earning good money, and doing all the night-time emergency work for the Thames Water Authority.

First Lesson Learnt Well (Springfield Park)

Some of the keepers and older work staff knew that I was desperate to earn extra money, and suggested that I put in a few leaflets around the houses near the park. They had to be near, for I was a good few years away yet from passing my driving test. Being only a couple of miles away from Stamford Hill, it was prominently a Jewish community. When it came to certain religious festivals, a lot of Jewish people would approach the foreman or whoever, and we'd have to go out and cut off huge branches (mainly laurel), these we were told had to be draped over conservatories etc.

One day when I was in the park an elderly Jewish man asked if I could move a few tons of soil, so I told him it would be five bob an hour (five shillings or 25p!). I shifted all that soil in just under an hour! and got paid my five bob – all that graft for that pittance! therefore I soon learnt to do priced work where I could.

It wasn't the man's fault, for he was only accepting the price that I gave him.

Another Jewish man came up to me one day and asked if I'd do his garden for him; before I had a chance to tell him of my charges he said, "I'll give you two bob and an old overcoat." I gave him a very firm NO!

Another Jewish man, elderly, should have got a firm punch on the nose from me and, in fact, reported or arrested. Back then, like now, I had long fair hair. Of course I was very clean shaven, and couldn't have mustered up a beard or moustache if I tried. I wore thin long-sleeved pale coloured jumpers, those worn like Phil May of the group 'The Pretty Things'. The man said, "How are your periods going?" I said, "What did you say?" and again he repeated himself. He did think I was a female! Had I been, I'm sure the police would have been called in. Of course it was a standing joke amongst fellow workers, even the lady gardeners got to hear of it. I was teased for several years after with that question!

The other incident I had, did actually concern the young and older female staff. Back then I wore what they called 'ice-blue jeans', they were tight, lots of lads of my age group were wearing them, and I certainly didn't give it a thought. It turned out that one or two of the women or girls did not want to work with me, because of the 'outline of what they could see *down there*'. I refused to change any of my clothing, and a good few of the men stuck up for me and told the foreman "why are they looking down *there* anyway, they should cover their boobs more in summer in that case". No more was ever said on the matter, but old Sid Butfoy said I was all bollocks and boots!

How Sensible! (Springfield Park)

I wrote about leaves earlier on, and jogged my memory again on something else hard that we were made to do – we had to rake all the leaves off the huge shrub borders, then dig out large squares that looked like mass graves. We hit on large roots from close-by trees and shrubs in the border and yet another strenuous job.

Once all the soil was dug out, all the leaves had to be raked back in, stamped on, and back-filled with all the soil, making sure there was something of a hump so that we didn't dig on the same spot another year. The brilliant idea behind all these 'leaf mounds' was that on these in two years' time when the leaves had rotted, we could then plant Rhododendrons, Azaleas, Camellias etc. with the already-made leaf mould.

Springtime at Springfield (Springfield Park)

After a hard winter, springtime used to wake up all the lovely crocus in bloom round the lake, many of which I planted. Dot one year planted crocus in a 1964 pattern, that did look good as you came up the hill from the Superintendent's house, for there was a small area containing an Evergreen Oak, these being a pain by losing leaves in summer, but never becoming bare because of the new growth at the same time.

I still have several photos of me and various staff at Springfield, and all the photos are of us all on a nice spring day in March, posing amongst crocus or Forsythia. Dot always gave a cheery wave to a smallish man who wore an American cowboy hat "Hi Tex!" She always seemed pleased to see him in his cowboy garb – she said that he was a famous Country and Western singer. The Jewish people soon filled the long line of park benches in front of the café. This area faced south, and they sat there from early morning to late afternoon when the sun went down, all were very elderly.

Two Near Assaults (Springfield Park)

I was big enough and strong enough to beat up someone, but never needed to for trouble always came to me! I was just fifteen and only at the park a couple of weeks when I was walking by the lake past the small rockery on the path (Dot planted a Zauchneria) when a small, very elderly lady was trying to hit me with her walking stick. She yelled abuse at me, not liking my hair, and shouted, "You look like a monkey" and tried her best to hit me with that stick. Sadly I had no witnesses to this near assault, even though it was a fine spring morning. It seemed odd, for papers at that time were always on about long-haired yobs attacking the elderly.

The next incident could have gone either way, and again had no witnesses, and after the incident reported straight to the office where I probably should have spoken to a brick wall. We were all in the middle of planting out a new bed on the far side of the lake, by another gate. We were planting up trays of Polyanthus, and I'd just made up a huge trundle pot of the new-on-the-market MAXICROP made up of seaweed (it did work brilliantly too!). when it was time for tea-break, there were around six of us on this job, and one suggested that perhaps one of us could stand guard over the pot plants and have a later tea-break, so I said that I wouldn't mind, so that's what I did.

The park had always been a quiet non-menacing place really, so what happened next shocked me to say the least. Suddenly through the gate came a group of black youths – two were girls, and I was threatened with more than one knife and pushed up to a nearby tree near the bowling green. For some reason I was not scared, and have never been scared of cowards or those that go around mob-handed for back-up. They couldn't understand why I stayed calm with a knife just inches from my throat, but I wasn't scared, but just told them that I had a good memory for faces and that if I saw any one of them outside the park at some time, we would fight, or if I was with loads of my mates and they were on their own how I would reverse the roles.

One of the lads obviously hated white people and was telling me that I hated blacks. I retorted back sharp and told him about my mum who had multiple sclerosis since the fifties and how I knew and loved many of the black doctors and nurses who have looked after my mum over the years. Strangely, they backed off of me, and all walked out of the gate. I did expect to see them when I left out of the main park gates that night, but no I never saw any one of them again.

When the staff came back, they found it hard to believe what had taken place all in a spate of a mere twenty minutes. They could easily have come back and seen me severely injured, or worse… DEAD. I reported to the office, but strangely nobody was unduly bothered about my experience.

Rustic In Homerton! (Springfield Park)

When the very likeable and hard-working Charlie Swaby retired from Springfield as the park's bowling green keeper, another near-retiring man we only knew as Mac took over. He again was from the old school and knew his craft well. Once again, because I worked hard, I was to work alongside Mac on a very interesting project at Homerton in the East End of London. The first job was to build a hundred foot long, ten foot high intricate rustic fence at an old folks' home. All the lovely rustic poles, plus Mac and me went by tractor. Mac knew exactly how to start this complicated project, the likes that you don't see at all today, except for rustic arches on a far-smaller scale. I'd never done anything like this before, and as we slowly progressed, I got into it, and learnt what bits went where.

Carpentry has never been one of my strong points and my auntie Rita tells me that I take after my Grandad on that score… I'm very proud to say! My aunt reckons I lost my vocation in life making greenhouse benches for rockery plants, because they all tilted and were so rickety!

I did though, manage to cut straight when helping Mac and being under his guidance, he was a nice chap to work with and sorry this project came to an end. Needless to say since my teens I have never built another rustic fence!

It was always nice sometimes to get away from the Park and do projects elsewhere, like once a year a group of us would sit in the trailer and Johnny Johnson would drive all the way to Clapham Common (*not Clapton Common), Clapham was a good few miles away, and we did all types of work there for the forthcoming Clapham Show. We put out literally hundreds of chairs, benches, etc., banged in thousands of stakes and affixed miles of rope as a barrier for the arenas. We also placed all the red and white poles used for the Gymkhana.

A follow-on from building the rustic fence at Homerton I was to complete all the planting etc. for a brand new park built at Homerton. Everyone was busying themselves, and I suppose a few of us brought from Springfield helped hurry things along quite quickly. Only a short walk away was a group of shops, one was a florist or ironmongers, and I bought an impressive plant that I'd certainly never seen before. Very common now, and that was the unusual Primula 'vialii', this had bright red buds and mauvy pink flowers and looked like a sort of mini red-hot poker. Such was the plant's rarity then, I found it wonderful to see a plant such as this in the heart of the East End!

I Never Stood a Chance! (Springfield Park)

Back in the early sixties at the park, I dearly wanted to learn about propagation, but only the girls were allowed to do this, all under the eyes of Annie Hanks. I liked Ann, she was a no-nonsense lady and the nursery was her domain. Some of the girls in the park remained sweeping all day, and had to work in two's; the men when sweeping had to work alone, and all of us hated the besom broom, or birch broom as it's known. When the nursery got very busy in spring, all the ladies would be in the green houses and sorting out the cold frames.

The only males that worked in the nursery were always the well-spoken ones, a bit 'plummy', many not sorted to hard manual work. The only times I was in the nursery was for any lifting and lugging, or digging over the border that stocked the forthcoming sowings of wallflowers etc.

It was also the lady gardeners mainly that did all the shrub pruning and planting out, so unless I pestered Dot, I was never taught the names of shrubs and I had a head start than most. Dot taught me the names of unusual shrubs that the park had back then, unusual then of course, like the "Judas Tree Cercis 'siliquastrum' that stood to the left on the border to the café's grass area, and the huge "tree of heaven" Ailanthus 'altissima' that stood to the other side of that grass compound. It was therefore inevitable that I would be more or less self-taught in all I know now, for I could clearly see that I was not to be taught propagation and unless I lost my cockney accent, cut my hair, and not so big in stature and energy, I never stood a chance of doing lighter duties in propagation, for it seemed I was far too valuable for the muscle side of park work, much I know as my own doing to avoid the dreaded boredom of the besom broom! Well-spoken and presented lads too seemed to work on the bowling green like John Growcott and Ken Crowther.

The Work Force (Springfield Park)

Springfield Park was a very much hidden away park, and never really overly packed even in high summer. It is a very pretty park, being hilly, had some fine views over Walthamstow marshes, and the very pleasant sight of huge barges up and down the River Lea (sometimes spelt as Lee) and you'd see the occasional horse pulling a barge along the towpath, and where the barge men and other rowers would stop at the café – an old wooden quaint shack back then. Just across the river from the café was a small island, we had a huge task one year to tidy the lot up, as we did on occasions with the park's own island on the lake.

I've spoken of many of the staff already by name, here's a few more for you; some I'm sure of my age still with us, but others have long met their maker, but I'll never forget them.

Those I'm sure still with us in 2009 are Tom Tansley, a lovely chap who kept his romance with Susan Mills top secret. Sue was a lovely girl, her dad was a C.I.D. man for the Parks Dept., a big chap, and friendly towards us all, and we went to Sue's sixteenth? birthday party. Tom and Sue kept it very quiet, but I think Sue landed up marrying my friend Derek Bobbin who worked mostly in the nursery with Sue, but also did a lot of labouring alongside us, his mum and dad were lovely people. Derek I think went on to work at a park called Kenwood. Older lady, Lily Nash, was very pally with Bert Dearing (the Dennis man) and became a mother figure to not only Sue, but Theresa (Terry) Peck. Terry eventually married a parks foreman elsewhere. Then there was Brenda, a shy young, girl. I still have photos of them all.

One old chap that I really liked was Sid Butfoy. He was the bothy man, he made sure the tea room was spick and span, you'd never be let in he'd just washed the floor, which he did about four times a day, for the keepers had their tea-breaks and dinner hours different times to us, and Sid kept it spotless. Sid, I think, spent his working life as a coalman, he certainly was a tough old timer, and wore a 'Romany' type scarf at all times, and looked like a typical old style rag and bone man. Sid was always angry about something or someone, nearly always serious, yet I got on so well with him and made him laugh. I think he saw me quite different from all the other chaps, what with my long hair, etc., the Beatles now on the scene, our transistor radios with Tony Blackburn etc. on the airwaves, and Leapy Lee singing 'Little Arrows' always seemed to be playing when we were clearing out a shrub border or down that dark cellar in the yard where we chopped wood with large axes all day long, a place too where I etched my name on one of the bricks in that cold cellar.

Sid always had a dish cloth at hand, or a clean tea towel over his shoulder awaiting the next thing to dry up. The only other man I knew who met Sid's temperament was a lovely chap called Les (he was the handyman at Chigwell Public School, Essex), he moaned, groaned, flew up in a rage, but never with me, for Sid and Les I took as friends and we just sort of had that understanding with each other. I was different and so were they. Sid was also the man who was responsible for the cleanliness of every toilet block in the park, therefore a full-time job, and Sid had his routine, and you got to know his times on where he'd be if you wanted a quick chat.

Sid had a special liking for Dot, he always had a smile and a cuddle for her, he called her 'Dolly'. Sid lived with his sister at an area called 'The Bakers Arms' because of the pub of that name, and was literally on the boundary of Leyton and Walthamstow.

Rumour later had it that poor Sid went blind. Isn't it sad that when you're young you never really think of keeping in contact with people once you've moved on to a new workplace.

Sid's best mate was George Patterson. George had a 'cauliflower ear', spoke with a slight mumble, but was a very funny guy, and couldn't stop laughing if something tickled him. During tea-breaks etc. George always had his face hidden behind the morning newspaper, and only looked up when all of us would erupt with laughter over something, and we'd all go into a loud rapturous cheer, which we were often told off for by Mr Galleyhawk upstairs, because we'd woken the baby up! We hardly took notice of his pleas though.

George's task in the park was just sweeping, all day every day; he hated physical work, yet in summer with his shirt off, was very muscular considering a man nearing retirement. George's quip was "I don't come here to work, I come here for the benefit of my health and to enjoy the bloody scenery!" and some other quips that I daren't print here, but do remember them well from my innocent teenage years! George admitted to having a lovely life in Australia and under his own admission was a hobo. Something quite strange happened to George, for after a time people kept saying that they saw George walking through the park after our official working day, and something that George would never do, once six minutes to five came round he was out of that gate like a shot! So many people told George that he was seen some evenings, he took a stroll through the park at the time when his 'double' was always seen and when the two men saw each other it was total shock, for it was his brother who George had not seen for forty-odd years!

Somehow this news reached the TV stations, and I sat and watched George and his brother being interviewed by Richard Dimbleby on his 'Panorama' TV show. I have often wondered if this piece of film is still in the archives somewhere? George and Sid had admiration for each other, yet worlds apart.

Terry Brown was slightly older than us, and soon went up the ranks. He was smart, knowledgeable when it came to plants, and became one of the youngest Superintendents and had a park allocated to him, he was a nice chap.

One really funny guy joined us at Springfield, a Yorkshireman by the name of Jimmy Walsh. Poor Jim had no teeth, so soon got the nickname of 'Gummy Walsh' or sometimes 'Gummy Gummy Walsh'. Jim was a really lovely chap, we too liked working together, and funnier still when he brought along his 'duck-call' whistle, he'd creep up behind strangers and blow it, or hide in the shrubs, even on the loo… a total nutter!

Harry was a nice guy, he had either just got over a breakdown or I was told he had one not long after I left the park for the last time. Harry came along as the main tractor driver, (we'd had several over the years) when we were away from prying eyes, I would pester Harry to let me have a go on the tractor if he could teach me you could see it in his eyes that he wanted to, but was far too risky in case we got caught, and I had to admire him for having to keep refusing me. I used to make Harry laugh though.

On the whole, I met some lovely characters at Springfield, and they really were characters too, and they didn't know it.

A young man called Peter Reason also was a part-time tractor driver, again went up the ranks quickly and become quite high up on the Parks Dept. at Waltham Forest E.17. Then there was John Grocott a very well-spoken chap and he too rose the ranks after working as an assistant to Charlie Swaby on the bowling green and went on to have his own green somewhere.

A chap called Ken, a very pleasant chap, occasional tractor driver, and noted cravat wearer! This was unusual for the swinging sixties garb, especially on a young teenager. Ken, like John Grocott, spent most of his time with Charlie Swaby on the bowling green, learning of all the trade secrets. Ken, like a lot of the others were well-spoken etc. and all had fairly well-off parents. In the late stages of his teenage years rumour were soon circling that Ken's parents had bought him his own garden centre in a well-to-do part of Essex, and had a thatched roof too. Many years later I was to see it for myself.

No, I don't remember where I was when President Kennedy was shot, but do remember where I was when one of our men told me about Ken's forthcoming garden centre. I was just alongside the park's theatre, making my way down the hill on my Dennis mower, and feeling so envious, for I'd always wanted a little growing nursery of my own. Sadly my finances have never stretched for such a venture, but I'm sure I would have made a good nurseryman.

Not long after our surprise meeting, Ken of course asked if I was still gardening, and told him that I'd been self-employed now for a good few years. I gave Ken my leaflet that listed all that I covered in the world of gardening, and he spotted that I restored old fruit trees. He asked if I'd like to do some work for him as he also had chaps out landscaping, and luckily there were fruit trees on this property where his staff were presently doing landscape work. I readily accepted, and Ken only had one stipulation, and that was that I had to somehow cover over the signs on my van, to let the client think that I was one of his staff. I didn't like that idea very much, but thankfully the signs were the easily removable ones, so there was no problem.

Ken showed me the lovely orchard that was to be pruned and let me get on with it undisturbed, for I was to carry out all the work single-handedly. I decided to work on an old very neglected 'Bramley' apple tree, and did the job meticulously to full restoration, and took one very long day to complete the job (this was a Saturday, as for the majority of my working life I have done seven days a week). I reported back to Ken at the nursery to let him know how I'd got on. I was pleased to tell him that I'd completed the big Bramley. His face was soon to change to one of disbelief, for then he said, "How many of the others did you do?" and of course told him "*None*, just the 'Bramley." – "One!" he cried… "Just one! You're supposed to do the whole orchard in a weekend!" He couldn't comprehend what I'd just said and vice versa, we were both now feeling very uncomfortable with one another.

I told him that I thought the whole idea of asking me to do these trees is because I know my job, and to do it well, and the 'Bramley' now is in perfect condition.

Ken ranted on that all the others had to be completed the next day – Sunday. The next morning came, and Ken had mustered up one or two of his staff and a tractor and trailer to put the prunings in – now, don't forget, all my pruning work was always carried out with hand-pruning saws, loppers etc.

The whole of that Sunday proved extremely embarrassing for me, and heaven knows what the owners must have thought, one man one day and six the next. I had to work very fast on each tree, removing just the obvious, like crossing branches, dead wood etc. The owners, I'm certain, must have thought I'd taken leave of my senses, being so very thorough on one tree and very random on all the others.

Back than I charged Ken forty pounds a day, but on talking to one of Ken's staff who was one of those sent along to help, said, "Do you know Ken charges to the customer a further ninety pounds per day, so has got ninety to your mere forty pounds for doing absolutely nothing!" I was truly astounded and devastated on hearing this, but it all made sense now why I had to take the signs off my van and become staff, because that way there was no fear of the client asking me what my fee was. I never worked for him again, and was taken aback that there was no real intention of doing a proper job for these people, for if they saw heaps of prunings, like most folk then think you're doing a brilliant job, I saw now how 'cowboys' get away with so much.

I had a conversation once with Ken, and we stood outside his very plush nursery, all nicely thatched, and I remarked how very expensive all his plants, shrubs and trees were. He stood back a little, pointed to the building and said, "This is why I'm able to do it, just look at the place, look at the area we are in." I'd still like to think that Ken looks back at that weekend, and thinks to himself that Keith really did know his stuff and hopefully feel ashamed of himself for not knowing what was really involved in fruit tree restoration. He did actually further his career by doing his own radio show and a slot in a local newspaper. One of those articles I have kept on fruit-tree pruning and despaired then on seeing it, knowing that if the readers had taken his advice it would have resulted in certain death for some trees.

Is this all a case that because he was given this huge business, you then stop learning your trade?

Ken most certainly had a business brain to take on such a venture so young, and I have regretted that we parted on such disagreeable terms. This was all way back in 1982, so might just one day drive out to rural Essex and pop in and surprise him again, but I don't think he'd offer me any work, and I wouldn't take it unless he agreed that I was allowed to do my job correctly and how it should be done to customer satisfaction, albeit they themselves may not be aware that the work is being done correctly, for if Ken or his staff had done it they'd still be happy?

Students Eh! (Springfield Park)

Every summer, students would seek summer work with the Parks Dept., and on the odd occasion in the winter too. But none… and I mean none… could do the hard graft that was dished out then, and the foreman and under-foreman were constantly coming over to us to make out 'to see how we were getting on'. They never had to do this to us normally, but were constantly chasing up the students. Now, although they were all extremely nice guys, we dreaded having them work alongside us, for 'A' we'd be the ones still doing all the work, and 'B' as I said, bringing the 'governors' over to look at us.

Just One Too Many (Springfield Park)

Adam Sennok was a Polishman, and was a nice chap and always a lovely smile from him to all whom he met. Looking back now, I realise that Adam possibly could have had a hard time during the war? for he was a persistent Meths drinker, often unshaven, and said to live alone in a dingy flat. Now whether due to drink or not, Adam drove the tractor and trailer at high speed through the park one day, and the trailer, which was a fair size, came off, left the path and skidded some twenty feet or more. Although nobody was hurt, he had to be quick-witted to somehow couple up again before any of the foremen saw the problem.

On arriving one morning, all hell seemed to have broken loose in the bothy, for somehow Adam had broken in and slept there all night. Whether Sid Butfoy was first on the scene or Chris Galleyhawk I can't say, but Chris being the foreman sacked him on the spot. We all saw him leave, he was in a terrible state. The hills at Springfield often oozed water out of paths and grass areas, and as the park's name suggests, was full of springs. Adam got stuck in these springs with the tractor on occasions.

Ron Barker (Springfield Park)

Ron Barker started his position as Foreman more or less the same time as the new Superintendent Mr Bailey.

Most of us got on with Ron, but again from the old school back then, and a very hard task master, so much so that he was called 'B-----d Barker'! (and he could be too!) for at Christmas time on the last day of work, it had always been customary to work only to lunch time, then you could either go home, or like most of the staff to the local pub. Ron though wouldn't give us permission to go, so a lot of the staff, moreso the men, became very angry, for it was only one afternoon out of the whole year.

Brian, alias 'the crow', became really angry, ran round to the nursery, grabbed several potted plants in *clay* pots, and furiously threw them as hard as he could at the office door!

Ron was then far too scared to come out! everything was getting out of hand. Eventually Ron did come out and told us to go home, and he daren't say anything about all the plants, broken pots and compost everywhere.

I was only just turned eighteen at that time, and Ron wrote a nice letter about me to give to the Judge at Crown Court, when the police planted drugs on me and two friends.

Ron had got to know me very well, and he had no hesitation in writing this letter (I still have a copy of it). Ron was hoping that I didn't get a prison sentence, so was I for that matter, but proved very difficult to prove our innocence because of the times we were in: 'The police don't do such things.'

Somehow it must have got to Ron's ears that I was slowly becoming quite a knowledgeable plantsman, a good worker and above all a good gardener. It did seem strange though, just suddenly getting recognised after all those years at the park.

Ron explained what was to happen, back then the system worked like this... You had to of course start at the bottom of the ladder, so to speak, and Ron told me that he'd put me in for my third class uncertificated exam, and would be in a year's time, and have to have a theory test and a practical test. All this of course gave me all the more incentive to learn a lot more. The time did come round, and I think three of us from Springfield sat the exam, both were girls and one of the girls was Susan Mills, and her dad was there too, as you remember he was C.I.D. for the Parks Dept. He was there talking to the examiner whom we were told was ex-C.I.D., and although I got on extremely well with Sue's dad, the other chap seemed to eye me with suspicion, and instantly knew that I was doomed to failure.

Sadly, I have no idea what 'park' we went to for this exam, but had to go by bus and train, and Sue's dad took me back to Springfield to make my homeward journey from there. (The park I think was at or near Southgate.)

The theory test was not a sitting down written test as I thought, but in fact was in a long narrow marquee. In the marquee was a very long table to match, and a row of twigs from shrubs, pot plants, cut flowers etc. all in a row, and each had a number, which were 1 to 100. We were all then given a printed sheet of paper which of course again was printed 1 to 100, and you simply had to write the name down of each shrub and plant by the appropriate number. I enjoyed this a lot, for I thought it was going to be a long written exam.

I found the practical test good to do too, for you had to show how to dig a circular bed, then the correct way of staking, planting and tying a tree in a circular bed.

I'm certain that it was spring when we had the exam, and the results came at the end of the year. The two girls passed both exams, and I failed. I use the word 'failed' very lightly, for Mr Barker told me that I'd got 100 out of 100 for the plant recognition, and failed on the practical. Everyone at the park felt sorry for me, and all agreed with me when I said it's funny how I passed when I was just a name on a paper among several others, yet where I could be seen and watched by the examiner, I failed. I could tell that the ex-C.I.D. examiner didn't like the look of my hair, and made it too obvious really, without him saying a word.

I was very angry, a whole year wasted. Ron Barker all along said, "you'll sail through", and he knew of my disappointment, and his thoughts must have gone back to the August with my trial at the quarter sessions, and how people wouldn't accept long hair, and that you were a villain or trouble-maker. I didn't get the prison sentence, but just one month on from that horrendous time, hoped that my luck would change and have that first rung on the ladder to be a top gardener.

Ron was quick to say "I'm putting you through again, Keith, I'll get the ball rolling straight away." I told Ron not to bother, but thanked him for having that great faith in me, for he knew I knew my stuff. Ron did put me forward again, but I did not turn up. Ron put me through again, but I left before the time came. Ted Ellis, one of the keepers knew how sad I was at failing, and told me that they were looking for a Head Groundsman at the Orient F.C. in Brisbane Road, Leyton, E.10, so I made arrangements for an interview.

So, folks, to this day, and now not too far from retirement (and death perhaps!?) I have no qualifications whatsoever, and now know I never will.

The Orient F.C. (goodbye Springfield Park!)

I did take Ted's advice and wrote to the Chairman of the then LEYTON ORIENT F.C., Mr Arthur Page, to see if I could have an interview. I thought what the hell am I doing applying for the job as HEAD groundsman at a major football club, I must be totally off my trolley, for like most, you all doubt your own knowledge and abilities, and felt way out of my depth, but I was so desperate to get away from my disappointments of failure at Springfield Park, so determined to try a new challenge.

I'd learnt so much at Springfield, even how to make edging board bend round to keep the soil or grass edges from falling onto the path, either Bill Brotherton or Albert Danahar showed me how it was done, just by making a long series of cuts all along the board and it virtually bent like rubber! Needless to say, when I'd mastered this, I was then the main edging board man for a time. In a way I was so sad to leave Springfield, for I'd been there since I was fifteen.

My interview day came, and still wondering what had possessed me to apply for such a job, but I thought I've done it now, 'in for a penny' and all that. Arthur Page was a very delightful man and put me at my ease, and seemed more like an old friend, than the big boss. Arthur explained to me that they hadn't had an official Head Groundsman for around twelve years, and if I took the job I'd be ending the situation. Arthur Page asked if I liked football, and I said "to be perfectly honest with you, I really can't stand it!" Arthur retorted back with a laugh and said, "What! and you're going to be our groundsman!!" so I quipped back, "Does that mean I've got the job then?" and Arthur happily said, "yes, you have!"

I went on to tell Arthur that it was the Ground work that I was really interested in, and what I'd really applied for. All this seemed music to his ears, I also went on to say "Just think about it, on match nights, all those hundreds of people wanting to go in, and me wanting to get out!"

I had two obstacles in my way, two men who couldn't or wouldn't let go of their *EX* positions, and having had that same problem at Wadham Lodge Sports Ground E.17 didn't want the same all over again. The man who had hold of the reins for the last twelve years was a certain Charlie Nichols (Nicholls?) and kept telling me when to go home, and other duties. Okay, I had to be shown the ropes, but when it goes on and on, you gradually feel as if you are not in charge at all, and had in fact someone still over you. Charlie was not an unpleasant man, quite the opposite in fact, but he was well past retiring age, but seemed to like the authority of still being in charge of the ground as sort of Head Groundsman and Head Caretaker.

Arthur Page had already told me that I'd have two grounds to run and that they'd recently taken over a ground formerly owned by Great Universal Stores… where?… Clapton!… where?… opposite Springfield Park!

I never did venture into Springfield Park again, and Ted Ellis never got to know that I got the job. Great problems came about here for me, in the shape of the second man, Sid was his name, very elderly, and had lived on the ground in a caravan on his own. He'd been the groundsman there apparently for years, now demoted because of my arrival to get the ground in good order, and a very badly neglected bowling green, which virtually faced the Pavilion that was now being modernised with disco lighting fixed into the walls and ceilings. Sid didn't like the modern changes to the old building, and no doubt worried about any late night revelry, for his caravan stood at the back of the Pavilion only feet away. Sid couldn't upset the main carpenter carrying out this work, although kept getting in the way.

Sid, though, started hiding tools, made out that he'd lost the keys to the shed, or put the keys in the shed door early in the morning, and on my arrival just appear round the corner as if my chance, he'd glance towards the shed door and then blurt out "Look, you've left the keys in the shed door all night!"

Sid clearly didn't like me, or moreso perhaps for what I stood for. Yes, it must have been very sudden change for him, for it seemed his world was now chaos.

It goes without saying, I had no choice but to report him, for all this could have rebounded on me so badly. I relayed all that had happened to John Falltrick, Orient's secretary. John too was a very nice chap, he was the one who got to tell Arthur Page what was going on. Sadly what could they do? Like Fred Bradley at Wadham Lodge, Charlie and Sid at the Orient were all retired or near retired elderly men, but certainly made my life very difficult, so I never really ever fully took charge in the sense that I would have liked, simply because these men wouldn't let go, or told to take a back seat now. Sad really, for I could never really leave my mark. I never had the chance to show them my true worth.

Sid continued to be a nightmare, and I kept a set of keys; he obviously had duplicates, but I did try to lock the shed in front of him each night. The Great Universal stores ground was now known as the Orient's official training ground, the equipment there was very ancient, and all left outdoors, one contraption I had no idea what it was but it was unmoveable!

John Falltrick came to see me one morning on the training ground, and asked if it was possible to restore the bowling green to the glory that it once was. He of course asked if I actually knew what to do, "Yes, without a doubt" was my answer. I couldn't hold back from telling John that most bowling green keepers treated their greens as if it was precious gold dust, and so they should, but no matter how you wrap it up it's still grass, very fine grasses, but nevertheless GRASS.

I told John that to do this project I'd need good equipment to do the job properly, plus a fair amount of materials too. I eagerly looked forward to doing this project, and needed to commence in Spring, around April time. As I say, I never got to start that project because I left soon after.

I have a lovely scar on my second finger, right hand, when a drill snapped when I was fixing a crossbar to the goal post, it looked pretty bad at the time. I did a fair amount of graft on the training ground, usually three broken-up days there, and the rest of the time on the main pitch at Brisbane road, ready for match days, weekends and week nights. I had to be there for all the matches which I really hated, and just wandered up and down aimlessly and longed for home time!

On match nights, I was a steward, for I had to wear an identity badge. I was solely there just to taken in the four corner flags at the end of a match, so then I was suddenly the Head Groundsman again!

My Grandad, Harry Bishop Ridley, was very proud of my position, and soon found out that he had supported the Orient for donkey's years, so on hearing that I was proud to be able to get Grandad tickets for all the matches – he was so overjoyed I can tell you!

The very first time that I had to cut the grass on the main pitch I had an audience of painters who were painting the chairs, benches and other woodwork; there were about five of them looking at me from the main stand. I found this daunting, as if I was being scrutinized, or someone waiting for me to do something wrong – and I did! Well, it wasn't really me, as you'll see. The mower I was pleased to see was a Dennis, and a machine that I'd used hundreds of times, so just knew that I'd be okay.

This grass-cutting machine did resemble the Dennis in every way, until that is I started cutting – I just could not make a straight line! It was so embarrassing, and what with all those eyes on me made it ten times worse.

I got the light and dark green stripes okay, but knew that I'd done it wrong when one chap (who I got to like later on – Harry) yelled out, "Looks like a bunch of bananas!" little did Harry know then that I'd remember his words all these years later, so deep was my embarrassment!

I did master the machine in the end, plus learnt why I couldn't go straight. It was the positioning of the engine, for over many years used the engine on a proper Dennis as a guide to join perfectly to the next line and so on.

I got to know a few of the players at that time, and football fans seemed to be envious of me and say 'do you know so and so' as if they were gods! To me they were just guys kicking a ball about for an actual living, and no more. Perhaps some of the players who never ever spoke to me thought that I was in awe of them like their fans… if only they knew!

Peter Barnes took over from Arthur Page when he retired, and there was always a cheery wave from him if we ever saw each other out, and long after I left Orient, and a player did the same, and was the most friendliest all through my time there, his name was Tom Walley (again, not sure of spelling of surname).

One thing that I did admire about all the footballers, and that was the arduous training that they had to do, very strenuous exercises they were too. In fact, even back on the main ground, I was told to pile the grass in the corners of the pitch, they would put the grass in very large bags and run up the steps and tip it somewhere on the Coronation Gardens side of the pitch. I never did look to see where it all went, but it was a bit of exercise that they had always done, and saved me my time to get on with something else.

Going back to Coronation Gardens side of the pitch, used to be hundreds of ornamental shrubs called Colutea 'arborescens' "Bladder Senna"; it had broom-type yellow flowers, which later died and formed inflated 'bladders' containing the seed. These shrubs were my only reminder of Springfield Park, of which they had only one!

When I left Orient, and a little later on around 1974 I went to work for the Haringey Borough Council and during my time there, met a great chap called Wally, an ex-security guard, a big-built chap, and found this an unusual job for him, for he was a shy sort of man, a gentle soul, but his stature no doubt got him the job. Leaving security, joined Haringey Parks Dept. and we became good pals. I always admired how Wally had grown some baby Christmas trees in a seed tray, and gave them all to me to sell on my flower stall, a new venture for me.

Wally, later on, got fed up with Haringey and heard that there was a job going at…wait for it!… Orient F.C. – the position was for a Head Groundsman and Assistant Groundsman, so Wally and his son applied for the job and got it! I have often wondered how long he stayed at the Orient, Wally may now be long retired, but did his son stay on I wonder, or did they get all the hassle that I did and stayed a short time?

When Wally told me about this ad, I then told him that I was once their Head Groundsman, and relayed all that had gone on, and how all my chances were spoilt. Wally was so surprised that I'd taken charge of Orient's ground, and told him that I left on very good terms, and told Wally to tell them that I thoroughly recommend you – this Wally much appreciated.

Haringey Parks Department

I really can't think how I learnt of this job vacancy at Haringey (WOOD GREEN), but got the job straight away. I used to travel every day from my house in Chingford Road, E.17, and had to sit in heavy traffic on the North Circular road. I'd branch off a few side roads and make for White Hart Lane, which would then take me to another series of roads to what was called Glendale Depot, and that was where we were based. We were all in 'gangs', although 'our gang' consisted of me and a chap called Bill Davies, a nice chap from Wales, and luckily being the two of us, we got on just fine.

Our work consisted of looking after all the gardens in old folks' homes, libraries, schools, toilet blocks and a host of other places. we worked each one in order, but the bigger places had to have fairly regular attention, and leave the smaller ones for a while.

When it wasn't the main growing season, or during dry spells in summer, when growth slowed down, we would be set to other projects, and where the other gangs were threes, fours, and fives, me and Bill did quite a bit of graft between us. Bill was a good garden labourer, but didn't know a buttercup from a daffodil, which actually suited us fine, probably how we came to work amicably together.

One task was to plant up trees and thousands of ground cover plants, at a place called New River Yard, a new sports complex, at the top end of White Hart Lane. Geoff Capes, the weight lifter, trained there we were told. The ground cover plants came in bundles of several hundred to a bundle, and consisted of Vinca 'major' or "Periwinkle", Pachysandra 'terminalis', and Hypericum 'Calycinum' or "Rose-of-Sharon" (all planted separately!).

Apparently the sports centre was built on the site of an old dump, and not long after opening, walls started to crack, roads and paths began to sink, at the time it was said to be due to metals and wood gradually rotting away hence a lot of underpinning had to be carried out.

Like most councils in the past, your starting times in the mornings were 7–7.30, and a five o'clock finish. In all my years on the various parks departments, the Haringey Parks Department was the easiest work when it came to working overtime in the weekdays and weekends, and had to lock the gates at ten o'clock at night, for I'd be in charge of a small park called Chapmans green, a lovely park with flower beds, bowling green, and tennis courts, and had a small pavilion which had window views of both the bowling green and the ornamental beds with various summer/spring bedding etc.

You had your own very small tea room with a kettle and cooker etc. and from there people would come and buy tennis court tickets from you, and that's all you had to do. The main overtime in the weekdays was when you took over from the main gardener at five, so from then on you had to try and occupy yourself. I'd nip over the road to buy newspapers and magazines, plus something for my tea; there was a radio too. All this was okay for the duller rainy days, but on lovely evenings and weekends it was up to you if you wanted to do anything, and I invariably did want to do something, so I'd dead-head flowers, hoe between the bedding plants, and mostly did watering. Being a smallish quaint park, it was always kept in pristine condition, for the whole area was totally manageable for one person, and extra help was really only needed during each of the bedding seasons.

If you wanted to you could just use a paper stick to pick up just the odd bit of litter, or perhaps empty the bins; everything was optional, or you could sit in the little tea room all day. When I think of all the years of graft at Springfield Park, it was all a very pleasant change.

When it came to locking-up time, it was dark, and although not a huge park, you always had to keep your wits about you, for we are talking about the Wood Green and Tottenham areas, where once a pupil threw a teacher through a plate glass window; the rough families who'd pull down their garden fences and gates to put on the fire indoors, they were given TV and carpets by the council, and the tenants would sell them, and as both were classed as a necessity so we were told, the council replaced all the items each time. We lost count on how many fences and gates one family had. We witnessed it, for it was our job to keep clearing out a nearby shrub bed that was full of junk and allsorts, hence faced their back gardens.

A yob from one of these houses, went to one of the schools where we attended the gardens; he'd be totally irritating and taunting me, Bill, and who knows who else? He'd climb like a monkey up the tallest tree in the playground and yell out abuse to one and all. One early evening I was watering all the beds at Chapmans Green, when all of a sudden the water kept going on and off, I looked up to see this yob and some of his cronies playing with the taps, and when he wasn't doing that he'd blatantly walk past me and jump on the hoses.

Back then, you could hit back at any yob without the fear of being done yourself, hence he got his comeuppance from me – he unexpectedly came round the corner to use the loo which was adjacent to 'my office', he looked shocked to see me so close up. I grabbed hold of him and shoved his face right into a hawthorn hedge. Boy, oh boy, was he in agony, and I thought "Sheer bliss!"

Not long after, one of the bowlers who had witnessed all that was going on, told me that there was a fire in the front of the Pavilion, the yob was seen running away for he'd grabbed several bins from the park, put them all under the seated under-cover part of the Pavilion, and set fire to the lot, where he'd hoped to burn the whole place down and all... including me... inside it!

We never did see this yob again, although for the rest of that summer, I expected him to return. Thankfully this was the one and only incident that I ever had in the park.

One very sweet old lady used to walk through the park every evening with her little dog, she was as cockney as old boots, and always looked none too tidy or clean, and always wore a dirty old coat. She'd come up to me and say "Shutcha eyes, open yer gate, and see wotchya granma's boughtcha" she'd then pull out an apple and say "'Ere, shuv this in yer gate!" and go to put this apple in my mouth from that dirty old coat. I'd always say "Thank you, Mrs Lark, but I'll eat it later." Another night it'd be old boiled sweets or soft toffees that had all seen better days. Even the greengrocers over the road turned your stomach, for they'd open a large bag of potatoes, that was okay until they moved the actual bag, for loads of awful cockroaches would scurry about in the shop, it was the first time I'd seen these creatures.

Chapman's green was also our meeting point each week to pick up our wages from a security van. We got to know these two chaps really well, a couple of nice guys, one went missing for a good while, and no one had said a word, but he suddenly appeared again one day to say that he'd been in hospital and nearly lost his life when someone shot him whilst delivering council wages.

I Fought for a Fiver! (Haringey Parks Dept)

I've been for numerous interviews in my life, and some pretty tough, most times I did get the job, but very often stuck as a garden labourer, even though your bosses know you are capable of so much more. They still put me on the more skilled work, and never a mention about upgrading you, therefore more money too.

Some of the chaps said that foremen and such likes were always wary of making someone up a grade, in case it put their own jobs in jeopardy. Garden labourers, and that meant most of us, were classed as grade 3, but I was told that because of my knowledge I should be the top grade of 4 which was to recognise you as a top gardener.

I had such a job persuading the bosses, but eventually got the rise. I had no idea how much it would be – fifteen, twenty or so pounds? I was shocked when it was a mere five pounds! I was worth just that bit extra against all of the other garden labourers who, with their own admission, were clueless when it came to plants, shrubs etc. and I had the responsibility on the more professional jobs that were allocated to me.

Like other places where I'd worked, they introduced the dreaded 'bonus system' which was always doomed, and never an incentive as we were led to believe, i.e. the more work you did, the more wages you received. The whole thing was a farce, and like at other places where I'd worked, I proved time and time again that the system was a failure and produced shoddy work.

I remember my first job at Haringey on the day the bonus system started. Me and Bill Davies were asked to prune a shrub bed. I'd got my 'top Grade 4' status at this point, so had to prove that I was worthy of the grade. I pruned each and every shrub how it should be done. At the end of the week, and of course, completing other pruning work, and other jobs of skilled work, we waited eagerly for our wage packet. It was laughable, all that work that we did, and hardly anything on top of our normal wages. I complained to the foreman, Ron Nunn, and the Superintendent, and asked what was the point of having the grade 4 status, surely it was so that I could do my job properly and skilfully, and now being penalised for taking so long on each set job. I said that it wasn't worth all my knowledge being used if the bonus system meant you had to rush and bodge each job to meet a deadline.

The bosses had no answers for me, and could see that they took my point and knew that I was 100% correct in all that I'd just said. Was I now to follow all the other garden labourers and simply just hack at the shrubs and turn them into a sort of box shape, or indeed rounded, as indeed you see exactly today on the majority of Council run parks, play areas, precincts etc.

I found it also an insult to my mate Bill, for although he had no knowledge on gardening whatsoever, he was a first-class helper to me, like getting all the prunings away from me as they slowly piled up, he'd weed and 'tickle' over all the beds, sweep up etc., etc.

One of the tractor drivers was also getting fed up too, for tractor work was of course multi-task, so how could his bonus be worked out? He was fetching, carrying, loading, unloading, pulling the triple mowers when grass-cutting and spraying. It's the spraying that I now refer. I was asked to help Fred on the spraying, Fred driving the tractor and me mixing the chemicals and do the spraying. We had to do paths, roadways etc. and I had to walk miles and miles.

Fred and I were talking about the unfair bonus system and he said that he'd had umpteen problems, for he too was a skilled man on many types of jobs. I said to Fred, do you fancy a laugh and have a mock at the system? He was all for it, and asked what I meant. I asked how the bonus was to be worked out on this particular job of work, and Fred said that you got so much for doing so many feet or yards, this was exactly what I thought, so I said, okay Fred, let's see what happens. Fred looked at me quizzically, so I said to Fred, "Watch this!" I gave one single squirt, and said "Right, Fred, book in 1,000 yards!" Fred laughed, and could now see what I was up to. We booked in thousands of yards for that week, and actually got a brilliant bonus for bodging! Most of our areas allocated had no weeds at all, plus I walked very fast with the spray full on, and even had the spray on whilst standing on the back of the tractor!

How ridiculous I thought, here we were, bodging, very unskilled, and getting a lot of money for it, nothing to show for our work either, yet prune shrubs etc. with the greatest skill and get nothing. I never did prune properly at Haringey after this, I just 'hacked' away as they'd always been done… crazy, isn't it?

I was for the High Jump! (Haringey Parks Dept)

Our foreman asked me to go to a playing field to prune all the shrubs on the boundary line – one section was Cornus or 'Dog-wood' and there were two coloured stems on each of the varieties, one lot red, the other yellow, and the brightest were some six feet high. I set to work to fully restore these very neglected Cornus which, I hasten to add, were crammed with crisp packets, bottles, cans etc. and a border well overdue for restoration.

The prunings when stacked made a fair ol' heap, I can tell you. As we were tidying up the last bits, the playing field keeper came over to me in a total blind rage, and was virtually screaming at me, "What are you doing? You've killed my lovely shrubs!" I told him in no uncertain terms to go and take his venom out on the foreman. Boy, was he in a rage, and yes, he said he was going to report me, and he did!

When I went back to the yard that evening, an under-foreman asked if I could report to the main office at ten in the morning to see the Superintendent and Parks foreman, Ron Nunn. None of this worried me in the slightest, for I knew that I'd done the pruning correctly. The next morning word had got around and all eyes were on me and the very agitated playing field keeper standing with me outside the office door like two school kids waiting to see the headmaster!

The keeper, who was notably agitated, probably wondered why I was not showing any sign of nerves, and probably unnerved him even more. Once inside the office, the Superintendent asked the keeper what had gone on, and of course kept furiously pointing my way, "he's done this", "he's slaughtered that" and so on, and I stood by just listening. Ron Nunn, whom I got on very well with, looked my way with a glint in his eyes, knowing the outcome of all this, for he knew I knew my job backwards.

The keeper had said his piece and asked to stand aside as they wanted to hear my side of the story. I explained to the Superintendent that the under-foreman had set me a task to prune and restore a long host of various shrubs on this man's playing field, my head nodding to the direction of the keeper. I then explained that I got to a long line of 'Dog-woods' that needed severe treatment. Ron Nunn then spoke up, "Did you say 'Dog-wood', Keith?" I said yes, Cornus 'elegantissima' and 'spaethii'. The keeper gave a very shocked look my way when those words came out. Ron then said very magical words, "Aren't Cornus shrubs supposed to be cut down to more or less ground level each year, Keith?" I then took the greatest satisfaction of agreeing with Ron, and told him that's exactly what I'd done, but now, being March, was the perfect time for this work to be carried out, and that this time next year you would see all the brand new bright stems where you can see them, and not neglected and seeing them 6–8 feet high on top of very old dark wood. I then said, hence next March I'll need to cut them back again, to ensure good winter colour for next year too.

The keeper by now was feeling very foolish, and the words 'swallow' and 'hole' sprang to mind for this man. Just before I left the office I turned to Ron Nunn and the Superintendent and said… pointing to the keeper… "I think this bloke ought to stick to cutting grass, don't you?!"

The keeper never ever spoke to me again, but something very funny happened not long after, for I assume Ron or the 'Super' went along to see my work for themselves, albeit Ron himself had seen me do other types of shrubs many times, but perhaps not the Cornus that had always stood on a very prominent main road position on this keeper's field. Ron then asked me to restore all of the Dog-wood that were at the main entrance to Glendale Depot, and when I was in the middle of it – guess who came round the corner?! I bet he wanted that hole again!

I'm Made Up Again! (Haringey Parks Dept)

I'm not saying that it was because of the 'Dog-wood' incident, but must have contributed for me to take on the role of site foreman for one of the Job Creation Schemes. I wasn't a first choice, but whoever they chose, made a right muck-up of it and didn't know which way to turn, then someone put my name forward, so they made me up to a sort of site foreman plus my grade 4. The foreman's job did actually boost my wages quite a bit. It was 1975 and there were three million unemployed at that time, so you'd have thought that I'd have the cream of good workers, but no, well, not to the very end of the project.

The project being to create a small park. The very neglected gardens had formerly belonged to the gas company, and prior to that was a girls' school. I was shown over the site of 'Woodhall House', and the foreman, me and the architect got together to discuss my plan of action. I was later to have a disagreement with the architect, he was a nice chap but should've really stuck to architecture and not plants, for he chose all the completely wrong plants for the gardens. I told Ron Nunn of the problem, and never saw the architect again, and everything was left to me!

My only big regret on this project were the young labourers. I had yobs, and I mean yobs, they were wasters, mickey-takers, lazy, late-starters, and so totally arrogant. And had no choice to slowly but surely have three of them removed from the scheme. Yes, I was threatened, and what they'd do to me if they saw me out, but they'd picked on the wrong one in that score, so asked them to settle it *now*, and pointed out that I didn't want them to be disappointed if they never got to ever see me again. How frustrating that would have been for them! Of course it came to nothing.

The yobs would Kung-foo posts, young trees etc., and one day they tied up one of the more placid lads to a scaffold board and put the board over a four foot deep flower bed that they then tried to fill with water. If I hadn't have got back from dinner earlier, the lad would most certainly have drowned (he was face down)!

I was so angry, I'd moan to all the bosses and say "three million unemployed, and I'm left with wasters who all, under my teaching, could have gone on for a very promising landscaping career." I was left with three nice lads, all very keen to learn, but remained three lads less, and I worked just as hard as them – I had to, so that the project kept moving, for the Job Creation Scheme on this particular project was for only six months.

The bosses offered me three more lads, but I refused, by saying that we'd already lost very valuable time, and I did not have the time or the patience to see what a new lot of lads would be like, hence I kept the same three labourers to the end of the project.

The Start of the Project (Woodhall House)

The site to start with had to be cleared of every conceivable piece of rubbish. When that was gone, I used very powerful trade weed-killers over the whole site to rid of nettles, thistles, Convolvulus, Ground Elder etc., yes the very worst in the weed world, not to mention the dreaded blackberry!

Whilst all this was dying back, I put the lads on digging out clay and rubbish soil from the original rose beds, each were 10ft long x 5ft wide, and got them to dig out to a depth of four foot (hence the depth that could have drowned the lad mentioned earlier).

I set my task to restore a massive very old Wisteria that had grown to an enormous size in all directions. I was highly praised on the completion of this job, for I'd done the lot on my own, for I affixed new wires to the wall, and tied in the wisteria. It looked then like it had always looked like that, in so good condition, boy did it flower well the following year, you could almost hear the climber calling out to me... THANK YOU!

Once all the beds were dug out, all the weeds on site now completely dead, I ordered in some very rich compost that had come from old cucumber beds, this stuff looked superb, lovely and dark, so I couldn't wait to plant up, the dark soil obviously a nice background for all the green leaves and flowers. The flower beds had literally tons of this compost in them, and I was to have a big surprise later that summer, and will tell you what it was in a minute!

Whoever I had taken over from when starting this project was totally clueless when it came to garden restoration, for these same beds on my arrival were just hoed, and the roses a hacking job, yet was *supposed* to be the finished job! The roses, which were very old, I dug out, did a 'hard' prune on them, and removed *all* of the old wood, plus a root prune too for easier planting. I washed all the sticky soil from the roots, thus making sure there were no bits of bell-bine, or couch grass amongst the roots, for if there were even the tiniest bit would start to grow, and soon invade the new beds.

On the subject of old roses, or shrubs for that matter – when I've been on an interview for a job, say for a private house, I've walked round the garden with the owners and the subject comes up about the gardener who had to leave or retire, and the owners would say "We were sorry to lose him/her, for he/she was such a good gardener" invariably I'd glance down, especially to the roses, to always see a 'Bodge prune with loads of dead-wood amongst new growth. I'd think to myself they weren't *that* good really, for you could see that they only *thought* that they'd pruned the roses correctly, so straight away just knew that only the roses alone, I could make a big impression. Still today, even parks have clueless gardeners. I only have to look at the roses, and that tells me all I need to know, for you've either been taught how to garden properly or not!

Never Judge a Book... (Woodhall House)

From the very first day of work at Haringey, all the blokes used to point out to an older chap, "Watch him" "Don't give him a lift, drive past" etc. and always wondered why? "He's trying to cadge a lift" was the most common sentence, especially at knocking-off time when driving out of the yard.

I remembered similar words being spoken about my pal Michael Neale on my first day at Springfield Park, I never listened to the chaps back then, and we became good pals. I seized my chance with this chap and said, "Hi, mate, would you like a lift?" The reply is what I expected, and I wondered then if I'd shot myself in the foot so to speak, and perhaps should have listened to what the other blokes had said. The chaps it Seemed had got the man all wrong, for we got on very well, and I had no hesitation in giving this new found friend a lift whenever he wanted one.

This new pal was George Gwarys, a Polishman, and had retained his strong accent. I was soon to learn that George was a very skilled stone mason. I thank the Lord that I did make the effort to befriend George, for I had a lovely surprise when I found out that he was to work with me on this project at Woodhall House.

We were both overjoyed, and as we got to know each other, we had great admiration for each other and also of our two different styles of skills. We worked so perfectly together. George was a very warm-hearted caring man, and had a brilliant sense of humour, his accent making some of the English 'rude words' even funnier. We'd go to a café in Wood Green about three times a day, and the banter between the lovely lady owner Edie was hilarious, and with her grown-up daughters too, I daren't print any of it!

As I said earlier, it's so sad that George and I were having to try and train total yobs, and they could have learned a fantastic trade, but George and me knew that it was hopeless. George laid beautiful paths, steps, raised beds etc., he was a craftsman indeed.

George and I not once had a cross word, we would discuss what we were doing each day so that we were never in each other's way. Something I dearly wished, and that was to know more about George's health, for George always said that he thought... or was told... that at some point he had had a heart attack, and he'd very often ask me, "Do you think I've had a heart attack, Keith?" I could only say that there was no way that I could tell, but pleaded with him to see his doctor in case he'd mis-heard, for I said that "if you have had one, should you really be lifting all this heavy stone?" I'd also point out that he was never breathless, and worked hard, so perhaps George had heard the diagnosis wrong.

George, I'm sure, never did check with his doctor, and poor George died sometime around 1986 I think.

I was devastated hearing the news; I'd now known George a good while, I even took my then little daughter Heather to see him, and he made a fuss with sweets and money – to Heather's delight. I also got to meet George's wife, Maria, she was an Italian lady, very pleasant, but her English wasn't that good, so felt a bit silly and tended to go into another room after a cuppa was made.

If there truly is an afterlife, then George is one man I'd love to see again. Rest in peace, George... until then.

We soon got to the planting stage, all the outer borders backed mainly by Yew trees were planted with mixed shrubs, and each side of the steps and ramp I planted Santolina 'incana' also known as 'Cotton Lavender'. All the main floral beds had mixed bedding plants, but in the centres planted the tall "African marigolds", and this is the point that I'm now able to tell you of the big surprise that I spoke of earlier on. The cucumber compost must have still had lots of goodness in it, for the "African Marigolds" just grew and grew! in fact to 4½ feet high – their stems were like mini tree trunks, and what a magnificent sight.

I was very fussy when it came to laying the lawn and made sure that the turf sat an inch or so higher than George's paving, this making it so easy when mowing and of course using the long-handled shears for the edging. (See photo)

By the August or September, the park looked so amazing, full of vibrant colours, George's stonework, the seating bays that George made now had park benches on them, the huge "Tulip Trees" Liriodendron 'tulipifera' were in full bloom, along with their saddle-shaped leaves, and a tree that you don't really get to see flower until at least its eighteen years of age. George had built a raised bed round these too, and I planted these up as well, with flowers.

Apart from the jobs in the earlier part of the project, the only other bad thing to happen was when I walked round to the area where we stored all the plants overnight, and a security guard came round the corner with his Alsatian – it was on a leash, but on seeing me took a frightening leap towards my face. Thankfully I turned very quickly, the dog bit through my shoulder. Pandemonium broke out, loads of blood, the security guard in complete shock, and pulled the dog back as hard as he could.

Luckily at this point, we were still in a very cold January/February, and I wore several layers of jumpers; the reason for the layers being that it's not too restrictive when working. I was rushed to the nearest hospital for treatment and a tetanus injection. It was not long after it came to my attention that the dog was going to be put down, but I protested and said that it wasn't the dog's fault, for it obviously hadn't been trained properly, for it should normally have attacked on command. I never knew the outcome. I *had* to be in the Union, and I was told to make a report out for compensation – I never received the price of a jumper, and from that point on, never paid to be in a Union again.

I managed to get the gardens in pristine condition, for I was told that the gardens would be opened by the local mayor. The flower beds looked so superb, for the foreman, Ron Nunn let me have what I wanted. I chose Cannas, standard Roses, standard Fuchsias, standard forms of Plumbago, Lantanas etc. The gardens were 'rich' looking, if I had to put a description on it, and proud of not only my mark that I put on it, but equal credit to George Gwarys and to the three remaining lads, for these three I'm certain now knew the reasons why I had to have good workers to complete such a project.

When I think of the overgrown junkyard that I first walked into, and the other person's very weak attempts to try and take on such a project, to now this wondrous and dare I say it... quite an atmospheric lovely garden!

We finished up on the Friday I think. George had already gone home, sadly, and I'll tell you why.

As I was making my way to the bus stop, one of the lads came running down the road, frantically calling out to me to come back, for I was supposed to be actually meeting the mayor (Councillor Vic Garwood) and to be at the official opening of the gardens, but nothing had been mentioned to me all day when we were doing the finishing touches.

I went back, and met the mayor and other dignitaries and told them all what the project had entailed. The mayor and other dignitaries did a few speeches and declared the gardens open. I walked with the mayor as we had our photographs taken for the local newspaper and the three lads just behind us, they too proud to be in the photo. So it's more's the pity that George had gone home, for he should have been with us in that photo, for he certainly put his mark on the place.

We all said our goodbyes, and finally made our way home. It wasn't until the next morning, Ron Nunn asked what happened to me yesterday afternoon. I was puzzled and asked him what he meant. It turned out once again that nobody had told me the procedure of the day, for I and the lads were supposed to have followed on and gone back to the Town Hall for tea etc.

Now the project was completed, and hopefully I'd put a feather in the Council's cap, then wondered now that they'd seen what I can really do, what they would set me to do next. I was totally shocked to be put back with just me and Billy doing our rounds again, and a separate task of picking up large stones etc. on a new site that had just been seeded over. After about three weeks of doing this I was really fed up, and even more shocked when my site foreman's pay was stopped. All the other chaps in the other gangs just could not believe it either, for each of them went to see the gardens after they were opened and said how beautiful they were. Needless to say… I left.

I'm Too Classy… fied!

Quite a few people over the years have asked if I have any qualifications, i.e. certificates etc. and of course always give a resounding "No!" for after the unjust treatment at Springfield Park, or should I say the ex C.I.D. Examiner, just felt that at that point that I was now one year behind all the others – the others being the girls… who had prettier faces than me!

The exam was to be as I'd mentioned, for a third class uncertificated, hence that first rung on the ladder. If I'd passed that the following year would sit for third-class certificated, and each year so on, that being second-class uncertificated, second-class certificated, first-class uncertificated, first-class certificated, by then you'd make your way up by means of promotion, i.e. under Foreman, Foreman, then superintendent.

Finsbury Park Training School (1960s)

FINSBURY PARK back then was classified as a first class park because of its size. The council decided to use a large area of the park to build a new training school, and training gardens. We started off very basic, with just a new hut or large shed, and Mr Galleyhawk, our one-time Foreman at Springfield Park, was our teacher for a short while, and we'd be shown round all the gardens and shrub borders at Finsbury, and be tested and taught plant names. A Mr Cooper soon joined as a teacher, and took over from Mr Galleyhawk and Mr Cooper was a very likeable chap. we had to dig out our own plots, which were fairly large oblong shapes. The turf that was taken off to form these beds was piled high in a large square shape, to make a loam heap. When rotted down, did make good loam.

162

The drainage system was still being put in for the new building and the trenches containing the pipes, were only covered with corrugated sheeting. We had to walk on these to get to and from the hut. I sadly trod on the two adjoining pieces and my leg went through, gashing my leg very badly and trapping it too! (A scar I still have.)

The new school was bright and cheerful, but didn't learn too much from Mr Cooper, for he was more on the 'chemical' side of gardening or to be precise, the scientific side, of which I had no interest. It's just that this would have no use to me on the type of gardening that I wanted to do.

When I first went to Springfield Park in 1964, you *had* to do day-release college, in fact a college for further education, at Mornington Crescent (Camden Town). I hated every minute of it, for I'd just left school, and it felt like I was back there again, and to the fact that we were doing similar lessons too, and was definitely miles out from learning anything but gardening, for Mr Cooper who later came to Finsbury, was one of our main teachers at the college, and virtually I refused to learn anything and knew I was wasting my time and theirs, for I'd waited all this time to learn about plants, trees, shrubs, pruning, propagation restoration of the same. I wanted to also learn more about the grafting of fruit-trees, how to prune a fruit-tree, how to go about making a pond, rockery, etc., etc., but all we had was science, that's all.

We even had maths classes, my very worst subject at school, and have always had 'number blindness' if there is such a term! Then a total nightmare, we had to play basket ball in a large gymnasium! I've always detested sport, because I'd rarely seen sport as a sport, only anger, rage and disappointment of players, none rarely smile, and that the players *had* to win every time. Look at the abuse and rage thrown at football refs for instance, and hard to believe they're part of a GAME, no matter how you dress it up.

The man in charge was Mr Berryman (Berriman?) and was told that he was an ex Mr Universe in the 1950s, but he released his anger on me because of my long hair – yes, it's that old subject again. He was always saying to me, and another chap who had long hair – "be a man, cut that hair!" He always flexed his muscles when saying these words. I mucked in when playing basket-ball, for like all sport at school, not one teacher actually taught you how to play football, cricket, rounders etc. Just everyone else seemed to know except me! and probably another good reason for my lack of enthusiasm.

One day, Mr Berryman told me and this other chap (who resembled the looks and hair of 60's pop singer Dave Berry) to both have our hair cut, and if we didn't we'd be thrown out of the college and out of the Parks dept.

I couldn't believe my ears. Here I was, left school, in the world of a working man, sent to college not of my choice, and told I'd lose my job because of the length of my hair. I was fuming I can tell you!

I did no more, but rang the County Hall in London, to ask to speak to Mr Gardner, the very man who took me on when with my Grandad at that interview. I relayed all that had gone on – I was quite proud of myself for sticking to what I believe. I don't remember exactly how old I was at this time, but the group 'Unit 4 + 2' were in the charts with their hit 'Concrete and Clay' and one evening at the college they had a 'college dance' and the group who starred was 'Neil Christian and The Crusaders' also known as 'Christians Crusaders' who too were riding the charts with the song 'That's Nice!' which I still have!

Mr Gardner's reply was the one I wanted, and I must admit I was so totally surprised that he actually remembered me with my Grandad when I came for an interview – "As I told you then, I'm telling you now, you can have your hair down to your arse for all I care, as long as you work hard. Get back to me if you get any problems from Mr Berryman."

Well, off I went to college that day, still not knowing if it would be my last day, until that point when it was time to bring Mr Gardner to the fore that is!

On my arrival, everyone was now waiting with baited breath to see what was going to happen, for I walked in, then the other chap, and he'd cut his hair off! They all had a real go at the poor chap who, I suppose, only wanted to save his job and continue college. "You should have stuck with Keefy" in hindsight though, looking back now, perhaps he thought I'd too come to college with a short back and sides.

Mr Berryman came over to me straight away as we got to the changing room. "What did I tell you last week? I told you what's going to happen." Then to the shock of not only him, but to all the others, told him of my phone call to Mr Gardner and what his reply was, and if there were any problems to get straight back to him. Mr Berryman and all the others stood there amazed. Nothing did ever come of it, and no more was said. I secretly liked to think that Mr Berryman had a little admiration for me after this, for I would often see him in a canoe on the River Lea at the bottom of Springfield Park; he'd always give me a cheery wave and broad smile.

I had no idea where he lived, but one day many years after saw him cycling down White Hart Lane, when I was at Haringey Parks. I still looked the same, hair even longer, and he still waved and smiled.

Probably he was now involved with the new sports complex that I spoke of at New River Yard?

I Become a Barrer Boy

Many years down the line I decided that I'd like a plant stall; well, it wasn't my idea to start with, for a chap and his wife that I knew asked if we could start up a plant stall. Little did I know then that they had no plant knowledge at all, but hoping to 'feed' off me. The chap even wanted to call the stall 'The Hybrid Plant Company'! We fell out very quickly, for he was a cocky big-headed sort of chap. I kept the stall on, and made a real go of it. It was the winters that really put paid to it, for like all gardening in the eyes of the public, comes to a dead end, and no one wants to buy plants in bitterly cold weather, even though I tried. At the start you had to pay one week in advance, therefore you missed a week, your week in advance was forfeited. So it came about that you turned up every week so's not to lose that money. The only time you saw that money again was if you decided to leave the market for good and never be able to return.

I lost my money through being ill with flu, and had nobody to take over my stall. I used to buy sacks of bulbs and plant them up in bowls; they were sometimes mixed bowls with perhaps a primrose or hyacinth added to the main bowl of daffs. My pal, Peter Blackford, took me to the famous Spitalfields Market and the newer Nine Elms; these were huge flower markets. I was introduced to several of the sellers whom Peter had done business with over many years, and Peter's words to each of them was "Look after him!" Peter hoped his words helped me, for he said to get the best deals you normally have to show your face over quite a few years, they had to get to know you.

Laughable nowadays, but they used to sell the branches 'greenery' … of the popular 'Leylandii' conifer, it was sold at £30 a bundle, such was its rarity back then. The 'Leylandii' and Yew were used as the green backing to floral bouquets etc.

I had to be up at 4 in the morning to get to the flower markets for 5–5.30. Within the markets were small shops where you could buy all items for the floristry trade, i.e. florist's wire, baskets, ribbon etc., and I bought a few novelty items to spruce up my mixed bowls. I also bought thick reams of paper, in all patterns, all ideal for wrapping, or to surround a bunch of flowers.

Funnily enough, one of my biggest sellers were not real flowers at all, they were dried sprigs of 'butcher's broom', stuck in a pot to make it look like they were growing, in turn the sprigs were sprayed silver, gold or whatever, sprayed again with a glue, then straight away minute balls of polystyrene were fired at the sprigs. The 'balls' would either be of one colour, two colours and so on, hence making each 'plant' look very different from the next.

I made a sign up reading… LOOK! the plant that needs no soil, water or feed, just dust once a week!… I sold every one I'm pleased to say, and helped to make a little money during those freezing market days.

I used to look over to another stall who were doing a roaring trade – they were fairground showmen, and sold hot apple and pineapple fritters, they looked so easy to make, yet had queues all day from the moment they opened.

I managed to buy some packets of seeds all past their so-called 'sell by date'. I pierced a hole at the tops of the packs and threaded them all on strings; these I strung to the 'beams' of the stall and the uprights, and made the stall look so colourful, moreso in the dull days of winter. I'd also sell the packets at a mere 5p or 10p, but warned the public that the seed may have lost its viability, therefore no great loss of money, but a real bonus if they germinated.

I soon learnt that I didn't really need to go to flower markets to buy my stock, and went to several garden centres and growers to get their best trade prices, and could do this in more sensible daylight hours, plus I'd pot up my own stuff from my garden with no real layout.

My stall often looked vibrant and well stocked, and made use of every bit of space allocated. We were on what they called 'The Lea Valley Trading Estate', directly off the main North Circular Road, so it was always a busy market.

Arthur and Amy Laws had a flower stall down Walthamstow's famous High Street for many years, and at one time in sort of partnership with John Harker of Northfields Garden Centre, E4. John did the growing as I remember, and Arthur did the selling. They had a disagreement over something and they parted company.

Arthur came to see me at my stall, and he praised me so highly for my great efforts. It's great when someone gives you praise, it lets you know you're going in the right direction. I remember at Northfields one year when Arthur lost over a thousand pounds worth of bedding plants after a late frost came, he was devastated. This was a nursery quick to learn though, for like all nurseries, they liked to start selling summer bedding quite early, moreso the hardier bedding plants like Antirrhinums, Calendula, Pansies, etc.

It used to be a recognised rule that you never plant out at least until the second week of June, so as the fear of severe frosts had gone. Northfields always sold theirs at the correct time, but suffered financial losses because they waited 'too late' and folk bought from elsewhere instead. The only time they came out on top was if there was a very late frost and people lost most of their plants, they'd flock to Northfields because their stock had only just gone on sale.

As mentioned, they were quick learners and eventually put up very sensible signs, more or less saying that the plants here are all for sale today, but we advise you not to plant out until at least the second week of June. At least the public saw the honesty of the firm and good advice. It goes without saying this all worked very well, and Northfields were very successful from then on, and John Harker's two sons very soon learnt the trade (David and Alan) and put their own mark on the nursery.

John Harker's brother, Gordon (wife Sylvia) has also a large garden centre over the road, and such were the frosts there, Gordon's words still echo to me today "If it survives here, it'll survive anywhere!" 'Chapelfield Nursery' must, I assume, lay in a frost pocket. Gordon and me are still in contact today. It was Gordon's plants and sundries that I used when creating the gardens for the Walthamstow Building Society, where we won the 'London-in-Bloom Competition' for many years running! The certificates were always on show above the customers' counters.

I hadn't had a holiday for years, so when the papers came to take my photo re: the 'London-in Bloom', I was away, so the lovely manager Pat O'Brien took my place.

Like so many garden centres, growers etc., they discard thousands of plants, shrubs etc. that supposedly look shabby and pot-bound etc. The whole of my life money has never come easy to me, albeit have always been an extremely hard worker – my only self-praise! When at Northfields one year I asked if there was anything that I could take from their dump, I was open with them and said that I'd nurture the plants back to health then try to sell them, they knew that little ol' me was never a threat to them so they gave me full permission, which was very admirable of them.

I literally filled my van with all sorts, and I was so excited that I'd forgotten to think about the weight that I could carry – had I been pulled up they would have thrown the book at me if I'd had to go on a weigh-bridge. Anyhow, some of the better looking plants were lilies, just the one variety, and each one still had a label in it and was Lilium 'formosanum pricei'. I couldn't find it listed anywhere, but then looked through one or two RHS journals, and by chance someone had done an article on it, and went on to say that it was a rare lily, and found so many thousand feet in the Himalayas, and mine had been thrown on a dump! I have not seen the name since, so possibly today still a rare lily?

What a Total Waste of Money

Going back to the Haringey Parks Dept for a minute, and one little story that I forgot to mention, and still to do with the idiotic bonus system, was when it was my job one winter to do tree-planting. I really loved this job, and love trees too, and wished the council back then had the same affection for them, instead of trying to flog a dead horse with the useless bonus system.

It was nice getting up each day knowing exactly what my job was. I'd know all the materials that I'd need to do this job properly, or *tried* to do the job I should say. Each and every day we were somewhere different, that is *we* being Bill and me. It could be a school, shopping precinct, housing estate, park, or just on a verge of a road in an ordinary street.

It goes without saying, soils varied at each place, and I always felt so sad for the trees that just didn't have a fair start in life, even though I tried, and refer to clay or very sticky soils, this type of soil is impossible to filter through a tree's 'anchor' and 'fibrous' roots, to stop any air gaps and a sure fire death knell for any tree.

I would explain to the yard foreman that as they know, I was given first class trees to plant, many twenty foot high specimens too at times, all done I think to perhaps deter vandals, each thinking that the trees were older ones and had been in for several years. I'd explain to the foreman that to try and plant a tree properly in clay or sticky soil was totally impossible, and a total waste of time and money, planting perfectly good healthy trees, knowing that they would soon die.

I asked if I could be supplied on site, some fine soil, but the foreman/Council, refused because of the time factor of the bonus system. Where I could, on the various sites, I'd nip over to the nearest shrub border and pinch some soil to filter through the tree's roots, to at least try to save as many as I could. Sadly, it was mostly the case where we dug a hole, put the tree in and backfilled with clay, even heavy treading would not push the clay through, and a large air-pocket would be created i.e. like making a clay roof for a 'tent' etc. We'd leave the tree perfectly tied and staked, knowing full well that the tree would die, all for the sake of half a barrowful of fine soil or compost.

I see so many things on TV today that I'm so unhappy with, for even with good fine soil, the presenters do not plant trees as I was taught, that method being to dig a hole slightly wider than the width of the tree roots, fork over the bottom, then place a mound of fine soil or compost in the centre of the hole, and sit the tree roots on top, spreading the roots if possible sloping down the mound. The stake at this point already being driven in with a sledge hammer or tree pummel, a heavy metal tube with two handles on each side that goes over the top of the stake, then either single-handedly, or preferably two people, lift this up and down hard, so the pummel drives the stake in. I did this mostly single-handedly each day!

Once the tree was on the mound you pour in the finest soil possible. The next stage was to lift the tree up and down, hence shaking and filtering the soil through the root system, and you keep doing this until all the soil has filtered through nicely and covered the roots. Now it's time to tread firmly, your heel was what you used to do this because all your weight can be put to good use. You then keep adding your soil until level with the growing point of the tree, and to never go over this point. You then water in thoroughly, the water still further pushing the finer soil through even more to fill air pockets.

The following day you can tread again, then top up with more good soil or compost. If frost is forecast, then tread each day when the frost fades, for frost can actually lift the soil, and once again air gaps are formed. This rule goes to *all* newly planted plants and shrubs.

Two old rules that seem to have gone out of the window, is that a garden cane would be placed across the hole to show the level point of where the depth of the tree should be at its growing point, hence the mound of soil made up to that level. The other golden rule was that the stake had to reach the more or less total height of the tree, allowing no movement, and as many ties as was needed, six usually, being the most. I'm not one for modern ideas, and correct planting of trees seems to be long gone, but modern staking does actually make a lot of sense.

The experts came to the decision that once the stake had rotted away, and the tree's being supported for the whole of its young life, were the very trees that fell down in even moderate high winds. The modern idea to use the short stake set at an angle with just the one tie, allowed the tree to sway in all weathers, and allow it to adapt. Over the years the tree would gain strength, hence would stand OK when the stake was taken away.

More Broken Golden Rules

Sadly, I don't get to see many gardening programmes, but when I do watch I am always critical, mumbling away either in my head, or the nearest people sitting with me – they get the brunt of my annoyance with "I was not taught to do it like that!", hence if I did sit for a practical exam today, I'd fail it again!

You never see TV gardeners really plant shrubs or plants correctly, just a couple of presses with the hands around plants, and a mild light step round shrubs where air must get in. Of course TV would not show you losses. Still today, 2009 I use a heavy turf pummer to pum down turf to aid a good level, to help bind to the soil, and level equal to the next turf.

Long before I used a turf pummer, I used to whack the turf with the back of a spade, and the vibrations from that alone contributed to painful knuckle joints even then as a young man. I look at TV gardeners today just lightly tapping the turf with the back of an ordinary garden rake; I find this laughable, if I'd done that then I would have definitely been classed as a 'cowboy' gardener, plus real cowboy gardeners see all this and see how landscape gardening, or turfing at least seems so easy today.

Whilst I'm in whingeing mode, I'll tell you of more modern-day ideas. My son Rowan sat for various exams in the world of reed management, chainsaw, weed-killing, etc., and as he'd worked with me for some time, I was able to show him the 'old' ways, or should say how I have always gardened. Rowan would come back from college and relay some of those jobs of work to me and tell me how the work is… or SHOULD be carried out now.

When talking to me it seemed that I'd gardened wrongly all my working life! and many of the new rules so totally ridiculous. Let's begin with weed-killing: I'd used weed-killers since first starting work in 1964, along with the chainsaw at the age of fifteen, and for many years used the deadly weed-killer Paraquat. We were taught how to use them safely and efficiently. Out of the blue a few years ago now I started to get numerous calls to do weed-killing, and very profitable it was too, but damned hard work carrying a large knapsack-sprayer on your back. One young landscaper offered me all his spraying work, mainly around factories, warehouses and such like, and told me that he didn't have any certificates, and hadn't realised that he had to have them. I of course told him that I'd used all types of weed-killers since 1964 and that I also did not have a certificate, I certainly hadn't been told that I'd need one.

The chap said that I didn't need one, and because I'd been using them since such and such a year, i.e. 1960 something, I had what they called 'Grandfathers Rights'. I'd never heard of this, so happily took on all the weed-killing work possible, and probably explained why other landscapers gave up doing this type of work. I then assumed that because of the amount of enquiries I was getting, thought that perhaps there'd been a notification in a magazine or newspaper?

I carried on doing weed-killing for another six years or so. My son Rowan rang me one evening, and at the time that he was training for weed-killing work, and said, "Dad, you mustn't do weed-killing any more, 'Grandfathers Rights' apparently went out three years ago, and if I was caught I could be fined a thousand pounds!" Rowan went on to tell me that I'd have to go on a course to get a certificate. I couldn't believe my ears, and there was me working on a building, directly next to the Ministry of Fisheries! They'd have thrown the book at me. There was no way that I was going back to a college to learn what I'd been doing for nearly all my life, and certainly could not spare the time to do it. The same goes with chainsaws, I'd worked them too since 1964 all without protective gear!

Chainsaws are dodgy to use though, and fully appreciate why protective clothing has to be worn, the same as with weed-killers. Where was I supposed to go to be told of all these changes? I don't buy gardening books or magazines, for I feel I know my trade, and do exactly how I was taught and self-taught, for who is going to knock on my door to tell me of all these numerous changes that occur now on such a regular basis?

I was also taught that pruning or sawing off a branch from a tree, to cut flush with the trunk, then paint with a pruning compound. Rowan says, "That's wrong, Dad!" they now say you should leave a snag of at least an inch or so. I showed Rowan in an instant how the old method should be done, and at that point was able to show him how the new method did not work, and could prove it on the very tree that we were working on. One snag of about an inch had died, and the die back had started to travel down the trunk a few inches, thus harming the tree. The old way would have been sealed and on the way to recovery. Another snag showed itself as re-sprouting, for the snag had a bud on it, the bud of course meant new growth, and therefore caused no die back, but at the same time you still had a 'branch' that in the first place was unwanted anyway, and again if it had been cut flush, this would not have occurred. Just a few years ago, a property developer whom I know, offered me some work to restore very old and neglected ornamental trees and shrubs, and without hesitation I asked if he wanted one particularly very neglected tree 'repaired' the old way or the new way.

The property developer promptly said, "Would you like to speak to a tree expert?!" I said, "Yes please, I'd *love* to speak to a tree expert!" The man dialled then handed the phone to me. The chap on the other end said, "How can I help you?" and I told him that it wasn't his help I needed, but just wondered how *he* would solve a 'problem'. I told him that I had an old apple tree in front of me that must have had a branch die at some point, or had been the victim of a 'hack prune' somewhere along the line.

The bad cut was now full of water and gungy dead leaves etc. The chap butted in quickly and told me that I must leave it as it is, for all the organisms in the water helped to protect the tree, I gave a little laugh, and said to him that I didn't want to appear rude, and said that he sounded like a young chap to me, and he said he was, so I went on to say that I've not heard of such clap-trap in all my days. The chap replied "Really!?" and then went on to ask me how I would go about it, and told him that my way was the way it had always been done. He then graciously asked about this old method, of which he knew absolutely nothing about, and I relayed it all to him, and he even agreed that 'my' way was so logical. I expect at this point he was wondering what else he'd been taught wrongly. I said that you just can't come into the 1990s and Millennium years, and change the rules of generations – all those bods sitting in offices all day, changing methods and plant names i.e. like the Hollyhock for instance, how come the name is now Alcea 'rosea' instead of Althea 'rosea', or the lovely Datura which is now a Brugmansia.

The chap listened to all I had to say on how I was going to save this tree, and 'my' methods have *never* let me down, and I could almost hear a tree or shrub saying "Thank you for saving me!"

The property developer was himself now listening to me very intently.

Step One: Push a garden cane into all the gunge.

Step Two: Take the cane out and hold it to the outside of the trunk from the top of the hole.

Step Three: Mark the trunk where the bottom of the cane rests, i.e. with chalk, coloured tape etc., take the cane away.

Step Four: Hand-drill with the widest drill bit 1½ inches and drill into the now marked spot. The drill hole should be level or very near level to the bottom of the hole, and the water should now start pouring out. You can poke a slightly thinner split cane in and out of the hole to keep the hole clear to rid of every drop of water and gunge!

Step Five: Once all the water is out you can then hose out the hole, or pour in water from a bucket or water can and thoroughly clean the hole.

I used to use the old winter wash Mortegg to do this job, this would kill off anything lurking. The hole now when it rains should never fill with water again with the now ready-made drain hole now on the tree. I'd also make every attempt with a chisel to clear any dead or rotting wood from the hole, you'll never get the lot out, but at least air was circulating and would stay dry.

Right up until they did away with the very large tins of tree compound (the same compound that was used for treating all pruning cuts over ½ inch) you could mix this compound with sharp sand, and make a cement-type mix; this would then be packed into the clean hole, not forgetting to plug the drainage hole, easily done by putting a piece of card or strong polythene against the 'drain-hole' and held in place with drawing pins or simply tied on tightly, this can be removed the very next day. You also do the same treatment to the now smooth top of the hole. You had now saved your tree, and soon see much improved vigour.

One, or should I say two of my successes were at Barsham Rectory, Suffolk, and restored from very poor health to great vigour, Magnolia 'Soulangeana' that had been pruned for no apparent reason. The second was Magnolia 'Campbellii', and had grown literally into a tree-like status; the blooms come out in February and a very welcome sight for that time of year.

The 'wounds' on this were of a fair size, and it was so pitiful to see such a magnificent specimen so neglected. I did all the cleaning out, chisel work etc. made up cement mixed with 'Arbrex' compound and filled the massive holes, but finishing off with the usual mix of 'Arbrex' and sharp sand to make a very smooth clean finish. The then owners didn't want to spend money for me to finish this job, so dearly hope this tree stands proud today! (They were multi-millionaires!)

Since the demise of the large tins of Arbrex compound and 'Mortegg', today I leave the hole open with the drain, and I can still wash out with the modern day equivalent of a winter wash, and paint as far into the hole with again the modern compound. Perhaps with all this work, perhaps it's no wonder that it is easier to leave wounds filled with gungy water – after all, no one wants to work hard anymore?

A Nightmare Pond

Sometime in the early 1990s I was called out by a lady to give her an estimate to restore her pond. The lady was very snooty la-de-dah, and didn't think for one minute that I'd get the job, and with her very off-handed tone on that first meet, I didn't really want the job! As always in cases like this, as most tradesmen do, we up our prices – this is done to lose the job, and if it's accepted, you are the getting paid for all the aggravation!

The pond wasn't that big, I'd say 8ft x 8ft x 3ft deep; the surround of the pond was made up of very old house bricks, about four bricks high so as to make a sort of path as well as a fairly natural looking edge to the pond with the old red brick that had a fair amount of moss on it, so it looked like it had been there years, and for all I know it probably had been.

The pond also had a seat built of house bricks, this too sat near the edge of the pond, hence your feet were on the brick path. There was hardly a drop of water in the pond, for it was choked with pond weed of all descriptions, and included various very congested pond plants. I had no idea if the pond was a concrete one, fibreglass or liner, it was in fact the latter.

The house bricks were set on a ledge, which in turn held down the liner, then built higher to eventually create this path edge and seat. I took out some ninety bricks or so, scrubbed them clean and stood them all in neat piles on the grass, until ready to replace them once the pond was thoroughly clean.

I kept in place the old liner, and put in a new one. All the pond plants had been split up and re-potted so that the pond had a very fresh start. I then had the task of replacing all the bricks carefully, starting with the bottom layer on the ledge, hence the first two rows or so stood actually in the water, then build up gradually from there, then proceed to build the seat, then the best bit, and that is to put in all the water, therefore a brand new nicely restored pond.

The snooty lady was very happy, and her tone over the three days had softened, and I was not someone for her to be wary of anymore, for hopefully she'd got to know me a little, moreso as we stood in her potting shed, where I showed her how pond baskets were made up.

Hers and my happiness was however short-lived., for I had an irate telephone call from her early the next morning, to tell me that the pond was EMPTY! To her I was a cowboy again. She ranted on about the cost and so on, and I tried in vain to explain to her that I was as baffled as she was, and that I'd put it right, or should say hopefully put it right, for as far as I was concerned I'd done the job 100% perfect.

On my arrival I was met with a stern face, and low angry tone of voice. Anyhow, I rolled up my sleeves and had a good feel round. The water was very clear, and thought that I would find something that had perhaps pierced the liner, but no, I couldn't find a thing. It then crossed my mind that it might be a thorn or piece of glass that had gone through the original liner then into the new one, and may have been the cause of the original water loss in the very clogged up pond, albeit still at the start was at least three quarters full.

I was now looking at a totally empty pond with a couple of mere puddles. I then dismantled all the brick seat, and all the many bricks and stacked them once again, took out all the pond plants and removed the liner, and still looking for a sharp object, I even hung the liner on the washing line to see any glimpses of daylight through it, but nothing. I ran my hands over the old liner, and once again... nothing. I commenced to re-build the pond once again with all the bricks, and put the pond plants back in position and then filled the pond.

Once again the pond looked superb, and at least put the smile on the woman's face, if only the fact that at least I turned up to put the problem right.

I was to be totally shocked the next morning when the woman was irate yet again, and told me that the water had seeped away, but had remained three-quarters full. I went back again and dismantled the pond completely for a third time, and each time as baffled as the last. This time when I took off the liner, I laid the old bits of carpet, cloth, bin and compost bags in the pond, then the liner, and once more built the pond complete.

It was at this point when re-building, I realised what the problem had been all along! It was the bricks! They of course being porous had soaked up all the water on that first occasion, for whilst I'd stacked them on the lawn for a few days all the water had drained from them, hence the second time, they'd absorbed a bit more and so on.

Later that day when I'd hoped that this would be my last time with this pond, I went to see a friend of mine Terry Coleman who had a homely aquatic nursery, and told him of my long saga, of which I lost out financially. Terry then said that he'd bet a pound to the penny that tomorrow when the lady rings, the pond would be full, for Terry said that years back he too had a similar mystery, for he said that he used to tie a couple of house bricks round his water lilies to hold them down in big buckets ready for sale, and the next day the buckets would be empty, and soon realised it was the porous bricks taking up all the water.

Terry was right, the lady did ring me to say that at last the water was at top level. I was then, with great relief, able to tell her the whole story. I said that the first two layers or so of bricks in the water took up a lot of water, then the rest of the water seeped into the brick seat which in turn sat on the brick path, which in turn again was partly built in the water!

I'm certain that the lady thought I was a 'cowboy' worker all along, for nothing went right for me, but I'd like to think that after the explanation she thought better of me?

I'm Talking a Load of Rubbish!

No change there then, some of you might say! But on a more serious note, getting rid of garden rubbish today is a great problem, and each and every Council throughout the country is to blame in my opinion.

Because I am a landscape gardener I'm classed as a trade, and therefore have to pay to dump garden rubbish, which of course is paid by the customer. When first moving from Walthamstow to Kessingland, I had to find out where the local tips were, and when I did, I was told "You can dump just this once but never again!" The same words were used at all the tips that I went to.

I contacted one of the heads of the Council, and said that I'd like to ask a few questions, and he agreed. I asked that if they'd had complaints say about an unkempt garden, i.e. there were rats, mice etc., and someone like me comes along and clears it, then I'm not allowed to dump it simply because my name is on my van or trailer and classed as a trade. The customer is a rate payer and so am I, so because the client/ratepayer has no means of conveying the rubbish themselves (which would be free), I have to take it instead for them.

The Council then argued that I was getting paid to take the rubbish away, which I'm not really. Yes, it comes in with the labour charge, but the rubbish side of it was a real menace, and only something that needed to be done so that I can get on with the proper gardening.

I said too that the Council may argue that the client should have a skip, but these are very costly what with landfill charges etc. and why would a client want a skip when they're completely legal to take it to a tip free if they could drive or have a trailer without signs on it.

I also pointed out that on occasions folk could neither afford a skip or the Council fees for me to dump (usually on a weighbridge) so the pile of rubbish stays where it is and back come the vermin! I pointed out to the chap and said that this is why there's so much rubbish dumped in the countryside because you make it so difficult for people to get rid of rubbish.

Another thing I mentioned and that was that I was a rate payer as well as a gardener, and had to pay to dump the rubbish from my garden. He said, "You shouldn't have to do that, sir!" I said, that not all my garden rubbish could even come close to getting it all in the green bin, I'd need about fifty! I do in fact have to fill at least three of those huge bags that sand and ballast comes in these days, then pay to dump it. He then said, "Well, I don't make the rules," so I said that he should find out who does for this needs looking into. I said that surely if someone takes the time to load up a van or trailer and make the effort to come to a tip, it means they want to be clean and tidy, and the likes of builders and landscapers etc. are only working for other people, rate payer! and shouldn't be shunned just because we have our names on our vehicles.

One friend of mine, just an ordinary householder, had re-tiled his bathroom, and bagged up all the old tiles and bits of plaster, all into bags just about manageable to carry. He loaded his van up (he could so easily had dumped it in the countryside) took it to the tip, where they told him that he was only allowed to leave two bags a day! So he left the bags, returned the next day to find the same two bags, just sitting there where he left them! He then hoped that no one would come over to him, thinking that these were the bags he'd just dropped off!

We can only assume that the two bags a day was to stop tradesmen coming in with unmarked vans without their names on.

A lady asked if I could do her a favour and take away some household rubbish for her, so took it to a tip and a cocky bloke came out. "You can't dump that, but we'll take that, and that, but not those" or words to that effect. I couldn't believe it, for I only had items of metal or wood, so dumped the items that I was allowed to dump, and brought back the rest to my house. It was at this point that I saw the dustmen at the bottom of our road, so quickly put an old typewriter in the bin, and bent up the metal holders that hold fluorescent lighting, along with other items that so easily could have gone to the tip. Later, along came the dustmen, took it all away… to dump it at the tip where I'd just come from!

One chap where we live got so fed up of being turned away, again an ordinary householder, and turned away because he had a trailer with four wheels on it. The chap had a good idea and telephoned the local TV station to come and witness something pathetic! Hence the TV people filmed secretly the man being turned away because of the four wheels, and was filmed taking off two of his wheels and then they let him in – work that one out!

When I look back to when I was a boy in the 1950s, the dust carts used to once a month put on a large wire-meshed trailer, and they would take away your old cooker, beds, fridges, etc, all free of charge; no doubt the councils then had a buyer for it all? These days too when the chaps used to lift the bins onto their shoulders whatever weight was in them, they did it with such ease, real tough breed they were; now the bins are on wheels and no lifting when it comes to emptying into the dust-cart, they can also more or less today go to work in a suit!

I had to laugh one day, for one of the dustmen who came to our house, refused to take my bin over to the lorry just a few feet away, so offered to do it for him! He refused and wouldn't take the bin unless I offloaded it a bit!

I looked back at my working life, and still I'm working hard today, and wonder if it was all worth it, but as people tell me "Keith, you can certainly hold your head up."

Wealthy School 'Kids'

When I used to go to the day-release college at Mornington Crescent, Camden Town, I got very pally with a chap. He was a pleasant sort of chap, brilliant sense of humour and a good family man.

Every word of what I have just written, soon became the exact opposite, and turned out to be one of the nastiest people that I have ever met in my life.

To think that my wife and I had been to his home at least once every couple of months, and even the odd day out together. It was at the time that we were house-hunting to hopefully move to Suffolk, we had just been gazumped a couple of times, and it had just happened again when 'A' approached me about a job. I'll refer to him as 'A' from now on, for it's more the pity that by law you cannot mention that person by name!

The job, however, did sound attractive, for 'A' had got the job as the head-groundsman for a public school, some sixty-odd acres I think, and that didn't include the gardens, and that's where I was needed. Much later on 'A' admitted to me that he really did bluff his way when questions came up at his interview, and relayed to me with a laugh on what he'd actually said, and to a layman it did sound plausible but it was total rubbish!

My interview was with the Bursar, and above him was the Head Master, who in turn had two elderly secretaries. I passed the interview with flying colours.

'A' whom I now knew as a bluffer, soon saw that he was brimming with confidence and authority, for this was the first time in his life (he was in his very late thirties then) that he'd actually ever been in charge of anything in his life, and go to his head it did!

At first 'A' was finding his feet, and made sure that everybody in the school knew who he was. He'd secured a tied house, and the whole house was done up to his specification, in fact anything that he wanted he could have – house or garden.

I thought this a mystery, for normally you'd take a tied house and that was it, and you had to pay out of your own pocket for any other fancy work.

'A' would set me tasks to do, and quite enjoyed the authority over me, he fully knowing that I was quite capable of running the whole lot. At other times he did leave me alone, and I commenced setting about suggesting ideas to him and the Bursar, for being an old school, the place had character but everywhere was dark and dismal.

It wasn't long before I brightened the place up, not only with brilliant summer bedding which included 'dot' plants, but set about refurbishing old shrub beds, and adding new plants. There were small woodland areas, that I enjoyed planting up, and most certainly had not had any plants or shrubs in them for many, many years.

It goes without saying, I was getting praises from everyone, all the masters and mistresses (teachers!) stopped to talk to me and ask questions, and even some of the older pupils of 18–19 years old or so took a keen interest. I found all this very strange too, for I looked back to all that I had achieved by that age, and all the work that I'd done, to think they were still at school and even stranger to see them driving to school mostly in sports cars that 'Mummy and Daddy' had bought them.

It certainly made me wonder how they had any self-worth, how much more would be given to them without doing an ounce of work? One or two of the much older working-class men said that during both world wars, the conscripted public school 'boys' were the ones who had been so molly-coddled all their life, that army life and war drove very many to suicide, for none were streetwise and knew not even the basics of life. The pupils that were brought to school by parents all had very flash cars, all trying to outdo the next person, and the ladies all look like they were off to a fashion show! Most however, were very friendly, and spoke to me on many occasions and asking for gardening advice.

Over the past couple of years or so, the old school had introduced GIRLS! all sixth formers, and was told that a good proportion of the boys hated the idea, and I witnessed this myself on one occasion, when one or two were abusive to the girls showing their disapproval. I thought the girls certainly brightened the place up, one even sent me a Valentine card one year – I say sent it, it was handed to me by one of the girls, I had to discard that quickly at work in case my wife saw it!

The two labourers that 'A' had were both yobs, very cocky, and as much as I tried to befriend them, I was ignored, which suited me fine, as I knew by that point that 'A' was setting them against me. He was very put out by all the attention I was getting, for the gardens looked so nice, and this school I was told had not seen such beauty in years. 'A' by now was getting more arrogant towards me, and instead of him looking at me as a feather in his cap for getting me there, he became very jealous. Being a public school, 'A' tried very hard to get in with people, and there were plenty of intellectuals to try and get in with. I actually got on very well with the headmaster and his wife, who were both avid gardeners and did a lot to restore their garden (tied house) which was literally amassed with the early celandine, a menace of a weed, very pretty, but soon dies down after flowering and not seen until the following spring. The Head Master and his wife we were told, kept 'A' at a distance, hence he not being able to understand how I was getting on so well with them, but people are not silly – you can all spot a chancer or someone trying too hard to make themselves popular, and the Head Master saw through him like a sheet of glass, but wondered why the Head Master had no power to stop his antics, of which I'll now tell you about.

We have all heard of Freemasons, but to this day I do not know exactly what they do, only being told of the well known coded handshakes and trouser leg-pulling, and helping various charities, you had to have money and that they all helped each other in business etc. Now I do have friends today who are Masons, and have never asked what it all entails, but at this school I saw how Freemasonry had a 'power' amongst its members, a sort of hush-hush even when things were so very, very wrong as in the case of 'A'. The things that happened was certainly a case of turning a blind eye, and then set us all to wondering what other things freemasons could hide? for 'A' should have, without any doubt, have had instant dismissal.

It all came to light that 'A' was a Freemason, which probably then explained how he got his house and garden to an extremely high standard. His money came from owning a record company, and owning the sole rights to two long-dead rock musicians. The freemasonry side also did explain a lot more things that cropped up. One of the first odd things to happen was on the school's speech day, where anyone who was anyone to do with the school was there. All the staff had to be there too, i.e. maintenance men, painters, plumbers, electricians, cleaners, cooks etc., etc., then to our great shock 'A' came on stage dressed in a white suit! and ad-libbed a very embarrassing speech for the appraisal to the Bursar, Head Master etc., all to boost himself up by buttering up everyone.

None of the working staff could believe it. "What's he doing up there? He's only the groundsman!" In fact most of us were laughing. I look back now and wonder who actually gave him permission to stand up and do a speech, for everyone said that no other groundsman there had ever done such a thing before. He was so determined that each and every person should know who he was, he was also seen to be in a private select bar, that stood out away on the school field, and a place for Masons' events etc.

The school often took on two self-employed painters, both nice young chaps, but one of them came into the tea room one morning and said, "Someone's got into my car and wrapped a dead eel around the steering wheel!" 'A' proudly said in front of us all in the canteen, "It was me, what are you going to do about it?" The poor painter was fuming, "What am I going to do, you'll see what I'll do," (he reported the incident to both the Head and the Bursar) "if you ever touch my car again, I'll do you!" All of us in the canteen were stunned. Neither the Head nor the Bursar did anything.

Later the next day, the painter came into the canteen for the afternoon break, again fuming, and even wilder than before, he'd been out buying more paint when a vile smell was in his car and smoke from the engine. It turned out that 'A' had somehow got into the chap's car again, sometime in the morning, and put another dead eel on the engine, and with the heat, it had exploded.

Once again we were all astonished at 'A's remarks of "you can't touch me" but the painter fumed, "not here maybe, but outside watch your back" and the painter for a second time reported him and told what had gone on, again nothing was ever done. Later in the summer, everyone jumped back in shock when sitting round the school pond, for 'A' had put in several large American Bull frogs – he thought it hilarious.

Often staff would go to the foyer area of the school, and one teacher would ask where so and so was today, or what class they were attending etc. One of the teachers one day asked 'A' where Mrs Bird was, he'd obviously been asked this question before, so on this occasion reached into his pocket, threw down some bird seed on the main foyer floor and said, "now I've put that down she'll find it and be here in a minute!" – Yes, I'm *still* talking about the Head Groundsman of a public school!

A new young chap started work at the school as an assistant gardener, and was partially deaf, and soon cottoned on to how 'A' operated and the chap gave as good as he got, and was verbally sarcastic to 'A' when he was rude or arrogant. One day David was asked to give a message to a teacher re. her preference of choice of shrubs to be planted outside her classroom. The lady teacher was notably grossly overweight. David asked 'A' whom it was he had to ask for, so 'A' said, "Her name is Mrs Bigpeice!" David, as I said, was partially deaf, and had to double-check with 'A' regarding the name. David said, "How unfortunate to have a name like that and being on the big side too!" Needless to say, David got into a lot of trouble, for he of course asked for her by name. David said how sorry he was for the 'error' and told the teacher that it was 'A' who told him that it was her name; the teacher this time reported 'A' and again nothing was done about it.

David felt absolutely terrible about the situation, and disliked 'A' even moreso now for humiliating him, and of course the poor teacher. One morning in the canteen, 'A' quipped an awful remark to David in front of us all, and David gave an answer; not many minutes after, David almost just sat down when out of the blue 'A' pulled the chair away from him. David fell to the ground, banged his head and hurt his back. The staff were in uproar at David's harsh treatment, one older man stood up and said that this was "a very wicked thing to do, you deserve a good pasting." 'A' replied simply, "Yeah, you and whose army?" Again the older man, plus one or two others, reported the incident, and as you can guess… nothing done again!

'A' was making himself more and more unpopular, yet it never bothered him, for he was safe in the power of being a mason, his job and position was secure.

Rumours were out that the Head Master at least was far from happy with all that had gone on, and moreso when 'A' started to go to the private bar mentioned earlier, but we were told that the Head Master's hands were tied.

I carried on creating beautiful areas, which included a main car park that had an old wall all round it and old neglected beds, which I planted up with very many old classic roses. I fixed wires to the old wall for the climbers and ramblers etc. Sadly, I never saw any of it in bloom, for I left the school soon after I planted it all up, and was my last ever project at this school. I can hand on heart say I left my mark at this school, and even today, some twenty-five or so years later, wonder how the Bursar explained my absence. I'd shown some of the staff how to restore trees and shrubs, even making hand balls of sticky soil to stick in the likes of sedums, sempervivums and Linaria 'cymbalaria' etc. to the crevices of the very old brick work to add even more colour and 'oldness'. I planted unusual hedges, unusual shrubs etc., all made good talking points.

One of my most favourite projects to do was to plant up an area outside the music rooms, which were all at ground level, hence a fantastic view for everyone concerned. I planted thousands, and I mean thousands of mainly mini bulbs of every description possible, for the long year ahead, i.e. snowdrops, aconites, chionadoxa, muscari, scilla, cyclamen (both spring and autumn types) crocus, gladiolus 'nanus', anemone, Leucojums, Ixias, Tigridias, Lilies, tulips, daffs, narcissi, tritelias etc. The area was flat, so I suggested adding natural rock (Westmorland stone) for the illusion of height.

Sadly, I only got to see this spectacular sight twice. It was noted that this was the Head Master's favourite area, so wouldn't you think that it would have been a sacking offence to destroy it? for after I left, I kept in contact with the Head Master's housekeeper, and she told me how 'A' tried his best to destroy the area, for obviously he knew it was my creation, and knew that the Head and I got on, and also knew that it was the Head's favourite bit of garden.

The housekeeper laughed though and said yes he had tried to destroy the area, but said that I'd planted so many thousands, it was impossible to eradicate them all. She told me that this was the first thing he did once I'd left.

I found it strange that the Head master said nothing, for surely this would have been mason against mason, and no doubt why nothing was ever said?

One of the lady music teachers had loved this area too, for I'd done my best to keep the colour going all year with Colchicums, schizostylis, etc., for late colouring. This lady asked me if I could restore her own private garden at home, and I readily agreed. 'A' was mortified! for perhaps in his warped mind he thought that I was doing what he wasn't succeeding in doing by getting 'in' with the teachers! for the teacher was no doubt telling colleagues what I was doing in her garden too.

On the subject of private work, I worked privately on a job of work at weekends, and on my days off, and on one job where I used up my two weeks' holiday. This was a huge job where I had to single-handedly move 40 tons of sandy sub-soil, and spread it over the site before seeding the whole lot. The area had to be cleared of tons of rubble – the rubble I found out was from the bombed houses from the blitz in London's East End, apparently when all the clearing was taking place, it was taken out to the countryside to allow a clear way for rebuilding.

I was working away happily on this project when I saw a car pull up that I recognised – it belonged to 'A'. He had heard that I'd taken on private work, and made a point of finding me. I was flabbergasted when he asked what I was doing there, and that I was not allowed to do private work whilst working for the school Here was I in my own time, on my holiday weeks and nothing to do with the school whatsoever. He was of course envious of the extra money I was earning too, and quite a considerable sum too for this project.

Although he only approached me just once on the actual site (he of course said nothing of his private work in the music industry), he spied on me two or three times or more after.

On one of these occasions I came over to him sitting in his car that was hidden behind a hedge; it was my turn for questions: "Why do you keep spying on me, does the Bursar know you're spending so much time away from the school? Have you sneaked out before when we've all been working hard at the school? we also know your dad is dying, so shouldn't you be spending every valuable minute at his bedside to savour those last days of life, instead of spying on me all the time? You're disgusting!"

Apparently he did report me, but nobody said anything, nor did they seem to be concerned when I told them all that had gone on, and asked why he was even allowed to come out of work time to find me on my working holiday.

The chap who was the only one to work closest to me on the gardens was a nice bloke called Bill, he was an alcoholic and was a very sad case indeed. Bill had the small bungalow next to 'A' and was in very poor condition and Bill made it moreso because of his problem. Bill, because of his drinking, was not always on time in the mornings, but to me proved a good worker when he did come in. It soon became obvious that 'A' wanted Bill out, in fact sacked, even though 'A' knew of the very sad story behind Bill's heavy drinking sessions, and all done to blur out a very bad horrific memory which Bill related to me one day in tears. 'A' was a wicked man, and only wanted his own way. Jealous too that Bill and I had become very good mates, although we were complete opposite to each other, me being lifelong tee-total and a non-smoker!

Bill's nightmare began years ago when he was an aerial man; on occasions he took his little girl with him, and she always sat in the car to wait for him whilst Bill was high up on a roof. Bill always locked the car door to keep his daughter safe. One fatal day though, Bill was up on a roof when he heard his little girl screaming in terror, for the whole of the inside of the car was on fire. By the time Bill got down from the roof, the car was ablaze, the screaming stopped and attempts to no avail to open the door. Bill's little girl was dead, and the cause was Bill's matches that he'd left in the glove compartment. Bill's wife never ever forgave Bill and they divorced, and Bill, now homeless, found the now tied property at the school. Drink took hold of Bill, who I'm sure given the chance could have got better with help. I tried to help him by being a good friend. As the years had gone on I'm sure Bill's pain would have lessened a lot, not forgotten, but eased enough with time. Sadly, I left the school, 'A' got his way and outed Bill, and I think Bill found a council property, and not too far from the housekeeper who too was good mates with Bill. Vera the housekeeper left at a later date.

I was to have the biggest row of my life with 'A', and told him a few home truths – one being he mistook the word Head Groundsman, and thought it meant King!

As things were getting worse between us, and realised that things were never going to change, for 'A', the Head Master, and the Bursar were all Masons, so I then wanted to find out who else was, and it didn't take too long and my plan worked!

For some reason I missed the deadline to pick up my wages from the secretaries' office, so couldn't pick them up until the afternoon – as mentioned before, there were two secretaries, assuming one for the Head, the other the Bursar? It was at this point that I told them that the Head Groundsman was far from a nice man, and I'm sure they knew that already re. the usual grapevine. I told them that I'd got a couple of interviews to be a lorry driver; I told them that they were the first people that I'd told, and would appreciate it if they kept this to themselves, well at least until I'd got the job. How I thought all this up on the spur of the moment I'll never know!

It was about an hour or so after our afternoon tea break, and a mere hour since leaving the office when 'A' strutted up and said, "What's all this I hear about you getting a lorry driver's job?" I retorted back, "Who on earth told you that?" He, being 'A', had no hesitation in telling me that it was the secretaries, and that they'd asked him to go to the office. So, as I suspected, the secretaries were likely to be masons! They should have noted the first six letters of their title, i.e. SECRETaries!

From then on I knew that I could only trust my closest friends there, and especially all those who'd had dealings with 'A'. On the quiet, one of my pals there knew that I really wanted to leave the school now, and he told me that there was a job going in nearby Myddleton House, Enfield, Middlesex, and that they were looking for a Head Gardener to fully restore the gardens there – this was the old home of botanist E.A. BOWLES. I got a letter back to say that I was in the top three applicants to have an interview. I never got that interview, and truly believe that the Head Master or the Bursar had some say in it, for when applying for any job you have to write about your past and present jobs of work, and as I had to mention a public school, check-ups were no doubt made. I knew the Head and the Bursar very much valued me at the school for all the beauty that I'd now created, so I couldn't blame them for that, and was I suppose a compliment.

'A' was getting more and more annoying, and kept making excuses to come over to me and Bill, probably to try and catch us not working, but he'd picked on the wrong people in that department, and to the fact that we really enjoyed our work. Both Bill and I said he can't be doing any work at all, for he was either checking up on us to annoy us, or swanning it around the school talking to all and sundry. He would have lasted under a week if he had been Head Groundsman for Leyton Orient F.C. or Wadham Lodge Sports Ground as I had been.

After the massive row with 'A' that I spoke of earlier, I gave my notice in by letter, of which I delivered to the school personally at the weekend. In this letter I wrote about *all* that had gone on with 'A' from day one, even to the point where 'A' had admitted to me that he had bluffed his way in his interview and fooled the Bursar. I left nothing out of that letter, including my disgust on how 'A' could even have been considered to be a Mason, considering all the good deeds that the masons do. It was a long and very detailed letter, and sent a copy each to the Head and the Bursar, so each knew the full story.

I received a letter back from the Bursar almost by return post, and said he was shocked on hearing of my leaving and that he'd like me to see him in his office on a certain day and time, of which I agreed. I was dearly hoping that he'd taken on board my suggestion to split the ground work up, i.e. let 'A' have his 60 odd acres of sports ground, and give me the gardens to look after. I said that it made perfect sense, for 'A' was an unknowledgeable gardener, and made no sense for him to be in charge of me. I mentioned too that this would hopefully keep him on the sports ground area and had no reason whatsoever to come over to the gardens or that half of the school, only to and from his tea breaks and dinner hour. I also mentioned that since I'd proved more than my worth to the school I deserved equal wages to 'A' or even more, for I was always *working* and not swanning about.

I eagerly waited for this interview, and as always the Bursar was very pleasant, and told me that I was a much valued member of staff and how I'd transformed all the so neglected gardens to almost a paradise, and went on to say how much I was well liked. (liked that is except by 'A' and his two assistant cronies!).

Then, there was a knock on the Bursar's door – it was 'A'! the last person I expected to see. The Bursar asked him to come in and sit down, and the Bursar told me that he wanted 'A' to be there to listen to what he had to say (the Bursar that is). The Bursar then said once again in front of 'A' all the praises that he'd given me just a short while ago, "and with all consideration I feel that 'A' should be in charge still of both grounds and gardens." I stood up and said that "I'm sorry, but there's no way I'll ever work with this man again," me pointing now to 'A's very smug face. I bade my farewell to the Bursar and told him that he'd made a very bad decision, and I walked out to never return to that school again.

My Plant Sales

Not long after leaving the school, I picked up where I'd left off, and pursued my dream of living near the sea, something that I was doing when 'A' asked me to go to the school and little did I know it then… secure his position there.

We moved to Kessingland, Suffolk, one week prior to Easter 1987. Although it was April, it was cold, and had no idea how the central heating worked, and couldn't find anyone to show us until after the Bank Holiday. The garden was a blank canvass, being mostly lawn, today it's mostly flowers and a country cottage style garden with two ponds, 'bridge decking' that my eldest son Adrian had made superbly, along with picket fences, arches, seating etc. – clever lad!

All the locals warned us of "all those east winds!" then one night, a total nightmare in October 1987, big gales, and felt our bungalow move, the odd shrubs that I had planted were swirling about as if in a washing machine, a huge filled water butt took flight, and damage everywhere. Well, we were warned, and then wondered how we'd cope each year with this sort of damage. To our relief it was nationwide, and turned out to be a fluke of nature and became know as the famous '87 gales.

I'd always wanted to own a nursery, but work, inclement weather etc. all attributed to loss of money, so wondered if I could operate on a small scale. My plants were establishing well in the garden, and I'd use them as a source to start with. I took hundreds of cuttings, planted seeds, and went hell for leather at it, and still using an old 'plastic corrugated' greenhouse to nurture along some of the plants. I never used a heater, believed in natural heat from the sun by day and colder at night, but warm enough still to grow hardy perennials. As soon as the plants looked like they'd taken, I'd put them outside to harden off before sale. At one point I was selling 400+ varieties of plants, and our local Punch & Judy man made me a good sign to go onto our fence for random callers.

Apart from the many plants that I'd brought with me from Guildford Rd, London E.17, I bought many more, all now making my sign mean something – RARE, COMMON AND UNUSUAL PLANTS FOR SALE, ETC.

Every plant I had sold for 50p! and I mean *every* plant, no matter how unusual it was. My method was like the old saying – a quick tanner is better than a slow shilling – and I had hordes of people at my sales, 3 or 4 times a year. I'd buy a plant say for four or five pounds; once home I'd split it to as many plants as possible, if getting lots of cuttings was impossible, I'd make just half a dozen or so plants. I'd plant half in my garden to slowly increase, pot up for sale say the odd six, these then would be sold for £1 only, and once the plant in my garden had grown sufficiently and I was able to propagate lots from it, that too would join the 50p bracket.

All the plants that I sold for a £1 would be my money to buy in new stock. I never really worked out if I'd made any profit from my plant sales, for I had to really blank out all the bits that the public didn't see, like all the running about all over the place to buy plants, i.e. time and petrol, and the collection of very many bags of compost, flower pots, labels etc., and I'd spend endless hours writing out hundreds of labels – the botanical name one side, and a common name if it had one, on the other, plus the price. After a long period, I'd make up one very large label and leave a box of labels for the people to copy themselves. This saved hours of work, I can tell you!

I would also spend hours pricking out, taking cuttings, watering, weeding the pots etc. I would like to go back to doing this again, perhaps one day, for I met a lovely lot of people, I expect they loved me too, for they went away with box-loads of plants. Our road was filled with cars, and local folk thought that perhaps something was going on down the beach! I suspected that because of my prices, that nurserymen etc. were amongst the throng, for I was far cheaper than wholesale prices! One nurseryman I know did buy from me, grew my plants on, and later had dealings with Norfolk's famous Bressingham Gardens!

Many years ago now, my wife Debbie and me were fairly regular visitors to the Capel Manor Institute at Enfield, and used to see a lovely little plant that had seeded into the shingle pathways; the plant was Lapeyrousia 'cruenta', a small bulb, and pretty red flower, and always imagined me selling this bulb in small original old clay pots. It's just that to me, the plant looked quaintly old-fashioned yet relatively unknown.

I did put this dream into practice, and had a good amount of very small clay pots, and stupidly I suppose now looking back, sold these plants and pot for a pound too! Thankfully though they did not sell too well, and relied on people buying them solely because they liked the look of the plant rather than the actual pot. One day when I was at work, Deb was all very excited to tell me that she'd sold some perennial plants, and as she didn't know the name of the plants, told the people to choose what they wanted and bring them to the back door to pay. Deb said that they spoke really posh!

When I went to look to see what plants they'd chosen I was truly taken aback, for they'd taken the pound labels from the clay pots and replaced them all with fifty pence ones. Poor Deb was distraught, for she had no idea on what prices I'd set.

I'd always wanted to learn about propagation, and growing plants to sell was my chance to learn. I'd be self-taught, and experimenting, and of course books teach you the right way. I would also copy what nurserymen were doing with certain plants, and be pleasantly surprised on how cuttings of all sorts came about, i.e. tip cuttings, softwood and hardwood cuttings, semi-ripe cuttings, and even leaf cuttings like many of the succulents etc.

The people I got to know at my plant sales would bring me unusual bits and we'd do a swap, or they'd invite me to their gardens to have a 'pick and choose' – absolutely wonderful!

When the time comes, I hope I'm blessed with a long retirement to pursue a hobby or growing and selling plants once again. April and May was always a good time for selling plants and on really sunny spring days it was nice to see folk walking round my garden seeing the plants that they'd just bought actually growing! on many they could see the rough height and spread of a plant too.

I always kept a good supply of garden books handy too on sales days, with a notice up here and there pointing that out so if they wanted to see a picture of something they could, and then hopefully I'd get another sale. It's also a common thing to say "you can sell anything if it has a flower on it!"

Another thing I always did was to put one of my landscape stickers on at least one pot of which I'd sold, and got a fair bit of work from this too. At least if I got work from it the person would be certain that I knew my plants if nothing else!

Could've Been Manslaughter?

Back in 2008 I was restoring a client's small garden to make it manageable, a new shed had just been put up, and backed to the wall that was adjacent to the road, hence in front of the shed I planted it up with quite expensive large clumps of small shrubs and perennials, and set it all off with a good quality pine bark. On the main border I'd laid down a membrane, awaiting one of those huge builders bags to be delivered and filled with 'red' chippings. I planted up all the beautiful plants and was told that the chippings would arrive early the next day. That morning, my client telephoned me and sounded in an awful state and could hardly get her words out, she was crying "my beautiful garden ruined" and so forth. I thought at first that it was something that I'd done wrong, but knew that Maddie Willis and I had parted on good terms with the garden the night before.

When Maddie did finally manage to get her words out, it came to light that the delivery man bringing the chippings had the huge bag on a crane and levered it over the shed and straight on top of all the newly planted flowers!

Yes, the man thought he'd make it easy for me so as I didn't have to barrow all the tonnage from the road, but what possessed him to assume that there was nothing the other side of that shed and not even knock to check first?

We then thought of all the 'what ifs' on that very spot, supposing there was a baby in a pram, an elderly or deaf person sleeping or resting in a deckchair, were there plant cloches, a pond, the list of what ifs was endless.

The owner of the company could not believe what his driver had done, but did pay for each and every plant damaged.

I do Believe in Fairies!

Well, I do believe in their existence, for some of the information comes from good sources. My pal Tom Tansley, whom I'd worked with many years ago at Springfield Park, told me about one that he saw when staying at an old cottage in Sawbridgeworth, Hertfordshire. Tom at first was a bit reluctant to tell me at first, for like most, feared ridicule. He told me how he was resting in a deck chair one sunny day, and happened to glance near the shed. He said that he really could not believe his eyes for it was indeed a fairy. Folk since then told Tom that perhaps it was a dragonfly, but Tom always said that dragonflies don't have human faces! He also said that the fairy did actually flit in and out of the old open window of the shed, and Tom said that in hindsight should have got up and closed the window on it, and 'caught' it.

A good few years later, Tom was taken ill and almost died, in fact the hospital had confirmed that Tom did actually die for a short period of time. Tom described the usual tunnel of light that we are all supposed to see when we die, and loved ones waiting for you at the end of it. This is exactly what happened to Tom. After coming out of hospital, Tom went to South Africa to recuperate and stop with close family who had moved out there several years before. Tom shocked all of his family by telling them the names and occupations etc. of all the old-fashioned photos on the sideboard end walls. They all said "It's impossible, Tom, these people have been dead for very many years," but Tom told how he'd held conversations with each and every person in these old photographs. He also told them many things that they didn't know!

When my wife Debbie and I were on holiday many years ago, we took a coach tour, it was to Buckland-in-the-Moor. The driver told us that this was reported to be the last place that a fairy was sighted in England? at that point of time (1970s) or indeed the West Country.

One of the very best books that I was given as a present, and was all about the Boswell family of true Romany Gypsies, and how the gypsy children actually played with the fairies on the south shore at Blackpool and several of these gypsy children still alive to day to back the story up. Their parents never called their children silly, for no doubt they had played with the fairies too, and as the gypsy man said when he wrote of this, "I dare say now you are going to call me light in the head. We played with the fairies most days."

A few years ago a lovely film came out called simply 'FAIRYTALE – A TRUE STORY' – the true story of two little girls who played with and photographed fairies. The story was known as 'The Cottingley Fairies' (Yorkshire), a story known the world over. When one of the little girls grew up to be an elderly lady, she confessed that the photos were faked, exactly how they did it at that age no one knows. They told reporters that they took photos of figments of their imaginations – many people also knew that the girls said that the photos were fake, and this was to protect the fairies at Cottingley forever, for the press and the world's eyes left them alone after this.

When Debbie and I took over our then youngest son Dale to see the film, we found it very atmospheric, for we were the ONLY people in the cinema that day watching that film. This made the film even more special to us.

Debateable?

Around the year 2004 I was approached by a long-standing client to landscape their garden. They knew that I was strictly on the natural side of gardening, and that I was not a landscape stone mason, hence only dealt with mainly garden restoration and new planting etc. The nearest I ever get to stonework is rockery stone and shingle or grit for paths and rockeries.

I was given a blank canvass, the area being mainly grass, and could design it myself, and when I say design I use that word very loosely for I have never drawn a design in my life, and when I did, it was a very rough sketch that even a child could do! but I'd at least get over to the client what their garden would look like. My clients knew that I loved the country cottage style, and also knew that they could leave the garden in my capable hands whilst they were away on holiday. They left me a fair bit of cash for the very first plantings, if indeed I got that far.

Just prior to them going away, I weed-killed the whole site, for the lawn had never to my knowledge been weed, greened up or even fed, so the lawn was full of the deeper rooted pernicious weeds, therefore did not want all these coming up in the new borders or shingle paths.

Before the weed killer was put down I cut all the grass really short, so when the grass and weeds died, it was only the taller weeds that needed to be raked off. The dead lawn stayed as it was, without the need to dig or rotovate etc. The first job was to mark out where all the island beds were to be, plus the very large border that went round the perimeter of the site; all the remaining areas would be a series of shingle pathways, and you could view every bed from these paths.

The boundary borders were 'marked out' with box plants (Buxus 'sempervirens'). Once these were in it was then a matter of buying in, then planting, all the numerous shrubs, trees, plant, climbers, roses etc., and being the boundary was flanked with old hedging of Hawthorn and older trees, so here was my excuse to brighten up these old hedges, by planting up very vigorous climber and rambler roses. Some were one-off flowering, others repeat flowering, the visitor being quite surprised at seeing roses some 50–60 feet high in the old trees or spread throughout the old hedges, and very unexpected colouring to a somewhat dull and uninteresting background. Many roses are most suitable for shady or north-facing positions, therefore once again giving that odd splash of colour that perhaps no one expected from that dull area, for most folk think that roses have to be in the sun. People too often say that roses prefer clay sticky soil – quite untrue of course, for roses like a good soil like most other growing things, they just tolerate clay.

On the subject of roses, I (that is me and son Rowan) made a large rose bed of all Hybrid Tea and Floribundas and added height with a good few standards and half standards too. Now that all the planting was going ahead, I put bonemeal straight onto the now long-dead short grass, then planted up. Yes, it did look odd on seeing beautiful plants, shrubs etc. planted in a base of dead grass! but now it was time to mulch around all these plants. I used well-rotted dark mushroom compost, the compost of course now blanking out the dead grass and the ground was now rich and dark, and set off all the greens and blooms of anything that was in flower, and the borders now looking like fantastic flower beds and the gardens were really taking shape.

Several tons of mulch and shingle for the paths had to be barrowed in from outside the property, and I drove endless miles to choose and deliver each and every plant, and when pricing for the job forgot to add the cost of the petrol, but now my price was in, there of course was no changing it. A DEAR lesson for me in more ways than one, and made quite a hole in my wages at the end. Mulching is a difficult task to do, once all the plants are in, but I used a method that I'd used many years ago, but then saw it on a modern day garden programme, as if the presenter thought it was his idea! not that the idea that I'm about to tell you was my idea, but seemed a logical thing to do at the time and saved me lots of hard work.

The idea that worked brilliantly was to place various sized flower pots, boxes, buckets etc. over the smaller plants, then pour the barrow loads of mulch on top of these, use a rake gently to level, and glide on the top of the smaller pots. All you do then is to gently lift off all the pots, boxes etc. and the mulch then falls slowly to the bases of the plants without smothering them.

I have used this method all of my landscaping life, and saved many hours of filling a bucket and slowly emptying out between each plant. When I did the bucket method, I also used to tread the mulch round the plants before adding a second layer, my idea doing this helped to press the mulch down to stop any possible weeds coming through, or air-borne seed germinating because of the 'hard' surface; the second bucketful acted as a light mulch for effect, and acting as being too friable for any air-borne seed roots to really get a grip, and thankfully failing to germinate.

Most of the island beds we planted an edging plant; I've already mentioned Box, but others were dwarf lavender, Santolina 'incana', Teucrium 'Lucidrys'; other beds had mixed shrubs and perennials to act as a natural overflowing edging effect to drift onto the shingle paths therefore to not make an enclosed border.

We commenced this work about the mid-May, so couldn't add any bulbs until that autumn, and when we did Rowan and me planted thousands of all sorts! We also dead-headed each and every one of them, and to keep the beds looking tidy we tied up the greenery on the daffs etc. by using two or three 1ft or so split canes – this stopped the leaves flopping down and making the beds look messy until they eventually go brown and die, then of course they pull away with ease.

Sadly, most people can't be bothered to spend hours tying numerous bulbs, but the effort on this garden always paid off, and the gardens stayed very tidy, like in winter, I'd use a leaf blower to more or less get rid of *every* fallen leaf; there was no dead wood on any rose or shrub, this was one of several gardens that I have created over the years that I was proud of, and Rowan's first!

When I say I tied in the leaves of the daffs, the leaves were always kept very loose, and the bigger the clump of bulbs, the more split canes you used, and as many as was needed to run garden (thin) string around the canes, thus the leaves still being upright as if still growing and ready to flower!

Going back to TV presenters, my ears always prick up when I hear them say "I'm going to show you a good idea". These 'ideas' I had done many times a long time ago, and when I did do them I was to some, a 'cowboy' gardener, for my methods were not the traditional ones, and being very young then, made me look even more like a 'cowboy'. On watching a gardening programme in April '09, a TV presenter told viewers that if they had a tub or container that didn't have holes in the bottom, not to put holes in the bottom but put them 6 inches or so at the sides, thus leaving a small reservoir of water at the bottom. I was doing this back in 1968 or earlier! I also put deep saucers etc. at the bottom of hanging baskets etc. and even added a sponge inside that to hold even more water, the bigger the container, the bigger the dish, or I'd line baskets and tubs with thick old carpet or cloth, all these held far more moisture than plastic liner.

Right, let's get back to the project. The property was a Bed and Breakfast, and all the rooms viewed onto these now beautiful gardens, and a perfect added bonus for anyone's stay, and I got talking to quite a few, and several asked for gardening advice, or what such and such a plant was called that had just caught their eye.

One day a surprise was to come, and with it a dilemma – one of the client's relatives had an idea and that was to enter the garden for the Lowestoft-in-Bloom competition; this was done and the garden got a GOLD! Now, do we say I got Gold, the garden got Gold, or the clients themselves? for Rowan and I had not long just completed the garden, albeit the clients of course had all the outlay, some people said that the clients cheated by entering a brand new garden without doing any of it themselves. Most new gardens look new, but this one was crammed with everything imaginable, and looked so mature, hence the clients perhaps did not feel the need to tell the competition organisers that it had only just been created.

For a while on my leaflets I put 'winner of the Lowestoft-in-Bloom Competition' and 'four times award winner of the prestigious London-in-Bloom Competition'. But because more people saw the project as the customer's, so I decided to change the heading to – Landscapers for a Lowestoft-in-Bloom Winner.

The following winter following the garden's creation, disaster struck – extremely heavy rains fell, and totally flooded the garden, doing immense damage; the pond over-filled and all the fish washed away, a lawn that adjoined it was covered in slimy mud with millions of spuds all washed down from a nearby field. One of the owner's relations said that it would have to be rotovated, the owners agreed. This of course would have cost a good few hundred pounds to do.

I, as quick as a flash, said that rotovating was not necessary and that I could 'easily' restore this part of the garden and still save the existing lawn underneath, which I did, but told them that we'd have to wait a couple of days or so to let the mud dry a little. It did turn out fine weather, and everyone now was keen to see how I'd solve this problem.

The method was easy, hard work, but nevertheless very straight forward. All I had to do was chop the mud, work in a long line, then chop before the last slit, then it was a matter of shovelling it all off, then running a spring rake to rid and break up any smaller bits of mud. Job done, and lawn near normal. The clients were pleased, this eased their burden and let them carry on the task of drying out all their property which too had flooded very badly.

Now it was time to restore the garden, again there was thick mud, some of that, along with the mulch, had washed through the edging plants and mixed with all the shingle. We now had to mulch again, wash the shingle and top that up. Many of the smaller plants had been washed out of the ground and had to be replanted, others had roots all showing, some shrubs too were damaged and needed a mild prune up to repair. The garden was now back to normal and by that spring you would never have guessed what had gone on.

Several people said, "I bet you earned well getting that lot back as it was." I told them that I didn't, I was charging my normal fee of £88 per day, that was my then daily rate, and *included* back then Rowan's pay too!

People said, "Did they offer you any more money, or did you get a big bonus for righting it all again?" I said, "No," and told them all that I was surprised too, considering all that I'd done for them, and saving them many hundreds of pounds albeit at that point I hadn't even considered that perhaps I would get a 'thank you payment', and now leads me nicely to an incident that even today I find so hard to comprehend.

Because I didn't get a bonus, and because I was still running round picking up new plants etc., etc., I put my daily fee up to £120, forty of which would be for Rowan, the rest for me, plus now allowing myself to be paid for all the petrol that I was using to and from various nurseries etc., for the lady would say, "If you see anything for the garden when out on your travels, get it and I'll pay you," so I did, and I always worried, for the new plants were still coming to 50, 60 or 100 pounds or more, along with compost feed etc., so good money was still being spent, plus I was buying boxes and pots of bedding plants to fill every gap possible.

Rowan by now was taking on his own landscape work, and to keep his money topped up, still tried to work with me when he could. He'd really enjoyed this project, and like to think that he learnt a lot from me, so on the completion of these gardens took on a big project for himself. Rowan now was going to college to learn about horticulture, etc. I had used him on all of this project, and gave him a nice bonus for all his hard work, so kept him on for the now once-a-fortnight maintenance of this garden.

We were due to do a one-day maintenance on this garden, but Rowan either had to go to college, or go to his own garden project, so had to do the garden on my own, and like I always do, put my heart and soul into it. I wrote out my usual bill of £120 and the owners were always very prompt payers, and I'd virtually always get paid by return post, or pick it up on a Saturday.

I then got a telephone call from the lady, who was very upset at my charges, and I of course couldn't understand why. A little later on, both the lady and man came to my house, although the lady stayed in the car, visibly upset.

The man came in and said how his wife was so upset, he said, "How come you are charging £120 and there was just you?" I said that this was MY daily fee, and if I decided to pay a labourer out of it, it was my choice. If I wanted to pay two labourers out of it then again it was my 'choice' 'loss'? I went on to say that this was the very first time that Rowan had not been with me, and that he'd be here next week, so in fact they'd been very lucky that I'd often had other labourers with me over the good few years I'd done work for them. I said to the man, "The whole argument is all over Rowan's pay of £40, you'd better have it back them." The man kept refusing, although he didn't take it, I insisted further, for obviously this forty pounds meant a lot to them. The man then left, minus the £40, so why the argument?

Either at my house or by letter, I can't remember which, I wrote/said – that when your wife takes on a couple of people each day to make the beds for the guests etc., and one of the staff don't turn up that day, surely then your wife pockets that money for herself as there was no extra outlay that day, and you with your successful car sales/repair business, you may do routine each day but then have a big car sale or something major to do on a car, or whatever, this surprise money is all yours surely?

Quite a few people were stunned when I told them all that had gone on, and two separate people were workmen who worked on occasions for these people. One said, "Good God, I work like you do, Keith, I have a set daily rate, and if I decide that I need extra help it all comes out of that rate, that's my loss, but I get my job done quicker." Both chaps said that they'd have to be careful now if they go back to this house, for they both said that each time so far, they'd always taken a labourer with them, "but there's sure to be a time when we won't!"

The whole episode got me thinking about this forty pounds, for what about the days when on numerous occasions the lady had paid me for all the plants that I bought on my travels and far exceeding forty pounds; what about all the many hundreds of pounds I'd saved them restoring the garden on my still flat rate? What about all my petrol losses, although I'm certain they – like me – hadn't taken that into consideration. What about all my gardening 'talent' – was I not worth far more than £120 a day, for I could name every tree, shrub, plant in that garden; surely anyone would sway the odd forty pounds for that?

My mind then wandered back a few years working for the same people, I did the odd bit of maintenance at £48 per day and fifteen of that for a labourer if I had the need of one. These same people asked if I would prune and restore the very old fruit trees in their garden (the very same trees that 'centre' most of the now island beds), the trees had not been done ever I should think. Anyhow, it was winter, glad of the extra money, or so I thought, and did the whole task on my own, there were prunings everywhere, and the only bonus was that the lady said that her husband would shift it all at his own leisure. If no one has ever seen a very neglected tree(s) then they have no idea what timber comes from them. Anyhow, the job took three very long days and included the usual – prune, thin, shape, dead-wood, height reduction, spray with winter tar wash including main trunks, all wounds over half an inch to be painted with a pruning compound, and tree grease applied to main trunks – I put my bill in for four hundred pounds plus.

I got a call as soon as they got my bill. "What's this, you can't charge all that, it should be £48 surely." I asked of course if they were joking, and they couldn't possibly think that I'd do all that for £48 for each of the days, for this was not garden maintenance by any means, this was *really* hard graft, and a job of skill, for pruning is an art. They actually thought that I was going to do all this under the fee for mere maintenance.

It was the man who spoke to me again after his wife's anger, and once again I had to explain to him in layman's terms – look, if you do car servicing say every day, and earn virtually the same money each day, surely your eyes light up when someone wants a new head gasket, or axle, or gearbox etc., and bringing in a vast fortune for you. It's the same for me, my £48 was now £400+ for harder work, for you won't do those big jobs of work for the same price as a service? Back then, I'm sure my point was taken on board, but not on this occasion with the forty pounds.

Amidst all this, I had the highest compliments from folk, all thinking that these people must have been barmy to even think of coming to my house for such trivial money, considering what I was doing for them. They were right, for it should have been me that should've been very upset, not them. It was also said by folk that these two people have each very successful businesses and should have bitten their tongues on this occasion, and *perhaps* other occasions like it, for Rowan had only missed one or two days with me when at college and was there 100% of the time working with me.

The people's logic as they explained it to me that there was *always* two men doing two men's work in the garden (me and Rowan) so on Rowan not being there they had lost out on one of the men's graft for that day. I'll say that word again – one DAY! and I still tried so desperately to explain that I was paying Rowan out of *my* day's pay. The whole episode seems so illogical – what you think, reader?

As a last note on this saga, the people did get more GOLDS, but as people have told me, "it's yours and Rowan's work still coming into fruition." I hadn't thought of it that way, and I suppose they're right, for as plants, trees, shrubs etc. grow and grow, so does the display of heights, widths and colours of all that was planted. So *perhaps* it was me who won the Lowestoft-in-Bloom after all… don't you think!? (or is it still debateable?)… maybe I could claim that first GOLD as my own, a bit cheeky of me, but would give me recognition of my work, and something nice to put on my headed paper!

One of the loveliest people to walk this earth. I have never known her house number, but going by the photo, it looks as though she is the first house from Chingford Road E17, albeit the house is in Kenilworth Avenue.
Mr & Mrs Green's garden... see text.

Another photo of my dad, just 1 year on (1972) when he had a heart attack. The difference you can clearly see in him from the photo taken of him in his garden at Monkhams Avenue the previous year at home. Dad was also called Walter Herbert Edwin Nichols, the Edwin coming from his grandmother Minnie's father.

Some of Dad's achievements was designing and building modern houses, schools and churches etc., one being the Catholic Mother Church, at Lansing, Toronto, Canada. Also building and designing the then biggest power station in the world at Ffestiniog, Wales.

He was a Lecturer at Walthamstow Technical College, and Chief Architect for Harlow Council.

I just liked this little photo (1930s/40s?) from a photo album given to me after the death of 'Kit' Kathleen Jones (Leucha Rd, E17) my nan and grandad's near neighbour.

Kit's brother and sister both died very young, one died of scarlet fever, the other run over by a horse and cart in Hackney Road, East London.

I dare say there is a reference to this terrible accident somewhere in the archives?

Kit's mum lived to be 100.

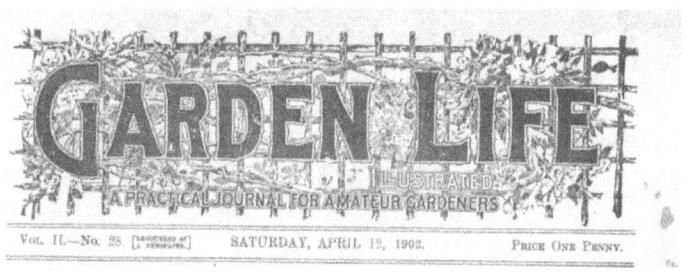

I bought these old gardening newspapers from an antique shop (Good Friday 2019). I was amazed on the amount of advertisers selling trees, shrubs, plants and sundries.

Youths held on drugs charges

Five youths, charged with possessing cannabis and amphetamine tablets at an Enfield house, were remanded until May 30 when they appeared at Tottenham Magistrate's Court on Thursday May 2.

They are alleged to have had the drugs at an address in Hertford Road on April 26.

They are ▓▓▓▓▓▓▓▓ ▓▓▓▓▓▓▓▓▓▓▓▓ ▓▓▓▓▓▓, Walthamstow, who is alleged to have had cannabis; ▓▓▓▓▓▓▓▓▓ ▓▓▓▓▓▓▓▓▓▓▓▓ ▓▓▓ ▓▓▓▓▓, who is alleged to have had cannabis; Keith Paul Nichols, 19, unemployed, of Coppermill Lane, Walthamstow, who is alleged to have had cannabis; ▓▓▓▓▓▓▓▓▓▓▓▓▓▓▓▓▓.

▓▓▓▓▓▓▓▓▓▓▓▓▓▓▓▓▓ Walthamstow, charged with having 17½ yellow amphetamine tablets; and ▓▓▓▓ ▓▓▓▓▓▓▓▓▓▓▓▓▓▓▓, ▓▓▓▓▓ ▓▓▓▓▓▓▓ ▓▓ ▓▓▓ ▓▓▓▓, ▓▓▓▓▓, charged with having three amphetamine tablets.

All were remanded on bail of £50 each until May 30.

One of the most awful times of my life, and still haunts me today, and will do forever (see my first two books for greater detail) being planted drugs by so-called 'police' a so-called temporary detective sergeant.

I have, since that day, searched long and hard for this low life that planted me, so that I can bring him to justice, and his cronies too.

It'd be nice to totally embarrass him in front of his family and friends as he did to me.

As you can see, I have erased my friends' names, as our names back then were seen by very many people, those also believing that there's no smoke without fire, and those that would not believe the police would do such a thing.

My second cousin Ann Green, née Ridley, poses with husband
Michael at the home of her mum and dad at Hackney Marsh where
Uncle George (my grandad's brother) was Head Keeper there. (He
and Aunt Flo had a tied house on site.) Uncle George was also prior
Head Keeper at Millfield, top end of Lea Bridge Road.
Photo shows Mike and Ann with Mike's Butcher Cup Trophy, for
bowls (1977).
Michael also worked at Finsbury Park, during my early training days
there at the Finsbury Park Gardening Training Centre, which had just
been built.
Photo by kind permission of Ann and Michael Green.

My lovely grandad Harry Bishop Ridley, chasing me down the front path, the alley between us and Ena and Arthur Cox (their front room window just in view).

I was 18 months old at this time, born 4th November 1948.

Little ol' me again, like today, always in the garden! The local council later put in a shed for all the residents, ours was at the top right-hand corner of the garden. We had the gardens of the maisonettes at the bottom of our garden, divided by a real cinder path. The bottom flat (left) was the home of the lovely Mrs Thornton (see text).

Photo circa early 1950s at 8 Chippenham Walk, Harold Hill, Essex.

My mum's grandad, Arthur James Axford, posing with his pipe – as usual!
He was Foreman at Hornimans Tea; his brother Henry also worked there.
Mum told me that her grandad grew the most fantastic Asters, mainly the
annual shaggy types called 'Ostrich Plume'.
My great grandad died after falling down whilst sweeping snow in the front
garden at 7, Bedford Road, E17 (now part of a car park); to this day you can
easily see where my grandparents' house once stood.
Sadly, the year this photo was taken is not known, but luckily the 15th
February is written on the back.

My dad's dad and grandad – Walter Herbert Edwin Nichols, and Walter Herbert Nichols. The children are very likely to be my dad and brother Eric (or is this perhaps a girl?). Photo taken in 1930s, also see text.

Me with my Acacia 'dealbata' ...Mimosa! Photo taken 1979.

Photo purchased from, and permission given via the *Walthamstow Guardian and Gazette* newspapers.

● Keith Nichols enjoys his tropical greenery. (X146)

Touch of tropics

ACACIA Dealbata is a rare beast in climates as cold as ours, but an impressive specimen is alive and kicking in a Walthamstow garden.

It's 20 feet tall, eight feet wide, extremely colourful and always thirsty.

Acacia Dealbata is, of course, mimosa.

the summer of 1978, never expecting it to survive, for it can usually only grow under greenhouse or conservatory conditions in this country.

But the small shrub grew quickly to reach its present height and last September buds began to appear.

It is now in full bloom and Mr Nichols'

Me with my Mimosa, photo used on the front page of the *Walthamstow Guardian* newspaper. I always sent them news of both my gardening exploits, and of my fairground travels with my vintage equipment, and the editors were always glad to print any news that I had!

Photo (March 1979) with very kind permission of the *Walthamstow Guardian and Gazette* newspaper.

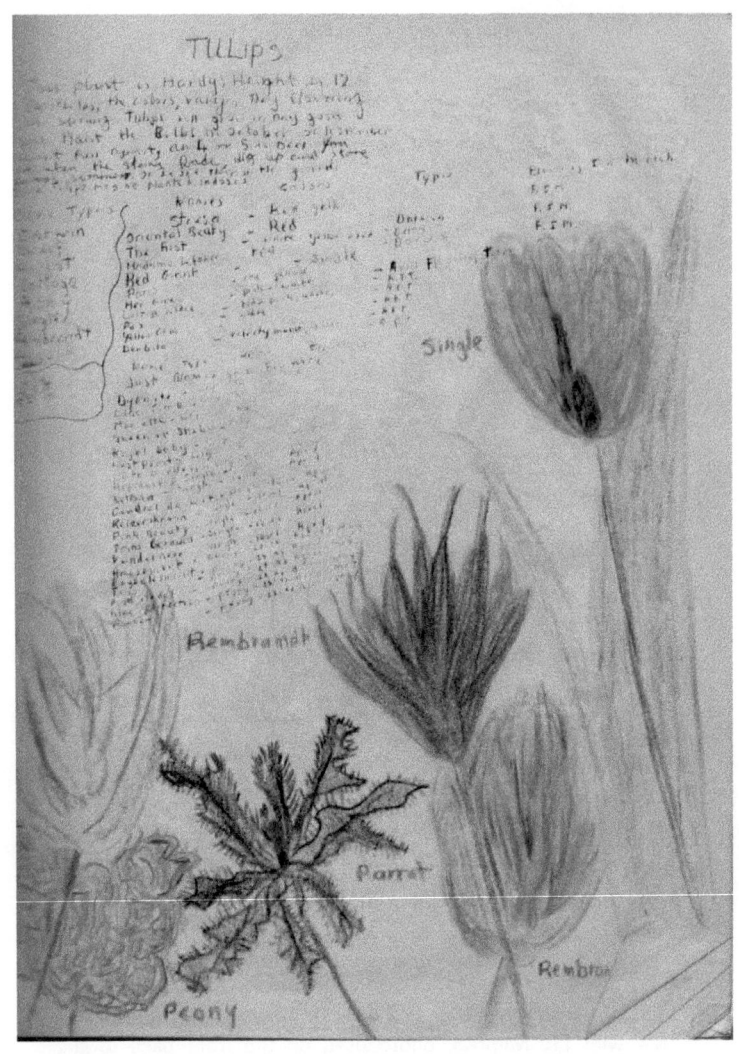

My first attempt at doing a gardening book! I was no Beatrix Potter, but I tried. I was about 10 or 11 years old. (One of several pages).

I've passed my medical to be a young garden labourer, oh to be called *young* again! (4th September 1964)

Coronation Day 1953

We all pose outside house numbers 6 and 7 Chippenham Walk. Me and sister Sandra munching away (just in front of the girl with the tall hat) and Alan Smith, son of Vi and Tom Smith just crouching front of photo. The alley at the back led to our back gate. I'm certain my dad took this photo?

Walter H E Nichols ARIBA

37 Bernwell Rd. Chingford Essex

Telephone : Silverthorn 0535

Another of my dad's advertising for his headed paper. Dad left us for new love elsewhere, very soon after we moved to 37 Bernwell Rd E4 from Harold Hill on the 7th March 1960.

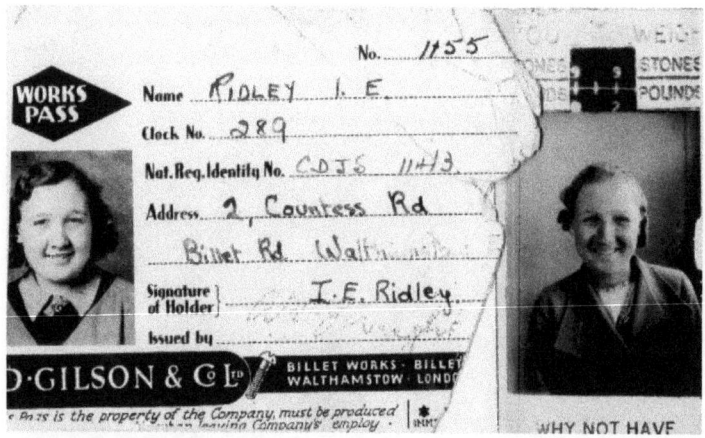

I like this photo and thought I'd share it with you...
My mum's works pass, she was around 18 or 19 years old, and made ammunition. She did actually nearly get blown up whilst at home at 2 North Countess Road, E17. The other photo is a weighing machine that told you your weight and took your photo too !

My friend Robin Barnard. Robin became Head Groundsman at Wadham Lodge E17 (Brookscroft Road). There were 3 more in charge before him during my time there. Robin and I had the most fun, yet took our work seriously, we enjoyed every day, a good mate still today. I became Head Groundsman at last after Robin left. Photo shows him at the Dad's Army Museum at Thetford, Norfolk, pictured with his mate Capt. Mannering. (Photo circa 2014 by Robin Barnard.)

My great grandfather Walter Herbert Nichols, always known in the family as the man who designed and built the Kingfisher Swimming Pool, Woodford, Essex (now a hotel).What was the occasion? Note the lady with the handbag and one craftsman, and also pictured a smartly dressed man. (June 12th 1934)

One mystery... It was said that he and my great-grandmother Minnie Nichols (née Robinson), lived in a big house in Chingford Mount Road called The Brambles, and said to have been built by my great great-grandfather? In much later years they resided at a property nearby simply called 'The Bungalow' at Westward Road E4.

Children Plant Park Trees

Newspaper clips, tree planting ceremony – pal David Bolton left of pic. and his mum on the right. He and I were chosen to plant this tree on behalf of our school (see text).

With kind permission of the *Chingford and Walthamstow Guardian* newspapers. (1963)

I took this photo of the lads when we were patiently lining up outside the office to collect our weekly wage. Left to right: Charlie Swaby (Bowling Green Keeper), Ted Ellis (Park Keeper) JOHN ____? Garden labourer, Terry_____? and Peter... both Park Keepers, all at Springfield Park.

My sister Sandra and me dressing up. Me wearing Dad's officer's jacket. Note Dad's rockery and crazy paving, and his screen... see text. Just in view Ena and Arthur Cox's garden next-door. Photo taken in the latter half of 1950s at 8 Chippenham Walk.

This lovely photo is of my Nanna and Grandad Ridley, my mum's parents.

The photo was taken at Clacton-on-Sea, Essex – June 19th 1957.

The shrub is Senecio greyii, this shrub inspired me to do a cutting demonstration in front of the class when still in the infants at Bosworth School, Harold Hill, Essex (see text); my teacher was the marvellous Mrs Gwither.

Our large garden at 37 Bernwell Road, E4 (see text). Pictured – my sister Sandra, my mum, and baby brother Barry, just born on 18th March 1960! And of course, yours truly. Huge allotments were at the back of our garden, all now built on. Note the huge lawn that I tried to keep cut, often with just shear!
Photo dedication to brother Barry and wife Maura Wallace-Nichols.

The opening of the gardens at Woodhall House, Wood Green, London (1975). We all listen intently to the speech of Councillor Vic Garwood (see text) ...and NO, I hadn't nodded off! PHOTO BY kind permission of *the North London Weekly Herald Newspaper Ltd*. Tottenham N17

Councillor Vic Garwood and me in conversation about the beautiful gardens that we created from a very derelict and overgrown site (see text). Note how I laid the turf about 2" above the path for easy mowing and edging shear work. I taught the lads landscaping for this Job Creation Project, and good mate George Gwarys, taught them the art and skills of stone masonry. He is still a very much missed friend.
Photo by kind permission of the *North London Weekly Herald Newspaper Ltd*, Tottenham N17.

Councillor Vic Garwood chats to the lads, and admires my planting, and the skilled work of George Gwarys, his brilliant raised beds, paths, ramps etc. George laid all the paving himself, all heavy York Stone. Photo by kind permission of the *North London Weekly Herald Newspaper Ltd*, Tottenham N17.

Another nice photo of the opening of the gardens. I was Foreman and overseer of this project. There was a lot of graft doing this site, but a real riot of colour in the end! Photo taken early spring to mid-summer 1975.
Photo by kind permission of the *North London Weekly Herald Newspaper Ltd*, Tottenham N17.

Me aged 1 year 8 months!
I'd just knocked over the now discarded Christmas tree! Photo taken at my paternal grandparents' garden at 80 Kenilworth Avenue E17, Rose (née Coggin) and Walter Nichols. Nan later married the delightful Percy Clayson.

Another picture of me, always in the garden! At my nan and grandad's garden at 80 Kenilworth Avenue E17.

Little me again! On the step of the alley leading to our kitchen at 8 Chippenham Walk. I've got my gardening gear on, and just a few steps where my new and first gardening plot was to be in front of me.

Albert Danahar, old time professional boxer, and one of the very well known fighting Danahar brothers of Bethnal Green in London's East End. After an injury stopped Albert's very successful boxing career, he took up the trade as a skilled furniture upholsterer; in his last years he became a park keeper and handyman at Springfield Park where we first met when I first started work.
Photo taken near the Park's lake, late 1960s.
Photo by kind permission of Albert's daughter Maureen Reilley.

A sad but happy photo, for it was the very last holiday for me and my sister (1959) with our mum and dad, and a last holiday for Mum as her MS took a firmer hold.

Dad left us for love elsewhere, Dad took this photo of us all at the B&B West Avenue, Clacton (see text). This part of the garden now sold off sadly.

Left to right standing – the cook/housekeeper, Mrs Newman... the owner, my mum, Jim Newman... owner, Mrs Newman's mum, then me!... little Glen with his mum (guests).

Front row: Susan Newman (owner's daughter) Glen's sister, and hers and Glen's dad.

A Powerful Light-Weight Ladder!

Being a tradesman, every day, or at least every week, we are in other people's homes, and you meet all types of people. One very strange lady many years ago now, asked me to restore her very neglected garden. All was going well at first, and I improved the garden no end. As I worked my way through the garden, I came across an old neglected apple tree, which had one branch around nine inches thick and about four foot from the ground, and the most obvious branch to come off as it was right over the path. So I set about removing this branch, hence now a very clear walk down the path. To my shock, the lady came out and said, "now how am I supposed to get down my path?" I said, "very easily now surely?" I then went on to ask her what she meant, and how did she get down the path before, and she said that she always stooped under it! I said surely this is far easier, but she was most unhappy.

I thought this episode very strange, but there was another problem yet to come, and was beginning to think that perhaps I wouldn't get paid at all. About two days down the line, I arrived one morning and she said, "Come with me, come and see what our ladder has done to my tree." I was taken aback, for I only had one small ladder with me, five feet long, extremely light aluminium, and you could hold the weight of it on your little finger, so… what had my ladder done, I wondered? The lady pointed to my ladder which was still resting up against the trunk of the old slightly leaning apple tree, "Your ladder has pushed my apple tree over during the night."

Astounded was putting it lightly, why would she think of such a thing, surely she had seen this tree at this angle for very many years? Without hesitation, I picked the ladder up with my little finger and said that this ladder hardly had the weight of a bag of sugar, let along push over an apple tree! I went on, with my labourer to push and pull this tree with all our mights, just to show her that her tree was perfectly stable. I sped the whole job up after this; yes, I did get paid in full, she then wanted me to restore the front garden. I did write out an estimate, it was accepted, but then made out I was far too busy to take it on!

Childhood Weeds

Some weeds do have a place in my heart, for we had very few flowers in our garden when I was a boy at Harold Hill (Essex), but an abundance of weeds, so they in fact made up for the lack of cultivated plants. Favourite weeds were… and still are… dandelions, Daisies, Buttercups, Chickweed, Speedwell, and always delighted if the Scarlet

Pimpernel turned up; the cultivated forms of the latter are much used nowadays in hanging baskets and tubs.

Clover is another nice weed, and again grow several cultivated forms of it.

I Don't Believe it!

By this above title, I refer to so-called hybridising etc., so-called 'new' varieties, etc., and perhaps what I'm about to relate will be explained to me one day? Way back in the 1980s I was watching a gardening programme, and the presenter was interviewing a group of elderly chaps in what was, I think, a gardening club, and the subject came up about 'new' varieties of roses that they had 'hybridised' (I'll use that word loosely as you'll see) for the chaps were talking about the rose Red Devil (year?), and this rose often 'sported'... hence had a 'sport' on it. I'll explain...

Back in the 70s I bought myself a batch of roses, I say batch, because I just used to buy the odd one here and there. Amongst the batch was 'Evelyn Fison', and so surprised one day to see this abnormal growth growing from an already flowering stem, but the new growth had a completely different colour flower and stood out like a sore thumb! I'd never seen anything like this before, so spoke to several older gardening pals, who too had never heard of this before, but luckily one or two had, and told me that I had a 'sport' of which I could possibly have a new variety. Now I was intrigued, for I assumed then that if I took the sport off at some point to have it as an actual cutting to then grow on to become a rose bush in its own right.

Even more baffled, what was I to do then – give it a name? If I did, who would know of it for there was only the one? Would I have to register it somewhere? Would someone come out and see it? These questions were endless, but pursued none of it, and all because of what I saw on this particular gardening programme.

As I say, all these old chaps were talking eagerly about 'Red Devil' and over time had got twelve different sports, and they had named each of them and I assumed took cuttings and marketed them?

Reading books written in the 1950s they suggest you try hybridising your own roses, and tell you how to go about it. So, like those old gents, many members of the public create new varieties and claim then as their 'own', how do they know 100% that it is indeed their own? Say like 'Red Devil' if just those old gents had got twelve new varieties, think how many 'sports' have appeared on that rose and sold all over the world for very many long years. Let's assume someone is able to register their rose as a new variety and put a name to it, how would you feel if you knew you had that exact same rose that you'd either hybridised or had a sport of and indeed how many more sports and new varieties have come from 'Red Devil' since that programme all those years ago, and what about the sports from many other rose varieties too? What about the rose colours and shapes, who is it that knows 100% that it is indeed a new rose? What about rose breeders themselves who are constantly hybridising, and no doubt getting sports too? How do they know that the new hybrid hasn't been created already – all too baffling, I say!

On speaking to a top Fuchsia expert, and he really knew his subject, fully agreed with me when I brought this up, for he said that he was *very* certain that lots of Fuchsias had exactly the same flowers and colouring, yet went under various names when going to Fuchsia shows all over the country and abroad.

On another gardening programme, there was a vicar who only grew Sweet Peas, and was seen to be doing lots of cross pollinating and he too claimed 'new' varieties. I mean, how many other pastel and dark colours can you get on a Sweet Pea? all that cross pollinating, surely other sweet pea growers and hybridisers all over the world are doing exactly the same, yet we are to believe that it's a new variety.

The vicar held up a pink sweet pea and said it was one of 'his' yet looked exactly like *all* other pink Sweet Peas!

In 2008 I bought the old-fashioned Nicotiana 'affinis' along with others that I kept from seed over the years, but the 2008 one was marked Nicotiana 'affinis' "Only the Lonely". It was exactly the same flower in colour (white), height and stature as all the others that I had. I have found these days that lots of old varieties are all glammed up, hence losing a lot of the old variety names, and now makes it so difficult to find favourite old varieties. Calendula 'Pot Marigold' was always sold in just two varieties, i.e. 'Art Shades' and 'Campfire' – today it's difficult to find either, although of course they are now masquerading under another fancy name! Going back to that Nicotiana, who decided to call in 'only the Lonely'?

I Chickened Out

I suppose I was around twelve or thirteen years of age when I first ventured with a friend to Petticoat Lane in London, and Club Row was a separate road where they sold all manner of livestock, many back then slaughtered right there in front of you. You could of course buy dogs, cats, etc., and all manner of birds, i.e. parrots, budgies etc.

Out of the blue I decided to buy some chickens, well actually… baby chicks, as I'd always loved the outdoors, and loved the sound of birdsong, cocks crowing etc. I don't recall what I paid for them now, not a lot I should think just doing a paper round etc. The chicks were put in a brown box, and brought them home by train from Liverpool Street station. I was told to keep them warm.

Mum was none too happy, and taken aback that I was going to nurture them in my bedroom at Chingford Hatch. I didn't have the usual light bulb to keep them warm, so used straw, old sheets and blankets and constant use of hot water bottles. All six survived my loving care (no central heating back then)! I built a very makeshift run to keep them warm and dry, plus an outdoor run area. Once again I used my meagre pocket money to buy feed for them. As bad luck would have it, they were all cockerels except one! and Mum was so worried what the neighbours would say, but very strangely they made very little noise.

One of the chickens, and assume this was the hen, kept getting picked on, and was in a terrible state, so I took it to the vet and they charged me seven shillings and sixpence for a brown powder that I had to make into a thickish very small amount of 'soup'. I made a small separate run for this chicken, and that chicken followed me all round the garden never leaving my side, and actually so pleased to see me each morning!

I loved my chickens, they were my pets, and suppose you could say that I rescued them from whatever fate had awaited them at Petticoat Lane, therefore so totally devastated on what was to follow. Mum had multiple sclerosis, and I'd forgotten that she had booked a holiday with the M.S. Society at St. Mary's Bay, Dymchurch, Kent, and Mum said that I'd have to get rid of the chickens somehow, for there would be no one to look after them whilst we were away. Mum pushed me more and more on this, but no one wanted them.

Mum must have spoken to our nice neighbour opposite and Mum said that Mr Tredwin would take two. He came to our back garden, picked up one and tried to wring its neck *several* times, and each time I tried not to look, but when I did that chicken kept looking at me – I'll never forget that moment.

As time neared a day away from our holiday, Mum said that I'd have to take all the others to the butchers at Hatch Lane. The butcher accepted them straight away and I was in mortal shock for after they took my pets to another part of the shop I was still talking to the butcher. I had no idea that they would be killed straight away, and my last vision of my chickens was them with their necks already broken and flapping about wildly as if in agony. I still truly believe even today that it might as well had been me that wrung their necks, and immense guilt since those days, it's never left me. Later that awful day, I cried and cried. Mum tried to console me, but sort of blamed her for not trying to find someone to feed my chickens for just one week.

The holiday did ease my pain a little, but on coming home to that empty chicken run I'll never forget, and this incident to this day stands as one of the very worst in my life. The guilt has stayed with me always, even though everything was totally out of my hands.

Had it not been for that holiday, those chickens would have seen out their whole life in my garden. Okay, so each one would have died anyway, but it most certainly would have been a natural death for them.

Don't Follow The Rule

I refer now to information given out on seed packets, i.e. sow thinly, pull out the weaker ones etc. Even as a boy I never ever followed this rule, for I found no 'weak' seedlings, correction… the seedlings that were weak I separated as with all the other stronger seedlings, and they very soon gained their strength and grew and flowered as normal, all because they were given a chance.

As a lad I had many more plants than my neighbours, just by using my initiative, for why buy seeds to then discard the majority of them, for if you only had a few seedlings that were strong you may just as well have bought dearer boxed or potted plants in the first place, for if a seed packet states that there is approximately 100 seeds, then there's no reason why you shouldn't have nigh on a 100 plants if you sow really, really thinly, all the plants have a strong chance of survival!

Try it and see!

A Poet and Certainly Didn't Know It!

I took my wife Debbie and daughter Heather shopping in Beccles, Suffolk and parked under some well-matured trees, and right out of the blue and out of sheer boredom, decided that I'd try to write a poem! I have never ever had thoughts about doing such a thing before, moreso as I don't particularly have a liking for most poetry, albeit there are some truly meaningful poems out there, especially to do with flowers, nature, and the great outdoors.

I had on that morning, been adding more to this book, so perhaps something within my brain had inspired me to create my first… and very likely last… poem! (See p.viii at the front of this book.)

Pipings!

Someone many years ago when I was a lad, and very likely to have been my grandad Harry Bishop Ridley (born 1899), showed me how to take cuttings of pinks and carnations, and told that they are not called cuttings, but pipings. What you had to do was take off some of the lower leaves from a three inch 'cutting' then trim the stem to a node, which is the small lump on the stem; on this node you make a small slit in it, then using just one of your trimmed-off leaves, slide the leaf into the slit. I was told that the reason for this is so that the piping has ready-made moisture in the thickish leaf, even to the point that the leaf as it rots also supplies a little feed for the forthcoming plant.

In all my working life I have never seen this method shown in books or demonstrated on any gardening TV programme. Modern day rooting powders today do the same job; some people even dip the powder in a tiny piece of moss and put that in the slit.

Grandad's Seeds and Shed

I was with my Grandad one day when he was sorting out his shed and he found several old packets of seeds, all in their original colourful packets. This was in the 1950s when I was a boy, and at that point Grandad reckoned those seeds to be at least twenty-odd years old! So they easily dated back to the 1940s.

Grandad gave me all the seeds, and believe it or not, many did actually germinate to our surprise!

Looking back now, I so wished that I'd kept those lovely seed packets with Suttons or Bees, Unwins etc. all written on the packets. The seed packets then were hand-painted and not photographs.

Today, always open your seed packs set in foil, for lots of seeds hide up in the sides and corners, so open the foil out completely flat to recover all the seeds. You will be so surprised on how many you would have thrown away.

Hyacinths

One of my most wonderful memories is being in the infant school (Bosworth Jnr. School, at Harold Hill, Romford, Essex). It happened each year when our teacher had planted up Hyacinths in bowls and put them on the windowsill. They must have been in full bloom for me to have this so nice memory, for it was a very sunny spring morning, the scent was out of this world.

Another of our classrooms had a Nature Table, this fascinated me, especially when a classmate had brought in some 'sticky buds' from a Chestnut tree, and now to watch those buds slowly unfurl. we also loved to see catkins at close quarters too! and the very many wild flowers in 'vases' namely… jam jars!

My school was apparently pulled down many years ago, and now all built on. I was told that a lot of the building materials at Bosworth had asbestos in it, if it hadn't the school would still be there today.

Honesty Was My Best Policy!

When we first moved from the East End of London for a life by the sea in April 1987, nobody knew me here and of course knew nothing about my quality of work. I had a very young family to keep, plus all the other very many expenses to run – a home, etc., so had to set about advertising in the local papers to start getting my name about.

One of my very first clients Peggy and Peter Cavill, and Peggy's brother Frank who lived with them, thankfully appreciated my know-how in the garden. These people came from Hedley-n-Arden and had a wonderful accent! The garden really was Peggy's domain, Peter was sadly very disabled, and Frank had his own interests (only Peggy is still with us in 2010).

For many years I had photo albums, eight in all showing various jobs of work that I'd done, all in stages, each job of work in pictures I asked for full permission from the householder if I could put their names just below, with their address and telephone number so that other new potential clients could contact them to see what my work was like and what sort of person I was. Most clients really enjoyed these albums, and there was enough proof of my capabilities in them to give a client total peace of mind. Nowadays since writing my own gardening column in the *Kessingland and Broadland Times* magazine, now for some 20-odd years. I photocopy each article twice, to go out in two separate large folders to clients who were interested.

I used to let potential clients keep a folder for a period of two weeks, then as the years have gone on and the size of the folder increases, the clients keep them for a month. I have now gone back to a fortnightly loan, for I have been so totally surprised when after a month's loan, the clients say "Oh! I haven't had a chance to look at them yet!" or "I didn't have time" or worst of all, "Sorry, I forgot all about them, they're still in the cupboard!" It's sad when you think that they could have been in someone else's hands who would truly have appreciated them, and sad too when you think that the whole reason for them having the albums/folder is to beat the cowboy, for they don't even come close when it comes to my vast knowledge on plants/gardening, and no, that's not being big-headed, that's plain honest, and laying myself open to one and all, and proof of the pudding that the client will be in very safe hands, and so foolhardy if they don't make full use of the time to at least read bits randomly to give them a bit of peace of mind.

I now loan the folders out in fortnightly stints, of course, because at present time there's twenty-three years worth of articles to read. It goes without saying that I'm not daft enough to think that every single article will be read. But on saying that, one lady, Anna Boggis, really did read every single word that I had written, and was adamant about that. Anna's husband Peter is very well-known in Southwold, Suffolk, or should say Easton Bavents, for trying to save his and other people's homes from falling into the sea through coastal erosion. Peter has battled with every known authority for help; locally Peter has the affectionate name of 'King Canute'!

Peggy Cavill (Cavell?) was the very first person in my new home town to borrow all eight photo albums with more or less information about each photograph. So you, the reader, will be so surprised at what I'm about to write, albeit this has happened many times before and since that time, so find it baffling that I as a professional gardener, get spoken to as a 'cowboy' would, so indeed how do 'cowboys' con so many people?

At the time I commenced Peggy's garden, she was still looking at the wealth of knowledge in my albums. I started weeding the first very unkempt flower bed, when Peggy came out and said, "Don't pull those out, they're my Honesty plants!" (Lunaria 'biennis'). I answered, "These are not Honesty plants, they are…" I was then stopped in my tracks by Peggy! "I'm telling you, my lad" (my lad, I was thirty-nine!) "don't you touch my Honesty plants."

I thought it now best to point out that she was wrong and that she'd employed me because I know my job, so I blurted out, "Peggy, these are weeds, it's 'Hedge Garlic'," but again she asked me to leave her plants alone.

At this point I thought it best to keep this situation light-hearted, so told Peggy that this then will make my job easy and find something else to do in another part of the garden, which I did. Soon after I started on the next bit I espied Peggy coming towards me with a gardening book in her hand, and couldn't wait to show me a picture of Honesty, "Look, Peggy," I said, "could I just pinch a bit off a leaf of the hedge garlic?" Peggy gave me permission to do so, I then rubbed a bit between my fingers and asked her to do the same. On doing this and putting it to her nose, she quickly drew back because of the pungent smell. "See, Peggy, hedge garlic!" Peggy said nothing, but saw her quickly thumbing her way to the weed section and no doubt to check on the leaf shape, which grant you does look like Honesty.

Peggy never did ask me to pull them out, so assumed that she would now wait to see what the flowers would be like, and indeed wonder why her Honesty plants did not put on fairly vigorous growth. The point I'm making is why have a dog and bark yourself? Why did she not accept that I'd given the immediate and correct identification? Why call in a professional gardener and doubt my words?

There was yet another very big problem at Peggy's – this time it was in her greenhouse, and so shocked at what I saw. Peggy had bought several tomato plants, and I noticed straight away that they'd all died, but oddly Peggy hadn't noticed this, but thought she was training tomato plants up strings. The 'tomato' plants were in fact the common weed that grows, mainly on dry wasteland 'Enchanters Nightshade'! Peggy had them all neatly tied on the strings and had even done all the usual nipping out of the side-shoots! This weed does have potato/tomato type flowers, all of course being in the same family.

The 'Enchanters Nightshade' in a garden is a fairly short weed, but because Peggy had fed and watered them they'd grown to the full height of the green house, some 6ft or so. Thankfully though the berries did stay small, for at first being green, then red (like a very, very small tomato) then black, hence then not anyone possibly making an attempt to eat one.

Once again I had to approach Peggy, gingerly, and show her the great error she had made. I had to point out that what a good job that the berries did not reach real tomato size and picked at the red stage prior to the black, or there would have been very serious health problems. Peggy insisted that I pull them out straight away, no doubt thinking back to the 'Honesty Saga' and she perhaps then knew that I knew what I was talking about. (Peggy is 91 in 2010.)

Doubt

Very many people have told me that it's such a good idea to have my work shown in photos or articles so now I'll tell you, the reader, why I decided to do such a thing. The idea came about very soon after I went self-employed many years ago now. A lady asked me to prune some roses for her; I went to estimate, the price was accepted and was about to set about doing the job when the lady said, "Now you do know what you're doing, don't you?" To say that I was deeply insulted is an understatement, but in an instant I thought… no, the lady is right in a way, I'd only just gone self-employed; she knew nothing about me or my work, the lady must have seen the look of horror on my face, knowing that I was being doubted.

From this point onwards I made a point of taking a camera with me on almost every job. I say almost, for every garden is different from the one before, so did try to pick a garden where there were different types of work. As an example, I'd take photos of the various sized ponds and rockeries that I'd made. I'd love taking photos of a totally neglected garden, and photographing it in the different stages to completion, then ask the client if I could photograph again in subsequent years to show maturity.

I also took delight in doing restoration on shrubs, ornamental trees, fruit-trees, roses, climbers and weepers of all sorts, i.e. Wisteria, Cotoneaster, Salix, etc. I'd photograph the neglected shrub say, prune it and take a picture, plus come back at some point the following year to show new growth and of course a final photo.

All these so different gardens in pictures could now give great hope to all those that had to look at their wilderness garden each day and not knowing which way to turn. You can appreciate now, reader, why that as now a 62-year-old man with vast experience still to this day get a good few doubters – unbelievable!

I have tried to give good advice to other up-and-coming gardeners, and also to other tradesmen who decide to take up self-employment. I always offer to loan them a copy of my 'terms and conditions' and another A.4 sheet with a guide to 'Payment'.

After only a few years self-employed, there were several pitfalls, but became a part of learning, hence now being able to do a detailed 'Terms and Conditions', these of course given to the potential client on my arrival to estimate. This, along with my detailed leaflet mentioning all the aspects of gardening that I carry out. I found it useless really just giving a client a business card with 'Landscape Gardener & Plantsman written on it, with address and telephone number.

The leaflet idea was a good idea, for it tells the client so much more, for many would look down the list and would say "Ooh! I see you prune fruit-trees" or "I note that you do lawncare" etc. They could then see that the walls, paths, and patios were not on the list for this should be left perhaps strictly for the Landscape Stonemason? Fencing, would not be there either and should be left again perhaps to a proper fencing contractor? All possibly not knowing a buttercup from a rose!

I'm not saying that landscape gardeners can't do these jobs of work, but I'd feel better in safer hands with someone specialising in one type of job, and knowing that job backwards, and rather less likely of getting a bodge job done, or being stumped with a problem.

Personally, I'm sure I would enjoy being a pavior or fencer if I'd had training, but I'd never make any attempt to try and take on such jobs of work. I had done a certain amount of fencing in my earlier career, and did do three jobs of work putting up a fence when self-employed. These turned out to be the last three fences that I ever did, and the reason being was that all three of these jobs of work were over different years, and on each of those days there were high winds; on my own and trying to put up 6ft panels, was no joke I can tell you! The very last one that I did was quite a long fence; I put in a good price, and all was going so well until the very last panel, and a post had to go on the very spot where a covered-up overgrown 3ft diameter tree stump was hidden, and took me three days on my own to dig it out. I have never put up another fence since.

When I did do fencing, I was lucky enough at the time to have a good pal who was a fencing contractor, and he was the one who told me how to do my pricing – he told me to charge a pound a foot, therefore to put in your first post would be six pounds for a six foot post, hence you need two posts so you got twelve pounds to put up the two posts needed to hold the panel. If the panel was six foot high, that would be a further six pounds, hence back then would be eighteen pounds to erect one panel. The client of course had to have to pre-buy the timber, cement, nails, etc., the pound a foot was for labour only.

If I was lucky enough to get trade discount, this on occasions helped boost my money up a bit, but it is more usual that the money you made from trade discount, covered a bit of time and petrol, phone-calls etc. collecting and delivering those materials.

I have had the most annoying clients over the years who know that I get trade discount, but expect this applies to them too, they sometimes want to come with you to get the materials and get the trade prices too, and worst of all it's those clients who don't come with you, I doing all the running about and they reaping the harvest. If I knew they were going to do this from the job estimation day, I would have put my labour charges up – at least this would cover some of the petrol costs and my time.

It rarely happens, but in a way it should occur more often, and that is for the clients themselves to buy all their own materials. Okay, so they don't get any discount, but it would really show them how much time and petrol they're using, moreso when certain items are out of stock and you have to run around elsewhere. It's like all these garden makeover programmes, that's the side they never show, for all the materials are on site and ready to be used, and no delays for the gardening teams.

Peace of Mind...

...Or should be if all clients read my terms and conditions carefully, for the purpose of it is to help them, and in turn really helps me, hence any job of work should run really smoothly.

I'll now run you through some of these terms and the reasons behind them. I'll mark my 'reply' with an asterisk; others are self-explanatory.

1) Children and animals must be kept away during work progress.

* The obvious dangers are there if tools or machinery are left on site. And there's nothing worse when you have done a good level, nicely prepared for turfing, and you come in the next morning to see all your hard work ruined, and you have to re-level it all again with no extra pay. Once I decided to add a terms and conditions list and clients hadn't bothered to read it. I simply lay the turf on the messed up ground where children or animals have been let loose. Some clients still let their kids or dog run about, even when you're there actually working, and the client can even see the problems being caused.

2) Cash payment for all materials, receipt given. A cheque or cash can be paid to delivery drivers marked C.O.D. for turf etc.

* It's always best to get the money up front for materials, for if you are knocked for your labour (yes, there is such a thing as cowboy clients, of which I'll go into later) – then at least you haven't been knocked for all the materials as well. Also, with ready cash, if you do have to buy alternatives or go elsewhere from your usual stockists you had the ready money.

3) Materials and labour are listed separately on your estimate sheet.

* I decided to do this when I noticed builders, painters, decorators, roofers, fencers etc., etc., put the prices together. For example, say a job came to £3,000, the client has no idea what is labour or what is materials. If say the £3,000 was too much for the client and your estimate is turned down, it may possibly have been because the material costs were high, for if you separate from the labour, the client can see what the actual cost is. Let me put it another way – say I've suggested forty pieces of rockery stone, eighty alpine plants, thirty bags of alpine grit, ten bags of compost and one hundred turf. If that cost was too high for the client, you could then hopefully save the loss of that job by cutting down a bit. You could suggest wider borders, therefore less turf, even forget bone-meal if you'd suggested it. Then you can break down further by having forty

plants, twenty bits of rock, fifteen bags of alpine grit (or none at all, and wait for the plants to do the covering), five bags of compost or none.

At this point the client can cut down a little more. I never alter the labour price though, for very little regards the hard work would really change. I've secured many jobs of work by separating, for the customer truly knows the cost of their job, and also it's a kind of honesty.

4) Payment for labour must be paid on day of completion. Failure to do so will incur a small charge.

* I mention this for it's surprising how when I've completed a job of work how the client just lets you leave without a single word about payment, so then you go home and have to write out an invoice that should not have been needed, for the client clearly knows what they owe you.

5) If you require a separate bill at the end of any work completion, I must be told prior to work commencement, therefore I can prepare a bill, so as not to delay payment further.

* Very similar to No.4 above. There's nothing worse when you've worked hard on a job, and at the end you should be getting paid at the end of the day, for it's so simple to pay cash or write a cheque, to then be told "could you invoice me". It's so frustrating when the client knows your labour charge that's in front of them!

6) Payment methods – cheque, part cheque, part cash, cash, cash payments receipted.

* I find this popular with clients.

7) The price of the labour is for the work done, not how long the job has taken.

* Boy! this has been a boon over the years, and now I'll tell you why. I would be a multi-millionaire if I, and other tradesmen could pinpoint the exact time a job will take, yet nearly every client will ask "how long will it take you?" There can be so very many problems on most jobs – it could be weather conditions, a rotovator breakdown, including leaf-blowers, chainsaw, hedge-cutter, materials not being at stockists, hours in a day, distance to a job, underlying problems not seen or noticeable on the day of estimating. Hence 7) above can work in the client's favour or yours, or indeed the job takes the exact time that it's been priced for.

Here are only some classic examples, gains and losses. Do you remember a few pages back when I did fencing, all going well until a huge tree stump was uncovered exactly where a post had to go, and how I lost out big time. Another job, many years ago, where I had to cut a holly-hedge, priced for one good day and took me three, but still only got the one day that I charged for the job. This was the first holly-hedge that I cut, or tried to cut with electric hedge shears, and proved almost impossible – the shears blocked with the thick leaves and stems, and made rips rather than clean cuts, so had to abandon the shears and do this huge hedge with secateurs and pruning loppers.

The client, needless to say, didn't pay me a penny over my price. I was in my twenties then, and did not consider the two words that would have got me out of trouble, and that is Estimate and Quote. Watching a TV programme one day, they said that a quote is a fixed price and has to stay as it is; an estimate is of course an estimation on what a job will be, so assume it is for labour and materials as two separate things. This does however leave plenty of scope for the cowboy worker to suddenly bump up the price at the end. I always let the client know in advance if materials or labour is to increase beyond the stated price and the reason for it.

On the subject of the wrong side of estimating, and that was when I was called out to price for a smallish tree to come out, and being small I priced it at a mere £12 which was to include the dumping fee for it at £2. The tree however instead of taking an hour or so to dig out, it took one very long day! The reason for that was that although it was only about six to eight inches in diameter it was in fact a 'new' trunk that had grown from the original 2ft diameter stump; the tree of course had been cut down at some point, and a fairly large tree, so someone either changed their mind and perhaps did away with the obvious suckers that would have appeared soon after it was cut down, one must have been retained to grow back as a tree?

Anyhow, I had a labourer to pay, so assumed the client would pay me more because of the dilemma… no, he paid me exactly £12. We'd cut up all the prunings small to fit in a trailer, we had to take it on a weighbridge, wait for it… yes, you've guessed… they charged me exactly twelve pounds! So having to pay a labourer a full day, I got nothing at all.

Total Bliss!

Many years ago now I did a landscape project of some size. They were extremely rich people, the man of the house was a gent, but the lady was really arrogant. At this point of time in their garden, I was pricing up several jobs, all at various prices, and at the end of one job this very posh la-de-da lady said, "What do I owe you?" I said one eighty-eight – now what I mean was one £88 as a good majority of the work was mostly at that price.

In an instant as this lady paid me with a good few notes I could see that there was far more than eighty-eight pounds, in fact there was one hundred and eighty-eight pounds, i.e. one eighty-eight!

I bit my lip and said nothing. I had unwittingly been rewarded if you like for the total rudeness over the past weeks.

Some Are Nosey!

I'm referring back now to my Terms and Conditions – Please pay labour payment away from labourers, remember this is your private business and most certainly mine! – Some labourers over the years always try to see what you're earning, and assume that all the money is mine to do as I please with it, they being totally clueless when not knowing what is involved in being self-employed. I should think that 99% of people who have helped me over the years have no rent or mortgage to pay, also don't run a car, own a phone (most own mobiles nowadays). I rest my case.

Squeezing a Bit More!

Once an estimate is accepted that's bound in my opinion, so over the years I've had to put? a stop to all the people who say, "Could you just" in other words, "Could you just cut that hedge while you're here?" or "Could you just prune that shrub?" etc.

All extra work added, but certainly not estimated for, and very often all these 'justs' added on a fair bit of time. Very few would carry on and say "add it to my bill." I soon learnt how crafty some of the clients could be, and added the following rule to my Terms and Conditions – Any work added to above estimate, no matter how small, the work will have to be re-estimated.

This soon put a stop to people suddenly having a lapse of memory at the time of estimating, these words now echo in their brain to think on *exactly* what they want me to do in the garden.

The Hard-up Rich

Now don't get me started on this one! for any landscape gardener will tell you the same, for money will always be found to buy a car, more than one holiday a year, and do up say a neglected house if a client has moved into a dilapidated property.

With all this done you hear those dreaded words, "We can't afford a lot in the garden" yet they want a nice garden. "We've spent such a lot on the house" is the other sentence that is uttered. Again, a perfect opening for the cowboy gardener. "Oh!" we'll do a nice cheap job, we'll make it look effective for the low price accepted." No, the clients don't hear these words, but that's what's happened or suggested between the cowboy gardeners.

I take no notice of all this hard-up nonsense, for you simply wouldn't call in a professional landscaper and expect to pay very low prices, and expect a top job.

Let me give you an example. A very well-off couple sold their massive house to buy something 'smaller', it still looked like a mini-mansion. The very first job they had done was to have every single window in this house taken out, and put in new double glazing, but it was double glazing that had the most beautiful glass very much on the style of stained glass, and of course was all leaded.

They'd called me in because they had a dozen or so very old neglected fruit-trees, and as I specialised in restoration of such trees, went ahead to estimate, going through with the customer about the procedure to carry out this type of work. The estimate was not accepted. "We found your price too expensive; if you could cut it down a fair bit we'll have the job done, only we have just had an enormous layout to get our double glazing." I thought to myself, no way – why should I subsidise my price because the double glazing was really expensive, those blokes got their money okay, so why should I lose out on doing my work professionally.

I coolly and calmly replied by saying, "The price will stay the same, and I can hold this price until this time next year. The trees are so badly neglected that one more year will make no difference. It'll give you plenty of time to save up your pennies." Gentle wording I'd say, to put the knife in and play them at their own game. Needless to say, I had a telephone call for me to go ahead with the said priced job.

On this very same job, the people gave permission to use their very luxurious new kitchen to make myself and my helper cups of tea throughout the day. They also let us have the use of their loo upstairs. Now I'll tell you about a rule that I give most of my helpers, and that is whether the client is at home or not, never look towards their windows, even if out of the corner of your eye you see a client at the kitchen sink or sitting directly in their front room in front of their patio doors... avert your eyes!

As I say, the people, who were in fact very nice, gave us permission to make tea in the kitchen. Their dining room was adjacent to it, then horror of horrors my helper stepped a couple of steps into their front room and said how beautiful it was. I called him back, with his cuppa in hand, and told him to come out of that room, even though he'd only made three or four steps. He asked me "Why?" I then said that the people had already put their trust in us to use the kitchen and the upstairs loo, where many other 'close up shop' when they go out, even if it's only half an hour. I said, "Supposing you turned round and knocked something over, or something went missing, moreso what about if bits of mud came off your boots or bottoms of your trousers and you hadn't noticed – the clients then would know you've been in a room that you're not supposed to go in, and any trust would go right out of the window.

Another odd thing happened on the actual day of work commencement, police pulled up outside of the house just behind my van and asked what I was doing as there had been a call to them. It was clearly obvious that I was a landscape gardener, for it was plastered on all sides of my large transit van, and still at that point unloading my van of work tools (note the word unloading, rather than loading as if items were being stolen to load up). The police themselves too found it very odd because it was plainly obvious what was going on. When the customer came home I relayed all that had gone on and the inevitable 'curtain twitchers'! The client said, "Oh, I know who called the police, that would be old Mr... I told him to give eye to the place as we both work each day, but it seems he's been a little too helpful this time. I'll buy him a bottle of wine."

I couldn't believe it really, the old chap was rewarded for stupidity. I never said that to the client of course, but did say that if I was a burglar or whatever, would I really do it in broad daylight, have my name and address and telephone number on the van, take time to unload various sized ladders, rakes, chainsaws, leaf-blowers, plus various journeys to and from the van to collect the tubs of winter tar wash oil, sprayer, tree grease, pruning compound etc. Would I or my pal sit in the van at various times to have our lunches etc? Would a burglar be seen to cart out and load up tons of prunings etc? I think not somehow.

The client did say she thought the client (neighbour?) was seeking praise for being observant, and even she thought that the man knew all along that we were genuine tradesmen.

I Need That Extra Push!

Don't believe all that you see or hear on TV, radio or newspapers – how many times do we all hear that? Especially on answering gardening queries, how come they know all the answers that the public put to them? With TV it's normally very scripted, for a viewer would have we assume rung in or wrote earlier, for the shrub or plant where the query lies, just happens to be right there in the studio! The presenter then can read the auto-cue or have a quick study of the subject in hand just a few hours before air time, for they are never failing in plant I.D., pests, diseases, pruning times etc.

Yes, they are deeply knowledgeable people, but doesn't it seem odd that they know about everything that's in front of them? It's probably more genuine if there is say a panel of experts, where some specialise in just the one subject, where others, and that does include me, have to learn a bit about all aspects of gardening and probably not always able to answer all questions.

Look at TV gardening makeovers where we're told they only have three days to do a garden, what's the three days all about? It can take me 2–3 days sometimes running around collecting materials, even then they can be out of stock; what about inclement weather – how come it rarely rains on these programmes, so you know that the programme can be cut to make the viewer believe that weather was good and it really did take three days.

I like to think that I'm a fairly knowledgeable gardener, but as a man now sixty-two years old, still undermine myself in so many ways. I never had the confidence to do a questions and answers, so when I did gardening talks mine was scripted and yet it wasn't if you know what I mean. One week or so prior to my engagement, say for a W.I. meeting, I'd send them an A.4 sheet with questions numbered 1–61 and I knew the answers of course to all 61 questions, choosing some that would give people a good laugh, or a question that was intriguing, some had short swift answers, others more detailed.

As I say, the chairperson would have the list and I'd ask them to photo-copy this for each and every member who was to attend that day, and the members could read all the questions or titles, put a tick by it and their name, hence on the night I'd simply look at each paper and say, "Right, Mrs Brown would like to know the story of what plant made me look a fool?" and I'd then reel off that story and so on. If someone had also picked that question, we'd go through each of the other members' questions, then ask those people who had chosen the same 'story' to pick another numbered question.

This was my script, so knew all the answers in an instant, where perhaps if it had been random questions as we're led to believe on TV, radio etc. I may not have looked so clever, with a "er, don't know the answer to that" or "sorry, can't help you there" etc.

Panelled programmes you have plenty of back-up, for if one expert gives an answer, another panellist could add a bit more, and possibly a third or even fourth person could add their two ha'porth, a programme then more believable.

Unappreciative Clients

There have been very many over the years but a few need mentioning, as all the following happens to me as a professional gardener. I do very often wonder how cowboy workers fare?

The first two incidents, if I can call them that, are two separate projects, and both old rectories. Both were massive gardens needing gross restoration and replanting and back to a former glory.

The first rectory had vegetable plots and a good-sized pond that needed restoring and replanting. I commenced this job in January, and one of the first jobs was to pull away blackberry that had grown up into the trees and had grown to a height of sixty feet! Whilst on the subject of blackberries, many years ago now some people who owned a launderette on the corner of Queenswood Avenue and Fulbourne Rd., E.17, and a new business venture for them, but the garden out the back was wall-to-wall congested with many years of dense blackberry. This was the perfect job for a before-and-after photo, the after photo showing the now perfectly levelled ground and new lawn.

Let me now get back to the old rectory – this was a huge restoration project, and even had to hire in pumps to empty the very large neglected pond. I planted all the edges of this pond with every type of moisture-loving plant that I could get my hands on, and looked superb, along with another area where I created a mini-woodland walk, and planted up plants that suited a woodland condition.

I really put my heart and soul into this, and once the garden was created, I was asked to maintain it. This meant of course planting spring and summer bedding plants, not only in flower beds, but also the numerous concrete ornamental pots that adorned various parts of the garden, and several were on concrete pedestals either side of steps etc., the added height gave me plenty of scope to use the many trailing plants that can be bought today.

I spent over and above my hours here, for I enjoyed it so much, and never charged an extra penny. I was to regret this by the time the darker nights came, moreso on the dark dank November days when it gets dark at half-past three/four o'clock time. It was the first of these dark days and had to pack up at 4.30, but the man owner was most upset by this, but it was near dark. My finishing time was fine, but he was very annoyed that I was going home, he had of course 'forgotten' about all those unpaid hours that I did back in the summer, for it was I hoped a bit of give and take.

Rather than argue or explain to the client, I never went back after that day, for to me it was a great insult.

The second rectory was about eight times the size of the first, and unkempt for years. This was a huge project, and we, that is two of my three sons, worked like Trojans to get the place up to standard, and on occasions barrowing and raking level around forty tons of mulch per week!

Once the massive clearance was carried out, this left massive areas of now blank ground that now needed filling. The people who owned it were millionaires – she a top lawyer, he was the highest in his position running one of our top banks.

The cost of the trees, plants shrubs along was £1,000 per week, hence with the trade prices I was getting helped boost my wages up and good bonuses for my two boys. Strangely, it was coming to the end of the main plantings when problems started to occur.

I had cleared a very old neglected herbaceous border, some 60 feet long and 12 feet wide, and was now ready for planting up. The man of the house came up to me one day and said, "We're spending an awful lot of money on plants each week, Keith." Luckily, although frightfully posh, the man of the house was friendly and approachable, so I could speak to him man to man. I did ask him straight out, "Why are we doing all this restoration, to then leave bare areas?" The chap then spoke about the cost, albeit did have the graciousness to say how beautiful the garden was now. I had to point out that it seemed like I was the bad guy in all this, and said that indeed costs could be brought down dramatically, if you want shrubs 8–10 feet apart I can do so, or perennials 5–6 feet apart, it will not look half as effective, and not nearly as nice as the rest of the completed garden with closer planting and marvellous colours, plus because of the close planting and heavy mulches, the weeds have kept at bay, hence cutting down maintenance costs, and not having to keep back-tracking, for the new bits of garden were looking after themselves, apart from watering. This all leaves time to restore and plant new areas. I also asked the chap, once we've cleared a neglected bed, what are we to do with it? I made a point of saying we could spend £50 a week and not £1,000, as long as I'm not blamed that the beds don't look nearly as nice, nor will the newly restored beds yet to follow.

I was now once again truly disheartened, and after the now two years of restoration, I decided to call it a day there. The man's wife thought it well below her to even turn on a hose to keep alive the new plants. "I don't do that!" she exclaimed when I said that someone would have to put water on them or they would all die. I was worried, for although the main bulk of planting was done and we were reduced to two days a week at the rectory, it seemed that no one was to keep the plants watered. I've carried out some wonderful gardening projects in my time, but it has been so sad that the clients have not always appreciated my work, and keep hold of a good worker and knowledgeable one at that, even if it does sound like I'm blowing my own trumpet.

Knock Knocked

"Beware of being 'knocked'," this was a term I soon learnt when I told people that I was going self-employed. Being knocked is a word to the layman meaning someone isn't going to pay you at the end of the job of work that you're doing, and had no intention of paying.

Have I been knocked I hear you, reader, ask?! Yes, three times in all my career. The very first time was when I was about nineteen I should think, and still a few years yet from passing my driving test. I mention this, for I was asked to do a lot of garden work at Southgate, hence I put various garden tools in a large hessian sack and travelled with this by bus! Boy, was that a task on its own, I can tell you!

Anyhow, I finished the job and the people were happy and promised to send on the money. After several requests by letter to them, the owner was always soon – 'soon' never came and they never did pay me. After a year or so, I made the journey from Walthamstow to Southgate again, but this time armed with a total weed-killer, the house had walkways and back gates to the properties, so I crept round, no one was about, and weed-killed the lot.

I only got this idea when friends of mine built a lovely front garden wall; they too got knocked, so my friends did some knocking themselves – they drove their truck over the lot, and took back some of the more expensive bricks, and the gates. You'd think it'd be legal to do this as you've not been paid labour or materials, and assume it's still your property. WRONG! The man had the nerve to report my friends to the police and it all got as far as going to court. My friends lost, they weren't fined very much, but as they said, it was the satisfaction that the man would have to pay someone to clear all the mess and added expense by having to pay someone to rebuild the wall, and pay this time he must have done for he couldn't risk another court appearance. The police of course did know the true story of what happened, and they too must have wondered why he didn't just pay my friends in the first place, for my friends always had a good reputation for their work. I think he thought he'd get away with not paying, but hadn't bargained for my pals to demolish his lovely wall.

So you see, we hear so much today about cowboy workers, but as you've read, there's plenty of cowboy clients too! My second 'knock' came whilst doing a restoration job, where rubbish, prunings etc., burnt for some five days in all, such was the neglect of this garden, and I had very long working days there until ten in the evening. I got well and truly knocked on this one. The lady paid me £100, then nothing for months, then a fifty pence postal order! I took her to the small claims court, but no money came until one day she turned up on my doorstep and gave me another £25. She kept saying how sorry she was, but was waiting for her brother in America to pay her some money. I never did receive another penny from her. I kept chasing up the small claims people to no avail, then out of the blue I got a letter from the lady saying how sorry she was that no money had come my way, but so thankfully she did write to say "how beautiful the garden now looked, and all the hard work and the results I can still see today." Well, I thought, at least on me showing people this, proved that it was nothing that I'd done wrong... no cowboy work.

I never did get another penny, only a letter from the small claims court some four years down the line when we first moved to Suffolk, to ask if I'd still like to pursue the case! and an enclosed letter naming all the other companies that she'd knocked, all wanting money from her. She'd knocked toy shops, clothes departments, furniture stores – the list was a long one. I could see some pretty big company names on that list, so little old me wouldn't have stood a chance of getting my money if they couldn't.

My next knock wasn't until we got to Suffolk. One very rich man asked me to give him an estimate to prune fruit trees and very neglected ornamental trees. On the completed job he just handed me some notes and said, "This'll do you." I didn't quite know what he meant by that, but on reaching home, he'd knocked me for seventy pounds. I telephoned him straight away, and he was very cocky and brash, and said that I should be happy with what I'd got. Unbelievably this man owned one of the very big amusement arcades on Great Yarmouth's sea-front.

My next knock was a total surprise. A job of work was accepted and priced for one long day, the job was to clear the garden and prepare for turf. The turf arrived late afternoon, and finished late. The bombshell came when I asked for my money. The lady quite blatantly and unashamedly said, "I can't pay you, my husband lost his job yesterday." I said, "So you knew yesterday that you had no intention of paying me today, you never stopped me coming did you?" I also went on to say that "if your husband only lost his job yesterday, that doesn't mean that today you're totally skint does it? You must have had our money at some point in the last couple of days, so where is it? You knew we were coming today."

The woman refused payment, so I said, "I'll get it somehow, you'll see." I knew of course that you can't get blood out of a stone, so decided on another tactic, for she'd not only knocked me but also the turf supplier, and I again lost out big time because I still had a labourer to pay, which I did.

I don't know if my tactic worked, but I don't think that I would have wanted to be in those people's shoes after I had done my deed! My plan was simple, I wrote a letter to them, demanding my money, and how the job was accepted by them, how they'd knocked the turf company and how I still had to pay my labourer, and in the letter I also mentioned about her husband's sudden job loss supposedly the previous day, and I further added that I'd billed them a further three times asking for payment to be paid in stages (there was of course no reply nor money).

I photocopied this detailed letter, some forty odd copies in all, went back to the road starting at the nearest end house, to see how the road house numbers ran on each side of the road, up to and past their house. I put each letter in, which I of course commenced with Dear Mr Mrs... (then their surname), but on my now stamped envelope accidentally on purpose 'forgot' to put who the letter was to, but then simply wrote on the envelope all the house numbers. Hence the householder couldn't fail to open the letter and read its contents, then realise that the letter hadn't been for them, but for the people down the road, opposite, or indeed right next door!

Hence forty-odd people in that road now knew what these people were like. It goes without saying possibly all those letters were returned to the people who knocked me, either posted by hand, or the unexpected receivers of these letters simply filling in the blank bit where the surname was left out, change the house number to the correct one, and put it back in the post with 'not known at this address, try number (?)' hence no stamp needed either!

These people must have had a good few come back through their door, and now knowing that they would be the talk of the neighbourhood. All this though, and I still did not get any payment, in fact some four years down the line, the woman made a point of saying "Hello" in a local superstore. How thick-skinned can folk be. It was a good tactic don't you think, and one worth remembering if you, the reader, sadly ever get to have a problem like this.

You, the reader, can now see why I get the materials' money up-front first, for if you do get knocked, you only lose the materials' money – I say ONLY, for this too can be quite a substantial amount to lose, let alone your labour.

There is one more thing worth a mention, whilst I'm on the subject of being knocked and that is how you get paid but knocked at the same time. How does this happen, I hear you ask? Simple, say you've given the client your price for the job, and you do that job as priced. Sometimes clients will say, "Oh, sorry, I forgot to ask you to prune my ornamental cherry, and to cut back that old Ivy, stick it on your bill at the end." Well, that's better to mention money, unlike all the "could you just do this while you're here, and do that, and that…" without a word about money.

No, the problem comes when you do bill them at the end, a point blank refuse to pay for all the extra work that you have done for them, with remarks like, "I didn't think it would cost all that!" and they do refuse to pay you too; they pay the original price, but none of the extras that they asked you to do. Now you can see why I now say to all my clients when they ask for extra bits to be done, I tell them that "I'll do the job first" and price the other and send you an estimate," thus now giving me a quieter life.

So many things happen when you're self-employed and dealing with the public, and this is how all my terms and condition, rules and regulations came about, and as you've read you can see why!

A good majority of my clients were, and are, real salts of the earth, they go that extra mile, so do I and then it's more like working for close family or friends, in fact several clients do become friends. Some clients over-pay or give a good tip, but this hasn't happened as much in Suffolk as it did in London's East End. But the clients that do, I am forever grateful to. One lady I had to charge twenty pounds to dig out a conifer and she gave me twenty pounds on top, and said it was well worth it, but I do state that they're making their job of work far dearer than need be, but how lovely it is to be really very much appreciated.

I've had some awkward moments too over the years. I'd priced to dig out a tree stump; I hadn't had a lot of work at that point, so was glad that this job came up. Tree stumps rarely are easy jobs of work by far, but anyway I got to work with axe, pick-axe, spade, crowbars, mattock etc., and set about the task with all my strength, and after an hour or so it came out. I'd priced it for our to five hours, so I was glad that it came out fairly quickly, albeit still some task on my own I can tell you.

The job done, I went for my money up to the house. The lady said, "What, already?" so I said yes, "all done!" "Well, I don't think I should pay all this," the lady said, so before an argument really ensued, the woman's father came round and asked what was wrong. The lady quickly said, "He's only been here for an hour and a half or so, and he's charging me" (let's say) "£80." So the lady's father said, "Is that the price on Keith's quote?" The woman said, "Yes." "Then pay him," said her dad, "for if Keith had taken all day getting that big root out, or indeed into tomorrow, it would've still been £80, wouldn't it, Keith?" I said yes it would, for that was the price for that particular job. I would be a miracle man if I could estimate 100% correctly, for no one knows which way a job will go.

Thanks to that lady's father, the daughter sort of understood, but was a reluctant payer. I was dreading that her dad was coming over to agree with her, and I would have had far less money, and not come away with my full amount, considering how slack work had been at that point. Hence another rule of mine coming into fruition – the price is for the work done, not the time taken. This alone has been a great boon for me over the years and glad that I'd overcome another problem. My rules were now truly paying off. When problems have occurred on odd occasions over the years, I can say "did you read my Terms and Conditions?" If they hadn't then of course the ball was in my court, and I could point out that the rules were there to help both parties and to help the total smooth running of their job.

I Could've Been a Billionaire by Now!

How's that, I hear you ask? Well, one day I had to go to the tax office in Walthamstow, for I had a tax query that I wanted sorting out, and to my total surprise after I gave them my full name and address, phone number job of work etc. they looked at their records and it said… Deceased! There it was all written down in black and white – I couldn't believe it, nor could they! I often wonder if I had stayed self-employed throughout and not taken the odd job on cards so to speak, I would never ever had to pay tax ever again, for the tax people most certainly would not bother to write to a dead man for money. This was all back in the 1970s, it's now almost 2011 and if I hadn't gone into the tax office that day, I needn't have paid a penny tax from that time, for I did no longer exist.

Chase Me!

Let me tell you about another bloomer regarding local authorities. I, even if I say so myself, have been an extremely hard grafter all my life, and certainly not one for handouts. It was one winter in the late 1970s, winter being mostly a very bad time for us gardeners work-wise. Snow and ice had laid for several weeks, hence no work came in, and nothing to commence, even if the ice and snow melted. The only thing I could do was to sign onto the dole to get some money, and that's what I did. Thankfully though at that time I had already been advertising in a local newspaper and the advert was still running when the ice and snow appeared. Strangely enough, even though in later weeks when the snow had melted and just ice or heavy frosts were about, I did receive about two calls for me to actually go and estimate, more calls came.

It was only about two to three weeks or so being on the dole, when I espied a ginger-haired man standing at the bus stop directly opposite our then house. He looked very suspicious and kept looking at our house. This happened every day for a few days, and I was very ready to call the police or go and see him personally to see what he was up to.

At last the snow, ice and frost went away for a good while and back to work I went, and able to sign off the dole, and hoping that the bad weather wouldn't return, or else I'd have to go through all the palaver of signing on again. After about three weeks back to work, a letter arrived addressed to me from the dole office wishing to see me. In the meantime I carried on working on the various gardening jobs that were accepted, but on driving to and from my work, and the various garden centres to pick up materials for each job of work. It was during this time that I saw the ginger-haired man driving in an almost identical coloured sports car in a dull orange! This man was on occasions driving behind me, alongside me, pulling out of turnings to follow me, then suddenly disappear. Who was this man? He was always just out of reach, he was never there when my van was stationary at various times.

I was beginning to think that perhaps I was imagining that this ginger man in his ginger sports car just happened to stand out, so I was able to spot him on fairly regular occasions, but then had to quickly remember that this was indeed the same man who had been staring at our house, mainly to my knowledge in the morning rush hour times, so it was baffling, so now I wished that I had approached him when I was able to whilst he was at the bus stop.

It was now the day to go to the dole office, suspecting that they'd either overpaid me, or perhaps even underpaid! I walked into a very crowded waiting room, and felt alienated, for although there were people there who really didn't want to be, but many others try to spend a lifetime on the dole and grow quite wealthy by it too. My name was called, and made my way to a plush office and was greeted by "Ah, Mr Nichols!" All I could say was, "It's you!" and there sat the ginger-haired man! I just couldn't believe it. I first made a point of saying that he had come close to having his lights punched out, but he gave a dull laugh. "You do know why you're here don't you?" I replied, "Sorry, no I don't." He then went on to say "I've been following you, and note that you've been working and signing on at the same time" (or a benefit thief in modern terms). Before I had a chance to speak, he reeled off all the roads and house numbers where I'd estimated or carried out work. "I lost you at one point, driving up Kings Head Hill." For you folk who wouldn't know Kings Head Hill, it's a steep hill in Chingford, London E4, and was on my way to my aunt and uncle's house at the top of the hill. I said, "How did you lose me? You in a sports car and me in a transit van?" "I don't know, but I did." So I had great pleasure in telling him that he had not lost me, he could have made a note of that address too, and later reveal to you that they were relatives of mine and simply paying a visit.

I was really angry now, and said, "Do you know that I've been signed off for over three weeks now?" He was shocked, "No, I didn't!" He reeled off some of the places where I'd been, and the times, all of the dates he had tallied with the actual times of estimating all during the worst of the weather, and the other dates tallied with actual dates when I worked after being accepted.

In an instant, the man closed his book and said, "Oh well, if you've signed off you can go." I was still angry and said, "No, you've accused me of cheating. I'm going home right now, and bring back my estimate book and work dates and what I got paid – these will tally with your dates." I also told him that "when I come back, I'm not going to sit in that waiting room for ages, I'm coming straight back in." He was now feeling very uncomfortable and very foolish.

I did go home and got the relevant papers, and yes I did go in straight away... well, more or less! The man kept saying how sorry he was, but had no answer when I asked why I had been singled out after only just signing on for a mere three weeks, yet others are on the dole for years. Again, he could not answer and I never went on the dole again, and yet it's something that I'm entitled to in dire times, but it's that same old story when it's the wrong ones being accused. The hours and petrol that the 'ginger man' spent following me for days on end must have been colossal, and shows you how the system had no idea that I'd signed off and told the ginger man's department. Oh well! Another of life's many sagas.

Talking a Load of Bowls!

Over the years and after leaving my positions as Head Groundsman for Leyton Orient F.C. and Head Groundsman at Wadham Lodge, because of the way Groundsmen are treated by the players of the various sports teams, vowed that I would never again take on any work involving sports work of any kind, even though I was told constantly how good I was supposed to be.

Sadly as I've mentioned, I can't take criticism, constructive criticism if it arises, yes, but not the critical whinges that I and no doubt other groundsmen get.

It was around the 1990s, and had worked for a retired couple, mainly twice a year pruning all their espalier fruit trees. Then one day the man of the house said that he was the Chairman of a bowling club (grass bowls) for Northgate Hospital, Great Yarmouth, Norfolk. He casually mentioned to me that he and others had become increasingly worried about the state of their bowling green.

The chap asked me if I would like two days a week on the green, albeit that two days I thought was pushing it a bit fine, for normally a greenkeeper's job was usually a full-time one. I mean, supposing it rained on one or both of those set days, surely the green would suffer even more? for my other days were of course back on my landscape side of things. The man didn't really answer my query, for I think that he was so keen to get me to take the job. I must admit I was reluctant and yet keen at the same time, and did lay my cards on the table with the man, by saying that I'd sworn that I would never take a job in sportswork ever again, as the players of whatever sport it may be always think they know my job better than me. One team member praises you, another member severe criticism, for you just can't have a good and bad job at the same time, it makes no sense.

Anyhow, my days that I was required, plus wages, were both worked out. I did have however just one stipulation, and that was if I had any bad criticism then I would leave without warning. The man agreed and said that he was glad that I was finally on board and shouldn't have any problems.

I was keen to get this green up and running again, yet still wondering how I was to perform miracles on just two days a week. I went along to see the green, and it was in a proper state, and you could clearly see that the players themselves had been having a go and failing miserably, and noted how they'd burnt sections of the green with the fertiliser. The rest of the green had bare patches and even small indentations everywhere, and wondered how on earth a game of bowls could even be played on it.

I had no doubts though that I could get this green back into pristine condition. The man took me over to the tool shed – I was totally shocked to see just a mower. I asked where all the other equipment was, they had no idea what I was on about, so I said that if a mower was all that they had, then no wonder the green was in such a state, so now I felt really confident that I could work miracles if the right equipment was bought for me.

One urgent item that was needed, and knew that it would be far too big to get into a small shed, and that is an item called a 'switch' or 'swish', and just could not believe that they had never had one. It is a simple item, a long 12–15ft bamboo cane, about one inch thick at the holding point, and tapering almost to a slither. The idea of the switch is that you simply switch it – or swish it – side to side, and used on a really dewy morning the switch knocks off all the dew into the ground, hence not just letting it evaporate and wasted. The switch could be used again when a rainfall finally stops, thus again the droplets now going into all the grasses.

The duller the day of course, the dew or rain would keep the green damper for longer. The switch also had another use, and on dryer mornings or just before the bowlers were due to arrive, and that was to run the switch over the whole of the green to break up the now dry encrusted worm casts; the casts are scattered like dust, and do so much good to the green, for the casts are rich in nitrogen.

Whilst mentioning nitrogen, a little tip for all of you who grow runner beans. At the end of the year when your runners are dead, just cut them off at the base for the roots often on occasions fairly plump and resembling the tubers of the smaller bedding dahlia, these tubers or small nodules are also very rich in nitrogen, so just leave them in the ground to rot away leaving their marvellous fertiliser. When you do cut your beans down, leave 2–3 inches of stem as a marker, and what I do then is to plant near that stem, and whether you plant fruit, veg or other plants, they are straight away being well fed.

As usual I've sidetracked, now back to the bowling green! Other vital equipment missing was an item called a True-Lute, a cumbersome item in my opinion, albeit did do a good job, but not if you have to use it all day. The idea of the lute is to use it for levelling and working in top dressings, mostly for ornamental lawns, bowling greens, cricket squares and such like. Top-dressing by the way if you're a layman, is a mix of sand, loam and peat, and extremely finely graded. You then put say half a barrow load of top dressing… let's say at one top corner of a bowling green for instance, you then knock it about to disperse the pile, either with the lute, rake or broom. You then work the lute backwards and forwards, say just working on a square yard at a time, the more indentations there are the quicker the top dressing disappears, the excess as your luting and satisfied that no more top dressing can be lost on that spot, you draw the excess top dressing to the adjacent spot but of course adding another half barrow of dressing, and so on until the whole area is completed.

Folk are often surprised when seeing a huge mound of topdressing, moreso for a bowling green, for they wonder where it's all going to go, especially as a green is so flat, or so they think. When you think how many times a green, wicket or garden lawn, is walked on in a year in all kinds of weather, you yourself cannot see what damage is actually occurring, hence why people cannot believe their eyes when they see a top-dressing mound 'magically' going into the ground.

The Lute, by the way, was a 2ft square approx of metal, that you simply 'spun' over, to use one side or the other, the grooved side was really to help disperse the dressing more evenly, and the smoother partly grooved side for the main levelling. I have not used a Lute since my time on the green, for I use the back of a three-foot hay-rake, much lighter, longer, more comfortable reach, and does the job just as good.

I find TV shows showing you how to top-dress lawns and use a besom or birch broom to work in the dressing, I find this only works to a degree, and does not in my opinion do the job 100%.

Other vital tools that were missing from the green's tool shed was a scarifyer (lawn rake, mechanised); the green had not been scarified for years, hence the bad condition of the green, and explained why the green had a lot of die-back in parts, where the grass had grown so thick. A scarifyer should have been used prior to applying any top dressing, for the scarifyer would rake out all the dead grasses, with drastically matted thatch, and even lift low mat growing weeds. The scarifyer does live up to its name, for on seeing this work carried out a dry day, folk are shocked to see so much rubbish coming out, and first sight often think you're a cowboy worker and have thoroughly wrecked their lawn, when in fact the harsh treatment is the total opposite.

Another two items missing were a spiking machine or aerator and as it suggests, aerates the ground so that water drains away easily from a flat surface; the other machine was a hollow tine, each tine or 'spike' was a ½ inch metal tube and when the tines went in the ground the soil is pushed up through; then out of each tine, the holes obviously wider than a spiker, albeit there was more often than not more spikes than there were tines. The ground after the tines had been over the ground, you saw hundreds of tubular soil plugs, of course these all had to be raked up.

You can now see the benefits of either spiking, or hollow-tining when it came to the top-dressing, for the dressing all worked its way down the holes, the sand to aid drainage, the peat to retain moisture, and the goodness of the loam to give it a bit of body too. So when it comes to the weeding, greening up and feeding of the grasses, you can now see why most bowling greens etc. look so superb.

Granted, every item I spoke of to the chairman he got for me, and as each item came I was able to start using them and to get the green back to its perhaps former splendour. My stay however, was very short-lived, for the chairman started to tell me that two or three of the people were already having a whinge about different things. I was surprised that the chairman was telling me all this, considering I had told him how I'd been so very reluctant to go back into sports work again. But when I did hear, I packed up there and then, exactly as I told him I would, and kept my word. The chairman was shocked.

I told the chairman that if the whinges were starting at this early stage, how bad would it get? The most baffling part of it was that I was doing so much more than had been done on this green for many years, using equipment that they never knew that they had to use. Lowly praise was all that I seemed to get. Were the whinges because I only did two days? Albeit their choice on that? had they wanted a full-time green-keeper but never asked me because I was self-employed and having to carry out other projects? Had they asked, I would have taken up a full-time position there, moreso because it would have been a regular wage coming in every week, come rain or shine, unlike my garden work.

The whinges though were fairly critical; one man did have the courtesy to say that their malicious talk was out of jealousy he suspected, for indeed I was a 'new broom', a new face, and perhaps showing them all up because of total incompetence, although never once rubbed their noses in it, and when I did it was only to the chairman sharing my disbelief on the so lack of obvious equipment.

Nothing he could say persuaded me to stay, for I again relayed all that had gone on at the Orient F.C. and Wadham Lodge etc., where all these people too knew my job better than me, they were, after all only players. Strangely though, never once have any of the top managers, secretaries or chairman at any of the places that I've been in charge of, have *ever* complained or criticised my work, and only full of praise; the complainers have always been with players, sports people, call them what you will.

At least I left very satisfied that I would never again work in sports work, and since the 1990s I never have. Sad, when there is someone out there who would've appreciated me.

Plants from a Penny!

No! This wasn't the price of the plants, for the plants were cheaper than that! For the Penny was Penny Hutch, a very knowledgeable plantswoman who at one time had her own plant nursery between Yarmouth and Lowestoft on the main road.

I hadn't long moved to Suffolk and was keen to sell plants, but only had the stock from my own garden and taking cuttings and seeds from these, which at the time were few, for our garden then was a blank canvass and badly needed filling.

As I just said, the plants were cheaper than a penny because they were given to me free of charge from Penny Hutch. It was virtually my first visit to Penny's nursery and was a bit hesitant at first whether to tell Penny that I'd like to sell plants, albeit only from home on odd occasions, and hoped I wouldn't be a threat to her as some would think.

Out of the blue, after I did tell Penny my intentions, she said, "I've got a lot of plants to get you started, and don't want anything for them." I couldn't believe my eyes when I saw the array of potted perennial plants that were now to come my way and ready for immediate selling and to split and take cuttings.

Penny, you see, was buying in new stock, hence wanted everything out of the way. Boy! I was so very excited, and crammed as many as I could in my van, and without a doubt my first time I broke the law by being over-weight? Well, it felt like it, but feared that if I didn't take them all in one go, someone else would come and take them all. Penny did assure me though that all the plants were now mine. One thing that I heard Penny say once, regarding the way that she gardens, "I float my own boat when it comes to gardening," (and funnily enough so do I!)

I know Penny has been on gardening panels at village halls, possibly radio? Now this I think is a brave step, for I don't feel I could do it, well that's not strictly true, for as I've said before, there's a lot I could answer on various horticultural subjects, but not necessarily specialising on one thing.

I often watch various TV gardening shows and one of the gardening presenters perhaps talks about a particular plant, or a method of doing a certain job in the garden, and I'm often left 'screaming' at the screen "Oh, you could have told them this, or that, or other," bits I felt viewers or listeners should know, and on occasions very vital information is left out.

What I find on panels is that you find another panellist sort of disagreeing with someone else's answer, for there's more than one way to skin a cat, but often a TV or radio presenter thinks they're right, and have given a correct answer, and very likely they have, for that was the way they have been taught or read from a book, so it's still good to hear of an alternative view don't you think?

When it comes to me 'floating my own boat' some of my answers would be found through total experience and perhaps a new method or way round a problem that no expert has ever heard of, because it happened to me, therefore can give the listener, viewer an answer never given before and not in any text book.

Sometimes though I unintentionally offend some experts who do know their subjects 100%, so don't really like it when I come up with something that they really hadn't heard of and feel quite put out for not knowing. I do remember talking to some tree experts a good few years ago now, yes they really did know their stuff, but I put a spanner in the works for I thought they all knew what I was on about, seeing as though there were so many experts all gathered together in one go.

I made a point regarding all this claiming lark, it's an offence to do this, that or the other, and how trade descriptions people were very hot on the tails of anyone breaking the law. So I felt obliged to ask these experts how they would categorise between stating that some plants, shrubs, trees, are classed as either 'evergreen' or 'deciduous' so they all said well there are the only two types when it came to actual leaves. So I said, "Well, what about the beech or youngish oak trees?" They straight away all said, "evergreen", but that's wrong, for the leaves are not EVER GREEN, for although the leaves do stay on the trees, they're certainly not green, for the leaves still hang on even when they're dead, and fall off when new buds appear in the spring. They all sat and thought about it, especially as I said that by law then every garden centre etc. is breaking the law by saying they are evergreen, when they're clearly not, where are the trades description people?

The tree experts were now truly baffled and did look a little embarrassed. I did put them out of their misery by saying that there are in fact three categories, those being: EVERGREEN, DECIDUOUS, and lastly MARCESCENT which is the correct term for a tree or shrub that retains its leaves, even though the leaves are totally dead. Oh dear! I bet I've now started you all off now making a claim!

Raphaels Park, Romford (Essex)

This park has so fond memories for me, and as the old saying goes regarding places of childhood, it doesn't always pay to go back, but I'll tell you, the reader, more about that a bit further on. I'm not saying every time... but possibly it was nearly always my lovely dear mum who would take us to this park and most likely when we'd been to the old market to do shopping, and to see all the lovely cattle and pigs etc. all in thick railed gating, of which were a permanent fixture for very many years, and now looking back, I feel most privileged to have seen such a sight, and now realise that I was seeing the old true market as in times of old.

Raphaels Park as you walked in through large ornamental gates, greeted you on the left with a very large lake, and always full of activity with the quacking of ducks and numerous swans – Mum always took us here to feed them. On the right as you came in the gates were immaculate lawns, and graced with the most beautiful circular, oval, square and oblong flower beds – these were truly outstanding to me even as a very small child. Just past these lovely beds on the right were groups of old mature trees, and the first time that I saw hearts cut out in their trunks, the hearts had an arrow through them with initials of the sweethearts. Of course I had to ask Mum what it all meant! On this spot was a Punch and Judy show, and it wasn't until we moved to Kessingland-on-Sea, and got talking to our local 'Punch' man Bryan Clarke, known as Prof. Jingles! – Bryan told me that it was him who was the 'Punch' man at Raphaels Park all those years ago, when he was first starting out, and even now in 2010 he's still working Mr Punch.

Mum would then take us further along to the play park, and remember looking in awe at all these tall beautiful plants that were in an area under trees, and if I remember correctly, a banked up area. Mum or Dad told me that they are called Foxgloves (the lesser known common name is 'Fairy Thimbles'. The colour range was superb, and very likely to have been either 'Excelsior Hybrids' or 'Foxy' unless these were unknown varieties back then?

I realise now that going back to places of childhood releases so many emotions, and think of all the very many people who have now passed on. It was in the November 2009 on a cold damp November day that I once again stepped back through possibly those very same iron gates. I was now 61 years old, and last walked through those gates as an eleven or twelve year old, then going through those gates with Mum and Dad; this time it was to be with my wife Debbie.

It was an odd feeling, when I thought of all that had happened since I last walked in... and out of those big gates, as a mere boy, and now as a man not far off from retiring years, and also having a wife with me and not Mum and Dad by my side.

Yes, the ducks and swans were still there, so were the trees where I watched Bryan all those years ago on a summer's day, but today it was cold and bleak. I was sad that those beautiful flower beds were no more, and just thickets of shrubs instead. I tried to find the playpark and rockery area that stood at its approach – I couldn't find it, nor the old bank that once housed those marvellous Foxgloves. I know that November wasn't the best month to visit a park, but feel that even if I'd gone in Spring or Summer, the scene would have been the same, albeit would like to take perhaps one last peek in more favourable months.

Again, leaving that park was sad for me, for I made a point of taking that ('last'?) step out of those gates, and my thoughts of Mum and Dad being with me as that small boy, but I was so glad that my wife Debbie was with me, albeit she had no real idea of those so sad thoughts going through my head.

When I was three, I was run over by a car outside Raphaels Park. The park's lake ran under a series of arches that made the slopes on the path and road outside. Mum had apparently asked me to hold the hand of her friend, whilst Mum took my sister Sandra across the road in her pram so that she could post a letter. I must have panicked seeing my mum going away from me, and pulled away from her friend into the path of a car. Mum obviously screamed, but had let go of the pram; the sloped path made the pram roll away, and thankfully someone was there to stop it.

Today I still bear a scar above my right eye, showing up more when I get hot! My wife Debbie and I did look to see if there was perhaps still a letterbox outside Raphaels Park, I wanted to get some idea on where the exact spot was where I was hit, perhaps indeed it was the other side of the road that the box once stood, and perhaps when Mum had posted that letter she was to cross back over to go into the park. Sadly, I'll never know.

Going back to the market place today, hardly any of the original dark cobblestones exist today, but found daft twisted bits of metal that passes as modern art, was dotted around this ancient market place – thankfully on that last visit in 2009 they had at last taken them away! I reckon someone heard me having a whinge or I'd like to think so, for I said these monstrosities were taking up valuable stall space, where rents could have been paid.

I'll keep on the subject of flowers and trees whilst I'm still writing about Romford. The first big chestnut tree that I ever saw, and must have been an outcry from the locals when it and other trees were taken down? If my memory serves me well, this small park stood opposite the old Romford Library. The library and the huge chestnut tree were both very sentimental to me, the library with dad, and feeding the pigeons in that small park with Mum. This park had lovely flowerbeds and a war memorial. You'll have to read the rest of my memories in my other book on Harold Hill, at Romford.

Holiday Flowers!

I didn't know it then, but in the latter part of the 1950s, I and sister Sandra were to spend our very last family holiday with both Mum and Dad. The great shock was when Dad walked out on us all, we as children never dreamed that Mum and Dad weren't getting on – after all, most couples have little squabbles now and again. It was one of the hardest things in life for me and my sister to bear, to see your dad walk away from you, and it was like a death not having that close loved one with you any more.

Today, it happens to thousands of people, and to think that those kids are going through the exact same emotions – it does get easier, but those feelings of that dread never go away…

This is possibly why the 1950s are so special to me and my memory, particularly sharp, and remembering so many things in that short time up until I was 12 in 1960. This last holiday was at Clacton-on-Sea in Essex. I won't go into the full details of this holiday, for I have covered this in my earliest memories book, but I will tell you about the flowers that were in the garden of that B&B.

On our arrival, I noticed a very familiar plant growing in absolute abundance, an annual that I'd grown on and off all through my boyhood, and that was the 'Night Scented Stock' Mathiola 'bicornis', a thin straggly looking plant, not much to look at in the day, but as soon as dusk falls, the pink flowers open and give off the most gorgeous scent. Luckily, we were given that very same upstairs bedroom where we could gaze down onto this wonderful sight. Even more delight came our way on mild evenings, the windows were left open, and in wafted that heavy scent.

Normally in most gardens you'd only see random plants from just the one seed packet, the then family (Mr and Mrs Jim Newman – aerial photographer/pilot) must have planted several packets to get such a big display, and I've never seen one like it since. The other plant was one of the Oxalis family, namely Oxalis 'acetosella rosea' with its shamrock-type flowers in a beautiful pink.

It wasn't until a good few years later as I was learning about plants that I found not only its name, but also found it fairly common, although it makes neat clumps, it does spread its seeds readily. The little girl who lived there, Susan, who was I think about the same age as me and sister Sandra, soon noticed that I'd taken a liking to this plant, and couldn't wait to show Sandra and I something 'odd' about this plant. She suddenly pulled off a leaf, complete with stem and touch the base of the stem with her tongue, it had an acidy taste, hence part of the plant's name – acet (acid). She told us that it wasn't poisonous, hence have shown this to many people since the 1950s, so thank you Susan!

In 2009 a friend, Peter Battey, the local Clacton Punch and Judy man, did some research for me, and also another chap contacted me. A 1950's advert was found with the actual B&B that we stayed in all t hose years ago in West Avenue, so me now having a contact I did not hesitate to contact the present owners to tell them all that I remembered about that last ever holiday with Mum and Dad. A reply did come back from someone – Julie Wayland – it was a delightful letter and she thanked me for praising up her lovely house! Sadly, she did not know where all the Newman family went to, but very possibly still in Clacton. Mine and Julie's biggest surprise was when Julie said that the Oxalis still grew everywhere! To think that those plants or its offsprings had been there since the '50s.

Julie has now said that I and my wife Debbie can go to see her, albeit she says that the house would have changed a great deal since we were there.

Again, like going in and out of those gates at Raphaels Park, as you read earlier, with both Mum and Dad, and many years later doing the same with my wife, I'll be going through those same emotions when eventually walking through and out of those same doors when that holiday came about in West Avenue all those years ago on that so very special last ever family holiday with Mum and Dad and sister Sandra.

Dad found love elsewhere a couple or so years down the line, maybe that is why this holiday stands out above 'all' others?

Scared Cat? Not Ours!

A modern variety of Coleus called 'scaredy cat', supposedly to keep cats off your plants – I bought one and as soon as I put it down on the path ready to plant, our cat laid straight on top of it, still in the pot, and went fast asleep! So we assume that cats have to lie on the coleus to leave all the other plants alone?

It Doesn't Pay to Write

It's a very pleasing thought when I get a bit of feed back from my articles that I write for the *Kessingland and Broadland Times* magazine, and some twenty or so odd years have now passed, and I still at this time of writing write my own gardening column for this magazine. The feedback that I just mentioned is of course regular readers of my column, and so very complimentary when they say that I really should have a much bigger audience, they know of course that I write from experience, not simply just copying from books.

Many a newspaper or magazine does just this, it's only a guess mind you, but I find it suspicious when you see a piece of gardening advice given, and no name given of the writer of that column, so I can only suspect that it's the chief editors themselves who simply just copy a 'month-by-month' gardening book(s) and therefore can save on payment to a writer who really knows what she or he is talking about. Anyone could really do it, they could just buy several gardening books, pick a subject, let's say for argument's sake you chose to write about Rhododendrons to start with, you could simply just pick up one of those books to start you off, then turn to 'R' for Rhododendrons in each of the other books to read up on further information that each of the other books didn't mention.

You can always tell an amateur on certain gardening columns, because there is a real feel that the person doesn't do it for a living, for very obvious things are left out.

When we first moved to Suffolk from London's East End our local paper *The Lowestoft Journal* only had an organic gardening section back in 1987. A friend of mine, Harry Dean, did this column for a good few years before we came to Suffolk; not long after this Harry gave up writing his regular column. I have never asked him why? A good few years passed, and nobody filled Harry's space, so I asked Harry if it would be okay to ask the Journal if they would like a regular gardening column, and checked too to make sure that I wasn't treading on Harry's toes in case he decided to write again.

Harry assured me that he would never write his column again, and that I should go ahead and write to the then editor. I did, to my total surprise, get a quick reply back, so had the feeling that they had missed Harry's column (albeit as Harry said, "There was no public outcry when my column suddenly disappeared from the newspaper's pages!") and as a few years had lapsed, it seemed that the editor was keen to get my column going.

I mentioned of course that I wrote for a local magazine, and that all my articles very much varied in size – some would be three, four or five-parters, others would fill a quarter or half a page etc. I also assured him that my columns in his newspaper would not be the same as in the magazine, and if it was used further down the line I could easily re-word it all.

One point that I did suggest to him and that was I could easily write 'topical' issues, for the newspaper column would be a weekly one, against the magazine which was monthly (now, bi-monthly). The editor then wrote to me to discuss terms; he asked if I'd either like to be paid, or have a free advert, or my telephone number added to the bottom of my column. I wrote back to say that I would prefer to be paid, for had I just moved to Suffolk I would have been glad of a free advert or telephone number added, but I was now reasonably established, and that regular payment would be very handy for the winter months ahead where all gardeners are just not wanted.

To my delight they agreed to pay me, and could send an article in straight away, with my own heading that they chose – KEITH'S GARDEN – by Kessingland Landscape Gardener, Keith Nichols – I was over the moon, for I had tons of material to use, and so much in my brain still unused! Okay, so the title they chose wasn't totally accurate, for it wasn't really about my garden, but would feature many plants and shrubs that I have grown.

I had once again a good feedback, by letter, phone or in person, congratulating me on my new column, moreso from people whom I did not know, so that was even more assuring, knowing that total strangers were enjoying it, and believe me, I had so much more to come, and also to my joy, nothing was edited out, and that was a surprise for a newspaper. Sadly, my column, after only five or six appearances over the same amount of weeks, suddenly stopped being printed.

I wrote to ask if I'd done anything wrong, for they had material from me right across the board. Strangely, I heard nothing back, and even though I asked, I never did get any form of payment for all the work that I did for them. I didn't get an apology from them at all, to my total dismay though just a few months down the line, they got someone else to do a type of gardening club, with special discounts etc. from various garden centres, shops etc. and like Harry I never had any public outcry asking what happened to my column either. The new gardening club column lasted only a couple of years as I recollect, and folded as quick as it had started. There has not been a gardening column in this newspaper for a good many years now, except on occasions when an odd random article appears where the writer does not give his or her name. One or two people have said that it's likely that, when my column appeared in the paper, the idea had been put into the editor's head, hence when I had made my offer to write a column after Harry's absence of a good few years, perhaps he sought out others, and I just happened to be a quick filler-in until he found someone. Why did the man who took my place suddenly stop writing – did he not get paid either, or did he have an offer of far better things? Perhaps we'll never know?

Thankfully, nice comments still come in from my monthly articles in 'Katy' K.T. *Kessingland Times* – someone then suggested that because of my prolific writing, not all to do with gardening, why did I not contact some of the really big gardening magazines, and see if they would like to take me on board so to speak, even as an occasional writer. So, as someone thought I was good enough, I thought I'd try, of course knowing that there are far better, and more knowledgeable gardeners than me around, but then thought yes, but would they want to write too?

I straight away wrote to my two old firm favourites *Amateur Gardening* and *Popular Gardening*, these I knew from boyhood at my nan and grandad's house in Walthamstow. Later on in my teens I bought *Garden News*, *Practical Gardening* and of course the later *Gardeners' World* magazine. Yes, each one wrote back to me to my surprise; they'd all at least answered my letters, but all said that they had their regular writers. I have bought all these magazines since writing to them a good few years ago now, and new writers appear on a fairly regular basis, so my name was never on a short list by any of them.

I was neither upset nor disappointed, it was literally a very random try, and of course there are thousands of gardeners out there who have tried just like me. Over the very many years I have sent all of them gardening queries, ideas, suggestions etc., and all have gone to print, and still have private personal letters to me direct from either the editors or gardening experts themselves, and have been so very helpful. Hence it's these very same magazines where I hope to put in one or two ads a year in the hopes of selling this book! Boy, my grandad would have been so thrilled to have seen me do a gardening book, and to advertise in at least two of the oldest of the gardening magazines that were his favourites.

What a State!

Aren't people rude? Haven't they got a cheek? I am of course referring to locals and holidaymakers alike. Why you may wonder? I refer to those who speak aloud and criticise my front garden! The summer of course when we have windows ajar and can hear every word spoken.

"…calls himself a gardener" says one, "a bit of a mess" says another, "you'd think he'd make it more of an advert considering what he does." Yes, my wife and I hear it all unbeknown to them!

Some of these people pass by several times a day. I hasten to add that they must all have small gardens that do not warrant too much work on them. Other folk are visitors or holiday-makers, so why say anything at all about a stranger's garden and know nothing of the circumstances?

I used to have a sign up advertising my landscape works, so was obvious that I did this for a living, and on occasions seven days a week, and also had two businesses to run (you'll have to read my other two books about that!). Yes, the painter rarely has the chance to paint his own house, and yes, a builder, plumber or electrician may also have slight neglect on their own properties.

Many trades like mine for instance are both manual and physical, and hard graft, and you face that every day of your working life, and all in the most severe of weathers – be it freezing cold or baking under a hot desert-type sun, and on the latter, my son Dale and I were on yet another project of restoration work in the hottish summer of 2010, and the sun became that hot we couldn't hold the metal tools, they were truly unbearable to touch, and not an ounce of shade in any part of this large garden; and where there was shade, it was at an area that we'd already restored. We had no choice but to pack up and go home.

Many people find gardening a chore in their own gardens, be it weeding or cutting their lawns, and can go indoors or relax in the sun and do their work at their own ease; a landscaper for instance has no such luxuries and have to do the job whatever the conditions.

Many people too never face 'jungles' to clear on almost a daily basis, digging, raking, pruning, dispersing tons of soil, etc., lifting bags of compost, sand etc. they neither work a rotovator, level soil, or on your knees all day every day, with a bent back, skimming off weeds or an old lawn, then laying hundreds of turfs, 'pumming' each one down with a heavy 'pummer', or loading or unloading tons of rubbish into a trailer or loading a skip. To think that you're so exhausted from one day, yet have to face another, and another, then finish a project, and start afresh on another job all over again, then again, and again, for the whole of your working life, and agony with not only aching muscles but on occasions just not feeling 'quite the ticket' to face yet another gruelling day.

I think what upsets me and my wife mostly is when running my second business, and me being the most upset of the two of us, because it's me doing the hard graft, but glad that my wife will always speak up for me if something is ever said. My second business, mostly at weekends and bank-holidays, and I'm often up and out from 5, 6, or 7 in the morning, and occasions back home about 2 or 3 in the morning – now they were very long days, and a manual job that 99 out of 100 people would definitely not do!

I, on getting home, obviously need a good rest and sleep. Later in the day I often used to walk through our village, and meet various people. "Day off, Keith?" "No work, Keith?" "Business no good?" or behind my back "his van's there today, nobody wants him." Yet I'd done, unbeknown to them, two days' graft in one, often too travelling many many miles, when these 'put down people' are all asleep in their beds! and most wouldn't know about a day's graft if they tried.

Ironically in spring when my cottage-style front garden looks particularly pretty, these very same people refrain from making a compliment, then it seems to be a touch of the 'green-eyed monster' and there's a lot of folk who suffer from this!

After completing one or other of these often gruelling landscape jobs, the last thing I want to do is to start on my own garden. Yes, I do have to do it at some point, but certainly don't want people telling me, especially as I can clearly see for myself that the garden needs a tidy.

I suppose I shouldn't worry about my critics who pass by my garden with often a venomous comment, for it's my paying clients who I have to impress, the ones who put money in my pocket. Only one lady has spoken to me face-to-face, telling me that my garden was a mess (to many, a cottage-style garden is always a mess, even at its best!). The lady was walking her dogs, a youngish woman; I told her that I worked seven days a week, told her of my hours and so wished that I could waste my time walking dogs three or four times a day as she'd been doing, and I'd get far more done in my garden now if you hadn't stopped me in my tracks to talk to you about my 'neglected' garden.

The lady was totally taken aback, and I must have sounded as rude as she had been to me – touché I say! Perhaps if my garden was always in pristine condition I would still get the so snide comments "…of course his garden's lovely, he's never at work," 'he must be retired or do part-time to get a nice garden like that." I really don't think I will ever win!

I Have a Reservation!

One winter I was put on a task to plant thousands of young hawthorns to inter-plant amongst the mature thorns to fill all the gaps on the central reservation of the A10 covering the stretch between the Haringey parks boundaries.

New House New garden?

I can give you the reader a good tip here. If you have moved to a new house... new to you that is, rather than a newly built property. I suggest you leave your garden for a whole year if possible before doing anything drastic, and I don't mean leave regarding the weeding, but take note on the plants that you can see.

If you say move into your new home in summer, you'll have no idea where those previous bulbs will be, or mid-winter perhaps when the previous owners had cut back to ground level various perennial plants, or perennial plants that fade back to nothing after flowering, don't hack at neglected trees or shrubs, wait to see what they are first, then read up or seek advice on how to go about restoring them.

Almost Did Two Jobs For The Price of One!

Now how did that nearly happen I hear you ask? It was way back in the early 1980s, and had a garden project in South Woodford, Essex, and in the same posh road that Lonnie Donegan, the well-known skiffle man used to live and not long moved away from.

I started to clear the back garden, and the lady didn't want any perennials saved and although I said "it looks like you've got a lot of them, there might be some unusual ones amongst them" but no, I was to out the lot, re-turf over the borders, but plant up shrubs only, elsewhere. This garden was a new one to the lady and her husband (who I never met) so was a blank canvass if you could call it that, for the garden looked like it was a lovely garden in summer, but this was March and all had to go!

One of the first plants that I spotted was the then unusual 'black grass' so I dug that up for myself. In later years at Chelsea Show, this plant really came into its own when the exhibitors decided to create out of flowers the Buckingham Palace guards, the thoughts soon came on what to use for the busbies... the 'black grass' did the trick and they clustered all the plants together, they did look great. Also in this garden I did spot a rarity, and luckily this was a big job lasting some three months, had I not been there that long I would have missed it, and that was the delicate looking Gillenia 'trifoliata', easier to obtain today perhaps, but not back then, so I had this plant too and add to the Planniscappus 'nigrescens Japonica' (black grass!).

One point I must make here – s'funny when I say the word Japonica how nearly everyone says "Oh I've got a Japonica!" when in fact there is no plant called Japonica albeit the "Japonica Quince" or Chaenomeles is referred as the Japonica, when in fact Japonica only means that a plant etc. comes from Japan. One lady many years ago couldn't pronounce Japonica and called it Jap on Eye Ka!

The project now over for me, but the carpenters who had previously done a lot of work for Spike Milligan were still hard at it inside the house with a new kitchen etc. It was now paytime! "You haven't finished yet, you haven't done the front garden!" came the cry from the woman of the house. I nearly died on the spot, not quite taking in what she just said, I told her that the work was completed as per estimate and was for the back garden only, she was insistent that the front garden was included.

I did no more than ask the lady to fetch my estimate, this would prove beyond doubt that it was for the back garden only. "I can't find it, you'll do the front or you won't get paid." I was furious, anyhow I went home that night, and thank heavens I'd done a copy! A lesson learnt here, which has stood me in good stead all my working life, and not 100% trust every client. I went back the next day with a big smile on my face, the lady stood horrified when as clear as day it read Back Garden Only – she did say sorry, and looked quite humble, and also proved that I wasn't pulling a fast one. The lady promptly paid me and asked for a quote for the front garden, which was readily accepted.

Had I not had a copy of my estimate I would have had no choice but to do that front garden, and all for nothing, for at that point there was no proof. I have made copies of each and every job since that day and no matter how low the price, I'll always have the proof.

On the very first day however, I was hurt badly by an old neglected climbing rose on a wall; it also had old large thorns, little did I know when restoring this I had to take three weeks off. I started on the restoration and cut away an old type (tie) as I cut away the tie that was slightly embedded in the stem, due to the long time it had been there. I was the next second in total agony, for the tie had held this rose back so tightly and me cutting it acted as a tightened spring and let go at an enormous force, right onto my knuckles, the thorns penetrated my skin and veins, the pain was excruciating, and the knuckles and fingers swelled up in front of me.

Need I say more? Another lesson learned and to watch out for in the future.

Out on a Limb

I wanted at one time to be a tree surgeon, but I couldn't stand the sight of sap!

Only Here for the Beer!

Another silly joke I can't resist saying to my clients, moreso when I've just laid a new lawn for them, "Now you have your new lawn, would you like to keep it really short and not to grow?" The answer is always a resounding "YES!" so then I say to them to go out and buy some bottles of beer, put it all in a watering can, and water it on your lawn, "What does this do?" asks the client, so I tell them, "Well, it always comes up half-cut!"

Clear Now of Crocodiles!

Back in the 1980s there used to be crocodiles in the River Thames... I tell clients. "Really?" they'd exclaim, "Yes, and it was me who got rid of them." I said that I mixed up Acorns all crushed up with the leaves and flowers of the common aster, added water and poured it into the Thames. "But there are no crocodiles in the River Thames." There I'd say, "it shows that it worked!"

Surgery Blues

I had to go to our local surgery yet again re. my back. After a while I got talking to an old chap sitting next to me, he was very jovial and we soon got on the subject of gardening and had a nice conversation for a good half-hour or so whilst waiting our turn to see the doctor.

The old chap's name was soon called out. After the old chap came out of the doctor's room, I would see he was very sad, and the jovial manner now gone, and as he'd been so friendly I asked what was the matter? He said, "The doctor has told me that I've got to take pills for the rest of my life." I said that lots of people have to take pills for the rest of their lives, especially when you're older. "I know," he said, "but he's only given me three!"

Quips!

I'm sorry, reader, about these silly quips, there really is no hope for me! but I do enjoy the banter between me and the clients that I know would share a joke, and if I can keep serious in answering their questions, so much the better! For instance, some clients say "What is the best time to prune roses?" I answer, "around four o'clock!" or another client would say "Why do you think my water-lily has died?" I reply, "I can see the problem straight away... you have over-watered it!" You'd be surprised on how many people say, "is that right?"

I remember having the dreaded flu one year, and was a slow process building myself up again, so I asked my doctor for a pick-me-up tonic. He said that "the best thing you can do is to walk six miles a day." I thought this was daft, for I was forty-two miles away by the end of the week!

A Grand Tour of My Garden!

Unless me and Debbie get too crotchety in old age, our Kessingland garden in Suffolk will be our last garden, hence hope we never have to move from our bungalow which is just a few minutes from the North Sea. We came here in 1987 in a cold April and a couple of days away from the Easter holidays.

I was now thirty-nine years old, so it was a very big step to move to an area where no one knew me or what my work was like; some would possibly say that I was foolhardy to start up a business as I was almost forty years old. I had always hated London, and the East End was changing rapidly, none to my liking – the dirt, grime, smoke and forever having to look over your shoulder because of crime etc.

We not only owed it to ourselves for a better life, but also our children, but I still taught them to be streetwise. Okay, so today on occasions our local papers of East Anglia do read very similar to the local papers of London's East End, for with so very soft punishments for horrendous crimes, gives the all go signal for many others to follow suit, knowing that prison isn't going to be too bad.

Our garden, on moving in, was a blank canvass, with mostly lawns and pathways; the existing borders of only about two feet wide, consisted of only Aubretia and Euonymus 'Japonica' of which I still have, now although I prune this back many times over the years a few sprigs of very bright yellow appeared, so I've kept all the green at bay, and nurtured a very bright shrub, and dare I say a new variety!? My shrub very much resembles the golden form of the shrub Choisya.

On moving to Kessingland from our home at 43 Guildford Road E.17, the removal men were so surprised on how many plants and shrubs that I was taking with me, in fact one removal man said, "You've got more plants than furniture!" and he was probably right too! The Guildford Road house was a nice house, all the road was lined with ornamental cherry trees, and all in full bloom not long after we moved in. Our house backed onto a railway line (Liverpool St. to Chingford) and crammed plants in to make use of the space. I still had my two sheds from our first house in Chingford Road (and still grace my garden right here in Kessingland!).

Guildford Road stood in the 'posher' part of Walthamstow and the area was known as Upper Walthamstow and fringed the boundaries of Woodford Green and the Highams Park. Epping Forest for us was a mere ten minute walk (I am a life member of The Friends of Epping

Forest). The forest is a beautiful place, but you couldn't get lost in it as days of old, for you soon come across a main road or motorway etc. What I found so extremely sad, was if you were a man walking in the Forest on your own, people would eye you with suspicion or caution, for there were many perverts etc. in the Forest, and found that nothing had changed, for when the Forest was less than a five-minute walk from our house at Chingford Hatch when I was twelve, all us kids would scream and shout, and residents would come out to tell the girls not to scream for it could be confused with an attack on a female, of which there had been several and the people who owned the houses actually facing the Forest itself always acted as lookouts for us, or somewhere to run to if a nutter was about.

Not long after we moved to Guildford Road, we were warned about a man who ran around our area of the forest stark naked, except for a mask and wearing ladies suspenders and stockings! As I say, normal men were always eyed with suspicion, if me and my wife were walking in there and saw some perfectly innocent chap just innocently enjoying the forest, we too threw that eye of suspicion, and of course the same was with me if I was on my own, folk would look at me oddly, and knew what they were thinking, for I'd thought the same about others.

I soon solved this problem, suddenly, by just having my dog with me I was 'legal' to be in that forest, and not looked at as a potential pervert, for I too thought no more about it if I too saw a man on his own with his dog.

I thought what a sad world that we now live in, and that me and other men couldn't any longer enjoy the simple pleasures of a walk in the forest on our own. It was also at Guildford road that I came up with another idea for what it was worth, and have told many people over the years, especially clients on how my idea worked. Now although the railway backed our garden, along with a part-brick shed that lay the length or should say width of the garden, this was our first house where we felt a bit vulnerable, knowing that someone could get into the garden if they wanted to, and found that indeed over the many years, all others, like us, who backed onto the railway, had indeed been broken into.

I put up a three-foot high picket fence and gate, about 10–12 foot from our kitchen door, with a specially made sign on the gate and facing any would-be burglar the sign simply said 'Beware of Dogs' (note 'Dogs' not 'Dog'). Two or three years went by, and by the way readers we never had a dog at this time, then one night snow had fallen. I was the first up that day and saw several sets of footprints from our shed all down the garden, and I could see clearly that they'd stopped at the picket gate and read my sign. The footprints then went right into my next-door neighbour's house; they ignored that and burgled the next neighbour. A lesson learnt here I think, so even if you don't have dogs, the burglars don't know that do they?

I remember right here in Kessingland and when I used to have my plant sales, and all the hoards of strangers that used to come through, so thought OK, I'm not in London, but burglars can be anywhere so again had a sign with a picture of a fierce Alsatian or Rottweiler, reading 'We live here' and again, note WE, hence more than one!

Our dog at the time, 'Bess', was a friendly soul, but then one day and possibly quite innocently (?) a man said, "Where's your other dog that's on the picture?" I thought to myself, why is he asking that I wonder? So, quick as a flash… and in case he was eyeing the place up, told him that we daren't let the other one out as it was very unpredictable. As I say, it may have just been an innocent question to ask by the chap, but if it wasn't, I'm certain by my remark, I'd made our home safe again by a simple deterrent.

Neighbours right here in Kessingland were burgled, so I gave them a huge roll of barbed wire to put on their back fence, this did the trick, albeit after such trauma for people in their eighties, the event stayed in the back of their minds.

Moving to Kessingland was a great thrill, especially when asking the children to collect smooth 3–4 inch stones and paint them up; I still have some of them. We could hear the waves so clearly when the sea was rough; not so much nowadays because the sea is out further. We could hear the toot-toot of the miniature steam train, and the roar of lions, all from the local Wildlife Park nearby. We were in heaven. Yes, several things have marred our stay here, but wish to keep this as a happy book.

Many people have asked me how I planned out my garden, well it wasn't – I knew what I wanted, but never had the money to buy what I really needed. Thankfully at least I had a good lot of plants that came with me from Walthamstow, so it was just a matter of working out the shapes of the borders, where arches could go, ponds, etc. In the many years that we've been here, my garden has changed rapidly over the years, and I'm always moving something or the other – in one area I had a lorry, caravan, car, trailers, etc., then one or two of them would go and something else would take its place, but the garden has always stayed in the cottage-style, and nearly always something in bloom all year.

Each year I look at a certain shrub, plant, bird-bath, shed etc., and think, 'Oh, that would look far better over there!' and because of my love of plants, my lawn now is miniscule, and the reverse when we first came here. I'd always loved trees, so this was always a priority, these gave height and interest to our garden, and doubling up the display moreso when a flowering cherry had lost its blossom for an old-fashioned rose takes over the colour for the rest of the year.

I have always made use of fences, walls, etc., to plant up climbers and add plenty of greenery to any background structure. I'll always cover a shed or summerhouse, garage, etc., fill every pot and container, add hanging and wall baskets.

One of my first trees here was Acer 'crimson King'; this and several other trees were planted in a patch, certainly I think no more than ten foot square, when an area like that would suit just one tree! The elderly lady who gave them to me said that her husband loved trees, and bought them all as quite young saplings, but sadly her husband died quite young, and now worried how big they would eventually grown, and that she really preferred to have a new lawn.

Today that Acer is a magnificent tree, and standing next to it is Acer 'negundo' "flamingo", and looks good, contrasting its variegation against the dark leaves of 'crimson king'.

One error that I have made in my garden, and that's where I positioned a lovely tree called 'the golden rain tree' Koelreuteria 'paniculata', only really blooming in good summers, mine throws out a few flowers on the branches just inches from the summerhouse roof, and flowers I'm sure because of the heat generated from the tar-felt roof.

My error is that on really good hot summers, two separate neighbours get the benefit of its flowers; one house is south facing, the other west, the northern and eastern side of the tree is my side, and barely produces a bud, but the rest is laden with colour, so I really have to crane my neck up between the neighbours' fences and my summerhouse to even know its in bloom!

I have three now good-sized Hibiscus 'syriacus' – two single pink, the other a double, and given to me by an elderly lady when they graced the front of her mobile home. "I don't want them, they're too slow growing, throw them away, cut 'em up." I asked if they could be thrown my way, so that's how I got them! One thing needed in gardening is patience to see things grow; if the lady had been patient, she would have seen the most beautiful sight around August time.

True, these shrubs become small trees (eventually!) are fairly slow to start with, and one of the last shrubs to produce its leaves in spring, hence why many people think they've died in the winter and discard them; they are also one of the very first to yellow-up and drop their leaves. These Hibiscus were the very first shrubs given to me by a client when we first moved here, and one of my first jobs of work too. These shrubs were then only about 2–3 feet high back then (1987); then came the '87 gales in the October – me and Debbie looked out of our bedroom window to see these shrubs whirling around as if they'd take off! Luckily, they survived that night, whilst nationwide there was total devastation. I wrote to Kew Gardens with an idea to raise money for replanting – I suggested that each of the trees that were blown down or severely damaged, and those same trees that had been planted by well-known people like royalty for instance, could the wood not be used to make into furniture, bowls, etc. and state – 'The wood to make this chair was taken from the tree blown down in the 1987 gales, and had been planted by Queen Victoria'.

I received a letter back from Kew and they said that they had already put this into practice (not because of my suggestion, I shouldn't think!?).

Over the years I have given second chances to sickly or misshapen plants, trees and shrubs, often like this because of the nurserymen or staff at garden centres. I have been greatly rewarded many times when they pull through to a fine display as if to thank me for saving them!

Because of total lack of money as a child, and couldn't buy all those wondrous plants that I saw in those 1950's catalogues, made sure that when I was older I would buy every weird and wonderful plant going! and still have some unusual 'gems' like say the two forms of Lonicera – Lonicera 'Pharoah's Trumpet, a beautiful climbing honeysuckle; and the bush form Lonicera 'infundibuliformis' "rockii". I would have to write a separate gardening book to list all the plants that I now have at present and in the past, but then there are so many gardening books out there listing thousands of plants and many photographs that I could never afford to do. Therefore this is why this book is more of my personal look at things that go on in the world of gardening, and my experiences.

Lettuce Prey

A good friend of mine helped me on the landscape side of things but had to leave me after only two days, for he started getting pains in his backside. He went to his doctor and the doctor was astonished to see a lettuce growing from his backside! The doctor, however, put my friend at ease and said, "Don't worry, this is only the tip of the iceberg!"

Twigged It

An odd thing happened to me too that very same year. I woke up in the night with a pain in my right ear, then out of the blue, a small twig grew from it. This grew to a small branch, then it blossomed and also came into leaf, then below that a small lawn, with mini-flower borders, beautiful scenery etc. Of course it goes without saying I had to get the doctor to come to me for I couldn't go out like that! My doctor straight away diagnosed it, "Don't worry, Keith, it's only a beauty spot!"

Utter Stupidity

Sorry reader, how much more silliness can you take! Right then, let's get back to the more serious stuff. I have, for as long as I can remember, when actually estimating, given every detail possible to the client regarding every 'do and don't'. Hopefully, I'd think that at least I'd let the client know what I'm talking about, and they feel confident enough to employ me to carry out their work for them.

I have a fair bit to tell them when it comes to the preparing of turfing sites, the laying and also aftercare. It goes without saying, that some clients shock me to my bones and so utterly stupid that you don't believe your eyes.

I went to estimate one such job – she was a nice lady, and was bright and cheerful, hence it was a shock on what was to come. I totally cleared this garden on my own, for the lady wanted only lawn. The lawn was laid, and left with my usual parting, "keep it well watered for at least three weeks until the roots take hold, then just keep moist until the grass is 5–6 inches high or as near as." You can imagine my shock then when I had a telephone call from the lady about five or so days later, frantically saying that her turf was dying. I asked her to explain in more detail what the turf looked like, and she explained that the turf had gone a browny yellow and had shrunk, each turf shrinking to leave 1" and 2" gaps.

I asked the lady if she'd been watering the lawn as I had asked her to do, and she assured me that she had, so now I was really worried, and now thinking that perhaps there was something in the ground – had petrol or oil or some other substance lain in the ground? But then I had to rule that out quickly, for the old lawn was still green, as were the shrubs and other plants prior to taking them out.

I made arrangements to see the lady straight away, and on my arrival the whole lawn was brown, with the gaps that the lady spoke of but all the turf was bone dry. I lifted up two or three and the underneaths were dry too, so I said, "But you haven't watered the turf, they have all dried up and shrunk." Again the lady said that she definitely had been watering. Well, I thought, I can't argue with that, for if she said she had… then she had! Yet it was so clear to see that she hadn't.

I was now baffled, but then something made me say, "Where's your hose and sprinkler, only I can't see one?" The answer I just could not believe. "I haven't got a hose or sprinkler." So I then went on to ask how the watering was done? "Oh, I've just been going out with a milk bottle." I was so dumfounded, for she really had just been filling a milk bottle and just flicked the water everywhere. I of course told the lady that there was simply no way this lawn would revive and she'd have to have yet another new lot of turf.

The woman still acted so surprised, and really thought the odd bit of water from a few bottles of water would suffice to keep one hundred and sixty turfs moist. The outcome I assume was okay, but the lady had a second lot of turf to pay for, plus the expense for me to take up, dispose of, and partially re-level again, and yes, this time she did buy a hose and sprinkler, and I never heard from the lady again, so assumed she followed my instructions, or did she forget to unreel the hose and turn on the tap! Going by the woman's mentality, it really wouldn't surprise me!

Horror of Horrors!

And as they say, there's more! I and a labourer laid a really lovely lawn in a back garden. We did the whole lot in one long summer's day, and told the chap that we'd be back in the morning to pick up the rest of our tools. The chap had two young sons of ten and eleven approx., and said how mad keen they both were on football, so I told them that they had a fair wait yet of 6–8 weeks before the lawn could even be walked on, yet alone play on it!

Anyhow, we went back the next day, only to find all the turf in a disgusting state, broken, trodden on, dents everywhere, and the chap just simply said, "Oh, they had a game of footy last night when you left. They simply couldn't wait eight weeks or so." The chap must have seen the look of horror on our faces. Well, the only good thing about all this is that at least the chap paid me on the previous day. My mind even today still boggles when I think back on what happened.

Shortfall

I remember doing a turfing job in Leytonstone, London. It was a big garden and the man wanted the whole lot turfed except for a three foot wide border at the back of the garden. These were the days of the old three foot by one foot turfs, not always of a good standard and often broke up, and hardly ever the same widths, lengths and thicknesses, hence many a time spoilt my good levels, hence back then often warranted extra expenses for the customers when I'd have to put on a top-dressing in spring or autumn to make up all the sinkages and unevenness of the turfs.

And so it was on this job, several turfs just crumbled and made it almost impossible even to place back together. I did, however, manage to turf this big lawn of some eight hundred odd turfs. The large lawn tapered as it got to the back. I'd marked in the three foot border that the man asked for, but I was now just six turf short of the border line, and all because of the damaged turf.

I showed the customer, and said, "Well, here is the marker for your three foot border, but we're six short – shall I make the border four foot wide instead, for you said you're putting in shrubs and they'll most certainly fill more than your three foot allocated border anyway in a short time." But no, the man wanted just a three foot border. I thought, how daft, for this was a huge garden, and this border was right at the back.

This chap was not for moving so had to order six turfs and waited three weeks for them, and the man wouldn't pay me until the job was done. After this, I always over-ordered on turfs to stop this happening again, and if the client asked about any leftovers I always said that it was courtesy of the turf supplier to allow for damaged turf. It wasn't of course, the client was unwittingly paying for it themselves. Some turf supplier today do supply free extras for damage, but not back in those days.

That Dreaded Mr Nichols!

Way back in the 1980s I pruned an elderly lady's fruit trees for her for a good ten years I should think. On going to see the job for the very first time, found these half a dozen or so trees in a state of neglect – anyway, I sent her my estimate and wrote down in full detail on how the work was to be carried out and what materials are needed. The lady kindly wrote back to say that she couldn't afford me, and that was fair enough.

About three weeks later I got a call from the lady to come and prune her fruit trees after all, for she'd called in someone else and he'd done a bad job. Now, quite how she knew he'd done a bad job I was keen to find out. On my arrival I could see for myself very bad workmanship and the same workmanship that every member of the public does to avoid paying a professional.

I couldn't wait to ask the lady, "How did you know that the man hadn't done the job right?" "I didn't at first, I let him prune one tree, still thinking that he knew his job, but when I took a closer look when taking over his tea, I knew something was wrong." She then related the whole story – it was when she saw the first tree, and spotted several crossing branches and the usual branches sitting one upon the other; the lady had also looked around for other 'items' especially when the man had completed his work, the items of course being the lack of all the materials!

The lady said in the end she had words with the man, and reeling off all that I'd put on my estimate. "In Mr Nichols' estimate, he said he would do this, or Mr Nichols was going to do that. Mr Nichols said you should do this etc., etc. The lady said that the man looked not only annoyed, but very embarrassed, perhaps now knowing he'd been caught out even though in his mind just chopping away thought his work would suffice. The lady kept saying that as I listed all the items on how you were going to do my trees, he kept grunting! Humph! Humph! and I bet he wanted to throttle that Mr Nichols! The lady went even further to embarrass the man, "You haven't put on pruning compound to paint the wounds, or put tree grease on the trunks, or sprayed with winter wash – Mr Nichols was going to do all that too!"

Needless to say, I got the job after this and put it right, but after ten years I had to put my price up, as had all the materials, and so the lady never had me anymore. I found this quite odd. The public I'll never understand!

Odd Job

One of the oddest jobs that I was called out to estimate was in Woodford, Essex, not many miles from my then home in Walthamstow, but far enough there and back, plus the time factor. The client said that he wanted a branch lopped off from a tree that was from next door; on seeing this branch, I found it not far off from looking like a twig! Yes it was hanging over the fence by two feet approx., but was only about one and a half inches thick!

I have often wondered if the chap perhaps did not own a pair of secateurs, even at a push you could've used a knife or hedge/grass shears. The garden next door was grossly unkempt, so it wasn't the fact that a clean cut had to be made, for even snapping it off would've done the trick.

The branch took just one quick snip, job done, but what could I charge? Even at that time (1970s), five pounds would seem a lot, so landed up charging him just two, hence I suppose just covering my petrol really. The only bit of luck that came out of this was that a couple had noted my telephone number on my van – the couple who lived just one road away from the 'branch' job wanted fruit trees and shrubs pruned. I got the job, and it turned out to be one of the well known (well, well known if you like cricket) and were the Wolstenholme family.

A Beast in a Walthamstow Garden?

Another extraordinary experience was when I got to work for an elderly couple well into their eighties I remember. Not a large garden by any means, but needed total restoration. We, that is my young labourer and I, found dealing with these people an unnerving one, for if Tony (Brayley) or myself had to ask to use the loo or to ask advice on how they wanted their garden, the lady would catch either one or other of us on our own, and talk about her husband relentlessly, but not in a nice way – she referred to him as a beast. "I hate him, he's a beast, I wish he would die."

The lady said this several times to each of us, and all we kept saying was "really?" or "how awful", moreso when she said that he used to interfere with very young girls, and this was the reason for her hatred. Oddly, the lady was saying these things within earshot of him, but he did not defend himself, so although he was a sweet old chap with a smiling face now, did he really do those things in the past?" Was his wife bordering on senility? Yet apart from her keep calling him a beast and wanting him to die, all other type of conversation was perfectly normal. Perhaps the old man was used to her saying all these things, but wouldn't you think he'd defend himself in front of us as strangers? or indeed had he actually done all these things? We were glad to get away really, for we didn't know who to side with.

Making up the Rules to Suit Yourselves

My son Rowan and I could never quite get our heads round a problem that occurred on a job in the mid-1990s and a lot of questions needed to be asked and answered, but to no avail as you'll read. The job of work entailed the cutting short of a massive lawn, followed up by clearing a five foot wide and 30 foot long border, plus replanting with new unusual perennial plants, and mulching around them with a dark compost to give the best effect.

It had been many years since I took a radio to work, for a radio does help you enjoy your work more and helps pass time quickly, moreso on the more boring jobs or on very dull days. Sunny days it's mostly just nice to listen to the bees, birds and all sounds of nature. This particular day it was half and half weatherwise. Rowan had a small radio and whenever we did use it, we kept the sound very low, in fact really just in earshot of us both. Of course it was nicer to be in the larger gardens where there was no one about for miles, hence could almost have the volume up full!

This particular day we put the radio on very low and, as I said, just in earshot for us both as this was a fairly narrow garden, so didn't want complaints from neighbours either side. The man of the house later came out to see us and looked quite horrified to see a radio! "Please could you turn off the radio, only we don't have radios or television." Of course, Rowan and I were taken aback, so I said, "Really? Why Not?" The chap replied, "We are a Christian family," and as I couldn't see the connection between being a Christian and radio and televisions, had no option to ask who made this rule up, for Christianity has been around a good while now, wouldn't you agree? and there certainly wasn't radios and televisions back then in the rules of 'do's' and 'don'ts, so assume the likes of other rules are made up by someone as years go along, and as things are invented or discovered. Now, although the people were totally pleased with our work, and it really did look nice too, plus the fact that I was able to tell them so much about not only their existing plants and shrubs, but also the host of new ones that we had planted, and of course we did get paid.

My conversation with the man though got me wanting to know more about this family's Christian ways, for I was using my eyes while on this job, but lots of things just didn't add up and needed explaining to me. The house was huge, so Christian religion allowed him to have this, and also whilst we were there the man asked us to leave a certain area for he was having built a two-storey extension to the house for his mother-in-law. So having plenty of money is okay too; the man also had a good job to earn all that money, for he had a brand new works van, two cars, but then these are mechanical and have electrics, therefore a radio, stereo, cassette, CD player? and just assume he doesn't use any of these? So how come that cars and vans were not around when their religion was formed, so how come they are allowed to drive and own anything mechanical? Why weren't these banned along with a radio or TV? Their religion doesn't state you mustn't have lots of money or allowed to buy big properties etc.

I think our biggest shock came when we had to go down their sideway, and there through the window for all to see were computers, laptops, etc! Why can't Christians watch TV or radio? For it's not all sex, swearing and violence on TV, especially with all these TV channels we have these days, with the most wonderful documentaries etc., we can all avoid the miserable soaps, horror films etc.

Radio and TV haven't been around that many years, and TV certainly didn't come about until the 1950s, and the programmes for very many years were so tame, and the people on TV were overboard when speaking the Queen's English, so when did this rule come about to all Christians I wonder? And last of all, sex, yes that little three letter word; the man had a nice-looking wife, and four children, so sex was not in the rule book, why did they not find that filthy, dirty, surely in *their* minds this was far nastier than any TV or radio? I rest my case, and said my bit, all the answers back to me from you the reader must be written on the back of a £50 pound note!

Today, I pass this same house on occasions, and as it fronts a main road, I can guarantee that every three years or so since I was there, the van (with the man's name on it) and the two cars, are always up to date. I think the couple should not have children, remain celibate, live in a small one-bedroomed house, travel by push bike, have no electric, especially for all the electrical things that they had in the kitchen alone.

Am I being barmy? Or do my rules sound as dumb as theirs. As I've grown older I can now see why there are so many problems amongst all the so many religions, the arguing, the wars, how many gods are there out there being worshipped every day? The mind truly boggles.

The really strange thing about all this is that during my very long years as a landscape gardener, have worked in two nunneries, have worked for bishops, priests, vicars etc., in churchyards or rectories and had a radio on in most of them at sometime or other, and never had a problem.

Look how many Christians watch and indeed appear in TV's 'Songs of Praise', so those that ban TV have we to assume have not a clue that this programme exists?

Whoops!

I really love old gardening books, they tell you so much, some of the reading very scary though, especially when you read of the chemical concoctions that were put either onto plants or in the ground, yet did no harm to many of our very elderly grandparents and great-grandparents, etc., plus other older folk who are still with us today. So it seems so strange in modern days with so many chemicals being taken off the shelves, where many had been used over so many years, yet did no noticeable harm.

On the other hand I've learned very good tips from old books, written so long ago but not strangely passed down the generations, and those tips still work very nicely today. It's nice reading about the tips given by the old gardeners too, little things that they themselves discovered or tried out, and much the same as I have done over the years.

As I've said before, I'm sure some writers of gardening books and magazines, simply just copy the ideas of others then repeating it so much it becomes gospel. Like say, when laying turf, still today you see when it comes to laying turf, and they say that it should be laid in brickwork fashion, i.e. lay the first row, but the second row should be laid half way over to the first one laid, then at the last turf of the second row, which should then have a bit left over, you cut this off and put it at the start of the second row where you moved over the first turf of the second row, you're then supposed to play about like this until all the turf is laid.

I remember the very first time that I laid turf back in the sixties at Springfield Park (Clapton) and was shown the brickwork method of laying turf, and I wondered why it had to be done like this, for it just didn't make any sense, so bravely asked one of the then under foremen Bill Brotherton, why the turf needed to be laid like this. "It's to stop the turf slipping." I thought this odd, we were on perfectly level ground, so where was it going to slip to? Was I to turn round and say, "Whoops! There goes another turf slipping."

When I eventually went self-employed, I never laid a single turf brickwork style ever again. In the early days of me doing this, several clients would ask why I wasn't laying it like brickwork, yet at the same time did not know that the answer was supposed to be… it's in case they slip… so they were simply only going by what was read in their gardening books.

Each and every client who asked me about the brickwork style, I'd tell them the reason about why it had to be done this way, because the turf will slip, so I'd gently push random turfs and say, "Look, not an ounce of movement!" and then I'd say "Can you see any reason why these turfs should slip… and where to?" Hence I got my clients all thinking and knew that I was right in my thinking.

The only time turf could slip, and brickwork style or otherwise would make no difference, and that's when turf is laid on a bank or steep slope. I then have only on occasions pushed in split canes, acting as 'nails', this would hold firm any turfs, and all this depends of course on the steepness, but in all these years have never had a turf slip yet, be it on a slope or flat ground. The split canes I only really used during hot weather, for when watering a slope or bank, or the event of a forthcoming storm or torrential rain, when water can get under newly laid turf and lift them perhaps slightly onto the next turf, but the split canes held them firmly in position until the turf knitted.

Slipping Again!

This time not a turf slip, but a time slip! For about three years I used to prune several fruit trees in a garden at Oulton Broad, not too far from where we live now. Somehow we got onto the subject of ghosts etc. The man of the house turned to his wife and said, "Tell Keith what happened to you about three years ago." The lady looked uncomfortable and was trying her best to wriggle out of telling me, and looking daggers at her husband for bringing the subject up.

Reluctantly, the lady gave up, and I saw that she was frightened of being ridiculed, but this is a subject I never laughed at. Anyhow the lady explained that she was standing at the sink in the kitchen, looking out in her garden, looked away a couple of seconds to put things on the draining board, then looked out into the garden again from the kitchen window. The lady told me that she had the shock of her life, for the orchard was as it would have been long before they moved there, and far more trees than were in her garden at present, and although a dry day, she saw ruts in the lawn, filled with water, the ruts were like those perhaps made by a hand-cart etc.

The lady said she was flabbergasted at what she was seeing, this so beautiful sight. The lady explained that she quickly turned to her daughter who was tidying out a drawer in a cupboard, and without thinking yelled, "Look at our garden!" The daughter, being quite baffled at mum's sudden outcry, and seeing her mum now looking quite foolish at what she'd said, for the garden was now back to normal.

They Should Go Away For a Spell!

Genuine signs that I saw on the roadside en route to Waltham Abbey, Essex: 'Tomaties for sale and Bags of SH.. Manure 25 per bag'.

Still the Rule?

In the whole of my landscaping career, it's been a never ending battle keeping up with rules and regulations made up of faceless and nameless individuals. Today there are laws governing the heights that a wall, hedge, or fence can be, and suppose this is one of the better laws, moreso since the introduction of the 'Leylandii' conifer, which has become the bane of most people's lives.

I remember seeing a programme on TV a good few years back now at the height of the craze through mainly the 1970s and early '80s. A chap got so fed up of his neighbour's overhanging conifers hanging on and over his fence, so started to cut them back. The neighbour next door saw what he'd done, and took the man to court – he was fined £1,000. This all came about because the neighbour had cut the other side of the fence line. If he had cut level to his own side or even half way on the top of the fence, then he would have been okay, but because he'd cut to the other side, he'd 'touched his neighbour's property'.

Golders Green Gold-Digger!

The title I did choose for this bit was GOLDERS GREEN GIT! Read on, and you'll see why. Golders Green in London, is mainly a Jewish community, and the client rang me to sort out his new to him but neglected garden, as he was away for long periods dealing in the fur trade.

Thankfully he was home for the duration of the time that I was there, as you'll read. The 'GIT' I hasten to add was not my client, but in fact his next-door neighbour! My client was a really nice chap, loaded with money, and had a really flashy car as I remember.

Firstly, I had to clear and turf the whole of this massive garden, plus prune and restore several fruit and ornamental trees, and some he simply didn't want and wanted them out, albeit told him that I could easily restore these trees, but no, they had to come out.

The client listened carefully to all my advice, and pointed out to him that his long garden had the gardens of several other houses down the left-hand side of the garden. The chap wondered what I was leading up to, so I pointed out that each house had windows of course, and people do look out of them; if just one set of eyes saw me taking out a tree of some age, they'd be straight onto the authorities and a heavy fine would ensue.

I had to point out that some of the trees may possibly have a preservation order on them, hence it's best to check what you can and cannot take out, and I can carry out my work with ease. The chap did exactly as I'd asked, so now we knew where we stood, and yes, there were a good many 'curtain twitchers' whist I was in the back garden. Let's now get to the front garden, and the neighbour on the right, and whose back garden too ran the length of the right-hand side of my client's garden. My client's front garden was in a bad state of neglect, so much so that the front gate had long been out of use, now covered in weeds and brambles, the main path buried with the same, and just a worn muddy path that many people had made by their own footprints to get to the front door.

The right-hand side of the garden was literally covered in very old massive shrubs, full too of weeds and the again dreaded blackberry; all this also scrambled over to next door's property, for this border of only one and a half feet wide, was the dividing border between the two properties.

The next-door neighbour, just like my client, also had his gate covered in brambles and weeds, etc., and also a much buried path because of dead leaves, weeds etc. and again like my client's, a well-worn 'path' of mud direct to his front door, such was the diversions of both properties.

At first, because of the density of the shrubs and undergrowth, had no idea that the width of the border was so small, there was easily eight feet in width of each shrub, i.e. four feet or so either side of the border, and similar in height too, in fact more like ten to twelve feet in height.

Anyhow, I got to grips and started all the clearance, the next-door neighbour was away at this point, so the client and I were hoping that when he came home he'd be so delighted. I filled an eight yard skip with what came out of that border, and it came to planting up time, so I ran a few ideas past the client, and settled for a nice mix of Hypericums (Rose of Sharon) Hypericum 'calicynum'. These I used as a ground cover to the taller Hypericum 'patulum' "Hidcote", these would grow possibly no more than a five-foot high hedge, and would take a hard prune every couple, or every year after establishing to keep tidy. I also used at random intervals to weep over the client's side of the border Hypericum 'moserianum' "tricolor".

After mulching with Somerset dark sedge peat, the border looked fantastic, hence now could re-turf the rest of the front garden. Our joy however was very short-lived, for when the next-door neighbour came home he went absolutely mental! and raged on how we touched his property, for apparently nine inches wide of that 1ft 6" border was his, in other words… half!

The chap threatened me and my client with a court summons, but my client said "Don't worry, Keith, I'll sort it." By this I understood that my client was to offer him a fair bit of money, which I'm certain is what happened, for the neighbour did calm down for the rest of my stay. The man gave no praise for this nice border, and probably wished he'd kept his mouth closed, for I suggested an idea, and that was to put in a low 3 inch high wooden edging board or one strand of wire to divide the two 9 inch strips, but we'd have to take out all the hypericums and use them elsewhere, and simply put in a row of annual bedding plants and he can sort out his side or let it grow back as weeds etc.

Sadly, I never knew if the neighbour rescued his gate or uncovered his original path, for he may have done after seeing what I'd done to the neglected garden of his new neighbour. As you've read throughout this book, in life, and dealing with the public, you most certainly come across some very odd people, and I seem to find a lot of them, especially when it comes to mere inches of ground.

I would have loved to have seen the man's face when the Hypericums were taken up, for it really did look nice. Perhaps later the neighbour did ask my client why they were taken up, for I'd already told the client that the Hypericum "Hidcote" would have made a fine hedge, and the 'rose-of-sharon' would have covered all the border and stop any weeds in their tracks, but now with the Hypericums gone, the weeds do as they like as they'd always done!

My Runner Beans Run Away!

In 2009 I grew some runner beans in a large tub, and they had grown their full height and more up eight-foot canes, a high wind came up one night and the beans and canes gone! We searched the garden front and back, neighbours checked theirs, and up to today remains a mystery. There is no way that anyone could get into my garden.

We're Here to Ask

It surprises me how many people tackle jobs in the garden and don't seek advice first. One year I got a job to trim back a tall hedge of the 'Leylandii' conifer; the other side of this garden was a new plot that had just been built on, the new owners of that plot said that they'd already cut their side back but asked if I could give them a look in as they had some work for me.

I went round to see them. "See, we've cut our side back." I stood in shock as they said it would soon grow back. "No, it won't!" I exclaimed, "for you have cut way beyond any greenery, you have to stay in front of the greenery for it to grow back as a hedge." The hedge was all brown, a thicket of brown growth and exposed trunks, I told them that "you've got to look on this for evermore, for it'll never grow back," so the only thing I could suggest, "to mask this ugly sight was to plant some evergreen vigorous climbers or build a large trellis framework about 3ft from the hedge and plant your climbers to that."

My clients whom I was working for had already seen as I was cutting their hedge, that you could see through to their next-doors garden because of the 'hack back', so I pointed out to them that at least they were the lucky ones, for after my trim, it would again thicken their side up, but the other people were looking onto an eyesore. It never did come to light who actually owned the hedge, and a good job it didn't or more trouble would have ensued.

Archaeology Stumps

One year I had two jobs come up to dig out large conifers, one in one garden and the other of similar size across the road. I've long forgotten what I charged for each now, so I'll use example prices. The first conifer was the easiest, I use that term very lightly, but easy compared to the second conifer over the road as you'll read. I set to work on the first, and like with all tree removal it's peace of mind to have an array of tools and a good strong helper with you when taking on such a job. I use sharp spades, mattocks, axes, pick axe, pruning saws, and crowbars for leverage.

First of all, you leave your tree, conifer or shrub for that matter, fully intact, for you then have the added weight when you do the rocking backwards and forwards to free the roots from the soil, plus you have something to hold on to whilst doing this task; the cost of the job £40 to include taking it away. When I went to the man across the road where I'd already given him a price of £40, his price now was £90. Why the big jump, I hear you ask? Because the man thought it would save him money, i.e. less than £40 and thought it would make the job easier for me, he'd cut the conifer down, so on seeing this on my arrival I had no choice but to tell the man of the new price.

I then had to say that it was because he'd cut the conifer down, therefore no extra weight to help it topple and weaken from the ground, but also had nothing to hold on to either, so this meant a lot of hard graft to continuously dig away all the soil bit by bit, just like a careful archaeological dig.

The man then could see all the problems exactly as I'd described, and realised that he hadn't saved any money at all. With a now low stump like this, you have to take soil away wherever you can, plus cut where you can, plus leverage with a crow-bar, in fact anything to make the stump lose its grip. If weight is there like the other garden, as it falls, it also exposes other hidden roots, and if you're very lucky you'll see a central tap root if it has one when its on its side; find this, and the tree will come away with reasonable ease.

My Magic Clematis!

As I've said elsewhere in this book, I 'float my own boat' when it comes to gardening, and garden how I want to garden; there are many ways to cut corners, and by that I don't mean a bodge! It's knowing your job, along with a little experimentation to try out things.

One such time came about when I bought my first house in Chingford Road, E.17. I'd bought myself a nice clematis, and a month or so after planting it, I went down the garden to inspect it, but found that the flower was trying to open, but was smothered in blackfly. Now don't ask me why, but I thought no, I'm not going to spray this plant, but try something different, and that's what I did!

The day was hot and sunny, and the ground dry, albeit the clematis itself was in light shade. I knocked up a fairly neat, concoction of systemic insecticide, watered the soil well around the plant to make it moist and not just put on the insecticide to just soak in and dry up. Anyhow, I poured the liquid away from the flowers and leaves, or should say almost open flower buds that couldn't open because of the density of the blackfly that were preventing it from opening. I applied the liquid to the root area, and assumed that the liquid would start working after perhaps a couple of days or so. How wrong was I? That very evening I thought I'd take a look, and there in full open bloom was my clematis! and not a sign of the many blackfly that were present earlier in the day. Systemics normally worked I thought just through the leaves and stems etc., but thought 'System' it could work through the system but take it up through the roots instead, and it did.

Quite how it worked straight away like that I don't know, I can only assume that the plant perhaps was thirsty in the dry ground, the stems being thin and wiry, the liquid went through the plant's system straight away. I'd never known any systemic insecticide work as quick as this. I experimented on other small plants in my garden and the effect was the same.

The Gunge Tree!

Strangely enough in a matter of just a few weeks I was to experiment again, but this time on a huge scale. A friend of mine and his family had just moved to a new house in Edmonton on the North Circular Road. His name was Eddie, a big strong likeable chap, and we met when he joined the Haringey Parks Dept. on my last few months there, and Eddie proved an asset when helping me do private work when I went self-employed again.

Eddie called me in because there was an unusual problem going on in their garden; it was something that I'd never come across before, but have seen it since in various nature programmes. The sight that met me was so extraordinary, and could see why Eddie and his family were concerned. The problem was with the huge weeping willow tree, or rather what was on it! The whole of this massive tree was covered in thick white cobwebs, containing millions of tiny caterpillars! So Eddie asked if there was anything that could be done, and seeing the desperation in his eyes I relayed what I'd done to my clematis, only a few weeks back, so suggested to Eddie that the same trick could be tried again but on a bigger scale.

I suggested to buy between twelve and fifteen bottles of systemic, soak the base of the willow with a hose, and to the width of the furthest branches. We flooded a big area, let it soak in, then knocked up bucket loads of the systemic and covered the whole area.

Unlike the clematis, nothing happened that night, so told Eddie to Keep me informed if anything does actually happen, and happen it did about four days later! Eddie rang me excitedly and asked if I could come over, which I did, and met the most ghastly sight – all the caterpillars had fallen to the floor, and the remaining ones gradually falling like raindrops. I had worked! and when you think how tall a full size willow is, it was indeed a miracle.

Later in the day, Eddie and I had the awful task of raking and sweeping the now soft gungy caterpillars into a big pile for disposal. The tree was now clear and my experiment worked 100%. I told other clients of my trial and of course tried it on other clients' trees, shrubs, fruit-trees, etc., and it worked each time, and all the people took the trouble to ring me to let me know that it worked.

I pointed out to them all that normal spraying could be very much hit and miss, especially where bugs have rolled leaves and hidden inside, or the unmovable scale insect or leaf-miner, for no matter where they hide because the insecticide was inside the system, there was no escape.

Yes, it was trial and error knocking up the right concoction, hence the more systemic you added, the chance of success was higher. Sadly, this brand of systemic was taken off the market, so I haven't to date (2011) experimented with other brands of systemic to see if they would work.

A Softly Softly Approach

When my son Adrian first came to help me on the landscaping side of things, it was a bit hit and miss on whether we'd ever get started on a project, for it turned out that planners had to be called in first from the council.

The garden wasn't that big, and as the people had just moved in, had a Victorian style conservatory built and took away a good chunk of garden, but I could see potential in there, if older shrubs and messy hawthorn and elder were taken out. I relayed some of my ideas to the clients and asked them to let me do the talking to the planning officer, instead of going in like a bull in a china shop, and tread softly, be precise, be accurate, keep calm and above all keep professional. The planning officer had already told them that certain things had to stay, but the things he chose to stay, still made the garden look so small.

The morning of the meeting came, the planning officer was a pleasant fellow, but like all in authority like to say a yay or nay and have to be in charge, and the more you push and insist what you would like, the more they dig their heels in and do the opposite. The man went ahead and pointed at various trees of fifteen feet high or so, and none worthy of garden merit, i.e. suckered ash, sycamore, etc. "You can take out that, and this, not that," were his ongoing words. Then further along was a gap of four feet, then an old conifer of some size, and very near the conservatory. The conifer was one that could come out, but insisted that a tree had to take its place. I asked if he had a tree in mind, and I couldn't believe my ears when he said, "Scots Pine". Had he any idea how high and wide this tree would grow compared to the existing conifer? So again I kept calm and said, "Wouldn't this affect the foundations of the patio and conservatory, plus cut out light?" Strangely then he agreed. I suggested a fastigiated type tree, tall, but thin, or perhaps some of the smaller prunus or malus species would suit? I listened to all his do's don'ts and cant's, hence had made a bit more progress, and asked if it was still okay to send him a plan (a 'cartoon' plan in my case!) and he agreed.

Later that week I sent him a detailed plan of what I'd like to plant and remove, and made suggestions how the other nearby houses would still have their privacy which was one of his concerns. I showed the client my planned out idea on what I could do; they loved it, but both doubted whether it would be agreed upon. We waited for about three weeks for a reply, and he must have liked my plan, for all the trees and shrubs that he said must stay, could go! For I'd chosen more sensible shrubs, trees, etc. to suit a small plot, yet give perhaps even more privacy than there already was.

The clients were so overjoyed and couldn't thank me enough, and we even invited the planning officer back to see the finished project – he *was* impressed I can tell you! Now if I'd got into an arguing stage with this man, the outcome would have been very different.

Careful What You Prune

I remember years ago when my regular work was in 'Millionaires Row' in Hampstead (also at Hampstead Garden Suburb) but it's the former that I refer to now. I recall one day when a few of the residents there were up in arms regarding the pruning of a tree. Now to be honest with you, I can't really remember if the tree had been pruned badly, or because it was pruned properly but without consent, for this tree had a preservation order on it, and at that time you usually had to be vetted as a qualified tree surgeon and someone would have to come out and show you exactly what branches could or could not be pruned.

As I never have dealt with larger trees, I'm afraid that I'm not an authority on the subject, so cannot give advice; the only advice I can give and that is always check with either your local parks department or planning officer before going ahead. I have had to call them out on several occasions, the last occasion a lady wanted an old silver birch of some size taken down and dug out, and as it was in a front garden and on a fairly busy road I knew that there would be a lot of eyes on me. Also there were some Maples on a side bit of grass and as the lady had just moved in, didn't know if the trees or grass area did actually belong to her.

I straight away contacted the Parks Dept., and told them all about the Birch and Maples, and could they come out as usual and check for me. I was totally surprised to find that they no longer came out to give advice, as every tree in every garden and in the street, is now on computer! Quite how this was done I don't know, for we are talking about a hell of a lot of trees.

Sure enough, before even getting my words out, the lady said a yay or nay there and then, yes it was okay to take out or even prune the Birch, and even told me that the Maples and the grass area did belong to the lady, and that I could prune to restore them. All this of course is peace of mind for not only the client, but for me too.

Get Knotted... or Knott!

The Polygonum family (pronounced Per-lig-er-nom) is a powerful family with a strong root system, and most are delightful garden favourites from perennials to rockery plants, and of course many polygonums are wildflowers or to put it another way... weeds!

The Wildlife and Countryside Act of 1981 states that this is the worst weed ever to invade Great Britain. It is illegal to introduce it anywhere in the countryside. The plant came from Japan in 1825 and used widely in 18th-century gardens, and a favourite as a background plant on an herbaceous border, growing from nine to twelve feet tall, and a rapid spread. Which one of these weeds am I talking about? It's the dreaded 'Japanese Giant Knotweed' Fallopia 'Japonica', anything from three to nine feet in height, and rarely seems to stop at the three foot height I can tell you! the other is Fallopia 'sachalinensis' reaching easily the twelve foot mark. The botanical powers-that-be have changed many plant names over the years, and rarely you hear why, for Fallopia is a new name really, for I and many others still call the

Polygonum family as, well, Polygonum! In other words Polygonum 'Japonica' etc.

If you, the reader, wish to grow a polygonum I'd choose the prettier variegated version, but grow it in a strong tub, or tub sunk into the ground, but make sure your soil in the tub is quite a bit below the surface, for if those tough rhizome roots get a whiff of other soil easily in reach, it'll be off like a greyhound out of its trap!

I have only come across this dreaded weed once in all my years of gardening, so I'll put you, the reader, in the picture so to speak, to show you how it would take four lots of neighbours to eradicate it. Draw yourself, or picture an upright cross (as a crucifix, not as a kiss); these represent four gardens. I was in the square bottom right, and this large clump of knotweed was up in that top left-hand corner, and without a doubt all the other three gardens at that point (centre of cross) would have the knotweed too, hence no matter what weed-killers you put on, the other three gardens we assume still had their plants, therefore all four neighbours would have to get their heads together and all treat the weed at the same time, and that was my suggestion to my client at Sybourn St., E.17 (bordering Leyton).

Like most houses today, we all seem to put up six foot fences, hence not at all easy to chat to a fellow neighbour, hence my client never did go to see the two separate neighbours at the back, so I never got to treat the weeds, so assumed the weed spread even more?

I will now tell you about a TV programme that I saw a few years ago now, and was one of these garden makeover shows where you're to believe that any size garden can be cleared and laid out in just three days, my mind set to wondering how they were going to tackle this particular garden and what advice was to be given, and strangely, although expected, they did not go back to show you the garden a year or so later, for I'm sure there was a huge problem, there had to be.

I'll tell you why, and unlike that clump of polygonum in the corner that I just told you, the reader, about, this garden on TV was top to bottom covered in 'Japanese Knotweed'! a total thicket of them, so this held my interest on how this job would be tackled. The gardeners got to grips with diggers, mattocks, spades, forks etc., all hacking away at these tough rhizomes, the cameras kept away when it came to all the knotweed growing at the very edges of the fence panels, and when the cameras were filming I said to my wife to look just beyond the client's fences in each of the neighbours' gardens, and sure enough as I expected, you could see this giant knotweed in each and every garden! So it goes without saying, every fence panel should have come out and deep concrete gravel boards should have been put in place to stop the invasion all over again.

After the gardeners so-called cleared the garden of each and every scrap of rhizome, they laid garden membrane only in parts, shingled other area, built patios, arches, paths etc., all the usual make-over stuff, and no, the concrete edging boards were not put in, and nor was any weed-killer used. Had that been my TV programme I would have made 100% certain that every bit of knotweed was dead, even if it took a full year to do it, just as I have to do with my own clients on badly weeded areas of problem weeds.

It would have been totally impossible to clear all the roots from the knotweed, considering the time allowed, for *yes*, the garden did *look* clear, but I could see quite clearly where parts had literally just been skimmed off and even cut down. The garden was far too big to do a proper lasting job in just three days.

I felt so very sad for the happy couple who looked so delighted with their new garden, believing that the knotweed problem had totally gone. Even when you saw the couple and their family celebrating, I looked beyond just adjacent to the fence-lines, the tall knotweed was there is the background wafting in the breeze, and waiting for their return back to the new garden!

As I've said, this is not a weed that crops up often in my landscape work, but have had telephone calls from folk, so can give them advice. If there is not too much of it I simply cut the thick stems, leaving about six inches or so, the stems thankfully are hollow, so devised my own way of eradicating this weed – I put a sharp steel rod down the hollow stem and tap with a hammer to penetrate into the thick rhizome, and long before I bought trade weed-killers that were far stronger than those sold at garden centres I'd then poured the weed-killer in neat. I've also used paraffin, and even paraffin and oil, so that it adheres to the remaining bit of hollow stem after it slowly drains away; you then know that the weed-killer has stuck on to do its job. Some modern-day weed-killers do eradicate it, and have to be a good trade weed-killer too for it to really work, and even then still needs more than one application. The only thing I warn people about is that if you do use paraffin or paraffin and oil, or sodium chlorate neat, it may be a couple of years before you can plant again. To test, I just used to throw a bit of grass seed down and a packet of mixed flower seeds, usually a children's mixture; if all these grew well, for they do grow quick and penetrate the ground easily, you'll know that you could safely sow seed, or lay turf and plant up, and just in case any 'residue' was a little deeper, plant up any cheap common shrub, something with a vigorous root system.

'Marestail' is another difficult weed to eradicate, but what I do here is to firstly get a long garden cane and slash at the plants, for this damages the leaves and stems. I then mix up a weed-killer, keeping it neat as I can so that the strength is there, then add a washing-up liquid to help it adhere, and preferably a lemon washing-up liquid that contains an acid, therefore you wouldn't use that on garden plants, but you can use ordinary washing-up liquid on them.

The slashing method works too on other bad weed infestations, for the cuts allow the weed-killers to absorb into the cuts straight away, and the weeds die far quicker.

Wing of a Bird

Back in 1971 whilst at the Lake District, I thought I'd found a black-leaved 'fern' growing wild on a grassy bank in the middle of nowhere. Today there is a black 'fern' for sale called 'Raven's Wing' – could someone have spotted that 'fern' and cultivated it to the fame it has today? I was tempted to dig it out at the time, for perhaps it was just a 'fern' growing that I'd never seen before. I'll never know!

Cart Before The Horse!

As you've read through this book you can see that I have to, at times, deal with very odd customers, and it beggars belief on how they get through life sometimes. On more than one occasion I've had a random telephone call from someone, "Do you do turfing?" "Yes, I do." "Well could you lay some for me, I ordered them the other day and they've just arrived." Totally shocked by this, I'd say that it was impossible, for a) I was already at the start of a job, and b) have no idea of the state of the garden, then invariably they'd say that it was in a terrible state, I'd then have to say that c) I hadn't even been given the chance to estimate for you to say a yay or a nay, and that I daren't start the job and just hope you'd accept my price right off the cuff at the end.

My client was now as taken aback as me, then told me that their garden was 60 feet by 80 feet or whatever, and told me that "It's old lawn, neglected borders, weeds about 2 feet high," etc. "What sort of weeds, bell-bine? ground-elder? nettles? creeping buttercup?" "Er, don't know" was the reply. I'd go on to say, "without seeing your garden, is it level? does it need a rotovator? do I need a skip? does top-soil need to be bought in to make up ground." My questions were endless. Imagine all those turf stacked there for several days whilst the ground was being prepared; they'd start to rot without doubt!

Dead End Street

One of the other strangest occurrences was when a potential client rang to ask if I could come along and give her an estimate. She gave me her address and I told her that I didn't know where her road was, so she told me, but prior to that she said, "which way would you be coming in?" So I told her and followed her directions. I found the road easily with her easily followed directions, but just couldn't find the house number, so drove right to the end of this long road which led to a dead end and just raised flower beds, so turned round drove up and down about four times and decided to park up so I could walk and see the house numbers easily. After about an hour and a half I gave up and went home to ring the lady; of course she wondered what had happened to me.

Again I went through the exact directions that she'd given me, and I told her that I'd followed the road to the bottom which had raised flower beds. Her next words to me I couldn't believe, "Ah, you saw the flower bed, well the road was blocked off two years ago, the road continues the other side." I bit my lip, for why oh why would she direct me to the dead end and not from another way in from the other main road?

So Short a Memory

One of my long-standing clients had moved house and wanted two separate lawns laid, but refused to take my advice when I said that she should use my good turf company (Tolleshunt Turf Supplies, Maldon, Essex) the lady chose her own turf supplier. After I'd prepared the area, and two very dodgy men got out of a battered truck, and quite honestly the turf looked awful, and everyone said so too.

The lady of course realised she should perhaps have listened to me, but was not prepared to admit she was wrong.

So, when it came to the second area, I stayed tight-lipped, for I could easily see that I was dealing with a lady who was going to do her own thing and not take valued advice. Anyhow, I commenced lifting the second lawn and found that the grasses in the old lawn consisted mainly of 'couch grass', so even when the lawn was taken up, vast amounts of it was clearly still in the ground. The lady then said, "I think I will try *your* turf firm, can you order them for me?" I told the lady that it was very unwise to lay the turf at this point, for the remaining lot of couch would soon grow through, and will spoil the top quality of the new lawn. But no, this lady wouldn't again take advice, and the work had to be done straight away, so reluctantly I laid this lovely turf on the top of couch grass roots, instead of weed-killing first.

As the year went on, the once beautiful turf of about only four months, started to look awful, and I said nothing for this now matched the dodgy turf that the two dodgy men had supplied. The lady this time wanted turf supplied; this time it was to be laid as a border so as to reduce the width of a large shrub border, hence two very long strips of grass.

I asked the lady if she would like the turf as last time. "No I don't, it was awful, and right outside my window too!" So I couldn't hold back, "There was nothing wrong with the turf, you didn't want me to kill off all the couch and come to that the dandelions too" (the latter of course having a deep root, hence when sliced off came back twice as strong). "No, no," she said, "it was bad turf! I don't know why you made me have that!" I really was taken aback, how many of her family and visiting friends had she told that to? (Tolleshunt Turf still operate superbly today, unlike those other dodgy turf men in the ol' truck.)

Couch Grass Tenfold!

I had done a fair bit of work for a young family who had just moved into a property that had just been built, and end-to-end of the garden was solid with couch grass, dock, dandelion and thistle; the latter three if just skimmed off come back stronger than before. As I've said, I suggested firstly to weed-kill the whole site, and as the soil was dented all over, could easily be solved with a good fine top-soil and layered on the top as a thick top dressing if you like, then rolled, and virtually ready to turf.

Once again the people wouldn't listen, and again to so-call 'save money' the man said he'd do the preparation, and I could come back and lay the turf. I wondered how he was going to do this, for his build or his job didn't suit manual labour, so knew something would go wrong, and it did… big time!

The man called me back for me to check to see how he was getting on; the man hadn't applied any weed-killer, and had *rotovated* the whole site! I had already told him that if you break off any part of couch grass root, and even if it was a quarter of an inch long with root attached – it will grow! Therefore after the very unnecessary rotovating, the roots had been chopped into very fine pieces.

The chap said that it'd be alright for it is after all still a grass, but I urged him to make some sort of level or pay me to do it, sit back a month or so until the grass grows, then apply a weed-killer, but no, he wanted the turf to be laid as soon as possible. The man wanted to level the ground himself, and thought at this very point I gave no further advice, but warned him that if he didn't level properly I wanted no come-back on this and asked him to sign my disclaimer form. He signed it and said, "But how hard can it be to level soil?"

I went back to lay the turf, and felt the ground sinking beneath my feet a little, thus spoiling the man's so-called level.

The man called me back after one month for his once 'clear' garden was a total mess, and so very glad that a disclaimer had been signed. I could see the sadness in his eyes and the so worrying look, so he knew that I knew that he'd shot himself in the foot, thinking that he knew a landscaper's job as well as his own. I could so clearly see that the couch grass had grown through the new lawn and really stood out compared to the normal mixed grasses in good quality meadow grass.

The other thing I spotted in an instant was the five-foot wide borders that edged this large lawn was of course a mass of couch grass, and as I said before, had increased tenfold after the rotovator had shredded it all up.

The man asked how we could get over this huge problem, so I said that yes, the couch grass on the borders could be killed off, but pointed out that the couch in the lawns had to stay, but the never-ending battle would be to try and keep the couch from creeping from the lawn into the borders, and a battle that no one could win.

The man did apologise to me for not listening to my advice in the first place, and even if the lawn and borders were killed off for a second time, top soil would again have to be ordered in as it should have been the first time round, and moreso now for because the chap had no idea on how preparation should be carried out, the turf was very uneven, something that in the trade we call 'rockery turves' – this is something that always occurs if preparation is not carried out correctly, and the only way out of this is over several years, the lawn must be top-dressed, all at a vast cost, yet if the lawn was prepared correctly, huge expense could have been spared.

If you do have to use a rotovator, you must realise that whatever depth your rotovator is set, it's still a lot of soil being disturbed. The art to a good solid level is to roll, rake, level and tread – not once, but several times. Yes, it is hard graft, but better off doing that than all the expense that would follow.

The treading part, known in the trade as the 'Gardener's shuffle' is a vital part of ground preparation; you do this by keeping your feet together and literally just shuffle along, your heel will find all the weak spots, hence you re-rake to level, then roll, rake again, tread and so on until you are satisfied that when you walk anywhere on your plot, not an indentation will occur. If you have done the job right you should be able to walk on your now-solid ground without placing long scaffold boards on your turf to work from, thus saving a bit of time and effort. I always end the preparation with a roll, for the ground should now be level, solid and flat. You can then make a 'key' with your rake to the width that the turf will be; this should now be a fine tilth, hence when you 'pum' or 'pun' in your turf, the turf will adhere to the soil.

As you can see, it's not the laying of the turf that's the real hard graft, it's the full preparation. Many 'cowboy; landscapers work as the client did, totally clueless, but by the time the lawn has grown and you then see problems, the cowboy is on his horse and well away!

Judas!

The 'Judas Tree' was one of the first of the unusual trees that I saw and learnt the name of when I first worked at Springfield Park (Clapton, London). Dorothy King 'Little Dot' as she was affectionately known, taught me the name after I relentlessly kept asking her so as the name would sink in my mind. The tree stood (still stands?) to the left of the Park's café garden where the outdoor chairs and tables were; this was enclosed with four-feet high ornamental iron fencing. The tree was only about eight feet high or so then, and never really get to any decent size in this country, but in its country of origin that's different.

Now, take note on the second part of the tree's name, for it will be relevant at the end of this section. The botanical name is Cercis 'Siliquastrum'; the 'Judas Tree' is a slow grower, and like nearly all members of the pea family, resent disturbance, therefore they are only seen usually supplied as very small 'shrubs' in a container (flowerpot, etc.) and not able to buy bare-rooted.

It surprised me how so daft some people can be, for I told a client all about the 'Judas Tree' and said that it would make a fine specimen tree for the front garden in the centre of the lawn. The lady asked how the tree got its name, so I told her that legend says that it was this tree that Judas is reputed to have hung himself from. The lady looked down at the two-foot high specimen that I'd supplied and quite seriously said, "that would be impossible wouldn't it, a tree only that high." So I thought to myself, well you ask a siliquastrum! I should have asked the lady if she thought that hanging was possibly a suspended sentence!

Strawberries and Not Nice!

Even after all these years of gardening, I find it so frustrating when I come across a shrub etc. that is not that well-known and I need to know the best time, and how to prune it. Yes, invariably the tree or shrub is listed, but when it comes to the section reading PRUNING, the shrub that you want info of reads – NO PRUNING REQUIRED and words to that effect, but what if you do have to prune it, when? and how? So you draw a blank, or take a chance and prune in winter which is the usual pruning time for most things, albeit I find it best to do it in the actual growing season whilst the tree, shrub or climber is in good active growth and had a far better chance of pulling through and re-growing within a few weeks.

A shrub, well, to start with, before growing into a small tree, now becoming a little less uncommon nowadays, is 'The Strawberry Tree' Arbutus 'unedo'. 'Unedo' means 'I eat one only!' for you'd never try a second one because of its awful taste, that's if you even manage to eat the first!

In all of our twenty-three years working in the Lowestoft area, I have only pruned and restored two up to 2011. Hence I was not familiar with the pruning time rather than the actual pruning itself. I searched through several of my gardening books, and each and every one of them said – no regular pruning required – but I did have to prune it, so when was I supposed to? for the same reads under magnolia and many years down the line I actually read that they prefer to be pruned in summer, albeit not having this knowledge, had always pruned in winter and the shrubs had never had any setbacks from me doing this at this time.

I thought I'd play safe on the first Arbutus, it was around April or May time, the front of the Arbutus faced the main garden, but the back of it backed onto a path that ran parallel with the garage. I thought if I pruned to the blind side of the main garden, should the tree not respond to pruning, at least it would be out of sight, so I set to work, and explained to the client what I was going to do. Thankfully just a few weeks later and the client rang to tell me that new shoots were sprouting out everywhere on all the different sized branches that had been cut back. I was now safe to do the main front half, therefore now all the tree was restored, and a lot more light now to that border and other parts of the garden.

I'm pleased I treated the Arbutus with 'kid gloves' for it could have been a tree or shrub that really doesn't respond easily to any pruning, and the whole tree could slowly have died back completely. Here of course is yet another case that had I been a 'cowboy' I would have just done what the customer asked, just to get the money and run and blow the consequences. My honesty and the way I went about the job paid off, for they gave me a fair bit of work after this and for one of their relatives too.

Part Repeat from Earlier and Added Bits!

No change here then I hear you say! Getting rid of rubbish from people's gardens has been the bane of my life during my landscaping career, and yet shouldn't be. Local authorities are in fact their own worst enemies, and make it so very difficult for folk to dump rubbish, be it household waste, garden rubbish, i.e. old turves, weeds, prunings etc., albeit whether you are a tradesman or householder.

My findings truly are an eye-opener on what I have seen, heard and experienced myself over very many years. In all my years in London, I never did find a place that would accept trade waste, therefore had to go to local tips that the householders used. The chap in charge there always let me in, and opened up an almost empty container for me to use. His eyes always lit up when I or other tradesmen came in, for you had to give the man cash, for after all we were not considered as members of the public, but tradesmen, and often our work vehicles had our names on them, and a big giveaway of course! If you didn't have your name on your vehicle you could do a fair few free unloading, for the man would think that the rubbish was from your own property, that is though until your face is recognised by the man in charge, and he'd either stop you going in, or to pay, which of course meant that the payment went into his pocket.

This didn't worry me, for I just wanted somewhere to unload the rubbish, and the money I gave him was from the client's pocket really, not my own. I kept the man 'sweeter' than other tradesmen, for I'd have a full transit van load of rubbish, plus four-feet high bundles of prunings on a large roof rack, and trailer load too, so on my very first visit to the dump and found that I could dump, providing I could pay him a sensible fee. Let's say then for this load back then he wanted say £10. I then of course knew what a full load like this would be, and what he was happy with, so to keep him sweet, even if I took two or three bags of rubbish in, I'd still give him his £10.

All my loads from thereon were £10; the chap was more than happy, and continued to open my own container, and £10 back in the 1970s was a lot of money, and I too was happy knowing that I had somewhere to dump rubbish for each job and peace of mind, and clients just pleased to see it all go so they didn't have to worry about it, albeit some of the bags of rubbish could have gone on the back seat of their car and they of course could dump for free.

Understandably, people don't want to muck up their vehicles, so the £10 fee was worth it to them.

I spoke to the head man of one council and asked if I could ask him a few questions, and he to give me answers. The conversation went something like this...

Q. "I understand that the council do get complaints from residents if a garden is unkempt and rats and mice have been seen and reported to you."

A. Yes, we're very hot on complaints like this, so what is your query?"

Q. "Right, let's say I've been called out to clear and restore a neglected garden, rats 'n' mice and all. I load the lot onto my trailer, take the first lot to the dump, and they refuse to let me in because I'm a tradesman with my name etc. on the side of my van, therefore I bring all the rubbish back, along with all the rest of it not yet loaded."

A. "Well, it's because you're trade."

Q. "Yes, but I am also a householder too, the client is also a householder yet they can dump free, and because they do not have a vehicle or other ways and means of disposing of their own rubbish, they turn to someone like me to take it away."

A. "But you can go and pay to dump at our trade waste place."

Q "But why should the householder pay me to then pay you to take the rubbish away. We're both householders, so should be free. Suppose the actual householder drove my van, how do we stand then, for you have the householder in my driving seat with his/her rubbish on board, but with my name on the vehicle... and me as a householder too."

– now a long silence...

A. "Well, I don't make the rules!"

Q. "But then you should find out who does and change them, for surely if someone has taken the trouble to load up a van, truck or trailer means that they want to be clean and tidy, and a responsible citizen doesn't it? This is why you see so much rubbish dumped in the countryside nowadays because you councils make it so very difficult for everyone."

The conversation ended there with both of us now baffled, for I certainly got his brain thinking! I'll now tell you, the reader, of three incidents to prove my point.

A friend of mine who wanted to dump his old three-piece suite, to be told that he could only dump one item per day. He couldn't believe his ears, so he unloaded the biggest item, the sofa, and thought well there's no way I can leave this on the truck all day and all night, so he took it to the open farmland and dumped it by a hedge, but actually in the roadside itself.

Another incident with an ordinary householder was seen by thousands, for he'd taken his small 6-foot trailer full of household bits to a local tip and they refused him entry because he had *four* wheels on his trailer! He said that at that point he was going to dump the rest in a lay-by, but decided to telephone a local TV station and asked if they could come along and film the situation, for he told the crew what would happened and he knew for definite what the very final outcome would be.

I saw that very same programme for myself, and sure enough he was filmed from a distance being turned away. The chap then drove off towards the secret cameras, then said, "Now watch this," he then got his wheel brace, took off two of the wheels, and drove back in, and twenty or so minutes after he came out and trailer emptied!

Here again why you see rubbish down our lovely country lanes, for you can see how hard it is to try and dump rubbish legally. I went to a tip with our own household rubbish, and two chaps came flying out of their cabin in a blind panic; they were friendly enough, and then said, "Oh, it's alright, you've got household, only your name on the side of your vehicle came up on our screen." I assured them that there was definitely no garden rubbish. So once again, had it been 'greenery' I would have been turned away because I'm trade.

An old folks centre was closing down and the lady who ran it asked if I could dump various items and of course I obliged. On reaching this particular tip, a cocky sort of chap said, "What have you got?" So I opened the back of the trailer to show him. "We can take that, that and that, but not that, that and that," and so on. I retorted, "But it's not greenery, it's household 'waste'; surely the timber bits go in the wood container, the metal bits in the metal container, I don't understand," and again he pointed at the items, very brash and cocky (he turned out to be a visiting inspector). I said, "That's totally ridiculous, do you mean to say I've got to take it all back?" He said, "Do what you like with it, that's not coming in here."

Anyhow, I did dump the bits that he said I could, and made my way home. As luck would have it, the bin men had just literally turned into the bottom of my road, so hastily undid the trailer, pulled out the small metal fluorescent light holders, and bent them in half and put them in my bin. The bin men lifted the lid like they do ready to empty, took the bin to their lorry and emptied it with no worry – so where were they going to take it? Well, I'll tell you – it was to the exact same tip where I'd just come from!

Back in London though, I only had a couple of bad incidents. 'My man' who I'd give the £10 to was in a right flap when I drove in with a good full load. The inside of the transit was full, as was the roof rack and trailer. "No, no, Keith, you can't come in yet, the inspector's coming today sometime!" "What time?" I said, but sadly he didn't know. I made five visits to that dump that day, each time being turned away by the worried 'tip man'. I had to sit in cafes and keep driving round to pass the time.

At last, very late afternoon, the coast was clear – he'd been! Not only had I lost all those hours, I lost my day's work, for I had to make my excuses to the customer where I should have been that day, so again saw the easy option of others to dump in the countryside.

A few weeks later, I went in with a fairly heavy load, but found that the council had put in an overhead rail over the main gates; this we knew was to make sure that it was only mainly cars or small vans that could get under – I just got under with barely an inch to spare. I unloaded as usual, paid my tenner, then tried to get out. Why try, I hear you say? Well, I couldn't get out, because the weight of my load was now off the springs, hence the van now was at its normal height. The man was in a blind panic, "Oh no, if the inspector calls and sees you in here, I'll lose my job for sure." The poor chap was in a state of worry, so I put him at his ease as soon as his ranting stopped a bit. "Don't worry, Les, it's not a problem, I can still get out." "You can't, you're already touching the barrier!" I finally put him at his ease again, "All I'll do is let a bit of air out of each tyre, then I can get out!" Boy, was this man relieved, I said, "I can soon put some air in later, and now you'll know what to do if it happens again!"

When I have spoken to the various Heads of Councils over the years when I have complained about either being turned away from dumps because my name is on my vehicle and/or trailer, or charge because I'm classed as trade, I have told each and every one of them how I have to pay to take my own garden rubbish away, they *all* said that "You shouldn't do that! It's free if you're a householder." I'd exclaim, "Yes, you've said the magic word HOUSEHOLDER! and a householder who has to pay to dump his rubbish because my vehicle with my name on is the only way I can get to dump my rubbish (rubbish being garden refuse). This puts me in the same position as a householder relying on me to take their refuse away because they haven't the means to." It all then puts things into perspective.

It's not everyone who can afford skips either. So you, the reader, now know what goes on, and of all the problems.

Cures for all – Super-Foods?

You often see odd snippets of news – either on TV, newspapers or magazines, giving out information on certain plants, then no more is said. I can remember reading that no benefits can be had from using the herb Comfrey and then being withdrawn, and here (in 2011) I'm still using Comfrey cream for my joints. Okay, it's doing no good, but certainly not harmful as the so-called experts suggest. It's almost daily now that you read of something that has been around for donkey's years, suddenly either being taken off the market or withdrawn from the market altogether.

The opposite is also the case too where suddenly we get to modern day to suddenly read of 'wonder fruit 'n' veg' like tomatoes, beetroot, blueberries, pomegranate and broccoli. We must assume then that tests have been carried out over a number of years to prove that all these things really do what they say they do?

They do say too that there really is a cure for all the world's ills in the plant world, either as single items or mixed with something else, but what? Research must be ongoing, for mixing and matching up the right concoctions from leaves, roots, stems, buds, seeds, bark etc. from the millions of plants is a massive task.

Some say that there is a cure for all the world's ills in the rain forests alone, hence the huge worry regarding the total loss of some species, and the very ones that could have cured the very worst of human problems.

It's Good to be a Scaremonger

Is there global warming or not? We no longer hear of the dreaded acid rain, what happened to that? 2010 and 2011 proved to be the coldest for one hundred years or so, and nowadays each year seems to be a record for one thing or the other, i.e. the wettest autumn since__? the wettest spring since __? the hottest summer since __? the driest spring since__? and so on.

Flooding though does seem a major problem today, and have put my own theory about this in several articles over very many years. The answer is a simple one, our country is almost full of concrete, be it where houses stand, pavements, patios, paths, buildings of every description, roads and massive long motorways, where each of these stand water would have easily sunk away. Today it has nowhere to go, except any remaining greenery, soil, etc.

If it rained heavy in spring or summer, the hedgerows and trees would soon take up water, or lay in very beneficial ditches. In warm springs and summers, all these would be very thirsty and 'drink' vast amounts of water, and when you think of all the millions of miles of hedgerows now lost, along with very many fields, the fault of flooding is so very obvious, for each and every structure was a place where water easily drained away.

No one can stop the progress of road building or houses, industrial estates etc., so the need to plant trees, shrubs etc. in their billions would... I'm certain improve the situation I'm sure. A spring or summer flood does not hang around for long in any major growing season, where trillions of plant life drink up water; the autumn and winter months prove a very different story, for the ground is already so wet and sodden, so where does excess water go to? At least the spring and summer has much longer hot dry spells to help soak away excess water.

It Could be the Death of You?

Well, in extreme cases it could be, for I refer to yet another article that I read somewhere, and this was a good few years ago now, and that was that every tree, shrub, plant, etc. sold, must have a label on it stating if the 'plant' is an irritant, poisonous, be it its leaves, berries etc. I have only seen this on very few plants etc. that have a label, for a plant should have 'poisonous to touch' or 'poisonous if eaten' or these berries, leaves flowers, roots, seeds can kill if eaten.

Many years ago I saw 'M' and 'F' written on labels referring to 'male' and 'female' on the separate pernettya plants. It can be confusing even with berries – are they edible, or only edible when cooked, and in some cases even poisonous until cooked or well ripened.

Since childhood I used to have thousands of tiny blisters on the inner sides of my fingers, and random large blisters appear on the side of my palm and knuckle areas. Doctors were always baffled. I've not had this problem for some fifteen years or so now. The blisters came once a year, usually in summer, although not always, so doctors put it down to either a chemical that I was using, or that had been on certain plants when bought, or was it something in compost or the top-soil itself at certain times of the year?

The sudden stop of these blisters could well be something that may now have been taken off the garden centre shelves, or indeed a certain plant, weed, tree or shrub etc. that perhaps I don't come in regular contact with now.

The garden can be a dangerous place, but the need for more information on garden labels I feel is so very necessary, especially as I have had two things happen to me and, had I been warned, would have worn goggles as I do now after a lesson well learnt. The first was in my own garden when I had to dig up a sub-shrub called Ballota Pseudodictamnus. It wasn't the height, but the spread of it, and worked out that I could have planted at least a dozen or so different perennials in that spot instead of the one shrub. I set to cutting it back, and pull away the prunings; little did I know that deeper inside the shrub, and where leaves had died and broken up, they had turned into dust-like tiny particles. In seconds all this got in my eyes and down my throat, and made seeing and breathing very difficult.

I ran indoors, drank as much water as was possible, and splashed my eyes too several times to stop the irritation. It was truly very scary. This minute dust does form on a lot of soft grey-leaved plants, like for instance Stachys 'lanata' or common "Lambs Ears" as they're known, and also Verbascum 'bombyciferum' to name but a few. Being soft and woolly and suited to hot dry conditions, does explain how the leaves die, dry out and fall to the centre of the plant and to the ground itself. Had it perhaps been the case that I'd dug the shrub up in the wet winter months, the incident may possibly not have happened, for the leaves possibly would have been a soggy mess.

Ballota 'pseudodictamnus' however is an unusual plant, fairly common, but many people do not know of its usage, and that being little wicks and used as either night-lights during a power cut or as a table centre during an evening meal to amuse your guests. Once the pink soft flowers fade, pick off a few during of course dry weather. Put a little olive oil in a saucer or plate, turn the flower heads so that the now-faded flower has its head in the olive oil, and the tip of the flower that was attached to the stem upwards. Let it soak up the olive oil until the 'wick' is wet, put in more olive oil as fuel and simply just light the tips – they'll burn away for hours!

Another shrub that was an irritant to eyes, also affected your face and arms or any other exposed areas, this shrub is Fremontedendron 'californica'. I first saw this shrub at the Chelsea Flower Show back in the 1970s and was unaffordable for a great many people, and even today can be on the pricey side compared to other shrubs. As my work picked up after moving to Suffolk, I wanted this shrub at last for our new garden. The Fremontedendrons are truly very beautiful shrubs with their two-to-three inch wide yellow sunny blooms which bloom for weeks on end, and best grown against a sunny wall or fence.

I planted mine next to a two or so foot path in a southerly aspect, hence you had to walk past it almost daily; it was when the shrub got larger, and being a rapid grower once it's settled in, you could not help for it to brush against you, and tiny hairs stick to your hands and arms and a really bad irritant to eyes as you can imagine.

Very sadly, because of this I had to cut it down, and doing this had to wear as much protection as I could. Strangely enough, this same week, a client called me in to look at the shrubs (mixed) that were against her garage, for she'd called in a painter to paint the facia of her garage, but the painter was off work as all his face and eye area had become very swollen and irritating.

I knew all the shrubs at the side of the garage for it was me that planted them all, and had no hesitation that it was the Fremontedendron that was the cuplrit; it had its own spot to grow as it liked, along with a large Garrya 'elliptica'; so had the guttering not needed to be painted, the Fremontedendron caused no problem to anyone, hence I had to go along and take it out, so now you can see why a lot more information is needed on labels and would have saved the life of two very magnificent shrubs.

Early Book

Something that I really treasure is an empty 'sketch'? book that my Dad gave me as a little lad when I was about eight, nine or so; the cover is dark red, and Dad had given me a bit of gold leaf to put my name on the cover, sadly now nearly all faded.

I did all the drawings myself with coloured pencils or crayons, but all the wording I'm certain I copied from plant catalogues of that time, and most certainly copied pictures from my *Observers Book of Flowers*, so it was always in me to want to do a gardening book at some stage in my life, so what better time than the end of it!

I also did drawings in pastels; the paper was black therefore all the pastel colours shown to good effect, the centre pages I drew all tulips in a park or garden.

Dad did the most superb picture for me of a wooden boat in water under a willow tree. He was indeed a superb artist.

The Client Who Wouldn't Listen – Now I Pay for It.

Throughout this book I have written about clients who refuse to take professional advice, but one stands out above all others, and the results of their idiocy I still have today, so I shall give you an account of what took place.

When we first moved here in 1987, one of the first of the bigger jobs was accepted at Station Road, Beccles (Suffolk) and on seeing this job, I was quite keen to show the client my abilities, and how to get over a major problem in his back garden, and when I told him what could be done he was totally overjoyed. So now I'll put you, the reader, in the picture…

The man and his wife were flummoxed on which way to turn, for their garden was just sticky 'mud' soil and clay; thankfully any weeds must have been removed by the man, and asked him what the weeds were, for if they were dock, dandelion, thistle etc. a slice off with a spade would strengthen them and they'd return without a doubt, but he assured me that they were not the weeds present. Of course, he may just have been saying that to hurry the job along, instead of having to wait a few weeks for a reappearance then a weed-kill.

On first glance, I could see that the garden was six-to-eight inches below path levels, hence they had to step down onto the garden. The man had made attempts to very lightly dig over the whole site to only a depth of three-to-four inches, which in itself must have been a task because of the 'soil' condition. It was at this point that I could run through the whole project with the clients, step-by-step.

"Right! Let me explain to you, your garden is like a clay bowl with no where for water to run." The man then said, "Could you not cut out channels at the lowest points for the water to escape?" So again, I repeated myself and said, "As I just said, your garden is like a clay bowl with nowhere to run to, and digging channels against neighbours' fences and flood their garden is not the answer!

Now, I'd hoped I got the man's attention again. "What I'll do is to do a basic level with a rake, not for levelling as you'll see, but to make it easier to walk on to reach the far sides of the garden. I'll affix either wooden or concrete gravel boards 'to' all the fence boundaries (a couple of inches in front of), then we'll barrow in a few tons of sharp sand, as this is the finest thing to break up clay or sticky soil, and aid very good drainage, then we'd need to barrow in a few tons of good top soil on top of this, and this should be prepared to make a lawn and be a mere half an inch below the pathway, patio etc. Therefore loose top-soil would need lots of rolling, raking, levelling and treading to get that perfect solid level, without fear of any sinkage; the turf can then be laid, and should then sit a good inch above path level, to make easy for mowing instead of scraping alongside a concrete edge, and far easier to use long-handled shears too for that nice neat finish. Job done, and your clay will be well below all the turf, soil and sand. You can now take away the wooden shuttering at the lawn's edge, and back fill with sharp sand and compost; all this of course is for your flower borders, and back-filled to the wooden or concrete gravel boards near the fence. So now you have a nice planting medium with again… the clay and sticky soil below." I then told him how to follow up… "A yearly top-up of your borders with compost, mulch, etc., plus a yearly top-dressing on your lawn, all problems… GONE!"

But do clients listen? NO! For after I did the basic levelling of the clay to walk on easier, which took all day after giving it a good roll to make it as flat as possible, I called it a day. It was a Friday, and heavy rain fell at the weekend, so returned on the Monday, and awaiting for all the tons of sharp sand to arrive. On my arrival I could see puddles everywhere on the clay, but all to be under sand by the end of the day.

All this was not to be, for as I walked across the garden – BOMP! My foot went down a hole about ten inches deep which shook me as you can imagine, and jarred my back very badly and I could hardly walk. As this happened, the man came out and saw me in dire agony, apologising profusely, and explained that he'd dug several of these holes all over the garden to help drain off the rain from the heavy downpour of the weekend.

I really couldn't believe what I was hearing, after all the information that I gave him, and that you can't drain clay, and how his garden is like a clay bowl, etc. We had to cancel the sand quickly, and I was off for several weeks with severe back pain. I was thirty-nine years old then, and now in my sixty-third year (2011), still have that same pain that has caused me many problems over the years and a loss of work and revenue, and when I do work, I'm always in some sort of pain.

Back in 1987, after a few tests, it was said to be a trapped nerve at the base of the spine. Dr Norcutt diagnosed it as that, and feels like a nerve without doubt. My own doctor also said that it was a trapped nerve, but as the years have gone on he says it's 'wear and tear', albeit the type of pain has never ever changed in all those years.

Medication – can you call it that? Pain-killers is the only answer it seems, hence have been in agony for most of the years, for as time goes by my doctor asks if I take pain-killers? My answer is always the same, "Doctor, if I'd been taking pain-killers for all these long years, can you imagine when my body gets used to one lot, I go on to another, what strength of pill would I be on today, and moreso what would my insides look like with so many years of pain? The doctor says no more. I explain that if I have to do ladder work, or bending with turfing, barrowing soil etc., I may take them to get me through a couple of hours at least, but then the pain comes back stronger, the pain-killers only mask pain for a while.

I remember when I was forty-six years of age, asking an elderly friend of mine, "when should you stop doing heavy manual work each day of your life, only I feel knackered?" My pal's reply I remember today, for he said your body will tell you when it's time to slow down.

When I was fifty-eight, my doctor advised me not to take on the heavier work, which I did start to do, but told him "but no gardening is easy, it's all pulling, bending, digging, climbing, even if there's no real heavy graft." I have asked him twice now since turning sixty if I could 'go on the sick panel', words I thought I'd never ask, and have always been a hard grafter, so deserved to take it easy. The doctor said, "Get away with yer, most of your pains will go anyway when you retire!" Everyone will tell you to do a lighter job, but few people take on older people; many are past their 'sell-by' at forty, let alone sixty-odd!

One thing I did ask my doctor and that was "how come some people (many in our village alone) have been 'on the sick' for years with so-called back pain, yet I see them carrying televisions, bags of cement, even out landscaping!" He had no answer, but pointed out that he knew 100% that I was a genuine case, for he knows what happened back in 1987, with no suggestion of putting me on the sick re-ill health etc. We come now to the winter of 2009/2010 and out of the blue, Bang! developed osteoarthritis in both knees, two elbows, one ankle, to join with the arthritis in my fingers which 'lock' when using secateurs and chain-saw/hedge-trimmer etc. I have no treatment for this, except for pain-killers once again. I was offered physio treatment, but I do active work daily, without the need for further exercise to make matters worse.

The pains I feel are dreadful and worsening; my future I feel is going to be a very bleak one, so I'll finish this book whilst I'm able to. Advice – don't do manual work for a living, for it just doesn't pay. It also looks like I'll really have to struggle to work until I am sixty-five, yet always hoped to work in gardening way, way past that.

It's all down to body make-up; you can either stay healthy or not, but I feel so bitter, being a lifelong non-smoker or drinker of wine and alcohol – I should be in top health!

The Royal Parks

It was a mere couple of months or so to the wedding of Prince Charles and Lady Diana Spencer, and I had been self-employed for a good while, but like always, you're either the flavour of the month with tons of work or none at all – this time it was the latter. I decided to look for work and get a regular wage with an employer, so wrote to the

Superintendent at Lloyds Park, Walthamstow (former home of William Morris) and a park I'd known since a very small boy.

The Superintendent telephoned me to say that they had no vacancies at present, but his friend was looking for a good gardener for the Royal Parks. I asked, "Is your friend Ashley Stephenson?" He replied, "Yes, Keith, have you heard of him?" I said I had and that he was quite a well-known chap, hence he gave me his address to write and ask for an interview, and a reply came back so I went for the interview. He was a pleasant man and gave me a bit of a 'grilling'; it was a tough interview and he asked many questions about names of plants, i.e. I had to name four or five varieties of Magnolia or name a deciduous conifer etc., etc. He seemed impressed that I knew the answers and consequently I got the job!

Ashley Stephenson explained that he wanted someone like me to be involved in all the mass planting out of flower beds, as this wedding was closely approaching, and that I was to be involved with the planting of tubs, hanging baskets etc., etc., and told me how I was here at a very exciting time. I was pleased too; okay, the money side wasn't brilliant, but it would be a regular job.

In one way I must have been bonkers, for I had to travel to Blackheath (or could have been Blackfriars? whichever was near the tube!) in London to get to the Parks Depts. base, involving buses, walking, and the dreaded underground which I hated. It was whilst on the underground that I thought, what on earth had I got myself into? Getting up at the crack of dawn to be at work there by seven, then all that hassle to get home again, and making a big hole in my pocket, money-wise.

I braved the first morning, thinking about this huge project that I was to be a part of, and arrived as the 'new boy' going into the bothy, taking a seat and possibly realising that I was now sitting in someone's seat who'd sat there for the last thirty odd years or so. Some of the men murmured a good morning, others kept their heads firmly buried in their newspapers, never looking up once – to say I felt uncomfortable was an under statement to say the least.

Anyhow, the foreman came in, a man small in stature wearing a cap, and quickly sorted out all the chaps to their tasks for the day. "Ah, you're the new chap," and promptly said to go with him. He showed me a locker which was full of various gardening tools, and a dept. with coat hangers etc., and asked me to pick out a rake and a hoe and go with him. At this point I thought 'rake... hoe...' and thought I'd be preparing one of many flower beds in and around London.

After a fairly long walk he suddenly stopped at this large overgrown shrub bed which was on a very busy main road with shops opposite, and promptly asked me to tidy it, I couldn't believe it. I had to ask about tea breaks and dinner hours, "Oh, you have them here, you can sit on that step." If I hadn't have asked, no one would have told me, so it was a good job I had a flask and sandwiches which of course I had to hide discreetly in the shrub bed where I was working. There I was, all alone, no help, no one to chat to, and hadn't a clue what part of London I was in, and would I know my way back to the yard I wondered.

I got to work straight away. It was disgusting – beer bottles and cans, meths bottles, paper, boxes, syringes etc., then thought, why then the tough interview? To top it all, I was grafting away with piles of rubbish dotted about the bed that was also full of weeds, and happened to glance over the road and there was the foreman looking at me! He turned to look in the shop window at the speed of light, but could tell by his head, movements that he was craning to catch my reflection and 'monitor' me like that. He never even had the decency to come over to talk to me, and promptly soon went away.

The foreman had earlier told me what time dinner was, but I thought 'blow this for a laugh', hence picked up the hoe and rake, found my way back to the yard, put the tools in the locker and thankfully no one was there to ask questions and made for the underground station at Blackheath and HOME! So I lasted half a day on the Royal Parks.

I was so overjoyed at being home, and was self-employed again that afternoon when a neighbour sold me a cultivator hoe and turfing iron that very afternoon (£10 the two) and still have them to day (2008).

The very sad bit about all this is that once again I never got to leave my mark on the Royal Parks. What a shame too that I hadn't been asked to fully restore that large shrub bed to show them my actual skills in proper pruning, then I wouldn't have minded clearing and weeding that bed as I went along, albeit a Parks labourer could have done that part, assuming that of course they had done a decent job of work to complement my pruning and restoration of the very old neglected shrubs.

It really breaks my heart on how I was treated that very first day, for after that interview I was really looking forward to sorting out all the floral displays all through the Royal route, but alas, it was very short-lived and just one more saga in life…

Hampstead

For a good three to four years I worked as self-employed in Hampstead, Highgate, Hampstead Garden Suburb and Finchley doing garden maintenance only, and stupidly working on an hourly rate and had to work hard to try and get a day's pay. I say *try*, for firstly I had to put up with such heavy traffic travelling to and from my home each day to the various destinations, and not arriving until eleven o'clock in the morning, travelling since around half eight, such was the congestion… *then*! What's it like now? So of course on my arrival, would have to park up, find a loo, have a bite to eat and a cuppa before trying to make some sort of day's pay.

How heart-breaking it would be if on my arrival rain would fall, and possibly not stop all day. I'd either come all the way back again or sit it out, wait for a break in the rain and try and do two or three hours to at least get petrol money back. Some of my days would be long and arduous, for certain times of the year there's more work in a garden than other times. I would arrive to a customer who'd usually only want me for one or two hours, then ask if I could do half or even a full day; this would be sprung on me on my arrival, hence having to let others down on that day, and hoping they'd let you come the next day. Others who would normally give you a day or half a day would spring on you "We only want you to do an hour today", which threw me right out on where to go to fill my day.

The hourly rate didn't work, for you didn't know what you were going to earn a day let alone a week, so did very, very long hours at £4 per hour, and many were not straight forward maintenance, but slid often into 'light' landscaping!

To think I was working for extremely rich people, some very nice – an Arab family, Mr and Mrs Yamini were lovely people, they lived next door to a Jewish lady, Mrs Weiss, another nice lady. She gave me a toy fluffy dog for our baby Heather, the dog is called 'Snowy' and she still has it.

Fire!… and 'Fire King'

As a little boy living at Harold Hill, Romford, Essex, I had two little plots in our back garden which Mum and Dad said I could have. I grew just the one wallflower, and old variety called 'Fire King', and the flower colourings look indeed like flames of a fire, all streaked in reds and yellows.

I had this same plant I should think for at least four years before it sadly gave up the ghost. It had, by now, a sturdy inch or so thick stem, a sort of bonsai wallflower! One day Mum, Dad and sister Sandra all just popped out to the shops for a short while, hence I had the run of both the house and garden to myself, and no doubt Mum or dad telling me not to go near the fire in the front room. But did I listen… NO!… for I went out into the garden, picked up the dead stem of 'FIRE KING' and poked it among the coals on the fire until it caught fire. I then panicked, left it on the coal, then to my horror it fell from the coal, bounced off the hearth… right onto Mum and Dad's carpet! I ran out in a great fear and panic… leaving the burning stem on the carpet! I remained terrified in the garden, and so frightened to go back into the house, thinking it to be ablaze. I was so scared when I went back into our living room, but by the grace of God, the stem had fizzled out and had just left a scorch mark of 2 inches or so on the carpet. I took the stem straight out into the garden and I *think* I hid it!

I cannot now recollect the outcome, whether I told Mum and Dad what I had done, or if they perhaps thought it was just a spark that flew out of the grate. I learnt a very dear lesson that day, not to play with fire.

I have never seen 'FIRE KING' sold either as packs of seeds or in plant form, yet when driving around still see many gardens with them in, and obtained my ones from a lady who was a costume designer during the heady naughty days of the windmill girls (Windmill Theatre). The lady is Evelyn Mathias.

What's That Strange Word?

My mum's (Irene-'Rene'-Eunice nee Ridley) favourite plant was the Gladiolus, and no doubt the red ones, being her favourite colour! Mum always had a vase full of them each summer.

As a boy, I always had plant catalogues sent to me (1950s) and never did find out who had them sent to me. One particular one had a centrefold of Gladioli, and it didn't matter where the staples were! The lovely colours went across the two pages, and still to this day 2008 I can remember some of those names. My firm favourite is 'Mabel Violet'. I say *is* rather than *was* for I found it still being listed in a modern gardening book, along with others that I remember like 'Spic and Span', 'My Love' and they have all it seems have stood the test of time, but found it sad that the gardening book did not say that they were old varieties and even possibly around before I was born (4th November '48).

A variety that I do remember (not listed in the gardening book was 'Silhouette', and as a boy I had no idea how to pronounce this strange word.

The Wight Plant!

My wife, Debbie and I visited the Isle of Wight way back in the early 1970s, and on that very first visit we noticed a very pretty plant literally growing everywhere, every nook and cranny, roads, paths, hedgerows and of course gardens. It was, we found out later Centranthus 'ruber' or Valerian.

Today I have the deep red and the paler pink variety, and did grow Valerian 'phu' with white flowers and bright yellow leaves. I also grow today the 5' – 6' taller Valerian 'officinalis' with tiny white flowers, all seeding profusely!

I grow many plants to day from memories of places or people that I know now and many who are no longer with us, but thankfully all had that wonderful gift of life, and all lovers of our wonderful nature.

Don't Turn Round!

If you grow the Christmas or Easter Cactus (my same plants bloom *both* times) never turn the plant like you should when growing other pot plants on a window sill. If you do this with the Zygocactus 'truncatus' giving it its correct name, you'll find the buds drop off, so leave the plant alone once in position. (Also now listed as Schulembergia.)

Baffle Your Friends and Neighbours

If you grow Lupins, Delphiniums, Pyrethrums, Oriental Poppy etc., as soon as the blooms fade (assuming you don't want seed) cut the whole lot down to the floor as you would in winter, give them a good feed and up they'll come again, and bloom often in August and September, but remember to feed again for the plant will need replenishing.

All the people who see them out of season will think they have either bloomed very late or far too early for the following year!

No. 8 Chippenham Walk – Harold Hill, Romford (Essex)

Having a Piece of Wedding Cake

As you came in through our back gate on the left, was the rockery that dad made. On this rockery was a rampant creeper and it had little white flowers and grey woolly leaves. The botanical name is Cerastium 'tomentosum' or 'Snow-in-Summer' as it is popularly known today, but let us again go back to when I was a little boy, and being small used to smell all the lower grown plants that you just assumed adults couldn't reach! The flowers, to me, smelt just like icing, and I was told by a family member that the plant's name suited it, being called 'Wedding

Cake'. Once again, I have never ever heard anyone use this common name, it was always 'Snow-in-Summer', no old books ever used 'Wedding Cake' as a common name.

Many years later in the 1990s when I started growing plants for my own plant sales, on one such day and the crowds filled my garden, a lady suddenly exclaimed "You've got some wedding cake!" I couldn't believe my ears and exclaimed back "What did you call it?! Again she said gleefully, "WEDDING CAKE, I've always known it as that!" I told her that she'd made my day, for I'd never heard it called by that name since the fifties.

How many people too have never smelt the sea-salty scent of Sedum 'acre' or 'Stonecrop'? As a child I loved it!

My suggestion to you, the reader, is because a plant does not radiate scent doesn't mean it hasn't got any… get closer! Be that small child again!

We're Going Past!

A gardening programme strictly about herbs – the presenter said rub the herb penny royal on the ground making a circle, put some ants in the centre, and they won't cross it. I tried it, and all the ants went through the circle with no problem! The idea was to rub penny-royal near a doorstep, to stop them going indoors – perhaps these ants had no sense of smell!

Burglars Watch Out!

I first saw the plant Agapanthus on a day trip with the college that I attended at a place called Mornington Crescent. Our trip was to Savill Gardens at Windsor. The Agapanthus plants were tightly grown in massive pots of some four to five feet high and also in width. Everyone admired them and we were told that they were a tender bulb, also known as 'African Lily' or 'Lily-of-the-Nile'.

The old method was to remember to cover them with straw or any protective mulch, but through climate change people rarely do this nowadays, but no doubt you'd have to cover your plants the further north you live.

Many years ago now, a certain Lord Berner had the novel idea of keeping intruders from his house and estate, for at the entrance to the gate, he had a sign put up on the lawn, reading: BEWARE OF THE AGAPANTHUS!

Attention all Bee-Keepers!

One of the prettiest shrubs to flower in winter is the winter-flowering honeysuckle, namely Lonicera 'fragrantissima'. My plant usually starts to bloom in early October when the sun is still warmish from the previous month, and bees are still in abundance. The shrub blooms right through to early March, and has bees on it every day until that time. The odd part about this is that the bees diminish in great numbers, hence only one or two visiting the shrub daily.

It still seems strange on seeing perhaps a butterfly sitting on a daffodil or early tulips on the odd warmer days in the coldest weeks of mid-February – to early March. Just a few degrees warmer on these months also brings out the odd flies, ladybirds etc., then completely disappear during the ongoing colder snaps. Perhaps bee-keepers should plant this shrub in abundance near bee hives and would this make any difference to the taste of perhaps a new type of honey?

Passers-by always admire my large shrub of winter honeysuckle as they pass my front garden, although do not see my rare specimen in the back garden facing our kitchen windowsill, called Lonicera 'infundibuliformis rockii' albeit the bees have declined so far to visit it.

Sweet Peas

Now the scent of this annual is my most favourite, I know the scents of most plants are different, but this seems to be in a class of its own!

Lathyrus 'odoratus' as it's correctly known is one of the easiest climbers to grow, but after sowing you must make sure the soil is kept moist so as the seeds shell splits open to commence its germination, or better still, place in a saucer of water, and in a day or so the seed shell breaks open ready for planting, although the moisture must be kept up or seed will shrivel and die.

My early sowing in 2007 produced fine plants all year, and the majority dying completely by the end of the summer, but one plant carried on growing… stopped… and remained green for the winter and no doubt would have resumed growing had we not had what they call a 'diamond frost' around mid-February (2008).

One little tip I can give you, and this is when your plants reach 6"–8" high or so, pinch out the top 2"–3" to just above a leaf joint, then plant those pinched-out tips. It's a good way to increase your stock of plants without costing another penny, the plant too benefiting from the pinching out to make it bush out, thus resulting in further blooms. Also when pinching out 3"–4" side shoots from tomato plants, plant these up too – they soon get going to grow fine plants!

My Favourite Tree

This just has to be the Paulownia 'tomentosum' or better known as 'The Foxglove Tree', and the flowers resemble the foxglove albeit are lavender blue and scented. The tree comes from China, and I've known of this tree since the day I started work at Springfield Park, Clapton London (1964) where one was planted on what we called the 'main lawn'. It was 1964, and a lot of things were new to me then, for I was now training and had to learn numerous plants, trees and shrubs.

Soon after this tree was planted... I can't remember now... but either it died or was vandalised, but I helped plant the second one, and would like to think that now it has reached a full-size tree? The flowers never appear usually on very young trees, but as it's fairly fast-growing it's not long before they do. The flower buds always form in the autumn, and if not killed off by too heavy a frost, will give you a fabulous display on still leafless branches around May.

The heart-shaped leaves are on the large size and soon form as the flowers fall away. Many parks departments used very young Paulownias as 'dot' plants amongst summer bedding schemes – a 'dot' plant is any plant that grows a lot taller than your main bedding plants, and as the name implies and that is to dot it about in a flower bed; for example, a bed of say petunias then the added height of say Standard Fuchsias or Geraniums (Zonal Pelargoniums).

Now back to the Paulownias used as dot plants, these would be on say a 3'–4' stem (stool) and be pruned hard, this then would produce 2'–3' huge leaves! but at the expense of no flowers. My own Paulownia is about seven years old now I should think, and every year the tree produces more buds each autumn, a far cry from the first seven buds that appeared when the tree found its right time to produce them. I wanted my own tree so much that I didn't take my own advice and warnings from plant books, that it was not advisable to plant on windy sites, for as the leaves get to a fair size they would rip in the wind.

I had no option as to where to plant mine in my garden, and only five minutes to the beach, have the east winds to deal with; so far my leaves have not fared too badly considering. One strange thing about the Paulownia is that some of its properties are supposed to stop grey hair! Perhaps it's never been followed up by scientists.

The best specimen that I've ever seen was at a very small park called Chapman's Green, Tottenham, and stands at the back of the tennis courts and where the park's compost area stands. This tree must have been at its full height and spread of some twenty-five feet or so, truly a magnificent sight in spring. I was called out to do an estimate at a cottage in Lowestoft, near Carlton Marshes nature reserve, and found to my great horror that the owners wanted me to cut down and dig out a Paulownia! I thought not in a million years would anyone want to even consider digging out such a tree, but sadly I got the job and it was so heart-breaking to do, for the tree was in full blossom too.

The reason the people wanted it down was because the roots were lifting the patio. I think if that had been me, I would have built the patio a little higher up; they probably did not plant the tree deep enough in the first place, for any root even slightly above ground will of course grow thicker, hence raising any path, patio or even lawn. That silly mistake took the life of that lovely tree.

Surrounded by Grass and Water!

Sadly now, I cannot remember how I got the job as a gardener for the Thames Water Authority in Coppermill Lane, Walthamstow. I remember nothing of the actual interview whatsoever! To start with, I use the term gardener very lightly, for I wasn't a gardener as such, well not in the early stages of the job.

When Dad left us as soon as we moved to Chingford Hatch, we then moved to 87 Coppermill Lane, so when I was working at Springfield Park, Clapton I passed the newly-built waterworks daily, then on to Walthamstow marshes, cross the bridge on the River Lea and be at the bottom of Springfield Park, then had the long haul up the very hilly but picturesque park, until I reached our bothy at the very top of the park. (Bothy is an old term for tea-room.)

The waterworks took up a massive area, and a lot of it was still under construction, making filter beds etc., so all our work consisted of grass-cutting with large motor mowers. We covered vast areas of grass on that site, although the mowers (not all) were self-propelled, you still had the walking to do, then whatever you cut, you had to rake up with a wooden 3ft wide rake. So you had to set yourself targets – cut, then rake.

We're now talking around 1974/75 and the old-fashioned 'bone-shaker' Allen Scythe mowers, for some strange reason fell out of favour, and were destined for museums. Thames Water thankfully had retained theirs, so I used them on the grass banks at the Coppermill works. These machines, although so superb at cutting the longest and thickest of grasses, were hard to steer and control, hence I made a few 'slips' and cut off newly planted trees some 3"–4" thick.

Being such a huge place, I got to know a lot of chaps there, all having so many different trades to run such a site. One chap on the gardening section was nicknamed 'nature boy' for he loved the open air. He wore a T-shirt and shorts at every moment he got. I'm not sure of the spelling of his surname, but Arthur Vears was his name. I nicknamed him 'a pint of light' (referring to light ale), therefore 'arfer Vears and a pint of light!

Another chap, a nice guy, very slow moving and took life as it came! Everyone knew that I would have loved to own a small garden centre and to grow and sell plants, a proper garden centre… selling *only* plants, shrubs etc. One of the workers told me that this quiet chap had lots of land, rotovators and other equipment, including a tractor all rusting away, and had no interest in the land at all, and the land was apparently a wilderness. I used to dream about what I would do if all that was mine.

Another chap, Mac, who was the man in charge of our 'gang' at a later date, owned at one time a lovely small nursery at Manor Road, just off Higham Hill E.17. He got fed up with that and he too took a job with Thames Water, and he never understood why I would love to have had a little nursery like he'd had. Mac's nursery I think is all now built on.

I was to be in three 'gangs' during my time at Thames Water, before my 'talents' as a proper gardener was recognised, although at interview do remember being told that there wasn't any gardening as such, but I decided to take the job because it was actually very good pay, or what was considered by me as good pay compared to other authorities of which I worked in the past.

My wife too was working then, and earned even more than me, hence with our combined pay, knew it was time perhaps to buy our own house, which we did, and bought 162 Chingford Road, E.17 (almost opposite Walthamstow bus garage – tram depot).

Because the pay was pretty good, sort of understood why the likes of Mac, and the 'quiet chap' took a full-time employed job without all the hassles and worries of self-employment. They were still with nature and their beloved outdoors, plus a good wage, plus single men, so had a few bob in their pockets.

Let me tell you about the 'gangs'. The first gang I joined (a gang of just three!) was working under the gang leader Brian Powley, married to the daughter of one of the top men in charge at Thames Water. Brian was a Yorkshireman, and very brash at times, for even if I made just a mere suggestion on how to do a certain job, he'd wag or prod his finger to my chest and say, "Don't bloody tell me ah nor?" in the broadest Yorkshire accent.

I liked Brian though, but as he was getting to know me more and finding that my 'talents' in the gardening world didn't stop at grass-cutting! he perhaps thought that he would lose his position and I'd be in charge of him instead.

As the new Thames Water site at Coppermill Lane (E.17) was nearing completion, Arthur Vears eventually had his own gang to run that massive site. We, on the other hand, were now free from that very boring open site, and took on the grass-cutting round very many pumping stations, and reservoirs of all sizes, some were massive, one was that big that each of us with large mowers could just get round the whole perimeter three times in one day, and if the grass was extra long, we'd only make it round once only. All the pumping stations, open and closed in covered reservoirs, all had to be raked off and put into huge grass piles, all hot hard work, especially in the height of summer.

Wherever we went, be it Chingford, Botany Bay (Enfield), Ponders End, Highgate, Hornsey, etc., etc., it was always the same farmer who came to our sites to load up all the 'hay' for his animals. we assumed he had it free, for it saved Thames Water on what to do with it. In winter our work consisted of mainly hedge-laying, the ancient art. Brian had done this in Yorkshire and showed us how it was done. We all mastered it very quickly, probably to Brian's dismay, and losing the upper hand again! Don't get me wrong, Brian and I got on well, and liked a joke – he found me amusing rather than the other way round!

Brian also drove a flash car, and mentioned how all the women looked at him in it, all probably thinking he was loaded, but one day we had to go to his house as he'd come out without his lunch, and we were surprised to see that he lived in a very tiny terraced house in Courtney Place (E.17), these were very old properties, as my great-grandfather's brother had lived there. Hence Brian's car gave him delusions of grandeur – what a show up for him!

Our methods for getting from place to place was in a Land Rover and large covered trailer, that carried all the gear, which included the large mowers etc., plus shelving for smaller items like the petrol cans, hand tools etc.

It was now high summer, and we were way out in the Essex countryside, and we'd gone there solely for weed-killing with a knapsack spray on our backs. It was a pretty little reservoir, all hidden and, as so many of them, mostly had fruit-trees for some reason. At the end of the day we'd obviously taken off our protective goggles and gloves, I was putting the sprayer on the large shelf in the trailer, when suddenly the arm of the sprayer fell back down, and splashed the weed-killer on my face and bare arms. We all knew it was dodgy stuff, everyone was in a panic, and we realised that there was no access to an outside tap to wash off the weed-killer. I then came up with a bright idea for what it was worth, we'd only just had our tea-break in the afternoon, and I made for the tea pot, and thankfully the tea bags were still in the pot with a little tea left too! So, quickly rubbed the tea bags on my face and arms, dipping the bags in the now cold tea. The next day, and the next, proved worrying, for my skin was peeling away leaving sore red skin. My face wasn't as bad, for I had concentrated on that first, but it was peeling nevertheless. It was no good, I had to see my doctor, for the skin was peeling and spreading all up my arms.

My doctor's first words were, "Have you put anything on it?" I told him that I hadn't and he went on to say that I'd done right, and that you should never add a chemical to a chemical, and that I should dab on salt water only; he was right, for within a week the blistering stopped spreading and soon dried up, and my skin healed within the month. I'm so glad that the arm of the sprayer did not flick back in my eyes, as who knows what the outcome of that would have been.

As mentioned before, some of the reservoirs and pumping stations had fruit trees, and I was stung on more than one occasion, mainly by wasps when fruit was falling, but the long grass still had to be cut. One day when mowing, I dropped my arms down a little to turn the mower, and was stung under the arm; it was sudden and painful and the mower crashed into a tree! another wasp had gone up my trouser leg and stung me on the inside of my leg – boy, was that painful too! On another occasion one got on the back of my neck. When I was a small boy, I was stung by a wasp, Mum said, "Have you put anything on it, Keith?" I replied, "Don't be silly, Mum, it'll be miles away by now!" Or the time I wanted pet flies, I asked the man in the shop for some and he said he hadn't got any – I retorted, "Well, you've got some in the window!" Right, that's enough of my silliness. I don't suppose you readers believe a word!

Right in the centre of High Beach, was another covered-over reservoir, covered that is, with a mound of soil then turf. Brian Powley said that if we came through the reservoir very quietly, as it was a hot sunny day, he said a topless lady may be sunbathing in her garden – they had obviously been here before! We sneaked in, and sure enough she was sitting at her garden table typing, apparently she was a writer.

The lady was middle-aged I should think, we knew that she would be embarrassed(?) so we unloaded the trailer, started up the mowers and made sure we came in full view of her. She then stood up and went indoors! We were trying to save her embarrassment by making a noise with the mowers beforehand to let her know that someone was on the reservoir, to give her time to prepare an escape. Instead, she got up quite casually without looking at us.

My other two 'gang' pals were George Stratton, a man nearing retirement, and hard grafter, and Mickey…..? a nice chap with always a smile on his face. We'd often tease George and say, "Look, Georgie Stratton, hasn't got his hatton!" (hat on). He took it all in good part, and teased us back as soon as he had the chance.

I soon made it clear to the 'governors' that the atmosphere was not always good with Brian, for he flared up from time to time, and wasn't that popular with a lot of people, so Mickey, George and I were based down at Lea Bridge (Leyton) on that large site, and Brian dropped us off there and picked us up each evening to get us back to Coppermill Lane.

The three of us all got on together, no one having anything to prove. We loved our time at Lea Bridge. It was at Lea Bridge that we really got to know, and like very much our main Head Gardener Chris Burke, a lovely guy, easy-going, a good laugh, he had lots of children six or seven (or more!). Chris lived in a tied house at Lea Bridge. I'll tell you more of Chris later.

Either George retired, Mickey left, so I had to go to yet another 'gang' a gang of two! One being in charge of the other, hence we're back to Mack again whom you read about earlier and known as 'Mac's gang'. Now it was me, Mac and Ken; again we all got on well together. Both were older than me, Ken being a little younger than Mac. It was here that I was to learn of even more pumping stations and hidden reservoirs, not only in London, but also the outskirts. we had a huge round, cutting grass and raking it all up in summer then mainly edging with a spade all winter, trimming off all the overhanging turf that covered edging stone or paths and driveways. There were the odd shrub and rose beds to prune and tidy at some of the places.

It was at the pumping station at Waterworks corner on the Walthamstow (Forest Road) Woodford borders that we all had a narrow escape. The day previous I had been pruning and restoring all the old roses there, and Ken and Mac were very impressed with my skills in pruning, and both realised that pruning is an art. Anyhow, the next morning we came to work there was commotion, for the IRA had got in, planted a bomb, and blew up the station! The explosion had torn through the roof, plus later we were shown round by some of the workers. They showed us the huge water pipes that had massive cracks in them, and so much carnage inside.

Very soon after, on that same site, they sent a photographer down and we had to sit for a photo so that we had a pass card (I still have it even today!) and we had to show it each time we visited the stations and reservoirs, albeit all knew who we were, we didn't mind of course, things did lapse after a long period. Had I stayed with Thames Water, I would have had my HGV Licence, for Thames Water granted a lot of free time for Mac to teach me to drive the large walk-through van; again, all were impressed on how I took to driving.

I had no idea why Thames Water wanted me to have an HGV after hopefully passing my test in the 7cwt walk-through. The walk-through I could understand, for Mac was not that many years from retirement. Ken had no interest to want to drive, so perhaps they wanted me either to replace Mac in Time, or start another gang. I can't think now why I gave my notice in at Thames Water. I have tried hard to think of the reason for wanting to leave, only to the fact that I wanted to be more involved with actual plants and flowers and not vast acreages of grass.

I know that some of the grass-cutting work was dangerous and at times I hated being big and strong, for over the years I have done strange menial jobs of work, some even at my own request I might add!

I assume not a reservoir? only we were asked to cut the very steep incline of grass that was side on to what is still called 'Suicide Bridge' at Hornsey. It took three men at the top pulling on a rope that was tied to the outside spindle of the power mower, the spindle of course revolving to turn the fan belt to drive the mower. I of course trying to not only steer and keep the mower from turning over because of the incline, but had to get a foot grip to hold myself up too!

The lower I got down the steep bank, the harder my pals had to pull to keep the rope taught When I was at the bottom of the bank, my pals at the top were still holding the ropes as tight as they could. It felt like I was at the bottom of a mountain looking up at them. Boy that was hard graft!

Thames Water Authority soon introduced a bonus system. Oh no! I thought, I've never ever seen these systems work, not to be unkind, but the majority of gardeners on local authorities are unskilled, and can only work as general labourers, good ones most of the time, but still unskilled all the same. So the bonus system was *always* so unfair to skilled gardeners who, when they know their job, have to do their work skilfully, and to do this you certainly cannot rush if the job is to be done properly, and in my long experience local authorities want at least a good few knowledgeable gardeners, but they are unable to earn good money on the bonus system. The majority of the unskilled go like a bull in a china shop to work as fast as they can, without an ounce of skill going into it.

One day we were told there was going to be a meeting at one of the pumping stations about the bonus system and a Mr thorn was coming down to talk to us as a gang. I had already had a whinge to Ken about my grievances about bonus systems and a moan about Mr Thorn and told Ken what I thought of Mr Thorn and his bonus system, but to my horror Ken called out, "my mate Keith here says you're a thorn in his side!" (Mr Thorn) I could've died on the spot, for I didn't think Ken would broadcast what I'd said!

Let's now go back to the very likeable Head Gardener Chris Burke. Chris straight away recognised my skills as a proper gardener and plantsman and sorry to say that I do not now remember Chris interviewing me although he must have. One day, out of the blue, Chris asked if I would like to go along with him to see the Thames Water's nurseries at Laleham in Kent, and of course said a hearty "YES!" He asked Mickey and George if they'd like to come along too, I think only Mickey came along(?) Chris asked us to meet him at his house at Lea Bridge at five in the morning, which we did.

On our arrival Chris introduced us to the Head Nurseryman, and told us to wander where we wanted and to enjoy our day there. About half way through the morning I spotted the darkest colour 'Decorative' Dahlia that I'd ever seen. I called Chris over with the Head Nurseryman to ask the name of it, Chris and Mickey were intrigued too! The nurseryman said it's called 'Eusebio' after the black footballer who had great football skills so I was told.

Later in October, Chris came up to me with his usual broad grin. "A surprise for you, Keith." What was this all wrapped in newspaper? "It's some tubers of that Dahlia that you liked, I went back to Laleham last week and the nurseryman asked me to give these to you! I was over the moon, I couldn't believe it.

I couldn't wait to plant them up in late spring; sadly after a couple of years the tubers died, but during the 1980s decided to try and find this Dahlia again, for 1975 when I first saw it seemed a long time now, I thought this was going to be an easy task being an actual named variety – how wrong I was to be, my discovery led me to search out varieties of other types of flowers and bulbs and was truly an eye-opener.

Let me begin with the saga of 'Eusebio', surly anyone having a tree, shrub, plant, bulb named after them must be as pleased as Punch, and would obviously have the said plants themselves to grow in their own gardens and without a doubt the close friends and relatives of Eusebio himself, let alone possibly in the gardens of his numerous fans.

I wrote to the national Dahlia Society to be told that no such Dahlia is listed! or to the fact has never existed. What, I thought would Eusebio think being told that?

Too many years have now passed for me to remember how 'dark' the dahlia now was, and the only Dahlia I know sort of resembling it is 'Arabian Night'. Had the name changed because the name of Eusebio was long forgotten, but then no more than Violet Carson or Susan Hampshire, or who is E.H. Morse? Get the picture?

Many years ago I did a landscape job in Epping, Essex. It was around January/February time, and I spotted some lovely daffodils in full bloom. No, I know it's not much to get excited about nowadays, with all the so-called global warming, but this was in the '70s.

The lady whom I was working for said that the variety was called 'Early Bride' and she promptly gave me some bulbs as a surprise later in the year. After about three or four years, the bulbs disappeared, so, like 'Eusebio' I decided to do a search for it by writing to the Daffodil and Narcissi Society, and a reply came back to say that there is no Daffodil called 'Early Bride', that letter I still have today.

Many years later when we moved from East London (Walthamstow) to Suffolk (1987) and a few more years down the line to the 1990s, visited a local nursery, in fact the first nursery to offer to give me a trade discount in answer to a letter that I sent them when telling them that I was moving to the area shortly. I went into the nursery one morning and my eyes gazed at a huge sack of bulbs, full of 'Early Bride'! (The nursery was Early Dawn.)

Back at Thames Water I was enjoying my time with Ken and Mac. We seemed to be doing the gardens and grounds of even more pumping stations and travelled a good few miles to all of them, covering Ponders End, Enfield, Botany Bay, Waltham Abbey, Buckhurst Hill. It was probably at this time that I was letting my capabilities as a gardener be known and shown, so somehow my name had gone forward to be taught to drive the large walk-through van (C.F?). Mac taught me, and I was allowed to drive round the safety of the much larger empty pumping stations with no other traffic or people about. They wanted to train me for H.G.V. and no cost to me, but a benefit for Thames Water at a later date, and of course for me too.

Another really nice time came when I left Ken and Mac for short periods, again Chris Burke now knowing that my knowledge far exceeded just grass-cutting at pumping stations and reservoirs. He asked me if I would like to work at Thames Water's main head offices at Roseberry Avenue, Islington, and to help a man called Bruce, and to help with all the spring and summer bedding schemes (twice yearly). I did not hesitate to say yes, for I was so keen to do proper gardening again.

I met Bruce, and we instantly liked each other. He was truly a jolly man, large and overweight, and could see that he was no longer a man who was agile or energetic and possibly nearing retirement, he always had a broad smile on his face and loved a joke. In Bruce's tea-room gardeners' 'hut', Bruce had his own large comfortable armchair Other chairs were there for 'visitors' who would all stop by for tea-breaks or dinner hours, be it painters, electricians, handymen, plumbers, in fact all staff who kept Thames Water's main offices in order, and *all* a great bunch of chaps.

Bruce had spent all of his main working life in private service, known as 'Mansion gardening', and gave up when the owners either died or moved to smaller more manageable premises. Thames Water's main gardens were adjacent to the Sadlers Wells theatre, hence the gardens and theatre looked good standing side by side, and complemented each other nicely.

I can't remember now how many flower beds there were, but all were dug over twice a year and different types of fertilisers were applied prior to the mass plant-up. The worst of the fertilisers was the lorry-loads of pig manure – boy, I was so embarrassed getting on the bus each night! Nearly as bad as leaf mould!

In the autumn we'd dig this in, then plant up thousands of bedding plants, like wallflowers, polyanthus or maybe primroses, bellis, and forget-me-nots, etc., then vast amounts of daffs, narcissi, hyacinths and tulips, and I always remember Bruce being so worried about the disease 'tulipfire', and believe he'd come across it before when in private service. All this was hard graft, and I remember also the lighter boring work of running a narrow hoe between each plant to keep down weeds and keeping those beds in tip-top shape. I often wonder if those gardens are still there – the public could view them from outside the ornamental cast iron railings, but had no access to the gardens.

I always loved the spring displays best, and particularly loved the good mix of tulips and wallflowers, and seeing all our hard work had paid off. As Bruce was getting less able, I prayed that I could stay with Bruce, for I as a young man could handle the gardens single-handedly, but once I'd completed each bedding scheme, it was back grass-cutting once again, for the lighter hoeing and dead-heading Bruce could manage, along with the immaculate lawns that graced around the beds.

Bruce and I became very good friends, and he found it very amusing when I came out with those awful botanical names, he'd get a great thrill by saying to the chaps, "ask Keith what that shrub's called!" His face would light up with an "ooh!" when I rambled off some long name. I was very saddened to part company with Bruce, he was a very treasured friend; they were his gardens, but *none* of this I'm in charge attitude.

Some years I was kept on longer to deal with the pruning and restoration of other shrub beds etc. at Roseberry Avenue, and soon asked to come in very early each morning to water all the indoor plants in the main foyer and all the very many offices. I enjoyed this job too, but again hard work running to and fro with a large water can of water, up and downstairs etc.

The year was 1976, one of the hottest years ever, and a Mr Black was the man who came on TV each day to ask people to use water wisely, and to save washing-up water to water plants, not to fill baths and sinks too high etc., hence whey I was shocked to still be asked to water all the house plants, and more shocking still when going into Mr Black's office and other men in charge, to see that each office had its own private shower unit and all had been used!

I also remember panic stations when masses of very expensive rolls of carpet intended for the main offices were so casually stolen, but quickly re-ordered and new rolls were there in a few days. We all found this strange as we all had to report to a security officer to get in and out of the main gates which had a barrier arm, so was a great mystery on what happened to these huge heavy rolls of carpet.

Another thing that has shook me through to my bones on working for several local authorities over the years and that is the total waste of materials, i.e. plants! I'll go more into depth with this later when talking of the places where I've worked, and my findings.

After spring had passed and all the bulbs and bedding plants lifted, all were put into a skip. Every daff, narcissus, tulip, bellis, polyanthus, dumped – all could have gone on for very many years. Okay, so forget-me-nots would not survive after lifting, nor would wallflowers, but the latter, in a private garden, could go on for four or five years or longer.

Summer bedding the same – come autumn, again a skip would arrive, and we'd fill it with geraniums, begonias, busy-Lizzies, spider plants etc., etc., it was criminal. Thames Water though would let you take home what you wanted, and plenty of staff would fill carrier bags, etc., but still thousands of plants were dumped, and such a pity to see thousands of bulbs all on a skip – each could have gone on for very many years.

As mentioned before, Thames Water paid pretty good wages, far more than any other authority for whom I'd worked, but on talking to one maintenance man one morning, I asked him what his job consisted of, for I noticed he always had a very tall ladder with him. He told me that his sole job at Roseberry Avenue was to clean all the light shades, holders, and put in new light bulbs, that was his full-time job! and was paid £100 per week, which was a fortune for the 1970s. I remember Bruce and I being totally taken aback.

I did regret leaving Thames Water, but I decided that I wanted to leave to become self-employed, for I really wanted to go back into landscaping and was so fed up of just grass cutting for the majority of the time.

Chris Burke and the 'Govnors' of Thames Water wanted me to stay, but they could not offer me anything; many thought that perhaps I should have been given my own round to do all the correct pruning, planting on the very many pumping stations, and leave the grass-cutting solely for those cutting grass. Then there was poor ol' Bruce, he was nearing retiring, why did not someone say that if I stayed I'd be in line for Bruce's job... and have his big armchair!

I ended my days at Thames Water, and was based at Chingford South pumping station at the junction of Kings Head Hill, and Sewardstone Road, E.4, and heard the first time mention of 3–4 foot giant puff balls growing on the sides of the massive King George VI reservoir nearby (my dad helped design it). I never saw these puff balls, but they were the talk of our little group.

I got pally with a chap of my age, and into pop music, he was delighted knowing at that time I was a roadie for my friend's world-famous group 'Atomic Rooster', later to be known as 'Vincent Crane's Atomic Rooster', he had chart and album hits. Vince co-wrote 'Fire' (No. 1, 1968), with Arthur Brown in 'The Crazy World of Arthur Brown' – see all details online, i.e. YouTube etc. So this new pal and I were on the same wavelength. He was not in the gardening section, Chingford South, this was a busy 'station' and a base for all types of trades within Thames Water. We did the gardens and grass there, but believe that Mac said that at tea times and dinner times, the bothy was far too crowded, so we made our base at a quieter sub-station.

I preferred the more countrified pumping stations, and particularly liked the Ponders End one. The old chap who lived in a tied house had a nice country-cottage garden, with plenty of fruit trees. His name, if I remember correctly was Costas; he was a serious man, 'moody' and moany, I thought I bet he won't like me!... Wrong! we got on great, I accepted him as he was, and a delight if I did manage to get him to laugh! I loved the ol' chap.

Like most authorities for whom I've worked, you *had* to join the Union. I had no idea really what they were all about, all I knew was that being a member never made me well-off, and always had to do hard graft. I was often told that the unions were there to help you... wrong!

for the one and only time when they could have helped me, I was let down so very badly – you've possibly read what happened earlier in this book. At the time I was working at the Haringey Parks Dept.

Anyhow, Costas wanted to go along to one of these meetings (albeit could have been about the new bonus systems). I said, "I'll take you." Costas was pleased that I came all the way from Walthamstow, picked him up at Ponders End, then onto the Coppermill Works where the meeting was to be held, then back to Ponders End, then home again!

Costas was a funny guy, so serious, and certain that he tried desperately *not* to laugh, for at this meeting they came up with some long word, and under his breath but 'loudly' talking to me he said, "What the f****** 'ells that when it's at 'ome?" All the nearby chaps heard him, although they weren't really meant to, realising he'd been heard, gave a wry smile. I say his name was Costas, but it *may* actually have been Sam Costas. He was always moaning about something, but in a nice way that was funny. I don't think he realised he was being funny, but everyone liked him very much.

I enjoyed most of my time at Thames Water Authority and have often wondered how I would have fared, had I stayed on. I look back now and realise that perhaps I should have stayed on, if only to see if Thames Water really could have made use of my gardening skills.

It's sad really when they can't see it at the time, for it's not everyone who takes to hard graft, for 99% of people go out of their way to avoid it.

Plants that Really were Down Under!

Two clients of mine had bought around fifty bare-rooted perennial plants, and by mid-spring they hadn't come up. I saw the problem straight away, and that being they had planted every one of them upside down! So how all the frost and snow hadn't killed them all was a miracle in itself. When I lifted them, the greenery or what should have been green was bright yellow and blanched white! Once they were planted the right way up, they all survived, and even flowered that year.

If I hadn't been called out to rectify the problem, I'm sure the Australians down under would have seen the blooms! The strange thing about all this is that the clients hadn't planted even one the right way up, even though the roots and dead-stems stood out like a sore thumb!

Wadham Lodge Sports Ground – Brookscroft Road E.17

Like so many things to do with memory, some things are as sharp in your memory as if they happened seconds ago, others very sketchy to hazy, even forgotten until someone reminds you of something you said or did years ago, and because you don't remember what they're on about you convince they're confusing you with someone else!

This all leads nicely onto who I actually thank for getting me a job at Wadham Lodge to train as a groundsman. It could have been my dad, knowing that I was looking for work and keen to get going in the great outdoors for which I was born! I was either still working as a Bingo caller, all indoors with all the cigarette smoke (124, High St. E.17) or I was still a timber porter at Laburnum Moulding Mills, Sutherland Road, E.17, both mundane jobs and not choices of jobs that had any possible future for me.

Dad's brother Eric (my uncle) lived with my aunt Margaret née Lucas, and two cousins Robin and Ann, in the third house to the left of Wadham's main gates, so perhaps Eric had heard of the vacancy that had come up for an assistant groundsman to the then Head Groundsman Vic Oliver.

This was a private sports ground owned by Sir Terrance Mallinson (wife, Lady Mallinson). I was told that the eight-acre sports ground and Pavilion was a birthday present to Sir Terrance, from his father Sir Stuart Mallinson – they were apparently huge timber importers. Sir Terrance was also a JP.

Again, hazy, but certain that my interview was with the secretary, Leslie Golding, a grand chap and we got on well. Leslie was at one time a famous runner. Leslie died some years ago now, but his wife Anne and I still swap Christmas cards and news each year, (2008) we have been in contact since those heady latter days of the '60s, my meagre wages then supporting my thirst for going to see all the big groups (bands) of that time, and had wonderful times without drink, drugs, cigarettes etc., not one of those had the slightest interest for me, nor have they all through my life.

At the age of eighteen however, I was planted with drugs by the police, regardless of the amount of evidence proving my innocence, I was found guilty.

Although I have no interest in sport, I loved everything to do with nature or the soil, so I was a quick learner and Vic Oliver was pleased that he had a hard worker too.

Maths right to the present day baffles me, and have mental blocks and nothing registers; of course folk find this amusing when I can pronounce and spell long botanical names. When it came to marking out, i.e. running tracks, hurdles, football, cricket wickets, hockey pitches etc., I found it all daunting; some 'markings' were easier than others and I mastered most of them, albeit not liking sport (except wrestling) of any shape or form, had no idea what some of the 'lines' 'boxes' 'half circles' penalty spots etc. were actually for. To me, *all* the white lines that I did, were JUST white lines!

Leslie Golding knew that I was having difficulties but was so willing to learn, so Leslie used to help me with the marking out, moreso the large running track and hurdle track. I quickly learnt about groundwork, and when Vic Oliver decided to leave for a better paid job, much later on I was made up to Head Groundsman – wow! Eleven pounds a week! My Head Groundsman's position however was still a little way off yet, for I had to work under three further Head Groundsmen before I could take the title, for there was still a lot of training up to do, although some of the groundsmen had to be taught a lot by me instead, for some were not familiar with sports ground work, and were just like me and fancied having a go!

I had to learn how to drive a tractor, everyone seemed surprised on how I picked this up in an instant, even reversing the large trailer, or good judgement when using the 'triples' or gang mowers to cut all the acreage. I learnt how to get the right mixture of lime and to mix it up in a large metal container called a 'trundle pot' – you have to pour in a couple or so heavy bags of lime and mix it with water, the trundle pot was on wheels and quite a heavy old lot to push about all over the field, and of course used to fill the white line marker.

The mixing had to be right, for if the lime was too thick the marker wouldn't go along, and too weak a solution it would make no impact on the grass. When putting any lines down for the first time, although the lime burnt in on the grass, I would add a little creosote or total weed-killer to the lime and that usually sufficed.

The tractor, a small grey Fergusson was driven by petrol and T.V.O; the latter I believe was a type of paraffin, you had to start the tractor on T.V.O., give it a run, then turn a switch for petrol, but you daren't stop the tractor on T.V.O. or it would do all sorts to the engine and we then had to call out a mechanic to fix it.

The method was, start off with T.V.O., give the tractor a short run, or let the engine run awhile, turn to petrol, but remember to switch back to T.V.O. before stopping, or at the end of your day, again giving the tractor a good run so as the T.V.O. is in the 'system' to start your new day.

I soon learnt of the types of weather and that you had to choose carefully before doing certain jobs on the field, i.e. grass cutting, rolling, chain-harrowing etc. You could make a right old mess if your judgement was wrong; yes, I made errors, but these were easily noted after driving the tractor only a few feet, this was enough to tell you that conditions were not right.

Spring and summer was lovely doing the tractor work, but winter was awful; there was a top covering that you could affix to the tractor, but the cold that blew up from under the tractor and gearing was often an icy blast. I used to have great difficulty getting out of the tractor when making for the Pavilion to have my tea-break or dinner-hour, for I was frozen, but the job had to be done to prepare for football and hockey matches, for not only visiting schools, but also adult teams at weekends. I was given a fixture list for both.

My judgement too had to be more or less right when giving a decision to an early morning phone call to decided if the ground was okay to play on because of weather conditions. They had to know in an instant so that calls could be made to other team players, hence I had to be in the Pavilion most Saturday mornings if there had been a night's heavy rain or whatever.

Sadly, as the main decision maker, you were damned if you let them play or damned if you didn't, they'd argue the toss with you. If Leslie came down they'd listen to him and he'd say, "You tell them, Keith, the ground is unfit." The players were unwilling to listen to a mere eighteen-year-old. (I left Wadham at 21 and they still didn't like being told!) They never argued with Leslie, being the secretary and an older man.

Sir Terrance and Lady Mallinson I got on well with. I kept my distance, but they always sang my praises, particularly on the one and only sports day of the year when all the schools joined in, and had a good chance to show what I could do to greater effect, but boy was it hard graft to do so. Thankfully all of the sports days were sunny or at least good weather, and Sir Terrance and Lady Mallinson were always the 'guest stars' at their own event. I got the praises from them, being announced to the scores of people watching their speech.

Although I was proud, I was never naïve to think that these praises only went to me, for as I said before, there were several other Head Groundsmen before me who must have had praises too?

I'm going to side-step a bit now and tell you more about Leslie Golding, and heard it all first-hand from Leslie's wife Ann, now 90, when I telephoned her at ten o'clock in the morning of March 7th 2008 – the same day that we moved with my mum and dad to Chingford hatch E.4 from Harold Hill, Essex in 1960. Ann told me that Leslie was England Team Manager for the Australian (Perth Games) and assistant team manager for the Great Britain athletics in Mexico and Tokyo.

Ann still has the letter that was sent to him asking if he would consider escorting the torch bearer for the Olympic Games (1948) – the year I was born! – when the games were at Wembley. Leslie of course accepted the invitation, and Ann has proud photos of him as he escorted the torch bearer all those years ago. Ann still has stacks of Leslie's letters, 'bumf' and memorabilia, and numerous medals that he'd won.

Although Leslie took on the job as secretary at Wadham, he had to take on another job, so Ann became assistant secretary. It was also Ann who paid our wages to us each Thursday.

I remember telling Leslie how much I liked my job at Wadham, and how it felt homely. Leslie agreed with me and said, "It's not a bad little job is it, Keith," sensing that Leslie loved it too.

Terrance's father, Colonel Sir Stuart Mallinson only visited the ground once to my knowledge during my time there. I was walking down the main drive (tennis courts one side, the bowling green the other) with George, the retired carpenter, who did odd jobs around the pavilion, as we walked together an elderly well-built gent was walking towards us. George politely said, "Can I help you, Sir?" in a quizzical way, the main said, "I'm Sir Stuart Mallinson." George, like most people, changed his voice a little to sound a bit more regal – George's voice sounding now quite odd as if he'd met the Queen! George then said, "Oh! I'm sorry Sir, I didn't recognise you," as quick as a flash, Sir Stuart said, "You should do, for I've looked like this for eighty-four years!"

As I said, George was the carpenter and worked odd mornings, and Arthur Bollam was the cleaner, but was always sweating and overdoing it. Arthur died whilst on holiday abroad with his wife. He was never replaced all the time I was there, so have no idea how the place ever kept clean after he died. Arthur would always be at Wadham at five in the morning, and finishing by the time I started at seven.

Retired men always seem eager to please, possibly to hold on to their job, but no one expects them to work as they did as younger men. Mind you, I'm a good one to talk, look at me in my 60th year and still grafting like a good'un; if it's born in you to work hard, it's not easy trying to slow down.

At Wadham, I did many hours over and above my time. Arthur too would be surprised to see me on the tractor or marking out white lines at five in the morning or first light on spring and glorious summer mornings – everything is so fresh and peaceful at that time, except when the tractor started up that is!

Why did I work for nothing? Well, as I said earlier, the place was homely and I really did take great pride in that job, and my wages were a pittance for all the hard graft, but then on real rainy or snowy days could sit and listen to a radio or read all day in the Pavilion all in the warm. I very often though got bored doing that, and made for the huge shed-cum-garage, and clean it all out, re-stack and tidy large bags of grass seed, weed-killers, lime and fertilisers etc., I'd cleaned and greased up all the mowers, tractor, triples etc. Hence on the days when I really did sit down all day in that Pavilion on the harshest days, me coming in *very* early, I felt I was making up for it, and believed in give and take.

Certainly Leslie Golding never complained, for he could see the place was running well, and no doubt my early mornings and of course staying on after five if I felt like it, never missed the eyes of the likes of George, Arthur and the 'troublesome' Fred Bradley! Now this is the first time this name has come up, so who was Fred Bradley?

I was first introduced to Fred by the then Head Groundsman, Vic Oliver or indeed Leslie Golding.

Fred had been the Head Groundsman at Wadham for over forty years, he too now working mornings and solely in charge of the bowling green only. He also had a tied house, his back gate leading onto Wadham's car park. Sadly, Fred became a real pain! Constantly coming onto the ground with either advice or criticisms, with his constant, "I'd do it this way" or "I'd do that first before that" all how he would do a certain job when he was in charge. Fred too would appear on Saturday mornings to give his judgement on whether to cancel play because of adverse weather conditions; it was not now his decision anymore, he used to force me into a decision, often to cancel or play, when each in fact should have been the opposite, especially if Fred said the ground was unfit and he'd pass the buck to me to make the calls to the various team leaders. Very often a team captain would still come along and say, "why is the ground cancelled, there's nothing wrong with it?" I'd get it in the neck through Fred's wrong decisions. Fred did like the power to say a yay or nay and revelled in it, the – Don't argue with me, I'm in charge here – many of the players called him a 'Jobsworth' moreso a 'little Hitler'.

Fred, and Arthur who lived a few doors from each other in Brookscoft Road, were always 'curtain twitching' to see what I was doing, who I was talking to, what time I arrived or left work, baffling them more because I was actually a young man who didn't mind hard work. In fact well used to hard graft long before I came to Wadham Lodge, they all had that resentment towards me saying little niggly things to show their disapproval, yet I never did do anything wrong. I think they anticipated that I would, but they had a totally different person – me – to deal with!

Each of the groundsmen whom I was under, all had the same, for Fred just couldn't let go, and was responsible for them leaving, for none of them, including me, ever felt totally in charge. The real crunch came one day when I was eventually running the ground, and really had enough of Fred milling about on the ground in the afternoons with his criticisms and words of wisdom on how I should be doing my job, yet I was well instructed and taught under the previous groundsmen, thus learnt from them. Fred had run that ground for so long, and how he did things, that he did not approve of the slightest change.

I finally rang Leslie to let him know of all that was going on, and asked if he and Terrance Mallinson were happy with my work, and they were. Leslie said that he would have a word with Fred, but Leslie said, "the trouble is, Fred has been here for over forty years and treats the ground as his home, and the tractor as his baby." Similar words were spoken to me a few months down the line when I took over as Head Groundsman for Leyton Orient F.C., Brisbane Road, E.10, for I had slight problems there, but more problems at the Orient's training ground at Clapton E.5 of which I was also in charge, as you've already read earlier.

Fred did make himself scarcer on the ground in the afternoons albeit now and then could see him at the Pavilion windows upstairs looking down at me. He'd made his way from the bowling green entrance to the back stairs into the Pavilion hoping not to be seen!

Now to the Groundsmen. As mentioned, Vic Oliver was the one who fully trained me, he was a quiet man, and liked a bet, for his brother who worked for a local removal company often appeared on the ground talking of the day's betting. Vic was a friendly soul, and we got to call each other UNCLE!

When Vic unexpectedly left... probably because of the low wages or Fred Bradley, or maybe a combination of both! another nice chap called Charlie started – his two sons worked on the much larger Wadham Lodge Sports centre on the main Billet Road, E.17, very nearby. Charlie and I got on very well, but you could see he was not only getting on in years, but had great trouble walking, and difficulty stooping down just to paint in the penalty spots. Very sadly, Charlie gave up his job almost as quick as he started it. Charlie did come and say a cheery "Hello Keith" from time to time thereafter.

Who was going to be in charge of me next? So I thought I'd better act quick and perhaps find somebody I know! and somehow managed to contact a chap who was a park keeper with me when I was a trainee gardener at Springfield Park, E.5. How we met up again I cannot remember, but he was always a nice chap, back then a man in his twenties, me a mere fifteen-year-old. I'd always known Ron Platt as an immaculately dressed park keeper, who always came to work in a smart suit and a briefcase, and although a common cliché, yes, they had sandwiches in them and that was it! I had never known Ron to be a manual worker, he was also, well but (softly) spoken.

Ron had been under my recommendation regarding being a likeable and honest chap, hence Leslie Golding took him on, but often wondered what answers Ron gave to Leslie when being asked about ground-work. From day one, Ron was apprehensive about the job, and I was his guide to show him sports ground work; he did not seem to know a thing, so it seemed that he'd only got the job on my 'say so', so to speak.

Ron and I got on well, and like when assistants worked under me, I never had that upper 'I'm in charge' attitude; they were equal, that's how it was with Ron, two pals working together enjoying each other's company and our work.

A little later on cracks did appear, for Ron still came to work – all those years later – in a smart suit, tie and briefcase! and change into working garb once inside the sports ground, as if to perhaps impress friends, neighbours or the unknown public that he had a grand job somewhere.

It was one day that I walked into one of the men's changing rooms, and Ron was changing into his work clothes, his trousers were already off and he quickly... after seeing me, grabbed his briefcase and hid his private parts albeit well covered in his underpants! He spoke in a shy, girly way, "Stop looking" although still smiling. I thought it odd the way he said it, and his mannerisms trying to hide himself, where 100% of men would not have taken the slightest bit of notice of a man simply getting changed – after all, this was a sports ground! He acted like this in other situations and made me feel uncomfortable, for this was not the Ron that I really knew.

I eventually met someone whom I worked with at Springfield Park, and told them that Ron was now the Head Groundsman where I worked. To my surprise they asked about the suit, tie and briefcase! for apparently he was doing that even as a park-keeper, going to work in a suit and then changing into park-keeper's garb.

My pal said, "Does he *still* live with his mum?" I said, "Yes, he says he does." I then went on to say of all the effeminate mannerisms and slight innuendos etc. "Did you know he is homosexual?" I said that I didn't, "not even when at Springfield, Keith?" came my pal's puzzled face. I explained that I didn't know, and in all my years at Springfield Park did anyone ever say anything, he was certainly not ridiculed by anyone.

My pal said that it was common knowledge, and I suppose blatantly obvious that he was, so I suppose now working with just me all day, he was gradually letting his guard down, and I didn't like it, and I became somewhat 'mildly hostile' towards him, although he never made or said anything untoward, the mannerisms and innuendos were becoming more profound. Perhaps this was his way of letting me know. I wasn't worried what gender he fancied, for he was still a nice likeable chap.

I still treated him as a friend, and each dinner-time, Ron, plus me and my girlfriend (my wife now!) used to go to dinner together opposite Walthamstow bus station (Tram Stn).

Things came to a head when painters came to Wadham to paint all the Pavilion, three chaps in all, and they joined us in the Pavilion three times a day for the morning and afternoon tea-breaks, plus dinner hour. Strangely, all the three men soon somehow worked out what side Ron batted for! and started to give mild taunts, and was getting more embarrassing for all concerned.

Some days, one of the guys used to bring in strange age-old medieval instruments to play, and odd gadgets. One of these gadgets was a set of old handcuffs, and the chap asked Ron if he could show him a trick. Ron, I think, reluctantly agreed, and this chap chained Ron to the water pipes over the sink. We, including Ron, all laughed, but the joke went beyond that, for the chaps said, "We're back to work now" leaving Ron chained up! I couldn't do anything for I had no key. I told Ron that they'll be back in a minute, and I had hockey pitches to get ready, so I too left Ron.

A good hour or so passed and Ron hadn't come to help me. I thinking he'd got waylaid on the phone etc., I then went upstairs and Ron was still there in a blind rage, quite rightly Ron said, "I'm the Head Groundsman, I can hear the bowlers just arriving downstairs, what do I do when they come up here for their tea?" Boy was he fuming and pulling at the pipes. I told Ron that I'd try and find the painters. I did find them eventually, but then they were too afraid to go up and release him, especially when I told them what a rage he was in!

In the end we all went up to perhaps try to make light of it. The chap freed him, and possibly expected a punch in the face, the chap now feeling a bit silly too now. Ron was now still raging and eventually calmed down. Ron found the job more and more demanding and found the heavier work a task, so soon gave in his notice, and I never saw Ron again – how sad that the really nice Ron didn't just stay like that instead of slowly revealing that he was homosexual, very sadly in all those years of knowing Ron back to my very early Parks dept. days, I never saw Ron again.

It was back to the drawing board again, to look for Ron's replacement. This time I left it to Les Golding to find someone, he did – Robin Barnard, a really great fellow, and we're still pals today! He was/is a jovial man, full of fun, and we took the mickey out of people when it was needed. He took our work very seriously, yet not, if you know what I mean, we had lots of fun, and don't think we ever stopped laughing!

One day Fred Bradley asked us to help him on the bowling green, he was fixing on some guttering that had come loose, so asked one of us to hold the step ladder that Fred was on, and one of us to hold the tools, screws, etc. The laughter was contained, but we were both fit to burst, for while Fred was screwing in the screws, his tongue was out on one side of his mouth, and his face wincing with all the effort he could muster. Of course, Robin turned his head away from watching Fred, Robin looked at me and made the same face. Fred glared at us, but we quickly made out it was something else that we were laughing at. Fred carried on trying to get the screws in with that silly face – boy, we were aching with the effort not to laugh, Robin and I daren't look at each other!

Sadly again we lost another groundsman. Like most of us, we just couldn't live off the wages, mine only being about £8–9 (£11 when I left in 1972), so Robin reluctantly left for another job. I truly missed Robin when he went, like me, he knew his job, but also knew how to have fun at what you do.

It was at this point that I was made Head Groundsman, a strange title really, for I was only Head over one person, or Head over no one when assistants came and went. I had no idea that I was going to be put in charge, but Leslie could well see that I was more than competent, and had been for a long time, and could have taken over long ago, but then I would never have met Robin Barnard and that would have been a great shame.

Nothing was any different really, except the decision making was all down to me. I never was, and never would be a big-head, I was just another chap out to earn a daily crust as anyone else, and proud to say that I never had a cross word with either groundsmen whom I was under, nor the assistants that eventually came to help me.

Let's now go on to my assistants! and in no particular order – I say that 'cos I've forgotten! The first was school pal, Charlie Brennan, a brilliant musician, singer, song-writer, and like a lot of the real good musicians greatly underrated.

Charlie (still pals today) had his claim to fame with Great Britain's entry for the Eurovision Song Contest, and the group 'Co Co' – their song was 'Those Bad Old Days'. Charlie can be seen on today's 'You Tube', and you see Charlie on the drums and megaphone. Charlie was a fantastic drummer and did solo bits with 'his' band, the Walthamstow-based band 'The Tinted Aspex'.

Charlie was never built for manual work, and none too keen on early morning starts! Sadly for Charlie, Les Golding, the secretary, also did random calls in to see me as he'd always done, and Charlie was not there, and I could only cover for him for so long, but did in fact look like he was taking liberties as Charlie and I were really good pals, but it was me that kept getting it in the neck from Les, for it was one less person on the ground to help me, and I had targets to meet.

After Charlie left (or was asked to leave!) the next lad of 16 was a backward lad, with mental and learning difficulties. His dad came to see me, along with Leslie Golding, to ask if I was prepared to give the lad a chance, and train him to do some of the basics. I told them that I would be delighted to. I really, really tried with this boy, but he was to put it mildly… USELESS! He had no concept of anything. The ground work was suffering, for all the work load was on me again, and I certainly was not paid enough to do the work of two men.

Because we more or less *had* to work Saturday mornings, I was allowed half a day off, of my choosing, i.e. mornings, afternoons etc., and if the workload got too much, I could mount my half-days up and have several days off during the quieter less busy periods, which suited me well.

I did a morning, and showed this lad (Michael Barwick) a job to do for the afternoon, and showed him a ditch that had to be gradually filled with soil. So I set him to work and took my half day off and told Michael I'd be back at five to lock up the Pavilion. When I did go back, Michael was still standing on the same spot and had moved no more than a barrow-load! I told Leslie that this can't go on, and apart from that I'd missed conversation, a good laugh and a joke about as I'd had with Robin and Charlie. Michael was a nice lad, but hadn't a clue on anything; he stayed awhile, but at least I kept my promise to his dad that I'd given him a chance.

The ball was in my court again, and asked to find someone, rather than advertise, so I asked my pal Barry Gough – he was a nice guy, laughed at almost anything I said! but found him to be 'high' on all sorts of drugs. He took to the work okay, but he too would wander in at ten and eleven in the morning as if to say – Keith's a mate, he won't mind – but he too forgot that Leslie still made random visits to discuss fixtures etc., with me, and again I did my best to cover for him, but because of his lateness and total absences, the sports ground work was again suffering and certain jobs were not getting done.

The sports ground that joined on with us, and separated by a low chain-link fence, was the London Transport Sports Ground. My friend David Mole was Assistant Groundsman to Head Groundsman Arthur......? David took over when Arthur retired. Arthur had two assistants, one David as mentioned, the other Keith Williams a staunch Hells Angel, a good worker and valued member of staff.

Keith was on pretty poor pay, for Wadham paid a little better, albeit ours was poor, so he was it seems working for a pittance. Keith and I got on well, and longed to work with me for several years. He would often pop over from his ground for a brief chat, and asked if Barry was still there, for if he wasn't he'd love to be my assistant. One day Keith nipped over to have a quick cuppa; our tea-breaks being the similar times to that of the staff at the London Transport ground. we were just having our tea when Barry decided to turn up for work – he was very apologetic and said that his dad died that morning.

Keith and I both said how sorry we were, but we were puzzled that he'd come to work. Keith and I smelt a rat, so the next day when Barry never came in, Keith and I bought a nice bunch of flowers to take to Barry's mum – she was totally shocked, for Barry's dad was alive and well! Keith and I were shocked too, yet sort of knew that something was amiss. We never saw Barry again, and drugs killed Barry not long after. How sad, still a young man. I lost several pals through drugs in the late '60s early '70s and lessons not learnt even today.

Keith filled Barry's shoes when Barry left, and proved to be a good hard worker. Yes, he was a typical Hells Angel, really dirty, scruffy, but a good grafter. He had the odd streak in him though, for one day we had just finished drinking our tea and he picked up a dart from the dart board near the bar; I was sitting down, when he gave the actions of a dart player lining up for the main score on the board, except he was aiming towards my leg. I said, "You dare!" but in a split second threw the dart into my leg. My face must have been one of total shock, for the shock turned to blind anger. I took the dart out of my leg, which was now very painful to say the least, and he knew it was time to exit!

I did no more than run after him with a heavy chair and it landed with a heavy crunch to his shoulder and back. How I didn't knock him out was a miracle. He made for the Pavilion balcony, thankfully he and I calmed down later, me still not believing what he'd just done. He never did anything like this after, but knuckled down even more to the work. He did do something very funny once, George the carpenter and I were having a chat in the Pavilion kitchen where we had our breaks, and we both looked out of the window in total amazement – we looked to the chain link fencing that joined the two sports fields that was a good way from the Pavilion.

In the distance we could see Keith rolling about on the grass all on his own and oblivious to any audience. I shouted to George, "he's got a knife, he's fighting a giant snake!" so George and I ran out. Keith was stabbing away furiously all entwined on what looked like from a distance a giant python! As we got closer we could see that it was one long (10 inches thick approx.) line of very matted leaves, twigs, dead grass etc., and that it came from a gulley that ran round the edge of the outside of the London Transport's bowling green.

Keith roared with laughter when seeing our faces! but what intrigued George and I was how long had he been rolling about like this before we spotted him? Moreso how long would he have carried on if George and I had not seen him and we'd gone out of another entrance? Keith called himself 'crazy dog' and did all the foulest things that you'd expect a Hells Angel to do. If we were down Walthamstow High Street, E.17, he'd think nothing of picking up the remains of an old apple core and eat it, or go into a butcher's shop, buy the raw sloppy meat with sinew and entrails, hold it in his mouth, shake his head wildly and growl at the throngs of crowds in the busy High Street market on Saturdays.

After Keith left, he went to work at another sports ground. I never had any more assistants either, and paced myself to take on all the work, Leslie giving me overtime and Sundays. Keith and I stayed friends, but believe he had other serious 'mental' problems, for although the girls loved him with his long shaggy hair, ice-blue eyes, and even had a posh studious girlfriend once, he was certainly very different to other people whom I knew.

Keith and I often spoke seriously, and he'd talk about his mum who had left his dad and him when he was young, and how she tried to smother him with a pillow, the house where Keith lived with his dad was filthy, and the darkest dingiest, dirtiest kitchen that I'd ever seen, all thick dirty fat in a frying pan, and their poor little dog cowering in a corner.

On one occasion he showed me his bedroom, and on lifting the mattress were lots of very greasy motorbike parts, chains, nuts, bolts. The next thing he wanted to show me, I strongly declined and quickly made for the door, for it was a skull! which he kept on top of a cabinet.

I daren't ask if it was a recent one, but knew that Keith had been a grave digger at some point, for he lived in Queens Road, E.17 and the Queens Road Cemetery was a few yards from his house. He worked alongside yet another Hells Angel, called 'Filthy Frank the Vicar's Son', later to find respectability as a hospital orderly in Whipps Cross Hospital, and in fact helped care for my own mum who had M.S. and had spent nine long years in that hospital. Mum liked Frank a lot, yes, and like Keith, he was very likeable. Mum couldn't believe it when I said Frank was an ex-Hells Angel!

As mentioned earlier, my Auntie Margaret and Uncle Eric's (Dad's brother) back garden backed onto the yard and tractor shed at Wadham, so I saw one or other of them daily, including of course my two cousins Robin and Ann. Keith must have spoken to Auntie Margaret about a design that he wanted on the back of his leather jacket reading 'CRAZY DOG'. Keith knew the exact pattern and design that he wanted, and Auntie Margaret turned out a lovely job. Little did she know that in a short time the jacket would be urinated on by numerous people, draped in vomit and other disgusting things, and he did everything imaginable (or unimaginable!) to get his 'Colours' and the acceptance as a fully-fledged 'Angel'.

Keith and I eventually lost all contact, but many of my pals asked, "Have you seen anything of your mate 'Crazy Dog'?" all I could say was that as far as I knew he was on a sports ground somewhere around Leyton or Leytonstone. I hadn't seen him since 1971; it was now 1979 and Debbie and I had our own house and Deb was heavily pregnant with our first son, Adrian. A knock came at our door, and had just finished playing our newly bought record 'Heart of Glass' by Blondie, to my surprise it was cousin Robin and... Keith! He was quite the worse for wear, and didn't get a lot of sense out of him, for he was far from sober.

We blamed Robin for years after, wondering why he had brought him round in this state, but of course now realise that it was Keith who had insisted on coming round to see us, for Robin was still a young lad back then. After they left, we had a lot of clearing up to do, for he'd urinated all over the toilet seat and floor. we had a young family, so we were furious. We never did see Keith ever again. Rumours soon circulated that Keith had died – overdosed? suicide? heart? We never found out. I'd love to think he is still alive and having a nice life somewhere. I still have photos of Keith and cousin Robin at Wadham, and the 'Crazy Dog' design!

Now let's get on to the serious side of my work. As mentioned before, I do not like sport in any shape or form albeit had a relative

Rita Ridley who apparently ran the 1,000 metres? (not to be confused with my mum's youngest sister Rita née Ridley). I was a stickler for my work and took great pride in it. On sports days or other eventful days I would do the whole length of a running track and hurdles with the large 'Dennis' power mower, which could have a seat on it, which in turn was built on a roller, thus with the weight of the person the roller had the added weight. The 'Dennis' is a very heavy mower to operate all day long and you had to be physically fit to use one too!

I rarely used the seat because I was young and fit, hence doing a whole running track took some stamina. The 'Dennis' of course cut much lower than the gang mower triples pulled by the tractor, so was able to make those fabulous light and dark green lines, and what with the freshly painted lines with lime, was as good as you'd see on any of the professional grounds.

Fred Bradley never did it, nor to my knowledge any groundsman since, and that was to use a 'Dennis' on the two large hockey pitches, hence seeing a multitude of light and dark green stripes. The usual method was to use the gang mowers and to make half the pitch light green, the other half dark. I'd certainly made a rod for my own back, for everyone commented on it, and said how lovely the ground always looked – little did any of them know of my staffing problems!

From the Pavilion windows you saw the true beauty of the ground with the stripes and new lime, and my cricket wickets too were treated professionally. It took me a time to learn how to do a cricket pitch, and was measured out with a thin chain. The main pitch I had to work out which way the mower was to run so as to see the light grass showing from the Pavilion and run the mower down the two sides of that to make the dark green, then from then on carry on doing light, dark, light, dark etc. All the other cricket pitches I'd do as all dark green, hence really showing off the pitches that were to be used the following day.

In amongst all the praises, I took a fair amount of quite unnecessary criticism from mainly the cricketers, the team captains and their players, who all thought they knew my job better than them. If they lost a game I was invariably in the firing line and that the pitch hadn't been right, but the pitch strangely being so perfect for the winning team.

Disliking sport as I do right from day one when I was made to play football, saw that 99% of it was not sport at all, more like a shouting match, a sea of angry grimacing faces, (crowds and players) and managers furiously chewing gum, and the inevitable fighting, and I'll say it again… crowds and players. The pure hatred and rivalry and against fellow countrymen too and that's without trying to get good rapport with sportsmen abroad, who in turn are doing the same as our countrymen, the anger, grimacing, shouting – need I say more? So where is the game? I'll use that word again… GAME.

When a player came up to me to moan about the pitch… cricket, football, men's hockey… I'd say, "Oh, I see, you expect to win every single game do you? You win the next, and the next and the next, how boring, then when you lose it's the groundsman's fault." I'd then ridicule them more for daring to criticise all my hard graft and expertise. "Supposing you won *every* game for the next ten to fifteen years, would you really play each week, then after ten years or so lose the game and then blame the groundsman – oh! come on!" I'd rant on "Look at the size of a human being, look at the height and width of a goal mouth, then look at the size of a mere football, that so very easily finds its way to a goal; you see goalies diving the opposite way the ball is going or on occasions no goalie even in goal! The ball goes in and the crowds go wild, why? when that must be the very easiest goal to score, a baby could do it." I'd go on, "look at you all, you kiss and cuddle if a goal is scored, jump on each other's backs, wrap your legs round each other. Aaaargh!! All as if you've really done something so spectacular, but no, a ball into a net, or a ball hitting stumps." and look at the so miserable faces of tennis players too!

The *only* thing I admire in sportsmen, and that is the training, they do train so very hard, but after that it's where that old joke comes in – I went to a boxing match and a football match broke out! – or indeed vice versa!

Many hard men become famous for their aggression in supposedly non-aggressive sports, and cannot understand how an assault on another player, and not classed as a crime, is no different to an assault in the street?

The one thing that proves what I'm saying is correct and possibly there's not a groundsman in the country that will disagree with me, and the one chance to show up the criticiser. As I said before, it was compulsory to work Saturday mornings to prepare wickets, goal mouths etc., but it's the cricket pitch that I now refer to, for often the captain of the team would come over to see me with a "Well done, Keith, nice pitch" and promptly hand me a tenner! when eleven pounds was my whole week's wages! he'd walk away happily, and me even happier, then one of the players of that very *same* team would come over and say "rough ol' pitch, Keith, could you give it another cut and roll?" At this point I would take great delight in letting him know all what had gone on with his team captain not half an hour since, his face was a picture and was totally speechless not really knowing what to say next.

Even funnier still was an occasion when *two* players came up to me with the welcomed tenner, again praising the pitch, then later their team captain having a moan that the pitch wasn't good enough etc., so once again took great delight in telling him that two of his players had praised me highly and had given me a nice tip!

I suppose the funniest of all is when two men came up to me at the 'same time' (usually football) the two men approaching me at different times, i.e. the leaders of the two rival teams, one saying how brilliant the pitch looked, the other just a short time later saying how the pitch needed rolling, or the lines not clear enough, etc.

Once again I took great delight in telling them what was said by each of them, no doubt adding fuel to the fire with their rivalry on the pitch! So, you can now see how all these men over the years knew my job as well as their own. It was in many ways so soul destroying. I was a fully trained groundsman and told I was a good one too, yes there were times the pitches looked bad, but then I knew it and every player and team captain knew it, therefore *all* of us knowing there was a good reason for it, and always due to adverse weather conditions prior to match days.

Many years after leaving Wadham, I was waiting for a bus in Fulbourne Road (just of Brookscroft Road) E.17, and a chap said, "Hi Keith!" I recognised the chap as either one of the players or one of the team captains. He asked what I was doing now since leaving Wadham; I told him that I was a Bingo Caller – he was genuinely shocked. "Bingo calling, with all that talent and know-how as a groundsman!" I said, "I couldn't take anymore of the criticism, for I couldn't be doing my job right and wrong at the same time." He then said, "Yes, we did give you some stick didn't we? but hand on heart no one since has come close to what you did on that ground." I thanked him for his kind words, now sadly all said far too late. Nevertheless, I took comfort in his words, knowing that I had done my job correctly.

I often baffled the players on how I got goal mouths and wickets back to greenery so very quickly, and never told them my secret, and always had that look of admiration from them, me with a twinkle in my eye, and longing to tell them really, but keeping the so easy secret back, added to my professionalism in their eyes. This same method I still use today in my landscaping projects, or anyone asking how to deal with dead patches of lawn.

Just simply rake the bare soil, thus making a 'key' of fine broken soil, add your grass seed, then cover it with thin hessian, then water that and keep it moist at all times. The hessian keeps the ground and seed warm, and what with the damp hessian and any warm sunshine added, the grass seed germinates far quicker. When the grass seed pushes through the holes in the hessian by ¼ to ½ an inch, then slowly take off the hessian and again keep moist until the grass grows, which it will quite rapidly if looked after. The other big bonus with hessian is that birds do not eat the seed or make dust baths, and cats cannot scratch it up and do their 'business' in it! but will lay on it if the hessian becomes dry. If the hessian does stay dry for too long, then it's obvious that the seed will become dry and die underneath. And to keep my secret a secret, I always took off the hessian in the early morning, before any players could see it, thus enhancing the 'mystery'.

On the subject of mysteries and still a mystery to day and concerns a tree stump killer. Let me explain – when I first started at Wadham Lodge, there was a very long line of poplar trees, which were fully grown and apt to drop twigs at regular intervals all year round, and prone to suckering to quite a distance. The poplars did make a nice backdrop to the field, but sadly planted on the side of all the rows of houses (Garner Road, E.17). George the carpenter incidentally, lived there, and was also 'spying' on me when he could.

No doubt the people in the houses had complained about the trees, the leaves would have been a great problem if the wind was blowing in that direction and landed in their back gardens, and of course a menace and lots of leaves to clear up from the adjacent football and hockey pitches too, and of course the suckers too were the biggest problem I should think, coming up through lawns, paths, green houses, between sheds and fences etc., and without a doubt these suckers went across the pitches, and the more they were cut off, the stronger they became, so forming a ground-level 'trunk' that no doubt played havoc with the mower blades etc.

Tree surgeons were called in and cut them all down leaving a two-foot high stump. The chaps did the usual drilling of half inch holes in the tops and sides of the trunks. I never have found out what type of stump killer they put on, and never remember them covering the stumps to prevent rain entering the holes. The men assured us that the stumps would be totally dead in a year, and that the stump killer would find its way through each and every sucker to its very tip, the suckers would die without the stump killer affecting lawn nor flowers. These guys knew their stuff, for after a year you could put your boot against the stumps and they simply crumbled into dust! We then raked out the debris, backfilled with soil, levelled off and seeded. I have asked many tree-surgeons since those days, all have been intrigued, but none to date have known what was used.

The chaps took away all the twiggy leafy stuff, and cut the trunks up and stacked them for us, no doubt for Fred Bradley and his wife! (House with the job plus free fuel?) One local man who had heard that the numerous poplars had been taken down, and once or twice a week would come to Wadham and in a very broad Scottish accent would say "Wheresmalogs?!" all in one breath! He used to walk his dog some days round the perimeter of the ground.

I was in luck one afternoon for as I walked down the main drive to the Pavilion, I saw various coins on the floor, every foot I moved I was getting richer! I thought perhaps it was going to be a wind-up, but no, it seemed that someone had left the Pavilion and had a hole in their pocket. I had good unexpected wages that week!

Being a young Head Groundsman at twenty years old, wasn't always easy when trying to convince older people, like salesmen selling grass seed, fertilisers etc., they'd ask for the Head Groundsman, I'd say "It's me" but they still wouldn't believe me, and even more difficult when my assistant was trying to back me up, and was more or less the same age as me! So callers often thought it was two young men mucking them about.

An older man in his fifties I should think came to meet me as Les Golding had informed him that I was now running the ground. It was a company called Parkers, and to be honest they were a good reliable firm, and I did I suppose have 95% of orders with them, for there was little that they didn't stock in the way of sundries. I had my name down now officially with them, and had the biggest shock of my life, for near Christmas each year they would send me £100 plus as a 'thank you' for dealing with them.

It goes without saying, Fred Bradley had got it for years, and perhaps the other groundsman before me in my times of training. I was a millionaire, for even when I left Wadham, my wages went from £11, £14, £18, £21 and lastly around £24 in early 1972. I left there early that year, Debbie and I got married on 20th May 1972, and although I left, Les Golding let us have the use of the Pavilion hall for our reception.

I really can't remember my exact reasons for leaving, but I had so many problems in my life, what with Mum's M.S. getting worse, perhaps my time-keeping was getting bad, I really do wish I could remember, for I must have done something wrong, for a man called Tedder Ward came to take over my position! I know I was truly getting so disheartened with the criticisms, so probably my heart wasn't in it anymore, especially when I'd had an offer to return to Springfield Park as their main 'Dennis' driver, that park was on my first time there under the L.C.C. (London County Council, then Hackney Borough Council, I left, now I was to return under the G.L.C. Greater London Council.

Tedder Ward started on the wrong foot with me when he popped into the ground for our first meet one Friday afternoon, he appeared arrogant and bossy, with the last words, "See you sharp Monday morning." I never turned up, and arranged instead for an interview at Springfield Park.

Leslie was upset that I had 'walked out' but told him that I would not work a single day with that man, and that I was put out by demotion without a reason given. Leslie never did say why, but still pleaded with me to try and get on with Mr Ward. I made my apologies to Leslie, still hoping that I'd have an explanation why I lost my position when my heart had always been at Wadham. I was a stickler for time and the daily routine on how to run an eight-acre sports ground, yet another mystery that bothered me for years, and even give some thought to it even today.

I had had happy and sad times at Wadham. Charlie Brennan would occasionally ring me at Wadham during my dinner-hour for a chat, and play over the phone his latest composition, once on a piano where he'd made up a song that morning – 'You came in Like a Beautiful Sunday'. In 1970 I promoted rock singer Screaming Lord Sutch, and again used Wadham's pay phone to talk to all the agencies. Debbie had her 21st birthday party at Wadham, again a free hall, a gift from Leslie Golding, Les again giving me permission for my Uncle jack Cook (Fairground Showman) to try out the acoustics as he was an 80-odd-year-old D.J! Jack's face was a picture, he sounded good too.

Talking of D.J.s, Tedd Moss, next-door-neighbour to Uncle Eric and Auntie Margaret, an older man, but he was our D.J. for our wedding. I liked old Ted, I helped him move to Kirby Cross (Frinton-on-Sea) soon after his divorce. His niece lives right here in my new home town of Kessingland, Suffolk, when his brother moved here around the same time as us. Ted also told me that his daughter wrote 'Jumping Jack flash' the Rolling Stones hit record. Ted said that she gave the song to the Stones then manager Andrew Loog Oldham, and as Lorraine knew nothing about copyright, he changed the tune and wording a little, and someone, if not him, put their name to it.

A young chap whose name I've now forgotten, lived near the sports ground. I knew his mum, and really wanted to work with me and learn all there was to learn on a sports ground, but he had enlisted to join the army, but we had a good laugh and chat, and let him stand on the back or sit just on the mudguard – it was the latter where he slipped and his whole leg got jammed in the wheel, he was screaming out, I was in a blind panic, and thank heavens I was going really slow or without a doubt he'd have lost a leg for sure. Instead, I slowly went in reverse, thankfully drawing his leg out again. His army starting date had to be cancelled for a week or so, and he did come back to say that he was okay.

Another pal of mine, Del, I say pal, but just knew him if you know what I mean. He wanted a job on my friend's dodgems and to go travelling, so I fixed him up to see them at Edmonton Carnival. I said I had to work, but we could go by bus when finished at five. He gave me a hand on the ground all that day. A few years down the line he was foreman on the dodgems.

Alf Andrews was a nice old gent, and was the secretary either at Leytonstone or Leyton sportsground. From my first starting day to my last day, Alf would give a loud whistle and a hearty wave, a signal that he'd make me and my assistant a lovely cuppa! Alf too lived in Garner Road, and his house cornered where the L.T. (London Transport) bowling green stood. I rarely saw Alf's wife, but often saw his very elderly mum who lived with them.

Alf loved Chrysanthemums, and had a large patch in his garden dedicated to the growing of them. He admitted that he knew nothing about them and only did a little dis-budding; to the layman this means the removal of all buds and retaining one, which then makes all the energy go into that one bud to make a much bigger bloom. The same practice is done to Dahlias etc.

Alf had called us over for a 'cuppa' one morning, I mention morning, but if he caught us in the afternoons there would be yet another hearty whistle and a wave and we all knew what that meant.

Anyhow, this particular day, the Chrysanths looked pretty magnificent, and because they looked so nice I casually said to Alf "those Chrysanths look like prize specimens, have you thought of entering them into a show?" Alf said that he hadn't even given it a thought, but now I'd put the idea in his head, and he entered them in a (local?) show somewhere.

On the Monday morning, following that Saturday's show, as usual Alf gave the signal for tea, and he had a broad grin on his face and looked pleased with himself, "I won!" came his joyful reply, after I asked how he got on. Now this was back in the late '70s, so I can't really remember the *exact* winnings, but was certainly two firsts, a second and a third prize!

I took photos of Alf posing with his Chrysanths and prize cups. He was a very happy man, thanked me profusely for suggesting to enter a show. The really silly part of all this was to make me think about all judges at all sorts of entries/shows, for my thoughts on this had always been the same, and have always doubted all judges for this reason.

Firstly, what did I know about so-called prize plants? Absolutely nothing! for Alf's plants just looked really nice, secondly had I unwittingly adapted the eyes of a judge to spot winning plants?... no, I don't think so. Thirdly, Alf had done nothing to these Chrysanths, not before or leading up to the show! There were no paper bags or other protection over the flower heads, no individual re-curling of the petals, for Alf just planted them, dis-budded, watered and little to no feed whatsoever. we know that because from just the week or two prior was when I first gave Alf the suggestion, and how lucky too that he found a show going on and allowed to enter. Alf and I mused over him winning for weeks after, for look at all the time and fuss that every entrant puts in, Alf had done nothing, he had no time to! This happened every year after too, and Alf just split the plants, little feed, water, staking, and dis-budding if needed.

We wondered what the judges saw in Alf's 'untreated' plants, they of course thinking that he'd done all the other palaver like the other entrants – it makes you now wonder about all judging!

When we first moved to Suffolk in 1987, my wife Debbie and I went to a flower show at Otley College near Ipswich. When we went in there was a fierce row going on, either between two entrants, or a judge and entrant. Fighting over flowers or fighting over a game of football, there's no difference – they are all adult children in my eyes. I could play a game or enter a plant, if I didn't win it would not put me out in the slightest, it would be meaningless to me. You just know you're going to win at some point, no different to a winner who you will lose to sooner or later. Yes, I've won things in the world of gardening, but I stress that I have never intentionally gone out to purposefully win anything. Yes, it gives me a bit of pride I suppose, only to the fact that I have perhaps succeeded or been recognised as a good gardener. Yes, the financial side can be rewarding, but not lasting, for *every* day of inclement weather was a day that you can't work, hence you start breaking down your last payment, and kiss all your hard earnt goodbye!

On the same subject of judges, and before I go on about my time at Wadham Lodge, I must mention a programme that I watched on TV and was shown on Boxing Day around 1985/86 which showed various people who had entered their gardens for a competition. Just one in my opinion stood out over all others, it was an amazingly kept garden, whose owners I can only assume spent every waking hour to get such quality, a grand old cottage-mix of perennials and annuals, the most beautifully kept green lawn with border and lawn on a sweeping curve.

The judge was so very critical of it and very much nit-picking. I'm certain that it as a case of even the judge being quite jealous of it, and wanted to do a big put-down because the owners thought that they would be definite winners with a garden like this. The people seemed so nice and ordinary too. Our whole family sat in total disbelief.

The garden of course may not have been the judge's taste and may have liked the minimalistic garden with the odd rock or weird lump of metal or modern art in it, for had I been a judge, a garden like that wouldn't even be in the running!

Self-employment in landscaping or general gardening can be soul-destroying because of bad weather, and as just previously mentioned, your good pay soon very much evens out, or in winter when there are very good working days, yes, cold maybe, but usually 'dry' (and workable ground).

The other side of the coin is working for someone. The wages in gardening and sports ground work were poor, but at least regular, and you get paid regardless of weather conditions. Some weeks in winter when at Wadham and I'd done every chore possible to occupy myself, the winters didn't seem so long, unlike being self-employed and have to wait for the phone to ring, so nowadays spend winters either in my own garden or writing!

As a very young man from the ages of 18 to 21 (I commenced at Wadham during the latter months of my 18th year) found Wadham a pleasant place indeed for girls! especially of course the sixth formers of more or less my age group. One of those sixth formers a couple of months or so of leaving, was my girlfriend, who of course became my wife, we married in 1972 and our first-born, Heather, followed later in the very hot summer of '76. Then there was Adrian '79, Rowan '82, and Dale 1990 (our Suffolk baby!).

Prior to and after meeting Debbie, my soul drive was to look forward to my weekends, for these were the lovely days of the late sixties and early seventies, the 'hippy' era! and boy I relished in it and had the best times and could write a book about those alone! and didn't need booze, drugs or tobacco to enjoy those times, thus remember a LOT, where most hippies can recall little to nothing. My pal Mickey Casey (later to become my best man at our wedding) would meet me every Saturday at Wadham. Mick was also a hard grafter, a builder, who too worked on Saturday mornings and on occasions I would go home, change into my most outrageous hippy clothes and go and meet Mick at his boss's yard near Blackhorse Road Tube Station (new then, Victoria Line).

Mick too would meet me in all his finery, very long hair, fur coat, beads, bangles, bracelets, crushed velvet trousers, velvet or multi-coloured tie-died T-shirts. I'd go home and change into all my weird clothes – my eighteenth century jacket or the loveliest jacket that once belonged to the drummer of the group 'The Taste' (Rory Gallagher was the lead singer).

Mick and I would make for the famous Kings Road, Chelsea or Portobello Road, where it all 'happened'. That was the day covered, at night we'd be off all over London, often by tube, to far-flung colleges, seeing every band imaginable, our favourites being The Pretty Things, The Edgar Broughton Band, and the Scottish band Writing-On-The-Wall… Mmmm… I think I will do a book on the sixties – I think I'll have a lot to say!…

I worked very hard for my money, and boy I made sure, if I could, that each weekend was memorable – I did more, went further moreso when being given a tip from the players, this alone would cover train, bus fares, entry to see a band, plus eat and drink (not alcohol).

It wasn't only weekends we went out, for although my varied low wages over the years were very low, entries to see bands (groups) were often only five or six shillings to get in, even when decimalisation came in we could afford to go out, albeit did not do any great long journeys during the weekdays because we had to go to work. Those really were lovely times, YOUNG I think being the key word here!

On those Saturdays when Mick used to meet me, I used to hand the Pavilion keys to Fred Bradley (at his tied house) for safe-keeping over the weekend, for Fred would unlock or lock the Pavilion if there was a function going on, and there usually was.

Mick would come with me to see Fred and Mrs Bradley. I always remember Fred acting more normal and a lot friendlier towards me when Mrs Bradley was with him (standing at their kitchen door). I wasn't at that point that awful bloke who 'took' his job, albeit now he was over seventy, and couldn't do groundwork if he tried, for I'd often offered my services on 'his' bowling green when the heavier work was needed, like moving all the tonnage of top-dressing so Fred could lute it in, or I'd shovel out all the stones (graded) that made up the gulley around the perimeter of the green – all these had to come out to be washed with a hose then the gulley cleaned out before the stones are replaced.

Mrs Bradley seemed a dear little lady, and on taking the keys back, she always treated me and Mick like children, but in a nice way, like "Here you are Keethy, here you are Michael, here's some sweeties for you for your journey." She did this to Robin Barnard too, for he, Mick and I would 'mickey-take' an exaggerated version of the way she said it, and of course very much appreciating her nice gesture.

On the subject of 'mickey-take', Robin and I made up the wording sung to the tune of 'These are a few of my favourite things' – Goal posts and spikers and lines and markers, tractors and hayters and fertilisers to, I am a groundsman boo hoo hoo hoo!

The Charles family, who lived in the first house to the left of Wadham's main gates, were the bar managers at Wadham's Pavilion, a lovely family, but their lives changes dramatically.

One afternoon I spoke to their youngest son Chris and his fiancée, they were both excitedly showing me their engagement rings. The next day as I got to work, learnt that Chris' fiancée had come off his motorbike on the North Circular road (mere minutes from Wadham) and was killed outright. I still have the newspaper cutting, and have often wondered about the family, and how Chris has got on since. I shouldn't think families ever get over tragedies like this, time heals yes, memories never fade.

In those hippy days, the bowlers on the green were rarely friendly, and me with my long hair would look at me as if I was something they'd just stepped in! Probably Fred Bradley had a little to do with it too, for I was the young chap, and he was fully in league with all of his age group on the green.

One of these bowlers who gave the odd sneer and remark, was to stand out above all others – his name was Charlie Cox and lived next door the other side to my aunt and uncle. Charlie very often sided in with Fred when Fred was making snide comments, but one day there was a lot of bustling about with police etc. and one or two people asking if I'd heard about Charlie Cox one of their most respected players?

It turned out that he had enticed a thirteen-year-old girl into his house and got her to 'interfere' with him and he to her. I for one took great pleasure in giving him the odd sneer and not speaking when he spoke to me out in the street. He was a man at the latter end of his sixties to early seventies I should think.

I had agreed with Leslie Golding that I would give Fred Bradley a hand whenever he needed it, and said that if Fred wanted to retire properly from the bowling green, I would take it over. The suggestion was put to Fred, and don't think he was too pleased with the idea, and that I hadn't any training. How wrong he was, for I had done bowling green work at Springfield Park, Clapton, London, when I was just fifteen and sixteen years of age, and learnt quite a bit from Charles Swaby and later a Scotsman known as Mac, two nice chaps.

In the weeks to come I was to meet up with Sir Terrance Mallinson and Les Golding, when the suggestion arose again about me taking on the green too, and if I did, I'd have to be given more overtime, weekends, to allow time for other priority jobs that I had on the ground already, including all overtime for my assistant.

I was blunt with both Terrance and Leslie, and said, "the trouble with people who run greens, treat the grass like gold dust" and went on to say, "whatever you think, it's only grass, fine grass, but nevertheless GRASS" and of course I went on to say that I knew that there was only one special mower (an eight-blader usually) to cut the very fine grass, and that you couldn't walk on it with heavy boots or shoes, the latter throwing Fred into a blind rage one day when he'd applied fertiliser to the green and the next day came in to see the outline of boots and shoes, the weight of the person pressing on the fine grass and burnt the outline in. Yobs had got over the fence during the night, and had run all over it. We had to hose it heavily to try to wash out the new compressed 'burning' fertiliser, before the players came in during the afternoon, but sadly it was all too late, the damage done.

I never did take over that green; strange, for my praises on all of my work on the main field came thick and fast to the ears of both Leslie and Sir Terrance from all the schools and private clubs, yet I hadn't the ability to look after a bowling green! I'm certain Fred was the one to put the block on me taking it over, for after this, some of the bowlers volunteered to come in to assist Fred.

Not blowing my own trumpet, but I have always been a hard worker, and always ready to earn money, and do nothing underhanded – I like to sleep at night!

Decimalisation had literally just come in, maths was and still does cause a mental block in my brain! and really not the time to take on a new venture involving giving change! Let me explain. Leslie Golding asked if me and Debbie would be interested in doing light catering at Wadham and supply food and drink to all the footballers who were mainly Firemen and Police, plus other clubs, visiting teams, etc., for when play had ended all were tired, cold and hungry, so assumed that in the past they all just showered then went home, for there never had been catering of any sort during my time at Wadham.

Leslie said that we could earn quite well out of it, for the more teams that played, i.e. football, men's hockey, plus their family, friends, and supporters, the more we'd make with all those hungry thirsty people. Debbie at the time had a better paid job than me, doing offset duplicating for a large company called Gestetner at Tottenham, London, so we put our money together to buy tea-bags, sugar, coffee, bread, butter, cheese, tomatoes, pickle etc., etc.

We were allowed to use the kitchen (where I sat each day for my tea-break and dinner hour) so had all the hot water we needed, but had to buy our own washing-up liquid and other necessities. All a drain on our combined incomes, not knowing if a profit would be made at all. As this was going to be a little business for me and Deb, and no doubt our services would carry on through the spring and summer, for apart from the cricketers, the men's hockey teams still played all year round. Also we had archers and tennis players, the prospect did look good, albeit forfeited all our weekends, and also knew that if we did have a weekend off it would be adverse weather, we knew that because that was the days that I had to say that the pitches were unfit for play.

The very next thing we needed was mugs, cups, saucers and plates, again with little money searched everywhere for a bulk buy. I didn't have to go far, but I'll use the term 'far' lightly, as you'll see. I found a large ironmongers in Hoe St., Walthamstow (near the Rose and Crown pub, but on the opposite side of the road on the corner of either Greenleaf Road? or Jewel Road?). The chap sold me a huge quantity for very little money, all seconds that he'd had stored for years, and probably glad to have them off his hands!

All the crockery was put in what I was hoping to be a strong cardboard box, 4x4 I'd say – boy, was it heavy! I still wonder today how I carried that lot from Hoe Street to Wadham, a miracle I'd say, and look back to think how physically fit I was back then. I thought that I'd either pass out, or give up and leave the lot on the pavement! I did make it, of course with great relief. We never took any of that crockery when I left, perhaps it's still being used today?! In hindsight I should have done two or three journeys, for I was still a few months away from passing my driving test so it was Shanks' pony for me!

Deb and I were excited about this venture, and hoped for good rewards. Our biggest obstacle now was trying to work out how decimalisation worked. My Uncle Jack (Cook), on the fairgrounds, so kindly made me and Deb a conversion board to work from, we kept it just out of sight of our paying customers to make them think we knew exactly what we were doing! Jack also gave us an old enamel jug that he and Aunt Rose used on their Hot Dog and Candyfloss stall when they were travelling the fairs. They now ran their Hot Dog stall down

Walthamstow's famous market, outside Rumbelows (TV store) on the corner of Erskine Road. (I still have the jug).

Deb and I did well with the idea of doing hot black currant, this did sell very well to my surprise and helped our finances. The idea of blackcurrant came about seeing the sale of the age-old Sarsaparilla drink in the High St (E.17) market. I had no idea where to buy Sarsaparilla, so blackcurrant it had to be.

Deb and I made loads of cheese sandwiches, spam, corned-beef etc., but sadly they did not sell well, it was winter and no one wanted cold sandwiches. Deb and I were losing good money, we tried even adding cakes and biscuits to sell, but they still didn't want to know Then my Uncle Jack said, "Look, Keith, why don't you do Hot Dogs and Burgers?" I thought it a brilliant idea. Jack said that he'd supply me all the rolls, onions, cooking oil, hot dogs, etc. I'd go to pick these up from Jack's stall early on the Saturday mornings, and as Jack said, "as you know, there's 100% profit virtually in all that you buy, for each item was cheap, bulk buying cheaper.

So once again we were now starting a new venture, and boy did it take off. The money we earned now warranted our every working hour, and had chances even to make up on our losses, to think that just on that Saturday prior we'd told Leslie that it would be our last, for I had to work hard on the sports ground for little money and could ill afford to lose any more. Leslie was so delighted that we were going to hang on and try something else. Our great happiness however was soon short-lived, for to my astonishment a letter arrived from Leslie Golding – he had no choice but to write it officially to say that we must refrain from selling hot dogs as the aroma was upsetting the bowlers on the green downstairs.

Debbie and I were devastated, for we'd now found a formula that worked. The Police and Firemen were very angry about the bowlers attitude, and if put to the vote the bowlers would have been vastly outnumbered. By this stage Deb and I were asked to cover for all the evening fixtures too, again, Police and Firemen.

Leslie declined to say too much, for he was the poor chap in the middle, but we just knew he was upset, for he was so pleased with me and Deb, and we solved the problem of them perhaps in calling in outside caterers.

Leslie said that we could carry on as we did before we started doing hot-dogs, but we had to decline his kind offer, for Deb and I had been working at a loss. I still have Leslie's letter to us, and to this day find the bowlers back then so pathetic. The bowlers never ever ventured to buy anything from us, but always came up the stairs for the hot water

– they'd always done this anyway since my first day at Wadham, they'd boil their water for their tea, and there was always plenty of hot water for them to wash up, so assumed they bought their own eats, therefore they didn't need us, but they were determined to put us out of business and they succeeded.

One little story was concerning my aunt and uncle's very elderly neighbour – I heard chaos ensuing and I somehow opened the neighbour's door, the old man had a fire. I never saw flames, only thick grey smoke, and I made my way down the hallway and this dear old chap with grey hair and bushy beard appeared through this dense smoke holding a frying pan. I helped him out to the front garden, he walked slowly, and seemed completely unmoved by his trauma! The fire brigade came, but I have no idea how the saga ended.

My very last story about Wadham Lodge, and a chance meeting with a couple whom I befriended from my first year at Wadham up to the time the lady died in 2004. I had been marking out some lines on the hockey pitch that had a chain-link fence to the car park, and ran the length of the cottages along Brookscroft Rd.

All of a sudden a chap in his mid to late sixties said, "Hello, have you seen one of these before?" The man showed me a stag beetle that was living in his garden! (How many of those in Walthamstow now, let alone then?!) The man introduced himself as Arthur Golding, a retired electrician, and his dear wife Queenie soon came out into the garden for a chat; their house was on the top right-hand corner of the hockey pitch.

Their garden was a style I loved, real cottagey, with all the twists and turns, not knowing what's round each corner, all arches, trellis, climbers, in fact a real cottage garden. Over the weeks we got to know each other more, for we all loved gardening and nature, and soon I was getting cups of tea from Arthur and Queenie as well as Alf Andrews. I was 'swimming' some days!

I really liked this couple, they were genuinely friendly unlike the bowlers nearby! One day Queenie and Arthur asked, "Would you like to come round with your girlfriend (Debbie) one evening to see the garden properly?" I didn't need telling twice, so took Deb to meet them, we all got on so well, considering the vast age difference of us all. This became a regular thing from then on.

Arthur and Queenie were quaintly old-fashioned, inoffensive, and humorous. Arthur did silly, silly things – he'd be out of the room and come back in with perhaps a tea cosy on his head, and say "Queen, Queen, look at me!" Queenie would turn and laugh, call him a silly ol' fool etc. We'd all be laughing, for Arthur was a tall chap, so did look comical with that cosy on his head.

He'd show us little items that he'd painted amateurly like a salt and pepper cruet set or whatever. They both couldn't have children, but fostered a niece for a few years; the reason we never asked. They both longed to see that little girl again, but never did, how sad, for that little girl never knew that Queenie and Arthur died in their nineties. They also had a nephew who was a pop singer called Bick Ford. They used to proudly show us photos of him in 'pop pose', in a pop music book (magazine?).

A sad time came when Queenie and Arthur decided that they wanted to move out into the country, after seeing houses being advertised on TV's Eamonn Andrew's show, so put in for one and got it. The house was in Bretton, Peterborough. I helped them move, and travelled up in the back of the removal van with them, and helped with all the unloading, hence the removal men took me more or less back to my doorstep back in E.17.

We visited them many times over the years, taking each of our children to see them, and to see Arthur's antics! Their garden, like in Walthamstow, was created in similar fashion, and No. 3 Norburn, Bretton, Peterborough became a delightful cottage garden. They were so pleased with their little place overlooking lovely fields that they called it Great Bretton!

Arthur painted large garden canes a pale green and affixed them to walls and fences for climbers, and grew the climbing 'Masquerade' rose over the arch that led from the living room door to the back garden. The rose sprawled from the arch over their front room window onto the now painted canes – it looked a picture and set their house off a treat.

Queenie (Margaret) and Arthur were quaintly old-fashioned and enjoyed their life, they'd talk to all age groups and even yobbish teenagers endeared to them.

Arthur… like me… enjoyed wrestling and matches were held very close to their home. Queenie and Arthur were the nearest thing Deb and I had to grandparents. They genuinely enjoyed our company and we certainly enjoyed theirs.

Peterbrough, or lat least the Bretton area, was a real credit to the local council during the '70s for every nook and cranny was filled with trees, shrubs and flowers, the local motorways of the A1 had their banks crammed with ground cover shrubs etc. I was that impressed, I penned a letter to the council and said that I'd love to work for them if we moved that way.

The council had made many open parks, with outdoor swimming pools, boating lakes etc., swings and slides galore.

Sadly, as the years went by, Queenie and Arthur's lovely views of fields etc. was swallowed up by housing; they thought the view would be theirs to enjoy for many a year. It soon got to their ears that all the over-spill of London (Battersea was mentioned) was moving in, and lovely houses, all new, were trashed, many set fire to. Vandalism, muggings, rapes were all vastly gathering speed as in most towns and cities. We were soon put off from moving to Bretton, and noted the sadness in both their faces of what was going on all around their cosy little house. ('Thank you' lawmakers.)

We always tried to visit them at least twice a year if funds allowed, but our pens were always out. Usually Arthur did the writing, but either of them would ring for a chat. We were devastated when Arthur died, and Queenie a few years after, they'd been together for sixty-odd years.

We lost two very good friends, thankfully they had well deserved long lives and enjoyed it, after all life is a real gift, more precious than gold.

When I think about them in 2008, to think that our friendship started way back in the '70s at Wadham Lodge, when Arthur showed me that Stag Beetle, who would have thought that this would be the start of an everlasting friendship that would go on for years, so thank you Wadham Lodge for bringing Arthur and Queenie to us!

One in the Eye for Me!

Earlier on I wrote about the dangers in the garden; one I did forget to mention was when I went to cut back a youngish plant of Euphorbia 'Wulfenii' that grew in a crack between a fence and the path, it had been a seedling from my main plant nearby. I had actually attended to the plant to cut off the dead bits and must have cut through a live green bit, and as it sprung back I felt a tiny drop of the white resin go into my eye.

As soon as it hit my eye, I was in dire agony, so rushed across to the outdoor tap which was mere seconds from where I was standing, splashed water in my eye to no avail, for in these few seconds the pain was truly excruciating. The pain was like a million needles being stuck in my eye. I was in such agony and could hardly see and lay on my bed, writhing in total agony as the pain heightened.

All this took place at ten in the morning, and the pain suddenly eased dead on seven-thirty in the evening. Needless to say, my advice is to wear goggles and moreso there most certainly should be a warning label on each and every plant sold. What if I'd cut through a thicker

356

stem and the droplet far bigger? What if it had been a small child or someone elderly? I really dread to think of the outcome. I'm very wary of all Eurphorbias and tell all my clients, who have them all about, my sorry tale as a warning of what will happen if you leave your eyes unprotected.

Reader... you have been warned!

Pretending Bonsai!

I have a very unusual crassula, Crassula 'sarcocaulis' and all the clients that I've met over many years who grow bonsais, I suggest that they use this crassula, because it really does look like a mini-tree, and moreso when those minute pink flowers smother it. Crassulas are for sale virtually in all garden centres, but in all honesty I've never ever seen this one for sale.

I Wanda what that Was?

Most of you have seen the lovely mauve Primula 'Wanda', an old cottage garden favourite, but had never in my life seen a curious version of it called Primula 'Wanda' "Hose-in-Hose". It was its usual colour but had the same type of flower growing out of the centre of the main flower. I don't know, and have never found out what Hose-in-Hose means – does it refer to the 'stalk' of the 'parasite' flower leading to the stalk of the main flower? I expect someone will enlighten me one day?

Variegated Beauty

One of the very best selling plants at my plant sales was Malva 'variegata' "Variegated Tree Mallow" also listed as Malva 'arborea', even back in the 1980s I was getting a fiver for it. I really do not remember how I first came across this plant, and never seen it listed in any gardening books, so knew nothing of what to expect.

I assumed it was a sun-lover, and it does seem to thrive on the driest of soils. I grew this plant in Walthamstow E.17, and it reached a height of four to five feet, and similar spread, and indeed was a quick grower, making 3 to 4 inch diameter of trunk girth, hence 'arborea' – tree like. In our Kessingland garden tucked in a corner, just the one plant made a six foot height and spread, and sold one to a man who lived in Northamptonshire, and his grew to a height of eight to ten feet.

The think I first noticed about this plant, apart from its very rapid growth, was the way the seedlings too had variegated markings on them before the true leaves appeared, hence instantly knowing it indeed was variegated and not the plain green version of no real interest.

As it grows rapidly, it sheds its leaves very frequently to then form the thick trunk, the nice pink mallow flowers appear later in the year, albeit masked a fair bit because of the stunning variegated foliage, the flowers of course being more noticeable on the plain green version. After flowering sometimes the whole plant will die as a typical biennial, albeit can grow to maturity from a mere seedling in one year!

I have been lucky on occasions to keep mine for a second or third year or more, with neat 'pruning' of the die-back to healthy nodes.

The seeds are reasonably easy to collect, but I just let mine drop where they fall, or shake the dead plant about to then get seeds to fall and grow in the oddest places. Although even without doing this, and could be the wind or birds, the plants come up here and there, some years more prolific than others.

My front garden is in a harsh spot facing north and east, and they even survive there much to my surprise, but wouldn't trust to this if you only had the one plant for the possibility is you'll lose it. I took a chance selling it at a fiver, but this helped pay for all my compost etc.

'Court' in my Front Garden!

A friend said to me "how come the police were in your front garden?" I said a passer-by must have called them." "But why?" my pal asked. "Well, I was only doing what it said on the seed packet." "What did it say then?" my pal asked. "It said, prick out every two inches!" – Sorry, reader, couldn't resist that one!

Instinct

In my many years of going out to estimate for potential work, you sort of know after talking to the people, that you are only there for them to pick your brains, for they more or less require a step-by-step guide from you on how you are going to go about the job, and then tackle the whole job on their own.

It's a difficult thing this, for when you're estimating and giving advice, you simply have to be honest, more so for the customer's peace of mind, and also to perhaps beat the previous landscaper who had been there before you, and no doubt one after you leave. If they hadn't been as descriptive as me, it's highly likely that I'd get the job. This is why I make sure in so-called passing conversation with the client, that I mention botanically certain shrubs, plants etc. in their garden.

I will often say, "Oh, I see you've bought Ampleopsis 'brevipedunculata varietata'," and carry on randomly like this as I walk round their garden. I then secretly hope that anyone else estimating hasn't got a lot of plant knowledge, yet should have if classified as a professional gardener, or advertising as a gardener, for someone who doesn't know their job properly can land up costing you a hell of a lot of money. Strangely though, I still don't necessarily get the job, so what *do* people want I wonder?

I Can Do Everything!

No! No! I don't mean me, heavens no! but I am talking about a client that I went to only once – read on, and you'll see why. A chap called me out to prune a very old neglected apple tree, the chap did accept my quote, so me and son Rowan set about the task – me doing the main pruning and restoration, Rowan applying tree-grease, 'painting' the cuts or 'wounds', spraying and loading up all the prunings.

The man sat just mere feet from us in his conservatory watching us, but watching us intently. When he made us a cup of tea the chap quite casually said that when the job was done, our services would no longer be needed, for he said that he'd been watching me carefully and he would be able to prune as good as me! He said that he could look at *any* job of work just once and would know exactly how to do it.

I couldn't believe my ears, for it can take a good few years to have the confidence and know-how on how to tackle any neglected tree or shrub, especially the first ones that you do. Pruning is an art, and I've only seen pruning carried out correctly about three times in the whole of my career.

A Refusal often Offends – Good!

A man asked me to prune his pear tree. "Just snip off the top, hack at the sides, that should do." I refused, to his astonishment, I said that if he had friends or relatives round, or a next-door-neighbour, perhaps watching or seeing the 'end job' my own credibility would go up in smoke. I said that I'd prune it properly or not at all. The man decided on 'not at all', so I walked away with my pride and honesty still intact. The chap was quite put out, a 'cowboy' would have found this their dream job!

I'll Get Me Coat Then!

Many years ago now at Pakefield in Suffolk, an elderly couple wanted their massive shrub border all restored to peak condition, a job of course right down my street. I was lucky to have the job accepted and really did look forward to starting on the project.

I needed a really big skip, so ordered one when leaving home that morning. Anyway, me and a labourer unload all the various tools needed for such a task, then to our horror, the elderly couple came out of their house, and readily putting on their coats, hats and scarves, they carried two chairs, sat down by the border and faced the shrubs. One of them said, "Right, now where are we going to start?" I was taken aback – what did they mean by WE! They were only going to sit there on a bitterly cold February day and watch us prune the shrubs! I thought, no way, it's bad enough when you see people peeking from behind the curtains or standing blatantly behind glass patio doors, without a thought of embarrassment.

So as quick as a flash I said to my pal, "Quick, Ian, put the tools in the trailer, I've forgotten something," all in earshot of the people just sitting there comfortably. They said, "you can leave all your tools here, they'll be alright," but again made the excuse about health and safety, and leaving tools about etc. They did their best to keep the tools there, saying that they could go in a shed. So, quick on my feet again I said that "the tools are now more or less loaded, see you when we get back."

My pal knew why we were doing a very hasty retreat, for he too thought it was odd on what they were doing, for later I said that even when estimating, there was no inkling that they'd be our audience, or not a hint that perhaps I could give them a shrub prune demonstration, or were there any questions on how I was going to tackle a mammoth task. It was all a bit weird really, for because of their ages of eighty plus, they were never ever going to tackle a job like this themselves, not now, or even on shrubs that do need a yearly prune. THE SKIP! Oh heavens, what about the skip I'd sent for? We raced home, got on the phone to the company, and his wife said, "he's leaving, he's just gone down the drive. I'll see if I can catch him." Thankfully he spotted her in the wing mirrors, and of course had to give explanations about the cancellation. Phew! that was a close one!

Strangely, the old couple never did ring me, I was certain they would, so perhaps they did actually realise that what they did was wrong, and should have gone about it in another way.

Get Knitted!

Every outdoor worker hopes they'll have enough work at least up until Christmas. One such job did come in, and I very much looked forward to commencing it. The job was for a lady who owned a knitting shop or wool shop, and the job was the clearance and then turfing and planting up of the garden that lay at the back of the shop.

It was a week before Christmas, and to commence on the Monday of that week, Christmas Eve was the Saturday, so knew that providing the weather held up, I'd have six clear days to do the job. As the job was accepted, I turned up at the shop at nine o'clock that Monday, and said to the lady that I was going to start that day. "No you won't," she blurted, "I can't have all that going on this week, I'm busy in my shop." I then tried desperately to get her to change her mind. I said that she wouldn't even know we were there, for we would be in the back garden even behind the stock room, and that she wouldn't even see us until the job was completed.

I also pointed out that I too had to be busy up until Christmas, so that like her, had a wage at the end of the week. I also explained that I carried each job out in order of acceptance, just as I had explained to the lady on estimating, and she of course was next, and just another working week for me.

I was annoyed with the lady, for now what was I to do? Well, I did lose that day's work, but luckily the next clients on the list welcomed me with open arms, so did get a wage after all.

The 'knitting lady' did ring me after Christmas for me to start her work. I had to say my bit once again, and said how totally wrong it was to turn me away that day, and how we would have worked away in her garden without anyone knowing we were there. She did say sorry, and I just said that I had a full diary, and couldn't fit her in until much later in the year – all lies of course, but she'd had no qualms about me not having any wages that week, only that she was too busy to worry about me. I look back now on how this job of work was memorable for all the wrong reasons, and another reminder on how so very difficult it is to deal with the general public, and things happen that you just don't expect.

When the lady asked me to carry out the work after Christmas I should have said, "Get knitted!"

We're Off Home!

Whilst still on the subject of the general public, I must tell you about another very strange incident that makes no sense at all. Once again I was called in to give an estimate for a garden restoration, the estimate was accepted and I gave them the date and time that I was to commence the work.

I'd been out early to get to the garden centre to buy all the necessary sundries to use on this job. I'd told the clients to expect me around nine o'clock. On my arrival (five past nine) I was shocked to be met with a tirade of anger from the clients, "What time do you call this?!"

Truly taken aback being spoken to like this I said, "I don't know, nine, just after, why ?" "You said you'd be here at nine, it's five past nine, if you say you're going to be here at nine you should be, if you'd said five past nine, then five past nine it should be." I, of course, retorted back, firstly explaining that I'd been out early getting all the materials for the job of work.

The clients didn't want to know. "We've got to go to work." I explained that it didn't make any difference to me, for I'd already confirmed with them last night that I was coming in today, the back gate was a wrought iron one, and no lock or chain on, and the people had already previously told me that they both worked and that the gate was always open, all of this I relayed back to them with their own words.

I also pointed out to them that if they'd already gone to work on our arrival, they wouldn't have known what time we turned up, and supposing the garden centre didn't have all of the sundries that I required, I would have had to go elsewhere to buy them. Supposing a client had rung me prior to going out, or a neighbour stopping to chat, or the car wouldn't start etc., I just could not see what their problem was. It would have been a different story had the gate been kept locked if the clients weren't at home, but this was not the case, I told them that I'd be there 'around nine', would they have been just as annoyed if I'd arrived say at five *to* nine?

Well, I'd had my say, so I turned to my labourer and said, "Right, we're off home!" My pal looked stunned, but he had been with me on more than one occasion when I'd had weird clients, so he knew when I said we're off home, that's exactly what we'd do!

At that point, I was still clutching the sundries that I'd bought for them, and my pal had carried some of the tools on our way into the garden. The clients looked so stunned that we were leaving, but now it was my turn to be just as awkward as they, and pointed out that we'd now lost valuable time, listening to them ranting on about a mere five minutes late, and me explaining myself, and the time it took with us arguing – was it all worth it? They actually stood in silence as they watched us go out of the gate. It truly was an unusual situation, and I try even today to understand their logic.

Deadly Michaelmas Daisies

When I was a lad in the '50s I remember Mum reading from her magazine and telling me about a man who had died after getting a mere splinter from Michaelmas daisy stems – he had caught tetanus. I've kept that in mind since a boy as you can see, I do have tetanus injections when needed and wear gloves when handling splinter type wood. There's a lesson I learnt from a very early age.

Short Story of Morning Glory

I fully understand why garden centres charge mostly high prices for shrubs, plants, trees, etc., but I can never understand high prices on very easy to grow plants that take no effort to produce, and often grow like unwanted weeds. Many folk out there truly don't know a buttercup from a tulip, therefore if it looks very pretty they'll buy it no matter what! As I've done a lot of propagating myself for my own plant sales, know what's easy to propagate and what is more difficult; you also get to know what takes the public's eye and make sure you have an everlasting supply of that plant.

Sadly though, with my eagerness to please the public that came to my sales days, I used to snip away at certain plants in my garden that were guaranteed to sell, and would eventually lose my own plant through relentless cuttings! whereas I should have let the plants build up for a couple or so years. For instance the rarely seen Trollius 'minus' and the more common Euphorbia 'palustris' faded from my garden through my relentless taking of cuttings. The Trollius I've never been able to replace, for I have forgotten where I'd bought it now.

One of my biggest shocks in the very late 1990s was when I entered a brand newly built garden centre where they clearly wanted to reap back money for all that had been spent on the new venture. The very first thing I spotted was a good few elongated pots (like those used in planting up Clematis) all with five, six foot canes in them, clasped at the top to make a wigwam effect, the plants in them were the easily grown, very cheap to buy in seed packets, "Morning Glory" or Ipomoea 'heavenly blue'.

All five plants in each pot had over-reached the top of the canes and in full flower, and because you could see that they were all greenhouse grown, instead of in the garden, the leaves were a lush, fresh, bright green, and smothered in the most beautiful blue flowers. Whereas in the garden grown to that height, the leaves would have been a darker green, less flowers perhaps, but in the greenhouse they were truly lovely.

The nurseryman knew that he'd sell all that he'd put out, especially the lot all standing together made a very spectacular sight indeed. The nurseryman had put a handwritten label on each one, with both the common and botanical names shown, but failed to point out that this plant would die by the end of the year, and the only way to get that display back was to collect its seeds, and do your own in a green house, albeit really is an outdoor plant.

My shock was regarding the price that the nurseryman was charging… twelve pounds per pot of five plants! As I say, you can pick a packet of *fifty* seeds for under two pounds and they grow at a speed too! Imagine too when the client gets the plants home and puts them in their garden, and to spot deterioration in vigour and flowers, whilst the plants acclimatise to their new positions.

The nurseryman no doubt still does the same today, and the pot plants even dearer, because he knows for certain that he will sell each and every one. I suppose you can't blame him really, for a nursery still has to try and survive during the bleakest of winter months, when not one single customer comes through their doors; that, and wet springs, summers and autumns, money has to be made when possible. There is also electricity to pay for, staff's wages, heating oil and a million other things to pay for to run even the smallest of nurseries and garden centres. As I have also said elsewhere in this book, other nurseries have picked up on single potted items, that once you could buy a tray of, and far cheaper, like say Shizanthus, Balsaam, Calceolaria, Cosmo, and many others that are made to stand out above all the other bedding plants on offer, and as I say all once sold in seed trays of various amounts.

I'll give you another for instance – a 'strange' but beautiful little plant just appeared from nowhere in my garden, just a single plant, I was baffled to see this plant and had no idea what it was. I looked at it more intently as it grew and realised it was the very easily grown Godetia, but you only ever really see it in many colours grown from a seed packet, but this little plantlet was on its own as its own thing of beauty, and had that been a pot plant, and without knowing what it was, I would have bought it!

It's funny how the public over many years all seem to adjoin certain plants, how one variety compliments another. Clarkia is always mixed in with Godetia, candytuft with Virginian Stock, or Virginian Stock with Night-Scented Stock (Mathiola 'bicornis') or Night-Scented Stock with Californian Poppy, for when these close at night the stocks open along with their heady scent.

Night-Scented Stock however, enhance any seed bed, for they add that extra splash of pink in early evenings of dull days. Tobacco plants too always enhanced any mixed border in the evenings, for they 'slept' all day, then evening time would come into full flower in all shades of pinks, the white of course being the most whitest of whites, along with their scent, and make a glorious effect. Try tall tobacco plants with tall

Cosmos, then watch for those extra splashes of colour as evening comes.

Ceiling Up the Past

When we first moved to Suffolk in 1987, I had a call from a lady in Southwold, a quaint virtually untouched seaside town. She hadn't long moved in, her husband had died, he had been a top surgeon in one of London's big hospitals. My wife Debbie came with me when it was time to estimate, at the lady's request, Debbie being someone to talk to whilst I nosed around the garden to price it up.

The lady gave me and Debbie a nice cuppa and asked us if we'd noticed the ceiling, which we had, for it was really outstanding. There were lots of portraits of young children's faces, each face looking down on you and their faces surrounded with a puff of cloud.

The lady said that a certain gentleman who lived there decided to paint the faces of every child who lived in Southwold at that time, and painted around the late 1800s early 1900s. The lady said that one of those children was still alive in 1987 and very much well into her late nineties.

The garden was the biggest shock, for the lady assured me that when she bought the property, the agent said that the garden hadn't been touched since sometime in the 1700s! this was most certainly true, for you couldn't take a single step to get into the garden, and would agree that at least half of that garden hadn't been touched since that time, but suspect an area that did look like an old vegetable plot had in fact been used in the 1800s for there was one of those ribbed dolly tubs up in a corner by an old wall, hence still full of water.

This was a very difficult job to price up, and by a miracle I got it right and didn't lose out as I was sure I would do. I had to order the largest skip possible, and I think capable of holding thirteen cubic yards of rubbish, we landed up filling two! They were massive skips and you couldn't see over the sides because of the height of them, at least they had a large drop front, these alone were heavy to lift.

In the centre of the garden (when we finally found the centre!) was a total mass of blackberry etc., and when we cleared that we saw a massive tree three to four foot girth of a dead ancient cheery tree, and wound tightly around this was a live old rose... a *really* old rose easily eight to ten inches thick, as were the honeysuckles and the clematis dotted around. No, none of these at that time when I was there dated from the 1700–1800s, albeit the original bit of the tree was, and I'll tell you why. The cherry tree... once I cut back all the roses and brambles growing through it, found that these were holding up this long disintegrated tree, and as soon as the rose etc. was taken off, this huge eight foot high stump literally fell to total dust. When we cleared it, the hole was huge, for of course all the root system had long gone and left deep depressions. It took six cubic yards of soil to fill this hole and level for re-turfing. This alone gives you some idea on the girth of the tree that once stood there long ago.

One last thing about this job concerns my helper at the time; it's hard to explain really about money, for as the years go on what was a lot of money then seems a pittance now. But I'll explain to you, the reader, how it was in 1987. My labourer was paid £20 a day, and only figuratively speaking told the labourer "by the looks of this job we'll be here for weeks!" The job however took just three weeks.

The job was hard graft, and as anyone who works for me knows that I give very generous breaks etc. and can grab a drink or eats whenever they like, even between the normal break times – good workers need looking after, and if it is hard graft which landscaping is, it makes the work a lot easier to face each day. I enjoy it myself too, knowing that we haven't really got set times to eat or drink.

This particular labourer was a good grafter, so I thought I know, I'll give him a surprise bonus. I said, "Here you are, mate, a surprise for you!" He undid the envelope to see that I'd given him eighty quid, but instead of him being ecstatic with this extra money, he said, "I thought there would be more than this, you said we'd be here for weeks." I really couldn't believe my ears, I had to explain that I had been figuratively speaking when on first looking at the jungle before me on first sight, and made that remark as anyone would on seeing such a sight.

I did take a guess that it would take three to four weeks, so I hadn't been far off in completing it in three, hence the bonus that I most certainly never needed to give, and after his remark, I wished I'd never given it to him, albeit deserved it. I can assure you the reader that I never gave him a bonus again, even though he did many projects with me thereafter.

There was one other occasion when I again used two of those massive 13yd skips, and that was when I had the job to prune, lop, cut back (call it what you will!) a sixty foot high laurel hedge of some age, and no chainsaws used either! The hedge was cut down to three feet high or so, and left multitudes of stumps. A few weeks went by and little green growths appeared all over these 'stumps' and trunks to grow on to be a neat laurel hedge.

When Clients Lie

Like an artist painting a picture, they recognise their own work, as I do when pruning and restoring an old neglected tree or shrub. I have my own methods and would know my work in an instant.

It grieves me so much when say, I have been going to a client for several years, especially after doing a restoration job on a shrub or tree to begin with, and be involved in the correct upkeep of them thereafter, to then go into their garden to commence work on those very same shrubs/trees and find that someone else (usually the client or one of their family or friend) has had a go on the said specimen and totally spoilt all my hard work.

I would spot in an instant bad pruning. The client of course doesn't know this, and assumes pruning is just pruning – a snip here, a cut there… so why then had I been attending their garden each year, do they think that perhaps I'd been doing the same? But you see, a year had passed since my last visit, and they had long forgotten what the correct pruning should look like, so they do tend to have a clip about during the mid and late summer months to 'tidy' rather than prune correctly.

Of course it goes without saying, and that is to point out to the client that someone's done a 'hacking' job, yet they swear that no one has touched them since I left the previous year. How could they lie so blatantly? I have to carry on and show them that this is not my pruning, nothing like it! You can see by their faces that they know I've caught them out, yet for some very strange reason don't admit that they or one of their family have had a 'chop' around. One or two over the years have confessed that they did 'have a go', and like those that don't admit it, I simply just have to show them how I know. The tell-tale signs are so easy to spot, for none cut to a clear clean bud, especially on roses where die-back always occurs above the bud because there's no bud past that bud, just a bit of green stem that can't sprout, so dies back thus affecting a healthy bud, thus continues the damage all the way down the stem.

Shrubs too are so very often pruned wrongly, and folk cut off the flowering wood that was meant for the following year, hence no bloom that year, and if they did the same the next year the shrub wouldn't bloom then either, and so on.

Changes

Gardening has changed drastically in my lifetime, and most of what I was taught has gone out of the window. Where once I could do my job without question, I now have to make sure that the ball is firmly in the client's court. Whereas years ago you were told to cut perennial plants down to ground level after flowering in say late autumn or early winter to stop pests and disease going onto the dead stems, I now have to give the client two choices – either do it the age-old way just mentioned, or leave all the stems to take the brunt of the frost.

There is though, logic in this, for if you do leave all your stems and spent flower heads on, and go out after a night's heavy frost, the stems and old flower heads have actually taken off frost that would have lain on your plant below. After all we do it with hydrangeas, the large mopped spent flowers do take the brunt of the frost, thus protecting the green buds beneath it. Okay, so most non-gardeners don't know this and just take off the old blooms leaving the buds on show, and yes still come into flower without that protection, but it is best to protect if you can in case of a very unexpected harsh winter.

Because we had two bouts of snow in early 2011, I hadn't had time to go into my garden to do any cutting back. I just happened to be on the phone to my aunt Rita to say that I was about to go out to the front garden (January) and cut down the old Michaelmas Daisies, "Oh, don't do that!" Rita exclaimed, the birds like the seed heads." Well, at that point, I hadn't seen any birds on the many dead stems of all sorts in the garden.

Rita turned out to be right! For that very next day there were five beautifully marked finches all excitedly pecking away at the Michaelmasses! Hence now will leave these intact until March-time.

In all our years here, 2011 sees me now trying a new aspect of gardening and experimenting on my own plot, more to take the strain off my back than anything else. I decided that everything would be cut down as usual, but the big difference this time would be to leave all the leaves.

Yes I could have used my leaf-blower, but there is a method in the madness, for a good few years ago now, I must have bought a plant or plants that had the seeds of the weed Speedwell, and like chickweed it forms its seeds and invades very quickly. It's only a real menace when the crocus and other small bulbs are at their best, for the speedwell tends to smother all of them.

The leaves will act as a mulch to help suppress the small seedlings, for in other years when actually using the leaf blower in early spring, noted that when the leaves were blown away, the seedlings beneath them were yellow and very weak, and considering that the leaves were not at all deep, proved that even a light unintended mulch seemed to work.

The leaves during 2011 will of course also rot down and give my soil a natural feed, so I'll very possibly do this every year now, for as gardening 'rules' change, I'll no doubt have to follow, like with cutting down of those perennials mentioned earlier, if modern-day gardeners say it's okay to cut them back when frosts have gone, so perhaps dead leaves protect the ground and plants from frosts and may not indeed harbour pests and diseases as we were always taught?

I will still put on my well-rotted compost on top of the leaves that sit on bare soil, this then would be a potential planting spot all naturally enriched.

I Refer to References

When I took that bold step to move to Suffolk at the age of thirty-nine, and try to start up a new business, I suddenly thought, hang on, Keith, you'll need references possibly, for no one knew of my capabilities. So just a mere couple of weeks before moving to Suffolk at Easter week, April 1987, thought I'd better get my pen out and ask some of my present and past clients if they would do a reference for me to show all potential clients until I get established.

There were literally hundreds of clients to choose from, so chose a mere handful and just hoped that they all thought I'd done a nice job for them. To my great surprise they all replied with the kindest of words and I'm certain that what they'd written greatly impressed my new clients and helped me with my new venture, which I was keen to start on in our new life by the sea!

As you'll see, I have omitted house numbers and telephone numbers, many of the people by now would now be either passed on or moved. Where you see an asterisk (marked as *) these are my up-to-date remarks, hopefully as further interest to you, the reader.

I will also include other writing, for on the 12th February 2011 my son Dale got down from the loft all of my photo albums of some of the work that I have carried out, photos I took at the start of a job of work to see all the jungles, plus half-way through a project to the finished job. These have sat in my loft since 1988 or thereabouts.

I really had a shock reading and looking at all the photos and the details that I used at the time to describe what the work entailed. Sadly, some of the photos I have forgotten to put in where the jobs of work were, or perhaps I did, but the glue is now drying up, and photos plus any wordings may have dropped out at some point?

I have also so surprised myself on how far I went on my travels to various jobs each day, and some of the places I thought I had never been there in my life! But photos don't lie, and I or a labourer are in some of the photos, so there's my 100% proof!

A good many of these photos scare me now, and really does show me how young and fit I was, for after *looking* through these albums I felt knackered! After this it really does explain why I have such an aching body now!

Yes, since 'The Beatles' I've had long hair, and still have today, but I've most certainly not been a so-called 'long-haired layabout' as I was thought to be most times re. people who didn't know me, or know nothing of my very, very hard-working life.

No, these albums have certainly been an eye-opener to me, so dearly hope they impressed all of my clients.

Clients Who Did Surprise Me!

Myra and James Fisher, late of Underwood Road, E.4, still to this day stand out above all other clients, and they truly wanted a lovely garden. Because as I've said you have to treat all clients with kid gloves, I treated Myra and Jim exactly the same... at first! I was quoting for the least amount of shrubs, plants etc. the minimal amount of fertiliser, composts and mulches, the smallest amount of rocks and alpines for the rockery etc.

I was however shocked in the nicest way possible, with Myra saying to me, "Now look, Keith, I want you to do this garden exactly as you would do your own," (I had to explain to Myra that that would never ever happen because finances would never allow it) "so create some of your dreams in my garden then!"

I was still being so very cautious, for I'd heard millions of times how people want a nice garden, but on the cheap. Right at the start I ran some ideas past Myra, "I like that idea, Keith, do it." "But that's quite expensive, it's only an idea." "Do it, Keith, buy and do what you want, I've told you that already!"

"Well, Myra," I said, "let's really start at the beginning to what I would do, I suggest painting all of your fences either deep green to give an eventual green background to all the plants even in winter, or indeed 'dark oak' to throw out all those vibrant colours of flowers, leaves or berries." Now Myra hadn't thought of the fence, for although all the fences were sturdy, they were tired and dry looking, I suggested a double coat, for the first coat is harder to put on as it always just sinks in, but the second or even a third coat, the brush glides across with great ease.

I then said that I would put on strong 'eyes' to affix wiring that would be set at six-inch intervals to the height and length of all the fences, these were in place so as I could affix any climbers or wall shrubs etc.

I showed Myra some unusual honeysuckles, jasmines, solanums etc., all nicely potted and all nicely clamped with those thin pieces of plastic that they use to tie in plants and shrubs these days, and showed her at first glance how to get 100% out of those newly bought plants.

All you do is lay the plants flat on the ground, undo the ties and take your time and unravel each stem, then plant your climber and carefully put each stem to the right wire, making a fan shape if you can, do the next climber and the next in the same way. Eventually they will merge together giving you either random colour or several varieties flowering at once which makes a superb backdrop to any fence or wall, thus also making use of every bit of space to add colour or greenery.

When you follow what I've suggested, you should now have a fair-sized plant for your money, for most folk just put in their climbers and keep the ties and cane(s) intact and just let the top growths carry on to be the main climbing parts.

Right, let's get back to Myra and Jim's garden... I carried on buying the dearest and the very best plants as Myra and Jim suggested, and me *still* not quite believing that I had a free hand, and just couldn't stop myself from saying, "but that plant would be £20 or whatever", all the time checking to see if it was still alright, as I got more and more into the job with a total free hand, realised in the end that Myra and Jim *really* did want a nice garden. No, the garden wasn't massive, in fact it was a modest plot that if money was spent on it, then it would be truly outstanding, and you could easily see an end to the job.

Jim loved fishing and had an interest in fish, so he asked me if I could put in a pond – a big pond! I asked if he'd like a concrete one or fibreglass, Jim chose the latter. The one I used to choose for clients, or 'suggest', I should say, was a shape called 'swordfish', for it had lots of ledges, twists and turns and petered off to a point, but as I say, Jim wanted a big pond, and the largest in fibreglass at that time was a rare ol' size called 'Pacific'. Yes, Jim could have had a much larger pond had it been in concrete, but space was tight, so we bought the 'Pacific'.

Boy! oh! boy! did I have to dig a large hole for it! and even when the sand was put in to cushion and level it and backfill with soil, there was still loads of soil left for me to create a large rockery full of large pieces of Westmorland stone, plus hundreds of ferns, alpines and rockery plants – it truly was impressive, and it was a rockery that you could view all sides, so by the time the water and bog plants had gone in, it all looked so natural as if it had always been there.

Behind the rockery I put in stepping stones with good quality pea-stone, plus planted a good mix of several weeping trees, i.e. Malus species, Pyrus, Prunus, cotoneaster, caragana etc., and beyond that on the fences, many varieties of clematis. I also put in an arch leading to this area, bird baths, bird tables were also added.

Each day when Myra came home from her part-time job, she insisted that I had a proper dinner! Every day I had mash, carrots, cabbage, peas, etc. plus a sweet, she just wouldn't hear of me just having sandwiches! I sat with Myra every day and our sole topic was the garden, with me blurting out more ideas and not once did Myra and Jim tell me to stop spending (unlike the big man at the top of his profession running one of our biggest banks, whom you read about earlier in this book).

After the back garden was completed, they wanted the front garden sorted out. This was the time that a dear pal of mine, Bob Maddison, had just completed his building course. Bob was a perfectionist builder, and built a lovely wall in Myra and Jim's front garden. They wanted the best so Bob was the man I chose for the job.

Bob and his lovely wife Jackie were our next door but one neighbours when we bought our first house in Chingford Rd. E.17. I remember Bob showing me some of the photographs of some of his work during training, and he showing me one particular photograph of a brick arch, but at 'ground' level, hence sort of shoulder-height, and showed you how an arch is made and how it stays up whilst building it, it was something that I had pondered over, yet the answer was simple – well, simple if you know how!

Sadly Bob died quite suddenly in his very early fifties, yet had been a keen football player, as well as a hard grafter on the building side of things. Bob and Jackie have four now grown-up children – Daniel, Scott, Ross and Glen.

Myra and Jim's only son, Paul, is my son Adrian's Godfather. Paul helped me and Deb out at Christmas time, giving us *lots* of little gifts for us to put in our children's Christmas stockings, and really helped us save Christmas, for I've had a life of lean times, but when you had a high mortgage and a million and one other things to pay for in winter, life was never easy. Paul had been our saviour over several years at that time. He is still a very good friend even today.

FIRE! And The Number One Garden

My late dear pal Vincent Crane (real name Cheeseman) co-wrote with Arthur Brown (of the band 'The Crazy World of Arthur Brown') the No. 1 hit single 'Fire!' in 1968, a song that blasted from nearly every teenager's bedroom at that time, to the great annoyance of their parents, with those first words of "I am the God of hell-Fire, and I bring you... Fire!"

When the band broke up around 1970, Vincent formed 'Atomic Rooster' and had a number one hit with 'tomorrow night' followed by 'Devil's Answer'. I was a roadie for Vince for some three to four years I should think, whilst between the long tours, I still carried on with my fairground work and landscape gardening – it was all hectic I can tell you! Thank heavens for youth and fitness I say!

Vince and the band were to start a world tour of around fourteen countries, and Vince said that all the wives and girlfriends of the band and road crew could come along, and we'd all be staying in five-star hotels exactly as we did in Great Britain. I sadly, much to Debbie's disgust, turned the tour down, as I have never had any particular yearning to want to go abroad, for this country has everything you could wish for regarding scenery and quaint villages and seaside resorts, albeit our weather is none too clever at times, as we all know.

Vince and his first wife asked me to landscape their garden at Belgrave Road, Wanstead. They would both be there for the start of the project to pay for all the materials, and perhaps fly back home from time to time to see how the job was going, plus to pay me, plus if further money was needed for any more materials, hence everything went very smoothly.

Vince had the greatest pleasure in telling me that I was being paid for my landscaping from the royalties that had just come in for the Crazy-World-of-Arthur Brown (L.P.)

All this time I had been looking for someone to work alongside me, and someone who was capable of building walls, paths and patios etc., a pal John said he could do it. Little did I know it, but he was totally clueless, and don't think he was even capable of building a sandcastle!

How Vince and his wife ever paid me, I'll never know, for I learnt a very good lesson at that time, and that is that I should have been shown some of his previous work, and spoke with his clients, but now looking back, I don't think he ever had any, and my work for Vince was the very first that he'd ever carried out.

The 'wall' that he built and the excuse for a 'patio' was a total disaster, for he stood each of the fancy blocks on an inch or so thick layer of cement, and NO pointing to the sides! When we all pointed this out to him, he tried to squeeze the cement in after, it was as you can imagine a total mess.

His crazy-paving path was set on sharp sand on soil, plus a basic point up, I was so, so, ashamed, for this was all of my such good reputation going up in smoke before my eyes. Thankfully my own work stood out as looking first class or all would have been lost. Had Vince and I not been good pals, he could have sued me for a lot of money, for I would have had to take the full blame, for I told them he was a good builder, but that was my own assumption. I never ever got caught out like that again; since then I closely vet all those that I truly recommend, more's the pity that Bob Maddison hadn't gone self-employed at that time.

Vince had a big garden at that time, all the weeds had to be skimmed off, and digging out deep rooted pernicious weeds too. The garden was far too up and down, so had no choice but to use a large Howard Gem rotovator, which I worked all day long until 10.30 in the evening. Vince had rigged up spotlights for me so that I could at least get the site well-rotovated, then hopefully commence the levelling and preparation from then on the following day.

Just the one thing marred our stay and that was when Vince's neighbours, two doors down, had made a complaint or should say accusation to me and John, for Vince one morning said that the neighbours had knocked to say that me and John had stolen all the meat and goods from a fridge-freezer that they apparently kept in a shed, and we supposedly had spotted the red light on the freezer when the shed door was open.

John and I were dumbfounded. Vince and his wife, plus me and John, kept glancing towards their shed in daylight hours, then again as dusk fell, then dark, and none of us ever saw a red light, nor for the three week duration of our stay. Those very same neighbours up to that point, had always given us a cheery wave or a hello whenever they saw us, but I and John most certainly put them in their place when we did see them again. I'm sure they realised their great error, for we did get a mild apology, more so when I made the suggestion that the police should be called, for this again was my business and reputation at stake here, and certainly didn't want Vince and his wife that we could not be trusted. No, that wasn't a good time.

That Thing Called Trust

I have touched on this subject elsewhere in this book, and the likes of me and many other tradesmen have to be 100% trustworthy when going onto or into other people's property.

I can only vouch for myself on this subject, so I'll relay some of the things that have happened to me, and once again we're talking about items worth mere pennies, rather than hundreds or thousands.

One year I had to restore an old cottage garden at Wrentham, Suffolk, some of this work entailed the restoration of fruit and ornamental trees. As usual I'd brought every tool possible that I'd need for such a project, but I did forget to put on board one very small item, and that was a two-inch paint brush to use to paint the fungicidal compound on the fresh cuts that I'd made with my pruning saw etc.

Now at this point of the job, it was the very last thing to do to complete the full thorough restoration of this lovely old neglected garden, and the lady was thrilled. I then asked the lady if she had an old paintbrush or indeed a new one that could be cleaned easily after I'd finished with it. I told her that any sized small brush would do, any size up to say three inches.

The lady now seemed a bit put out to my surprise, but she did find several really old brushes in her well-stocked neat and tidy shed that was full of all sorts. I painted all the 'wounds' therefore as I've said, the final end to the two-week project. I then proceeded to load up all my tools, just as the lady was leaving to walk to the local farm shop, and bade me a goodbye and a thank you for all my wonderful work.

In mere minutes, the lady came back, with a furrowed frown as if I'd done something wrong and suddenly blurted out, "you haven't got my paintbrush have you!?" I was taken aback by her attitude, so I retorted, "no, I don't think I need your old paintbrush; I've put it on the kitchen step." She was taken aback, shocked and surprised.

To think that I'd been there all of two weeks and took anything out of that shed. I assured her again that I wouldn't have stolen her paintbrush. When I think of all the skill that I'd put in restoring this garden, yet if I'd walked off with a small paintbrush she was prepared to think the worst of me.

A good few years down the line (2008), I had a call to cut a large lawn, and restore flower borders etc. for an old couple in their mid-nineties. I asked them if there was anywhere for me to plug in my electric hedge trimmer, and assumed it would be a power point in the house, but no, they pressed a button and their garage door opened. The garage itself was quite empty, except for a fridge and fridge-freezer, and a handful of basic gardening tools.

After I'd made my third or fourth visit there re. doing the lawn now on a very regular basis, the old chap said, "Have you taken my watering can?" In a very accusing voice, so I said, "I haven't taken your watering can, nor have I ever used it, in fact I've seen it once and it was with your other gardening tools." I also told the old chap that if I wanted to use any tools I'd ask first! The watering can I remember being one of those very cheap plastic affairs from the usual tacky stores. I also had to point out that I use only my own gardening equipment, unless I'd forgotten to put on a certain item that day, and only then would I need to borrow a client's equipment. Strangely, no more was ever said, and now a good few years down the line, I'm still working for these people.

I was fuming at the time, and nearly went out and bought half a dozen watering cans for the man to prove a point, that I'd sooner give him something rather than take it.

Now we reach November 2010, and again a huge restoration job was accepted, and again for a very elderly couple; the ol' chap was completely housebound, but the lady was fairly sprightly. My youngest son, Dale, helped me this time, for this truly was a very neglected garden. On job completion the lady paid me, we had the very last load of rubbish to take away, so told the lady that I'd be back in the morning to pick up all of my tools that were in her shed.

The next morning, I knocked on the door to let the couple know that I'd arrived, but was greeted by the lady with a stern, "What on earth have you done to our shed!" Once again I was taken aback at yet another accusation, so I retorted, "What shed?" for there were two – one where we'd kept our tools in the dry for the duration of the project, the other was a shed at the bottom of the garden that had been almost totally masked with large shrubs and well-overgrown climbers, bellbine and blackberry etc.

It was the latter shed that she was referring to and again she exclaimed, "What have you done to the roof?!" I told her that I or Dale hadn't done anything to the roof whatsoever, but had to point out that I had to pick up all the fallen rotting felt from amongst all the old shrubs and blackberry, and most have rotted off a few years ago by the state of it. The lady still looked at me as if I was lying my head off, so once again I had to say my bit, asking for what would I gain by taking roof felt from a shed? and also pointed out that there was even more felt that had slid off at some point behind the shed too, but I couldn't reach behind the shed to retrieve it. I also told the lady that how come even when we were clearing the dense area, she hadn't spotted the missing felt, for it was so obvious to see.

I came away once again feeling guilty, for she still thought that I'd taken that old felt off the roof. About four months down the line, I got talking to a lady whom I knew, and she asked how work was, and then out of the blue she said, "that was such a fantastic job that you did for Mr and Mrs...... what a huge difference!" So I naturally said, "do you know these people then?" and she said, "yes, I'm a care worker, and it was me that put your name forward." So I thanked her, but without hesitation I told her how the job was marred by an accusation. "Ah, the shed roof!" she said. "So she told you that I'd damaged the shed roof did she?" and the lady nodded.

I then explained to this lady about the masked shed roof drenched in climbers etc., but the lady stopped me mid-stream. "Keith, don't worry, I know you did no wrong, this can be a problem when working for the elderly, and when they can't get about they imagine all sorts." This of course did put my mind at rest, but if the old lady had told the carer on what I had supposedly done, who else had she told?

I'd hoped that other folk had seen all the real hard graft that had gone on, rather than thinking I'd just out-of-the-blue randomly torn felt from a shed roof!

One last thing that I have found is so weird, and that is over many years since going self-employed, how several clients make a point of telling me that their son, husband wife or daughter is a policeman/lady – is this supposed to be a pre-warning to me? for very rarely to any of my clients tell me what they or their relatives do for a living. I don't need to know, so I wonder why a fair few of my clients had felt the need to tell me that their kin are in the police force, it's a real baffler!

Lift Your Buttocks Up!

Sorry, I meant Buttercups! I'm now going to tell you how I rid an herbaceous perennial border of the fast growing, thick creeping buttercup. This was in Woodford Green, Essex, many years ago now, and the people didn't want me to use a weed-killer.

This was at the time of course when PEAT wasn't a dirty word, and over the years I'd used tons of it to not only plant new trees and shrubs to get them going much quicker, but also as a superb mulch, which was so easy to weed when weed seedlings grew on it, for they were so easily removed, for they had no real grip. Irish moss peat and particularly dark Somerset peat were used as effect to enhance the flowers as well as any colourful greenery.

Luckily for me there were very few plants and shrubs in this border, so once I dug them out I commenced in washing the roots thoroughly, to rid every scrap of this weed menace. Creeping buttercup throws out lots of runners just like a strawberry, and wherever the tip of the runner sets, off it goes again, putting out new roots as it goes.

This weed, like most others succeeds well in clayey or sticky soils, where it takes a good firm hold and very difficult to eradicate. The border that I was to now work on had these harsh conditions, but there was a plus in my favour, and that was that the sticky muddy border was some nine to ten inches below the grass edge.

The buttercup had also grown into the grass edge/lawn, so had no choice but to use a selective weed-killer on this, for as I explained to the people, if I didn't kill this off it would most certainly throw its long runners back onto the border as it indeed was doing!

Now to the task of ridding this border of creeping buttercup, and the method was so simple. We're now going back to the days when Irish moss peat was sold in really large bales, and called GROWER, and meant to be sold to growers and landscapers only, and those directly involved in agriculture, but moreso horticulture.

I remember too how fit I was when I was a young man, and lift them to put them on my shoulder and carry them from A to B. The grower bales were eventually sold too for the use of the public, but 99% of people either couldn't move them or have the transport to cart them at a later date, lorry drivers too refused to handle them, that was one of the reasons that I was told was due to their demise.

For this job of work I loaded and delivered sixteen of these huge bales, and if I chose them very carefully, for when the machine that loaded the peat in the first place had given extra pressure for some reason, made a lot of the bags extra fatter with a lot more peat, and of course very much heavier too!

All these bales were put on the border, with raking and treading, the vigorous buttercup eventually buried beneath it all. When this was done, all we could do was to leave it for 4–5 weeks and see what would grow through, and yes, a good amount did die through the lack of light, but the rest of it wanted to survive, so pushed its way through the very thick peat, to then draw itself out of the sticky soil into something far better to make even more vigorous growth. It's at this point that you say "gotcha!" for now the roots were released from the stickiness and could then be pulled out so very easy.

Although the peat did sink a little, and of course eventually work its way into the 'soil' and much later, a good few ton of good fine garden grit, then lastly I topped the border up with eighty bags of good quality compost, before finally planting up and not a weed nor buttercup to be seen anywhere!

If you do have the patience like those particular clients, and listen to and take advice, the result is a good one.

Another way round this particular job would have been to cover the whole area with black plastic and old carpets, but this method can take a year or more to work, and if the weeds were 'bellbine', 'couch grass' or convolvulus and the likes, these would thrive in such conditions, so you'd need really to use a mulch to get rid of such weeds.

As an example, I managed to get rid of every scrap of 'couch grass' from a then two-foot wide rose border in my own front garden. Firstly I made a 'box' effort to enclose the peat; I put a 1ft 6" high board against the picket fencing to stop the peat falling through, then in front of the border. The roses stayed put, and I simply put in loads of peat, and kept it topped up each month.

I commenced doing this at the very start of the growing season when everything was vigorous and on the move! The couch grew and grew, and once again to survive from the dark base of the peat, grew out of my soil, into the friable peat, and gently pulled; the strands of roots were immense, and by the end of September of that year the lot was gone. What about the roses I hear you say? The peat was piled high round these too, and none came to any harm. The reason why I kept the peat at least halfway up all the stems, was to make certain that every piece of couch grass grew out from in between the roots of the roses, and grow into the dense peat toward daylight, hence once again I could say "gotcha!"

I Will Survive!

To do a job like the above would maybe a little more costly to do today, for peat supplied in those old 'GROWER' bales are no more, and peat had always been fairly cheap to buy. Today you'd have to use alternatives.

Sadly, though, alternatives are not only not that cheap, but also sold in not too big a bag, hence not much for your money, therefore peat is still sold today.

I have experimented a lot in the garden over the years, usually trying things out on my own plot first to see what the success rate is. Most older trees, shrubs, climbers, and conifers, when an age, and like us all, don't like to keep picking up sticks and moving! I have tried several things over the years to try and keep plants alive if having to be moved at say the wrong time of the year, or indeed shrubs, plants etc. that truly resent root disturbance.

Conifers in particular and most things in the 'Pea' family, really don't move well even when remotely established, let alone long term. I had to build a pond and rockery years ago for my friend Rod Dott, a brilliant builder with his pal Andy. In the way of this pond was a prostrate type conifer that I identified as Juniperous 'Pfitzeriana'. Rod liked this 4x4 spread conifer and asked me if it would move okay. I told Rob that the conifer is not the easiest by any means, but I had done some experiments with these and had a fairly good success rate, far more than I expected. The method I used was to obviously dig a bigger hole than was needed to take the root system, and not using any of the soil that was taken out, and to plant solely in fresh compost, using as many bags as was possible. Then keep moist at all times.

I've found that the lovely soft, warm, friable compost, made those so fine fibrous roots form very quickly and ensures then hopefully the survival of your previous plants. Many of us have had to move in the summer months, and the wrong time to lift your favourite shrubs, roses etc., so follow all that I have suggested.

If you move say evergreen shrubs, they usually have a thicker leaf, so do hold moisture in those leaves far easier, so still use my method shown, unless they are acid soil lovers, you'd have to use *ericaceous* compost instead, but keep that compost moist at all times until you're very certain your plant has survived.

When it comes to roses being moved, take off every single flower and bud, plus any soft now drooping growth to the more solid part of the stem, and plant once again in just compost and no garden soil – this can be added back when you know your plant has made it.

I use the same method again on climbers and other shrubs when it comes to moving perennial plants except those with thicker leaves (like say pinks etc.). Just simply cut the plant down exactly as you would in winter, and once again plant solely with good compost, and keep moist!

The 'Judas Tree' is in the 'pea family' (Leguminosae) and one that rarely survives a move, as does 'Broom' or Cistus (rock rose) or (Sun Rose) – Broom is Cytisus. I'd bought a large specimen of 'Judas Tree' some 5ft x 5ft for a special client of mine for her birthday (Iris Jones) of Darsham, Suffolk – and when she moved to nearby Yoxford, she wanted to take the tree with her. I assured her it would die, unless she wanted me to take a chance on one of my 'experiments', and she was prepared to take that chance.

Once again I dug a decent hole, planted the tree/(shrub at this stage) and sure enough die-back came very quickly, then new growth came a little, then more die-back elsewhere. The following spring I cut back even more dead growth, and tested to see if the rest was alive, an easy test this, just scratch the bark in several places – if it's green and sappy, the wood is live, if the stems are rattly and sap dark green, dry and non-sappy or brown, the chances are that part is dead too.

This shrub grew in fits and starts from then on, until the shrub after three to four years finally settled down again. No doubt the good compost got new fibrous roots going again, along with moisture, and a feed every 2–3 weeks or so, ensured its survival.

I did try to save an eight-foot high white lilac that a client didn't want – it was an old one, and although it did flower each year, each year too, great lumps of it would die. It gave up the ghost after exactly five years, this was the classic case where this shrub truly resented root disturbance.

In my own garden now, I have a Magnolia and Camellia that were discarded in two separate gardens; the Magnolia has had the biggest struggle to survive from a multi-branched specimen to now a single stem; the Camellia has had some scary times too in its bid to survive, but now seems to have settled nicely now. Again it's taken both shrubs seven or so years to pull through.

Rather than discard altogether it's worth giving a shrub etc. a second chance. Except where stated, remove all leaves, flowers and buds from any moved shrub, it then builds up energy.

The Oddest Bonfire!

As you've read, I've had some pretty weird jobs of work over the years; one of those jobs of work was travelling with my then labourer Rob (now a priest) from Walthamstow to Orpington, Kent each day. We of course had to have a very early start and a very late finish, before that long drive home, go right over to North Chingford to drop Rob off at his mum and dad's. Rob was still a teenager back then. I had to then drive all the way home to Walthamstow, get some sleep, then over to Rob's again, then off to Orpington.

I did this for a good three weeks or so as I remember, and the job was a sad one really, for the couple wanted every tree, shrub, plants etc. totally got rid of, and turn all these beds back to lawn, and to make a good level so that the new turf joined in with the old lawn.

As you can imagine, all these massive patches stood out like a sore thumb, along with other tinier patches where single specimens had stood just the day before. The whole garden now was put back to lawn. I don't think it was because the couple hated flowers, but they both worked and had very busy lifestyles, therefore much easier to run a mower over the grass, giving them perhaps more free time when they were home.

I was later on contacted by a property developer to turf a back garden in Muswell Hill, London. Strangely the area that had to be levelled and turfed was void of any weeds, and just barren ground where a lawn I assume once grew. We found that we couldn't dig it for the ground seemed solid with roots, and all from the very many trees that were in that garden.

Because of the look of the plot, it did look like the whole area had in fact been weed-killed at some point, but certainly not recently. I had no choice but to hire a large rotovator, and I'm glad I did, for this churned over the, luckily, very dry ground. Our surprise came when the rotovator brought up tons of fibrous roots, there were just a few 3–4 inch thick roots, but not many.

When we started to rake to prepare the level, we just raked fibrous roots only, it was very odd indeed, hence had a large bonfire of just fibrous roots, and boy did it take a time to burn! So much root came out that the level for the new lawn was now a fair bit lower, so we had to barrow through several cubic yards of topsoil to build the level up again.

The owner was very understanding at this unusual predicament, and paid me more money for our great effort. It turned out as I suspected – the garden had been totally neglected for very many years, in fact as much as thirty years as I remember being told. I've worked on very many totally neglected gardens in my time, but I've never ever come across a garden containing just fibrous roots and it's never happened again.

Steam Roller Rotovator!

One of the first lawns that I ever laid as a very young man, when doing private work and the same time being employed, hence still working on my weekends etc. I had a job of work accepted at a place called High Beach, in Epping Forest. I'd heard a lot about Essex clay, but hadn't really come across it at that point, that reason being that I hadn't done enough private work in that area to really know of its existence.

That time did come on this job. The clients wanted a nice new lawn on an area that had been an unsuccessful veg. plot and it wasn't long before I found out why! The soil didn't look too bad at first glance, but because the ground was so up and down I had no choice but to hire a rotovator; this was a bad move, for the soil turned out to be sticky soil and the rotovator then fetching up clay, thick yellow and grey clay.

The rotovator blades clogged up solidly, so much so that you could no longer see the blades, the blades now sliding all over the place, and now looking like the front of an old steam road roller!

Rotovating was totally impossible, and as a then young enthusiastic gardener, I had to put my thinking cap on and see how to overcome this great problem. I was certain that others would have given up. I remember distinctly all these years later, standing at the plot and thinking of my best move.

I decided to order in a few cubic yards of soil to backfill the deepest of the ruts, plus to part build up the rest of the plot. Then came my brightest idea, and that was to order in a good few tons of sharp sand, we barrowed it all on the plot willy-nilly, and just pushed the piles very basically with a rake to knock down each pile to lightly disperse.

Once all the sand was in, it was like a miracle forming in front of us. The sand was fully spread, now we could easily tread the area as the sharp sand bit into the clay, and no clay now sticking to our boots. We could now at last use both sized heavy garden rollers, and the area became as flat as any bowling green. All I then had to do was dust the area with bone-meal, make a 'key' with a rake so that the turf could get a nice grip. The finished job was superb.

Once again I was lucky to have very understanding clients, who had to have the extra expense of not only materials but labour too. They wanted a lawn come what may. But as you've read in this book, other clients would not have been able to or prepared for any hidden problems. The sharp sand addition has got me out of so many scrapes over the years, and I have and still have confidence that I can prepare any lawn on rough ground.

Many years ago in Walthamstow, my doctor came to me with a problem! No, not a health one, but a garden one! I went along to have a look, he too had borders that were made up of sticky and clayey soil, and only a few shrubs and plants managed to brave the conditions, so the large border was pretty empty.

Once again it was down to adding a good few tons of not only sharp sand, but also alpine or fine garden grit, all good ingredients to eventually break up any tough garden 'soil'.

The real test later on is when you start planting your spring and summer bedding plants, for as the sand and grit gradually works its way in, the more friable and easier to use becomes your soil. I forewarned that his garden would look like Brighton Beach once all the materials were down, but once it was down, you could then mask it with (then peat) well-rotted horse manure, pine-bark (½" type) and bags of compost, plus in subsequent years to still add a sharp sand, alpine grit mix, to keep that ground workable.

It is always a great pleasure to see the joy on clients' faces when you've solved a problem for them, and they'd not known which way to turn. Because the sharp sand method was so successful that very first time round, in *every* estimate thereafter, I always wrote that – sharp sand may be needed if ground is sticky, clayey, too wet, or it rain falls prior to or commencement of laying your lawn – thus the client had to be prepared for that possible extra expense. Another alternative in latter years that I use and that is sandy sub-soil – it rolls out and sets like concrete yet a touch of a rake, you can make a 'key' so easily.

My Dad's Headed Paper

My dad was a brilliant architect, and I feel so honoured that I still have three of his headed note paper; they read as follows re. the order that I think he worked, i.e. when he was in Chelmsford we were still living at Harold Hill, Essex. They are as follows:

BARON, NICHOLS AND PARTNERS
Chartered Architects
139 London Road, Chelmsford. Telephone 51979

WALTER NICHOLS A.R.I.B.A.
Chartered and Registered Architect
8, Chippenham walk, Harold Hill, Romford, Essex
Tel: Romford 562

WALTER H.E. NICHOLS A.R.I.B.A.
37 Bernwell Rd., Chingford, Essex
Telephone: Silverthorn 0535

When Your Back is turned...

I was working for a couple who lived at Ainslie Wood Gardens E.4, and yet another garden restoration job, and just random large old shrubs had to come out and not restored (customer's choice); a large skip was needed. Me and my labourer saw the skip arrive, which was great timing, for we were ready to start loading it. I got the money for the skip to pay the driver. As soon as we'd done that we went straight into the back garden and loaded a barrow each, taking less than fifteen minutes I should think, when we got to our skip that was most certainly empty on its arrival only moments previous, was now a quarter full! We just couldn't believe our eyes, we rushed in to tell the clients, who too were shocked with our findings, and we said that we would have to take out the rubbish from the skip and leave it in the road, for we needed every bit of space in that skip as possible.

Both me and my labourer yelled out to hopefully reach the ears of the culprit(s), that we were taking the rubbish out. Now whether the culprit(s) walked or came by van or car we can't say, but it had to be someone very close nearby to spot the arrival of the skip and put rubbish in so quick in so short a time.

Breaking it up!

Mrs Mcnamara, Woodford Bridge, Essex, a dear lady who so loved her garden, but age was no longer on her side, she openly said that she wasn't well off, but the garden did look bad, she asked me for an estimate. I then surprised her when I said that I could do the job in three stages for her. Her face started to light up, "How would you do that then, Keith?" I'd then explain that I had always worked this way, for then it suits the client's means (pockets!) and guarantees future work for me. "I'll give you an overall price for the two large borders either side of the garden, and a price for the back border. If you can afford the lot in one go, then so be it, but if it really is too much for you we'll break it up to three stages over three years. I'd do the left-hand border thoroughly for you first and make it so easy for you to maintain thereon, the other borders can't get much worse in the forthcoming two years, hence will do a border a year, and thereafter you'd probably never need to call me in again."

And… that's exactly what we did!

Clear Off!

One of the strangest jobs that I only got half way to do, was the total clearance of a garden some 800 feet long, and as wide! and have the photos to prove it, along with almost a mountain of rubbish!

It was literally a hands and knees job, with each of us with a spade each to skim off this long old overgrown lawn and borders, and supposedly re-turf and plant up.

We cleared the whole garden, and never got any further, for he told us not to come back! me and my pal thought about this for weeks after, for what on earth had we done? for the job could have been done quicker if we'd used a mini-digger, but that had been out of the question since day one, for the side entrance was all rubble and deep holes everywhere, with just a single scaffold board that you had to literally balance on getting from the front garden to the back, and vice versa, all the house was like a builder's yard, so had he literally run out of money! for we would have had to have around six eight-yard skips or more to put all the rubbish in, plus our labour time to get it there, then there would have been the cost of the massive amount of the actual landscaping, the rotovating, levelling, hundreds of turf and possibly plants for any new borders.

When I look at these photos today to see all the really hard graft that we'd put in, okay we got paid for all that we did do, but our 'dismissal' if you can call it that had had me baffled since that time in the mid 1980s.

The strangest thing of all is that the man always sang our praises, yet so very serious and a man of few words when it was time to say time up – or – clear off!

Wages Were a Sin!

Well, readers, there's an insight for my Head Groundsman's wages, running the Orient F.C. and their training ground. (See the following pages.)

A Moment's Thought!

And that's all it was! I nearly went into agriculture instead of horticulture, for Mr Khunes(?) our gardening teacher at school, really wanted me to go to the Writtle Agricultural College, Essex, and I truly believed I would.

When I attended the day release at the North London College at Mornington Crescent, Camden Town, we did have a few outings to different colleges and gardens, and indeed we did go to Writtle, and shown all over the college and their gardens, and was surprised too that gardening and greenhouse work was much to the fore as the agriculture. I was impressed, and certain (?) it was there that I saw a huge Camomile Lawn.

We were each given a slip of paper, which I still have. (See following pages.)

How Dare You!

An estimate is only an estimate, and a quote just a quote, and nobody is under any obligations whatsoever. So then, you'll be surprised on the abuse that I got from the man, who was the son of the lady whom I sent my estimate to, "How dare you charge my mum all that!"

I couldn't believe my ears, so I said, "I can charge anyone what I like, you don't have to accept it, I haven't insisted your mum has the work done!" and so a slanging match ensued. I said, "If you were normal you'd get three, four or more quotes, you don't just read one then lead off with a tirade of abuse, you can now most definitely go and find someone else, and when each of them quotes you... hold your temper!"

One of my early business cards after leaving Springfield Park.
The phone numbers were of my aunt and uncle, Rita* and Jack Fryett
(*née Ridley) and my dad's number too in Woodford Green. I had no
phone, yet I was still looking after my mum.

**One of my business cards whilst I was the Head Groundsman at
Wadham Lodge,** E.17. I always worked on my day off, I was always
working. The phone number here was that of Wadham, for the secretary
Les Golding, gave me permission to use that number... hence, keep
ringing! for it was likely that I'd be on the field somewhere.

ORIENT FOOTBALL CLUB

TELEPHONE NUMBERS
01-539 1368/6800

LEYTON STADIUM,
BRISBANE ROAD,
LEYTON E.10.

NAME.... K. Nichols ...... TWO WEEKS ENDING. 27.2.73...

BASIC WAGE	£ 48.00	
APPEARANCE	£ .	
BONUS	£ .	
	£ .	
INCENTIVE	£ .	
	£ .	£ 48.00

Less

NATIONAL HEALTH INSURANCE	£ 1.46	
GRAD. PENSIONS	£ 1.48	
INCOME TAX	£ 7.50	
RENTS	£ .	£ 10.44
	£ .	
INCOME TAX REFUND		£ .
PAID INTO YOUR ACCOUNT		£ 37.26

One of my payslips when I was the Head Groundsman here at the Orient FC (Brisbane Road, Leyton, E10).
Considering I was I was looking after two grounds, it was very poor pay.
I looked after their trading ground, once owned by Great Universal Stores... opposite Springfield Park!
Wages were always poor then for farm labourers, horticulture etc.

ORIENT FOOTBALL CLUB LTD.

Place of Registration - ENGLAND
Registration No. -248-1553-56

Registered Office
LEYTON STADIUM
BRISBANE ROAD
LEYTON :: E.19

Chairman: A. E. PAGE
Directors: H. S. ZUSSMAN
F. F. HARRIS, B. B. WINSTON
M. E. PAGE M.A.
Secretary: J. H. FALLTRICK
Manager: G. PETCHEY

STA/4/JHF/PS

8th May, 1973.

Mr. K.P.Nichols,
7 Mercooke House,
The Drive,
WALTHAMSTOW,
E.17.

Dear Mr. Nichols,

With reference to your application as a Groundsman here
at Leyton Stadium, will you please telephone us, as quoted on
this letter head, so that an interview can be arranged for you.

Yours faithfully,

J.H.Falltrick
Secretary

My reply letter from John Falltrick re. my interview with Arthur Page –
(John was Secretary, Arthur the Chairman of Orient FC) – two very nice
gents!
It was Park Keeper Ted Ellis, who told me of this vacancy (Ted lived in
Walthamstow) when I wasn't managing to climb the ladder at
Springfield Park. so applied for the job at Orient, and got the job!

Thames Water Authority

METROPOLITAN WATER DIVISION

Coppermill Lane, Walthamstow,
London, E17 7HE.

Telephone 01-521 3411   Ext. 30

Mr. K. Nichols,
7 Hancocke House,
The Drive,
Walthamstow,
London, E.17.

DIVISIONAL MANAGER
L.O. Wild, F.I.C.E.,F.I.Mech.E.,
F.I.W.E.

Please address reply to:
Senior Resident
Engineer,
Supply Section.

Your Ref:

Our Ref:
LEC/RD

Date:
5th April, 1974.

Dear Sir,

Vacancy for gardener at Coppermills Works

I understand that you are still interested in the above vacancy.

If so, would you please attend for interview at the above offices at 10.00a.m. on Wednesday, 10th April, 1974.

Yours faithfully,

D.A. Lott

My reply letter from David Lott: I liked my time at the Thames Water Authority, and passed the interview with flying colours. Chris Burke was the Head Gardener, a really lovely chap.

GREATER LONDON COUNCIL

CSF. 131

~~London County Council~~

TELEPHONE WATerloo 5000
Ext. 280

THE COUNTY HALL
LONDON, S.E.1

Correspondence should be sent to the Head of _____ PARKS _____ DEPARTMENT
quoting PK|A|

Dear Sir/~~Madam~~,

PART-TIME DAY RELEASE OF YOUNG EMPLOYEES

Mr./~~Mrs.~~/~~Miss~~ _____ K. _____ NICHOLS _____
(Initials)   (Surname)

The above-named, a ~~London County Council~~ *Greater London Council* employee in this department, is required to attend classes for one day per week until the end of the academic year in which the age of 18 is reached. He/~~she~~ has expressed a preference to attend your college and would like to take classes in the following subjects at the levels indicated:

Course for Gardeners _____ (2nd year) _____

It would be convenient for him/~~her~~ to attend on any day of the week ~~except~~ _____ I should be obliged if you would kindly enrol him/~~her~~ as a student and return the attached form CSF. 131A when you have done so. As attendance at classes is a condition of employment would you kindly inform me of any irregularity in attendance and send me a report on the student's progress in July.

N.B. Financial Arrangements

1. *In-county colleges*—No fee should be paid by the student. No charge should be made for in-county students. For out-county students, the normal out-county procedure should be followed.
2. *Colleges outside the ~~L.C.C.~~ G.L.C. area*—Please indicate on CSF. 131A what fees (if any) are payable by the Council on behalf of the student.

Yours faithfully,

Chief Officer

The Principal,
North London College for
Further Education, at the
Working Men's College
Crowndale Road, N.W.1

My heart sank when getting this letter, for I hated school, and this was just as bad in a way (see text). I did not learn a thing at this college. (1965)

GREATER LONDON COUNCIL

Chief Officer of the Parks Department, F. Hallowes, F Inst PA

THE COUNTY HALL

LONDON, S.E.1

PARKS DEPARTMENT

Telephone — WATerloo 5000
Extension — 280
Reference — PK/A.1

7 September 1965

Dear Mr. Nichols,

Further Education and Training

You have been selected to take part in a new training scheme which is being organised jointly by the North London College for Further Education and this department.

The scheme will involve your attendance for further education and training on three half days a week:

One half day — General education at North London College

One half day — Gardening, science and calculations at North London College (until the training centre at Finsbury Park is fully established)

One half day — Practical work at Finsbury Park

You will be able to claim a refund of any additional travelling expenses you may incur, plus up to 2s. subsistence on any day when it is necessary for you to have lunch away from your normal place of work.

You should take the attached letter of introduction and enrol at the North London College, Working Men's College, Crowndale Road, Mornington Crescent, on

Wednesday, 15 September 1965, at 9.30 a.m.

The half day on which you will be required to attend Finsbury Park for practical work will be notified to you later.

Yours sincerely,

Mr. K. Nichols,
Springfield Park.

I did not enjoy receiving this! But quite enjoyed my time when the Finsbury Park Training Centre was completed, I learnt a lot more here!

WADHAM LODGE SPORTS GROUND

BROOKSCROFT ROAD, WALTHAMSTOW, E.17.

L. Golding.
58 Love Lane,
Woodford Bridge
Essex.
504-1354

SPORTS GROUND
Tel: LARkswood 2444

Secretary:
HARRY WATTS
44 COBCROFT Drive
Woodford Green, Essex.
Tel: BUCKhurst 0315

14th June 1969

Mr. K. Nichols,
87 Coppermill, Lane,
E.17.

Dear Mr. Nichols,

Thank you for your telephone call and I
confirm your appointment as assistant groundsman at Wadham
Lodge Sports Ground.

The hours of work are 40 per week, you will
be expected to work from 8a.m.-12 noon on Saturdays but will
be granted one half day leave per week in lieu. This will be
arranged with Mr. V. Oliver under whose direction you will
work.

Your wages will be £14.10.0.per week this
will be reviewed at the end of our financial year in September.

Will you please let me have your tax certificate
and Insurance Card as soon as possible. If convenient you could
leave them in an envelope with Mrs. Nichols and I will collect
them when I attend Wadham Sports Ground on Tuesday evening.

Yours sincerely,

Golding

My interview letter from the lovely Les Golding, I got the job!

Dec 5th 1971

Dear Keith,

I confirm the points resulting from our conversation of yesterday Dec. 3rd.

1. That you will return to work Mon. Dec.6th and continue until the end of the year when the position will be reviewed by both parties.

2. I will put before the trustees your request for an increase in salary.

3. Having dispensed with the services of Keith Williams you will work on your own. Mr Bradley will however be willing to give help and advice as he is able if asked.

4. An attempt will be made to eradicate the short comings and waste of the past months.
   a. The minimum use be made of the tractor especially on wet days and so avoid making parts of the field a quagmire.
   b. The lines and spots of the football and hockey pitches marked clearly and cleanly well in time for Saturday's matches.
   c. The completion of the work on the wickets be accomplished with as little delay as possible and the soil well luted.
   d. The trench along the tennis court be filled in and the ground levelled.

With the last two items completed we could then plan the number of smaller jobs around the ground which need attention.

Yours sincerely

K.Nichols Esq.   Hon. Sec.

Les Golding and I had made some unintentional choices of Head and Assistant groundsmen, and a lot left on my young shoulders, hence falling behind on essential work trying to do it all (8 acres) on my own. I did walk out because of the pressure, but Les wanted me back, so I did... as you can see !

T. PARKER & SONS (TURF MANAGEMENT) LTD.

COMPLETE
TURF MANAGEMENT SERVICES
AND SUPPLIES

"SISIS" MAIN AGENTS AND
DISTRIBUTORS FOR SOUTHERN
COUNTIES

RANSOMES & HAYTER
SPECIALIST DISTRIBUTORS

WORCESTER PARK,
SURREY.

LARGE STOCKHOLDERS OF MAINTENANCE EQUIPMENT FOR TURF & ARTIFICIAL SURFACES

27th November 1970

Dear Mr. Nichols,

As you are no doubt aware in January of this year Mr. P. D. Lowe took over from Mr. R. Booth in the capacity of area representative. We feel that Mr. Lowe will now be known to you as enough time has elapsed for him to have made personal contact with you.

Nevertheless we are anxious to ensure that our records at Head Office are correct. To this end may we ask you to kindly confirm the following:

(a) You are still Head Groundsman to Wadham Lodge, Walthamstow.

(b) Your home address is as shown on the envelope. If not, please indicate new address: ....
....

Finally we are enclosing a prepaid envelope for your convenience and we would ask you to let us have this information by return.

Thanking you for your past business and assuring you of our continued desire to be of service at all times.

Yours truly,
p.p. T. PARKER & SONS (Turf Management) LTD.

Peter Simpson
Sales Manager

Encl:

I ordered plenty of sundries from this great company, a very good reliable firm who would reward your loyalty with a good sum of money near Christmas – boosted my poor wages up that week!

Walthamstow Building Society

869 FOREST ROAD WALTHAMSTOW LONDON E17 4BB   TELEPHONE 01-531 3231/6

Our Ref: JPO'B/JP   Office hours 9 to 4.30 Saturday 9 to 12
29th April 1986

Mr. K.P. Nichols,
43, Guildford Road,
off Hale End Road,
(Upper) Walthamstow,
London,
E17 4EA.

Dear Mr. Nichols,

Thank you for your letter of the 23rd of April and I confirm that your quotation is acceptable to us.

Would you, therefore, please carry out the grass cutting, edging to lawns, weeds, flower beds, pruning, Spring and Summer. Plant out flower beds etc according to the season. During the course of the year, carry out normal maintenance including scarifying and spiking etc. In addition, pick up and dispose of all litter around the car park, paths, gardens, etc on alternate week days and generally ensure that the surrounding area of the Society's Head Office is fully maintained.

I understand that you will submit an account to me each week in the sum of ██ which will be in respect of labour only. All seeds, plants, fertilisers, etc will be paid for by the Society and, as agreed, our gardening equipment is available for use around our premises.

Would you be kind enough to telephone me as soon as possible in order to arrange a starting date.

Yours sincerely,

J.P. O'Brien
Assistant Secretary.

A MEMBER OF THE BUILDING SOCIETIES ASSOCIATION

A lovely letter from Pat O'Brien, he was a brilliant chap, very many were so very sad when he passed away.
On doing these plain gardens, I turned it to a wondrous sight ! for I had won them the London In Bloom Competition!

396

01-520 4274

April 1987.

The Sisters of Charity
St. Mary's
42 Church Hill Road
Walthamstow
London E17 9RX

To whom it may concern:

Mr. Keith Nichols worked for me this year.
He pruned my fruit trees and rose bushes and also gave
me excellent advice.

I am sure he will give satisfaction.

Signed-

When we decided to move to the coast in April 1987, realised that nobody would know of my work, so decided to ask a good few of my old clients if they would kindly give me a reference, so that I could show my new clients, thankfully, not one refused my request, and all were delighted to do so! There are a good few, therefore impossible to show them all here in this book.
Photo here shows reference from Sister Peter.

18th March, 1980.

Mr. Keith Nichols,
162 Chingford Road,
E17 3DA

Dear Keith,

Thank you for your letter of 11th March and I
quite understand your reasons for having to
give up working in this area.

However, you have done such a good job into
getting my garden into shape that I am very
anxious for you to continue. I have also
talked to Mrs. Hsu and perhaps we could come
to some arrangement whereby you do both gardens
on the same day, maybe three hours each (or more
when required) and we are both happy to increase
your hourly rate.

Please be kind enough to telephone me as soon
as possible.

Yours sincerely,

P. Lester (Mrs)

Reference from Mrs Lester of Hampstead, London. She was devastated
to learn that it just wasn't profitable enough for me to travel to and
from not only Hampstead each day, but also Hampstead Garden
Suburb, Finchley etc. (I think the furthest that I travelled to do a
Landscape project was the hectic journey to and from Walthamstow to
Orpington in Kent.)
I found quite unexpectedly that I could get four pounds an hour in my
own area, without all that travelling.
This was such a nice letter, so for a good while I did do one long day a
week for these two ladies, and extra money too!

12 Carnanton Road
London, E17 4DA

15th April 1987

TO WHOM IS MAY CONCERN

I have known Keith Nichols for many years
and it gives me great pleasure to be able to
offer this reference as to his character and
workmanship.

I have always found Mr. Nichols completely
honest, trustworthy, sincere and thoughtful
for others.

His knowledge of gardens, plants and shrubs
is superb.

Reference to his pictorial records will show
his capabilities as a landscape gardener, but
he is always very happy and willing to help in
a small suburban garden such as mine.

His services will be greatly missed in this part
of the world but I wish him every success in the
future.

M. Lloyd

Reference from two nice clients Mary and Harold Lloyd.

Mr. Keith Nicholls has done a good
deal of work for us in the garden for the
past five years.

He is extremely knowledgeable on his
subject and shows considerable intelligence
and imagination.

He is a hard and fast worker and his
prices are moderate.

R. WOODTHORPE BROWNE,
Lieutenant Commander RN, Rtd.

Reference from R. Wood Thorpe Brown, Lieutenant Commander,
R T D. Very nice chap, we got on well.

CHARLES V. ■ & CO. LTD.

SURVEYORS · VALUERS · ESTATE AGENT
(ESTAB. 1953)

Directors: C.V. Sales, F.S.V.A. J.D. Sales S.V. Sale

226 Chingford Mount Road, Chingford, London E.4. Tel. 01-529 1116-8
(After Office Hours 01-529 3440)

Members of the Chingford and Walthamstow Ass. of Auctioneers, Surveyors and Estate Agents
District office of the Woolwich Equitable Building Society est. 1847

Our Ref. CVS/JWR.

22nd October, 1982.

Mr. K.P.Nichols,
162 Chingford Road,
London, E.17. 4 PL.

Dear Sir,

Re. 10 Salisbury Hall Gardens, Chingford, E.4.

Further to our telephone conversation of today's date, we confirm that
subject to final acceptances from the owner, you would be prepared to
carry out complete clearance of the front and back gardens of the above
property as per your estimate of 6th October, for £650 including Skip.

We will be in touch with you shortly confirming instructions. As you are
probably aware, the refurbishment of this property will have to be done in
stages.

Yours faithfully,

C.V.SALES.
CHARLES V. SALES & CO.LTD.

I carried out restoration work for several Estate Agents. They would
call on my services where neglected gardens stopped the sale of
properties. Once I put my mark on these places and gardens
restored, they were sold!
All the agents did was to add my fee to the sale price and got all their
money back!

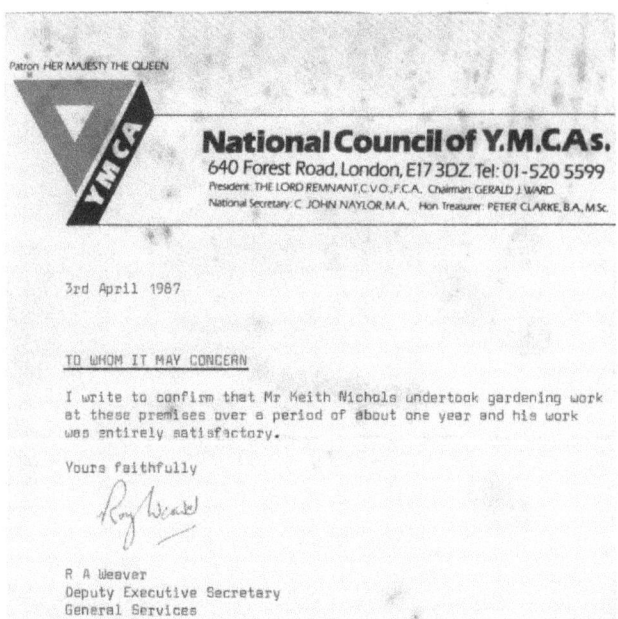

National Council of Y.M.C.As.
640 Forest Road, London, E17 3DZ. Tel: 01-520 5599
President THE LORD REMNANT, C.V.O., F.C.A. Chairman: GERALD J WARD.
National Secretary: C. JOHN NAYLOR, M.A. Hon Treasurer: PETER CLARKE, B.A, M.Sc.

3rd April 1987

TO WHOM IT MAY CONCERN

I write to confirm that Mr Keith Nichols undertook gardening work
at these premises over a period of about one year and his work
was entirely satisfactory.

Yours faithfully

R A Weaver
Deputy Executive Secretary
General Services

Reference from the Y.M.C.A., Forest Road E17. I did a massive restoration on the gardens here, on my own.

01 529 7501

Fairfields
Woodman Lane
London
E4 7QR

16/4/1983

To Whom It May Concern:—
We are pleased to
recommend Keith Nichols,
to you for gardening work
of all kinds. He is hard-
working, certainly knows
his trade, and gives a
fair price. We have
employed him on specialist
jobs on at least three
Occasions when he lived in Walthamstow
Mr Mrs Taylor

Mr and Mrs Taylor asked me to dig out a massive hedge – in its place I planted Buddleia 'globosa' as a free growing hedge needing little maintenance.

(Chingford E4)

402

CROWTHER

NURSERIES

Prop. CROWTHER LGC of CHIGWELL Ltd

Ongar Road Abridge RM4 1AA
Stapleford (040 28) 581

2nd April, 1987

Mr. K. Nichols,
43, Guildford Road,
Walthamstow,
London, E.17. 4 ER.

<u>REFERENCE</u>

I have known Keith Nichols since my years of training at G.L.C.
Parks, twenty years ago. He has kept in contact through the
years whilst giving me the opportunity of seeing many of his
garden projects. His work is always of high quality and
ably assisted by his indulgent enthusiasm for plants.
Since I have had a retail nursery Keith has purchased many
plants and sundries from us and always hasbeen most prompt in
settling accounts.
In fact our contact through gardening has always been a pleasure .

A nice reference here from friend and former workmate from
our first years at Springfield Park.
At this time Ken Crowther was taught the running of and
maintaining the bowling green at the park, under the watchful
eye of Head Green Keeper Charlie Swaby (Walthamstow).
Ken, for very many years now, has owned and run his own
garden centre.

September 15 1987

Mr Ian Williams
52 Jewel Road
Walthamstow
London E.17
(Now moved Kessingland)

To whom it may concern

I have known Mr Keith Nichols
and his family for around 20 years. And worked
for keith for about 4.5 years. He has always
been good mate and a great workmate.
I have worked with him on his mini fair
and his gardening work. I have never had a
cross word with him and he has always
been fair with me. Keith + Debbie always
welcomes you to there home. And they always
put thereself out for you.

Your faithfully
Ian Williams

A good reference from my friend Ian, who has helped me on and off
for a good number of years, in both of my jobs of work in not only
landscaping but on the fairground side too. A good grafter.

YELLANDS

Estate Agents, Surveyors & Valuers

EST 1930

B.D. Parmenter A.N.A.E.A.

272 HOE STREET, WALTHAMSTOW CENTRAL STATION
LONDON E17 9DD   Tel: 01-520 7334/5

OUR REF BDP/MH   YOUR REF

Mr. K.P. Nichols
43, Guildford Road,
Upper Walthamstow,
London, E17 4EA.   28th November, 1985.

Dear Keith,

Re: 43, Guildford Road, Upper Walthamstow, E.17.

I was very sorry to learn that you have lost, possibly your dream house in
Suffolk and that your house has now been officially withdrawn from the open
market. You mentioned in your brief letter that you will now have to wait
until the North Circular alterations have been completed but, I personally
feel that this would be not to your advantage as prices may in fact slow down
for properties near the Wadham Road area.

I haven't forgotten your kind estimate for my own garden and as we have now
chanelled as reserves into having the lounge and dining room sorted out for
this Christmas for the first time, it looks as if I will be calling you in
very early next year for your expert advice.

All the very best and love to the family.

Yours sincerely,

YES, gazumped on a property in Suffolk (1985) but had carried out lots of
work for Brian Parmenter, including his own garden. Brian worked on behalf
of Yellands Estate Agents E17 until me and my family finally moved to the
East Coast in April 1987.

01-504-4260

9, Hawkhaw Drive

Woodford Green

Essex.

15.4.87.

Dear Keith,

Just a note to express our thanks for all your work in the garden — it has certainly transformed the appearance.

We are both grateful for all the time and trouble you have taken both in advising and carrying out the work

Wishing you well in the new venture

Yours Alan Hitching

HH. JUDGE HITCHING.

A great reference from H H Judge Hitching, who I knew as friends Alan and Hilda. (Her family owned King's Florist E17) and Hilda was my daughter's teacher. Police followed me to their home (see text).

Walthamstow Building Society

860 FOREST ROAD, WALTHAMSTOW, LONDON E17 4BB   Telephone 01-531 3231/6
Fax No 01-523 2889

A MEMBER OF THE
BUILDING SOCIETIES ASSOCIATION

Your Ref

Our Ref

K. Nichols, Esq.,
43 Guildford Road
WALTHAMSTOW
London, E17

JPO'B/BMB

26th March 1987

Dear Keith,

Many thanks for your letter and we were all very sorry to learn
that you have to give up the work on the Society's gardens.

We shall miss having you around the place as most of us have
come to regard you as a permanent fixture.   Nevertheless we
quite understand your reasons for making the move and send you
our best wishes for the future with every success and also a
sincere thanks for brightening up our days with all the good
work that you have done around the office building.

Do remember that when you pass this way at some future date to
pop in and say hello and look at some of those lovely trees that
you have planted when they have matured a little more.

Finally, of course, I will be most happy to provide a reference
for you to use or to keep in your album and I will talk to you
about that in greater detail the next time I see you.

Yours sincerely,

PAT O'BRIEN

We did move to the coast, but I'd made such a lot of work for myself at
the Walthamstow Building Society, that they paid me even more money
to spend time on the gardens, travelling from Suffolk. A lady gardener
took over from me, but found the work daunting, and a big task, she too
called it a day.

Keith Nichols

Mr Keith Nichols worked, as a gardener, with me for three years. During that time I always found him to be honest, reliable and hardworking. His work was always of the highest standard. His relationship with the other staff was good and he was in charge of other gardeners working on a landscape scheme.

R Nunn

Area Superintendent
Parks Dept.
London Borough
of Haringey

April 1987

126, Higham Road,
Tottenham,
London N.17 6NR
12/4/87

Dear Keith,
As requested here comes one reference. Glad to hear that all goes well for you and I wish you good luck when you move.
Best Wishes
Ron

A really nice reference from my then foreman Ron Nunn (ex SAS) when working for Haringey Parks Dept... he was a great fellow!

CHAPELFIELD NURSERY
SEWARDSTONE ROAD
CHINGFORD
LONDON E4 7RE
Tel 01-529-1840

April 5 1987.

To Whom it may concern.

I have known Mr Nicols, as a customer of mine, for. The past eight to ten years. I have delivered goods to him. And, have had a chance, to see some of his excellent work. He puts effort + skill into whatever he does. I am very sorry to see him leave this area. I also wish him luck + success, in his new ventures.

Yours Faithfully
S. Harker.

Nice reference again from garden nursery owner Gordon Harker (wife Sylvie). All the plants, shrubs bulbs, and trees were bought from Gordon and Sylvie's nursery, E 4 All bedding plants too I bought from them for our entry for the London In Bloom Competition (won 3 years!)

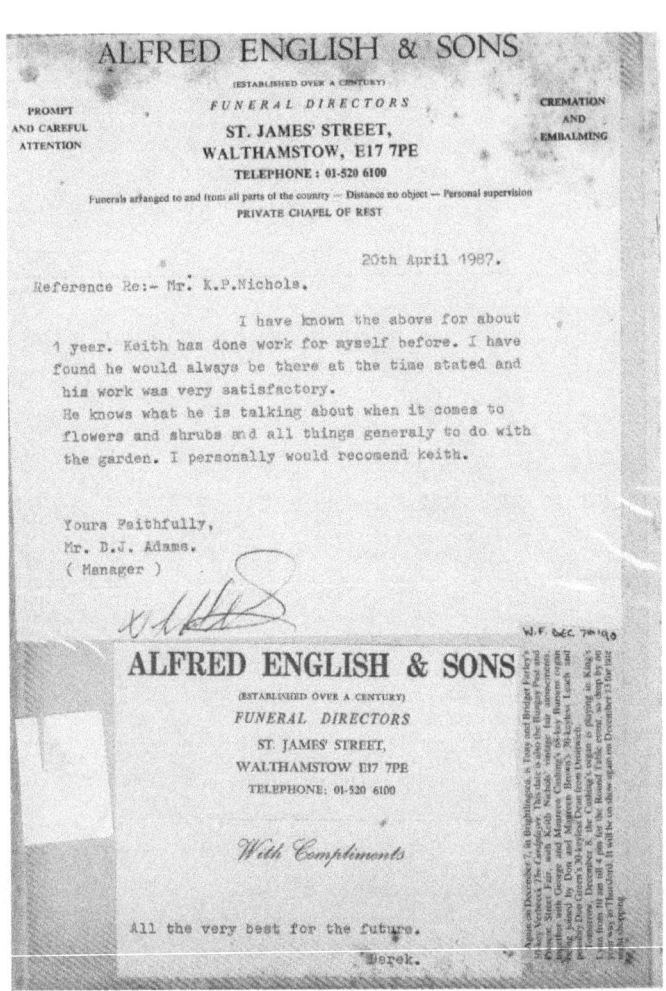

ALFRED ENGLISH & SONS

(ESTABLISHED OVER A CENTURY)

PROMPT
AND CAREFUL
ATTENTION

FUNERAL DIRECTORS

ST. JAMES' STREET,
WALTHAMSTOW, E17 7PE
TELEPHONE : 01-520 6100

CREMATION
AND
EMBALMING

Funerals arranged to and from all parts of the country — Distance no object — Personal supervision
PRIVATE CHAPEL OF REST

20th April 1987.

Reference Re:- Mr. K.P.Nichols.

I have known the above for about
1 year. Keith has done work for myself before. I have
found he would always be there at the time stated and
his work was very satisfactory.
He knows what he is talking about when it comes to
flowers and shrubs and all things generaly to do with
the garden. I personally would recomend keith.

Yours Faithfully,
Mr. D.J. Adams.
(Manager)

W.F. DEC 7810.0

ALFRED ENGLISH & SONS

(ESTABLISHED OVER A CENTURY)

FUNERAL DIRECTORS

ST. JAMES' STREET,
WALTHAMSTOW E17 7PE
TELEPHONE: 01-520 6100

With Compliments

All the very best for the future.

Derek.

A good reference from Derek Adams (see text) a grand chap!
Sorry to all the other nice folk who did references for me, so many of
you agreed to do a reference for me, they may not be included in this
book, but can assure you all that I've kept each and every one of
them... so, a very big thankyou to you all.

E STATE Agents

In between other jobs of employed work and being dissatisfied with most of these, dabbled in the early years going self-employed. People doing gardening for a living was still a rarity, and I easily recall how I was the only landscape gardener with an inch x inch box advert, the other few were only lineage.

Yes, later as work picked up a bit, I did go back to lineage and it was cheaper too, against my box advert which was exactly five pounds – a lot of money then!

The box advert did for some strange reason make the bigger companies get in contact with me, the companies were based all over, but wanted me to carry out work for them, not only local work for me, but also just the few odd miles away from my home. Most of these were big companies that had other ventures elsewhere, like extended offices, or for me to landscape gardens around other properties that they'd bought, and indeed properties for their employees etc.

The most welcomed work came from an unlikely source and they were Estate Agents, who actually had very good sense in calling in the likes of me to put right all the properties that had gardens that were in such a state, it was putting prospective buyers off from buying the property and moreso if the property itself was a bit dilapidated, and a very neglected garden is usually more daunting than a property that is probably just in need of a lick of paint?

All the agents with whom I carried out work for, said that some of the properties had been on their books for far too long, and the longer the properties are left they will quite rightly de-value. The agents all said that whatever my charges were could quite easily be added to the house sale, for I'd put my magic touch, the properties did actually sell very quickly. I'm not saying it's because of my work, but it at least made half of a major problem okay.

All of these problem gardens were real hard graft, but well worth it when I'd completed these projects to then see the agents' faces that were always full of delight, and now knowing that the property will soon be sold and out of their hands at long last. They all too wondered why they hadn't thought of calling in a gardener/landscape gardener before.

If they had called in earlier, my prices would have been lower, and perhaps the properties would not have de-valued quite as much. After some of my projects, some of the agents asked me to go each week and just perhaps keep the lawns cut and maintain borders etc. until the properties were sold, and as I say, that was usually within a couple of months, yet the houses had been on the books for anything up to 7–8 years and more!

The properties that did sell quite quickly were the agents who asked me not to just cut the grass short, weed the flower beds or restore shrubs etc., but wanted a new look, with a new lawn, new shrubs, trees and plants, and even a pond, rockery, arches, etc., plus a good mulch to show off the plants etc. to great effect. Now these did look good and the properties were sold more or less instantly, yet had been on their books a fair time.

Newly-built properties had more often than not just had a plain bare plot, sometimes weedy, as like today in fact, but some property developers nowadays do have a gardener to put down a lawn.

Many years ago now a property developer who was particularly memorable, but not really for the right reasons. They were clearly well off, and very flash, and almost totally impossible to talk to, for he was always on the phone (those early bulky mobile ones!) The very sad part of all this is that it looked like I'd found my feet at last, for the man had seen what I'd done for the estate agents, and wanted the same. I found him difficult to talk to because of his very constant busy, busy, busy business!

Where the problems came, was when I was trying to discuss the job of work entailed, and it had to be right so as I know what to estimate for, and that just had to be right. I most certainly didn't want any comebacks.

I found it so difficult even trying to discuss a job of work on their own property, he was constantly on the phone or having to 'leave me for a while' even when it was time to talk to his wife about their garden, he called her out to the garden, she was dressed in white tennis attire, and literally skipping about waving a tennis racquet.

This lady was even more impossible to talk to than her husband, for as you were talking to either of them, it was always eyes averted from my face, they were looking everywhere but concentrating on the matter in hand.

It goes without saying, I gave them a wide berth, and even with their phones and busy, busy lives, they never bothered to contact me to see why I hadn't got back to them with prices for each of the six properties concerned.

I couldn't even write out one estimate, for I had no inkling on what to estimate for, all because our meetings came in fits and starts, and no clear picture of what to do. I have no doubt that if the man had not been so 'busy' and actually listened to me, and had proper time to talk to me face to face, we would have had an extremely long working partnership, because the work looked like it would have been so interesting and most rewarding for both of us.

I've met actual clients like this, the worst being those that don't have the remotest interest in gardens or gardening, and not really listening to you at the time of estimating, and because they don't listen or prepared to discuss their requirements properly, that problems do occur.

This Book At Journey's End

Well, readers, I do hope you've really enjoyed my book, and even hope you've learned something from it, even if it's only about the general public!

There is much more to write about, for I have had very many clients and jobs of work over very many years and a story goes with most of them.

I promised you a gardening book with a difference, and hope I've achieved that?

Because of what happened as a mere teenager back in my training days with so much prejudice on appearance, rather than personality and knowledge, still to this day have no certificates of merit, and gone through life without any, so I have had to prove myself perhaps more than others? albeit hand on heart, I have never been asked if I do have any qualifications, so if you are an up-and-coming gardener and really do know your job, you'll not need to worry about a mere piece of paper! It's your clients who'll be your judge and jury.

Many people who actually know me have asked how come I have done so much in my life, not only as a gardener but also as a grower and plantsman, and my many years on the road as a fairground showman.

When all my pals were playing football or going to 'dances' 'discos' etc., I was always working, which included weekends and all bank holidays – actual holidays were almost non-existent.

Rainy and wintry days I spend time doing hours of writing. Yes I have had leisure times, but nothing like other people. So, I sort of look forward to retiring, but I'll hopefully still be active!

Keith Nichols

Footnotes and Extras

Earlier on in this book you read about when I was at school, and had a gardening class twice a week if I remember correctly, and my friend

David Bolton and I were chosen to represent our school – Heathcote Senior, Chingford E.4.

I still have the newspaper clip and photo that appeared in the Chingford Guardian newspaper, and 1963 seems about the right date, as I can see my 'Beatle haircut'! for I started work in 1964. Looking at this photo, David is pictured left of me, and his mum on the right. It also shows two of the dignitaries, and a good few of the pupils from the other schools too.

Most of the article thankfully is still legible, so I'll now show you, the readers, what was written. Where a word is now sadly faded I'll put in a dash. I expect the newspaper company does still have this photo etc. in their archives? The newspaper heading is…

CHILDREN PLANT PARK TREES

To give them a greater sense of responsibility for the care of trees in parks, a group of pupils from six different schools, planted six ornamental trees in Mansfield Park, Chingford, on Tuesday afternoon.

Chingford Secondary school for girls, Chingford High, Heathcote, Chase Lane Juniors, St. Paul's Catholic Secondary and St Mary's R.C. Primary, each sent two pupils at the invitation of the council. These trees were the last of 36 which have been planted round the park.

Before the ceremony, Chingford Mayor Ald. J.W. Nation, told the children "During the past few years many trees have been planted and obviously some get damaged. I myself planted one of those trees and every now and again I go to have a look at it. As you get older I hope you will do the same."

The Mayor asked the children to tell their friends not to damage the trees. The six planted by the children _____ Whitebeam, Japanese Cherry, and _____

Ald. Nation was accompanied by the Mayoress Miss Kathleen Nation, Parks Committee Chairman, Cllr L. _____ and B orough Engineer Mr G ___ ___ ____. [end]

The caption under the printed photo reads… Anne and David Thomas, of Chingford High School, fill in the earth round the roots of a Whitebeam, as Mayoress Miss Kathleen Nation holds the tree steady. Among the onlookers are pupils from other schools.

The Mayoress is just out of shot of the picture.

When I was in my late twenties, I did go back to find mine and David's tree – yes, it seemed as though all the trees were still there, but which one was ours was impossible to tell.

I wonder how many pupils have kept their news clip?

Last Writes!

As mentioned in this book, I wrote garden articles for a local magazine for 26 years. We didn't know it then but the very last one came through our door around Christmas week 2013, little did anyone know that that was the last edition, for there was no announcement to say that the magazine was to cease.

I wrote to the lady to whom I took my articles, and asked if I'd perhaps missed a copy, not dreaming in the slightest that the magazine would fold.

I never ever did get a reply back, no apology or explanation, and I was more annoyed because they still had umpteen of my articles yet unused that were for future editions; they have never been returned.

Other people I know e-mailed them to see what was going on, and no doubt some of the people who had paid for a year's advertising and still no replies.

I felt really let down, for Maureen Long had worked tirelessly to get this magazine off the ground, and sadly giving it up for her and her husband's ongoing ill health, hence she had to hand over the reins to a printing company who at first we all thought would enhance the mag. because perhaps they would have their own new ideas etc.

Rumour has circulated that the magazine wasn't paying, which is fair enough, but surely people like me and regular advertisers should have been contacted by letter or phone.

So much then for all my years of unpaid service!

Linda Harris

I would like here to give an enormous THANK YOU to Linda Harris, for her great professionalism in typesetting the manuscript for this book. I really don't know what I would have done without Linda's expertise.

Linda did a wonderful job on my last book back in 2009, plus a thank you to all those who were involved with PEN PRESS at the time, and sadly now they are no longer in business, for they did a grand job.

Linda and her very nice husband Andrew, we did get to meet, for Debbie and I took a coach trip to Cornwall to see the Eden Project and the Lost Gardens of Heligan. We were staying in Newquay, Fistral Beach, and Andrew and Linda came to see us there and have visited us here at home and I am proud to call them both friends. Sometimes you feel you are destined to meet such people in life.

Thank you again, Linda.

Keith Nichols (author)

By the time you read this book, I'm sure I'll have some answers –what do I mean by that I hear you ask? Do you remember earlier in the book I wrote of the so-called error that a TV programme made referring to Daffs and narcissi and their description of split 'Corolla' and split 'Corona'. Since this programme though, I've seen the latter written in several up-to-date catalogues, yet in all my gardening years I have only ever heard of split corolla. How come I've never heard of Corona except for the drink that actor/singer Dave King used to sing about in an advert many years ago.

Oh well! as I've said, I don't know all there is to know about gardening. I shall have to now look to see if presenters are correct in calling 'Monkshood' as Aconite!

It Was All Greek To Me!

I must add this last little story. I had a phone call from a man who lived in Palmers Green, London. He certainly sounded a jovial chap and most friendly, and spoke in broken English – he said in his own words that he was sorry for his lack of good English, albeit only very recent years studying English in his country of Greece.

He asked if I could come and see his garden as there was a problem with his roses. I'd never been to Palmers Green before, so it was a bit of a trek from my home in Walthamstow to try and find it. The chap was a nice man and like on the phone very friendly. Anyhow, I asked how I could help him, and his reply was one that I didn't expect – "Cock on Roses!" I said, "I'm sorry?" "Yes, cock on Roses". I asked him what he meant for now he was pointing to some rose bushes that did look a bit ill, but still I could not understand what he meant so I could give him advice.

He eventually called his smallish dog, picked it up and laid it belly arm in his arms, and them started to point to the dog's privates! and said "Cock! Cock on roses, dirty cock!" I didn't know what to say, then he said "Dog cocks on roses!"

It turned out quite obvious eventually that his dog kept urinating up the roses, hence the leaf colouring – but what a way to explain it!

I Treasure The Past

I love history and I love old things, and have brought up my four children to do the same, for these things can never be made again, they are unique.

One of my most favourite client whom I have mentioned a couple of times or so in this book, Iris Jones, Yoxford, Suffolk, a very kind lady of whom I wrote a lot more in my last book, she was the *only* client of mine that gave me a Christmas tip. I would get £100 and to our shock she gave my wife Debbie £50. Each year I would tell her what I'd done with the money, and one year she was as delighted as me! For what I'd bought I took along to show her. I put extra money to the £100 to purchase three Victorian albums – two were decoupage mainly, but the bigger book was a gem, it was full of the most glorious and unusual Christmas cards from 1906 and belonged to a lady named Olive Brear, and it seems she knew very many influential people going by the names on the cards and their abodes!

I bought the albums in Beccles, Suffolk, who sell really old books. They could shed no light on who Olive Brear (Brier?) was, or whether she had lived locally. Thinking back, I should have asked the bookshop owners exactly where they 'found' these albums.

I instantly noticed that nearly all the cards had flowers on them, but many not with the usual Holly and Mistletoe; a good few had other flowers too, most you would never associate particularly with Christmas.

A couple of years down the line I showed a friend these albums, and she explained that each of the flowers shown had a special meaning, each flower was giving a 'hidden message'. She advised me to buy a book called 'The Language of Flowers' and that would explain everything!

This is DEFINITELY THE END, FOLKS! T.B.N.A.

Keith Nichols

T.B.N.A.? There'll Never Be Another!